# CASTLE VALLEY
# AMERICA

To Sarah Alexander —
Thanks for all you've
done with the Peruvian
collection, and, most of all,
for your friendship.
With best wishes —
Nancy Taniguchi

# CASTLE VALLEY AMERICA

## HARD LAND, HARD-WON HOME

Nancy J. Taniguchi

UTAH STATE UNIVERSITY PRESS
LOGAN, UTAH

Utah State University Press
Logan, Utah 84322-7800

Manufactured in the United States of America

Printed on acid-free paper

Library of Congress Cataloging-in-Publication Data

Taniguchi, Nancy J. (Nancy Jacobus), 1948-
    Castle Valley, America : hard land, hard-won home / by Nancy J.
Taniguchi.
        p. cm.
    Includes bibliographical references and index.
    ISBN 0-87421-589-7 (hardcover : alk. paper) – ISBN 0-87421-590-0 (pbk. :
alk. paper)
    1. Castle Valley (Utah)–History. 2. Castle Valley (Utah)–Biography. 3.
Carbon County (Utah)–History. 4. Carbon County (Utah)–Biography. 5.
Emery County (Utah)–History. 6. Emery County (Utah)–Biography. I. Title.
    F832.C44T36 2004
    979.2'566–dc22

2004011982

To Darcy Anne Akiko—
Castle Valley native,
world traveler,
beloved daughter

# Contents

# Preface

Castle Valley is my home. Like thousands of other people who say that, I wasn't born there. But my children were, and their father, and their grandmother, and assorted aunts, uncles, and cousins. We still have relatives living there, and even though we have been gone for a while, we still come back to visit. Everyone's warmth and friendliness, the realization that we can always be ourselves because there's no point in trying to fool anyone, always remind us that we belong in Castle Valley.

It's hard to be honest about a place where one lives, to show it with all its defects and wrinkles and still reveal why it's so special. I have done my best. There are stories I would have liked to put in but didn't. Like the one about widow Isabella Birch Bryner, wrapped in quilts against the chill, riding an open flatcar to Salt Lake City to file on the land that became the Price townsite. Lynn Fausett even painted the scene in the mural in Price City Hall. But because Price became a town in 1892 and the 1900 census shows highly respectable Isabella with a two-year-old child, I don't understand the whole story. Was the child adopted? When did Isabella become a widow? Was she a plural wife? Did the townsite filing take place after the town was officially created? Why the rush—who was her competition? Why did local historian Ernest Horsley, who knew all the people involved, write that her father filed on the land for the townsite? I don't know the answers to these questions, and history has to make sense, or there's no point in writing it. If someone else knows the answers, please let me know.

The stories included here serve a purpose: to show Castle Valley's distinctiveness and, at the same time, how it reflected, shaped, or reacted to much of American history. This approach seems to fit a prevailing pattern which I just discovered while trying to select textbooks for next semester's classes. In the same afternoon I read David Hollinger's exhortation to globalize American history and "to speak to a nonprofessional public," and Joseph Amato's tribute to "local historians [who] provide a passionate attachment to concrete places."[1] I hope this book reflects both those ambitions to some extent. If I left out your favorite tale, write it down, honestly and factually. The *Carbon County Journal* is still in publication. The Emery County Archives is collecting all the local and personal histories it can get. Allan Kent Powell, a native of Huntington, now edits the *Utah Historical Quarterly*. Philip F. Notarianni, whose two grandfathers mined at Sunnyside, heads the Utah State Historical Society. Now is a great time for Castle Valley history.

This book has been in the making for over twenty-five years. Regrettably, many of the people who helped me have passed away and can no longer be adequately thanked. To others, I owe such a large debt that a mere acknowledgment will never repay it. Furthermore, I have not kept a consistent record of all of those who aided me. The list of those involved would be too long to set down here anyway, and I want you to read the book, not the preface. But you know who you are—and I hope you will find mention of your families, friends, bosses, neighbors, co-workers, and Castle Valley predecessors in this book, some of whose reminiscences have lain in my files so long I can't remember where I got them.

However, I must mention my deepest gratitude to my husband, Bob, and my children, Darcy and Dashiell. Without you, I would never have called Castle Valley home.

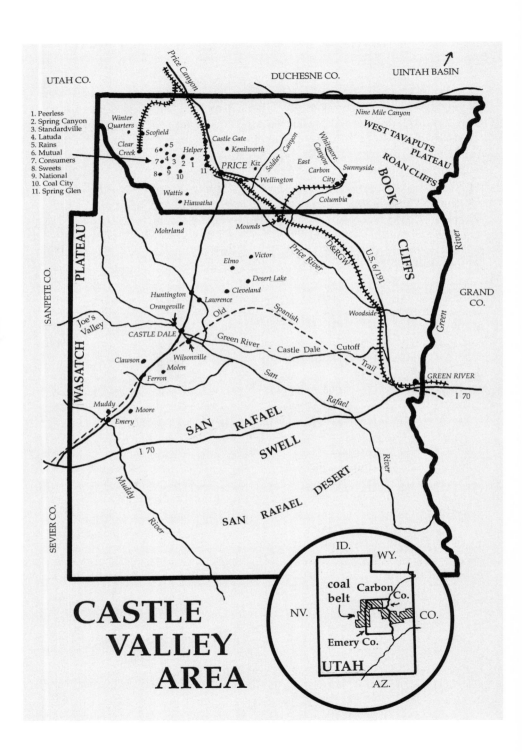

UTAH CO.

DUCHESNE CO.

UINTAH BASIN

Price Canyon

Nine Mile Canyon

WEST TAVAPUTS PLATEAU

1. Peerless
2. Spring Canyon
3. Standardville
4. Latuda
5. Rains
6. Mutual
7. Consumers
8. Sweets
9. National
10. Coal City
11. Spring Glen

Winter Quarters

Scofield

Clear Creek

Castle Gate

Kenilworth

Whitmore Canyon

Soldier Canyon

East Carbon City

Sunnyside

ROAN CLIFFS

6 ● 5
7 ● 4 ● 3 ● 2 ● 1
8 ● 9 ● 10

Helper

PRICE

Kiz

11

Wellington

Columbia

BOOK

CLIFFS

Wattis

Hiawatha

Mounds

Green River

Mohrland

Elmo

Victor

Price River

DeRGW

U.S. 6/191

SANPETE CO.

PLATEAU

Desert Lake

Cleveland

GRAND CO.

Huntington

Lawrence

Woodside

Orangeville

Joe's Valley

Old

Spanish

WASATCH

CASTLE DALE

Green River

Castle Dale

Cutoff

Trail

GREEN RIVER

I 70

Clawson

Wilsonville

Molen

Ferron

San

Muddy

Moore

Rafael

River

Emery

SAN RAFAEL

SWELL

I 70

River

Muddy

SAN RAFAEL DESERT

River

SEVIER CO.

# CASTLE VALLEY AREA

ID.

WY.

coal belt

Carbon Co.

NV.

CO.

Emery Co.

UTAH

AZ.

# Introduction

The poet wrote, "No man is an island . . . every man . . . is a part of the main."[1] The same can be said for places, literally and figuratively, and how and when they become connected indelibly shapes their history. Castle Valley remained an uninhabited island in the American West for generations, as more inviting areas were "discovered," inhabited, and "civilized." When occupation finally occurred, industrialization followed within a handful of years. Then, in quick succession, came the sort of change called progress, then cultural innovation, the effects of world-wide upheaval and, finally, self-recognition. Like so many people, in its maturity, after three score years and ten (more or less), Castle Valley started discovering what sort of place it was and where it fit into the continent of the nation and on the map of American and global ideas, creating new, multi-layered identities.[2]

Visions of American history normally come pre-scripted: the march of "progress" from Old World to New, from sea to shining sea, from autocratic institutions to true democracy. Traditionally, as a result, historians have viewed this process from the power centers (usually New England, New York, or Washington, D.C.) whether the approach is geographical, political, or philosophical. This book views a slice of America from a different perspective, in Utah's last-settled hinterlands. Even in the twenty-first century, Utah is a sparsely inhabited state (third in amount of public lands after Alaska and Nevada) and the last to be admitted to the Union in the nineteenth century. Only Oklahoma, New Mexico, Arizona, Alaska, and Hawaii joined afterward, but each of them had their own connections to other worlds—Spanish, Russian, or Pacific. Utah had none of those ties. It was (and is), in many respects, the edge of America, and Castle Valley is its last frontier.

But isn't Utah history all about Mormons? This skewed perception explains much of the persistent historical neglect of Castle Valley. Yes, it is, but also about Utes and Paiutes and Spanish and Mexicans and Finns and Greeks and Japanese and Italians—in fact, many of the peoples of the world came to Castle Valley at one time or another. And most were not Mormon. Some even stayed. So Utah history itself traditionally ignored this area—too late to be part of the usual Mormon pioneer story, too different to fit into the sweeping generalizations with which Utah is usually characterized. Even in the saga of Utah history, Castle Valley has remained an historical island.

Then how can Castle Valley exemplify America? As recent scholarship attests, America's story is not so much of a movement of white European stock westward as it is a flow of peoples into the interior of the continent from several directions, impelled by motives more varied than simple progress or conquest.[3] In historic times, continental penetration began first from the south, as the Spanish empire stretched out to claim increasing fingers of territory. Aside from Florida, ceded to England in 1763, much of Spanish expansion could be tied to the Old Spanish Trail. In 1776, Fathers Dominguez and Escalante initiated what became this well-traveled route. Their goal: the new missions of California; at their back, the 160–year-old entrepot of Santa Fe. The Old Spanish Trail runs through Castle Valley.

The next expansion came from competition between distant commercial empires. Their polyglot fur trappers associated sometimes with the French, or with the Americans, or with the powerful, long-lived Hudson's Bay Company. Men like the American Fur Company's Etienne Provost (for whom Provo, Utah, is named) traversed the region, trapping and later escorting caravans westward to the annual fur trade rendezvous. Compatriots left their names painted on a rock on the west bank of the Green River in the 1830s, at the very northeast edge of Castle Valley, and on the cliffs at its western border. Finding little of value there, they, like the Spanish, traveled on.

The third wave of strangers led to settlement—people of northern European heritage who usually star in the first act of America's historical pageant. Here, they came later. In Utah's case, most were Mormons— members of the Church of Jesus Christ of Latter-day Saints who had been driven from their homes by a succession of enraged neighbors. Their fellow Americans had been offended by Mormon clannishness, by their self-righteousness, and by rumors of repugnant practices: theocracy and polygamy. The flip side of these qualities—community solidarity, self-reliance, piety, and centralized authority—made the Saints successful in the West, and led to a well-rooted settlement in Utah's Great Basin. But while many of the Mormons initially sought a separate refuge in their protected Zion, American history would not let them rest long. While they ignored Castle Valley because of its awkward geographical location and desolate lands, they extended westward to California. In 1848, at Sutter's Mill, a handful of Mormon men helped discover gold, stunning the world and rearranging a good portion of its population. Trying to keep travel routes open, Mormons sought a corridor to the sea, founding San Bernardino—and between the excitement of Sutter's Mill and the hustle of California colony-building, Castle Valley's two leading pioneers got their early training.

With California gold came the clamor for a national railroad, which was completed in Utah in 1869. This monopolistic octopus wrapped its tentacles around Utah transportation until the coming of the Denver and

Rio Grande Western in 1883—right through Castle Valley, settled less than a decade earlier. The frontier was now open for settlement, up to its very edge.

A short decade later, historian Frederick Jackson Turner announced that the frontier had closed (in a much-disputed perception). At least the West was so settled that a frontier line could no longer be discerned on a map generated by the 1890 census. He noted the passing of several distinct frontiers: the Indian Traders Frontier, the Ranchers Frontier, the Farmers Frontier, and Army Posts (also, presumably, a sort of frontier). Castle Valley's history, while experiencing some of these types, proceeded in its own order as the grand American parade got somewhat jumbled by the time it reached this far-off region—definitely an island of barrenness among the checkered, settled lands of the West.

Once most lands were taken, American energy turned largely to their development and/or exploitation. The nation was buffeted by successive waves of change brought by the Industrial Revolution, progressive reforms, World War I, and the supremacy of business. These waves surged and crested in the national mainstream, and their crescendos crashed over the edge into Castle Valley in quick succession. No harbor of tradition existed to cushion the force of these blows, and Castle Valley had to devise its own ways to weather these cross currents. In the 1920s, national cultural norms and attitudes began to sink in, due, in part, to improved transportation, communication, and an increasingly mobile set of local residents. By the Great Depression of the 1930s, Castle Valley's history was entwined with the life of the nation, and the federal government had become a mainstay rather than a hindrance. National ties only strengthened in the 1940s and 1950s as Castle Valley minerals truly made the area "the arsenal of democracy." In this epoch, the "ties to the main" became two-way: not just outside influences rushing in, but contributions to the national welfare flowing out. As residents started assessing their home and its main significances, Castle Valley developed its own version of 1960s liberation, 1970s discontent, and 1980s economic revival.

In the most recent decades, Castle Valley has edged toward an economic precipice. Now very much entwined with energy production, its economy faces the practical dilemma of what to do when coal and gas reserves run out, as they are likely to do in the near future. Fortunately, Castle Valley has another kind of virtually untapped reserve: its history, geology, paleontology, archaeology, and its people, who have connections to virtually everywhere else on earth. The past remains near and palpable—you can almost hear it breathing. The future, however, remains a question, as it so often has in unpredictable Castle Valley.

# PART I
# CASTLE VALLEY CORRIDOR

# 1

# Passing Through, 1776–1869

*We rolled on down the creek a mile or two and then turned northward through Castle Valley, thirteen miles, mostly downhill, to Coal Creek, where we anticipated staying all night; but feed being poor, water bad and the bed of the creek quicksand, we rolled on.*[1]

—OLIVER B. HUNTINGTON, EXPLORER

Americans expected to create civilization in the wilderness; they just felt that they could skip Castle Valley. From the beginning of history, no one really liked the area: not the Utes, not the Spanish, not the Mexicans, nor the mountain men, nor the federal surveyors—not even the pioneers who eventually settled there. When Oliver Huntington penned his views in 1855, the valley's name and its unattractive reputation were both well established. Its dry, alkali soil and gullied landscape initially made only a convenient passageway in what became the American West. From the mid-thirteenth to the late nineteenth centuries, however, no one lived there permanently. The Utes, true, once traveled regularly through Castle Valley in their seasonal cycles through the greater southwest, leaving possessions at favorite campsites. In 1921, for example, a local schoolgirl's interviews with "old-timers" revealed that, "The early settlers . . . found poles of wigwams, pottery, weapons, Indian graves, bead work and rocks where they ground their corn."[2] Further south, circles of stones used to weigh down the sides of teepees and scattered pieces of broken pottery marked other old Ute campsites.[3] But these sites had been abandoned, perhaps because the Utes, like all other natives, had suffered greatly from epidemics introduced by whites, who had a resistance that Indians lacked.[4] Furthermore, the local environment had apparently deteriorated in historic times. One pioneer account related that although Utes "didn't approve of white settlers [in Castle Valley,] . . . because their own squaws became sick from drinking the

7

water, they would not live here."[5]

Permanent settlement came only at the command of the LDS Church (the Church of Jesus Christ of Latter-day Saints, or Mormons). In that, Castle Valley was not distinctive—virtually all of Utah and parts of Idaho, Nevada, Arizona, New Mexico, California, Canada, and Mexico were settled likewise. But within a handful of years after the first farmers scratched the soil for fields and irrigation canals, the Denver and Rio Grande Western Railroad built right through the valley. The railroad brought industry, a cash economy, and a flood of non-Mormon immigrants from all parts of Europe and Asia. From then on, American history ran on fast-forward through the Castle Valley corridor. This isolated, rural-industrial center of Utah, itself a most distinctive state, quickly became very different from its immediate surroundings but very like much of the rest of the country. In quick succession, Castle Valley fulfilled all the expectations of the passing age: exploration, pioneering, industrialization, immigrant adjustment, national boom and bust, Cold War development, an internationally-driven economy, and modern tourism. Yet it remains, to this day, geographically isolated. Other areas have a polyglot population and the trials of industry; most such are near urban centers. Plenty of America remains rural and traditional, but residents do not have to interact with a host of others from different traditions. None of the potentially comparable areas lie within Utah, a state that began as a separate nation: economically cooperative, polygamous, and theocratic. For this reason, a study of how forces and humans created today's Castle Valley, Utah, reflects a unique view of national aspirations as they played out in the most distinctive rural valley in America. Nowhere else was so diverse but so isolated, so industrialized but so rural, so fraught with labor disturbances yet leavened with religious tolerance. Castle Valley had all these qualities, because that is what people had to do to get along in this strange, remarkable place.

At first, Castle Valley was easy to ignore. Its natural barriers kept it separate from the rest of Utah. On the west, the Wasatch Plateau rises to some 7,500–10,000 feet above sea level, dividing the western Basin and Range Province, with its salt flats and Great Salt Lake, from the more eastern red rock Colorado Plateau, home of Castle Valley.[6] From north to south, the Plateau's heights give rise to five major, perennial, eastward-flowing streams: Huntington, Cottonwood, Ferron, Muddy, and Ivie creeks, the last a tributary of the Muddy. The first three of these creeks drain into the San Rafael River, which flows westward out of Castle Valley, cutting spectacular canyons in the northern reaches of the San Rafael Swell. This uranium-rich geological uplift houses secret springs, water pockets, and fantastic rocky shapes with weird names bestowed by lonely cowboys and defines the valley's southeastern edge. The San Rafael River's snaking course echoes that of the more northerly Price River, which enters Castle Valley through a canyon separating the Wasatch Plateau from an east-to-west-running pile

Castle Valley's ancient inhabitants left intriguing traces, including unfired, mud figurines, paint-ed rock art that sometimes resembled them, and pecked-in images portraying recognizable animals and fantastic figures, such as these at Rochester Creek, near Moore, Emery County. Photo by the author.

of uplands: the southern Book Cliffs and northern Roan Cliffs, together called the West Tavaputs Plateau. (Northwest of this region lies Utah's dom-inant Wasatch Front, contrasting with the "backside of the Wasatch Front," where Castle Valley lies.)[7] The Price River flows down through its canyon and southeast through Castle Valley (through a portion also known as Clark Valley), watering two or three tiny meadows amid a vast expanse of alkali and dirt until it, too, curves east to join the Green River. To the south and southwest, cradling the Swell, lies the San Rafael Desert, completing the circle around this remote area where the last dinosaurs once came to die.[8]

Castle Valley's last known, permanent, human inhabitants had been the Fremont Indians, an understudied group who inhabited the area over a thousand years ago. Fields of cultivated corn, beans, and squash generally grew near their clusters of pit-houses which sheltered extended family groups. Using stone tools, they fashioned unique hide moccasins with dew claw hobnails, rabbit-skin garments, and clothing made of tanned deer hides. They left behind gray and black pottery and unfired clay anthropomorphic figurines. They also decorated nearby cliffs with miles and miles of rock art whose meaning has been lost. Archaeologists, however, speculate that the Fremont may have had a developed shamanistic religion, featuring powerful figures with horned headdresses, swords, and shields. The Fremont rock art also features numerous zigzags, spirals, and stylized animals, including mountain sheep, deer, elk, and snakes. Based on a total of only 1,300 excavated sites in 1979, the Utah State Archaeologist "guesstimated" a peak aboriginal population around 1150 A.D. of somewhere around 50,000 inhabitants in Castle Valley. The Fremont, however, started drifting away in a dry cycle beginning in 1215 and culminating in the Great Southwestern Drought of 1276–1299.[9]

For the next five hundred years, Castle Valley appealed to few who saw it. By the 1800s, the Utes had named the area Blow Valley for its swirling, dusty winds. They avoided its poisonous water that killed horses and gave Ute women "big necks" (goiter).[10] Later called gyp water, (named after the Gypsum Formation), it was "so hard that if soap flakes were mixed in it, it would curdle," said a later rancher. He added, "A man can drink it for about two days only; after that time, he has to avoid sudden moves."[11] In 1830, a hardy mountain man traveling through Utah to California summed up the general opinion of Castle Valley: "the most desolate forlorn dell in the world—Everything about it was repulsive and supremely awful."[12]

Recorded history of the area began in 1776, a year currently better-known for an eloquent Declaration claiming independence for a ragged scrap of Atlantic coast. At that time, however, the greatest New World empire lay to the south. Spain had first grandiosely claimed Castle Valley in the middle 1500s, although none of the Spanish had seen it. By the late 1700s, however, Spanish policy makers pushed to secure its North American borderlands against other expanding European nations, such as England and France. Spanish officials in Mexico City sent an exploring party to forge a road from its northernmost outpost, the 150–year-old pueblo of Santa Fe (now in New Mexico), to its recently founded missions on the California coast. On July 29, 1776, Fathers Francisco Anastasio Dominguez and Silvestre Velez de Escalante left Santa Fe at the head of a party attempting to reach California. They never reached their intended destination, and their journey sensibly circumvented Castle Valley. They traveled north of it on their outward journey and, driven by winter, fled back to Santa Fe by a more southerly route.[13] Nonetheless, the Dominguez-Escalante Expedition forecast a route that bisected Castle Valley, a route romantically (and inaccurately) called the Old Spanish Trail because of their journey.

The Dominguez Escalante Expedition marked only one phase of human movement into the Castle Valley area. As noted, Utes had made seasonal forays, particularly when snow blanketed the surrounding highlands. United by a common language, various Ute bands ranged widely over some 225,000 square miles in far-reaching arcs, throughout parts of Utah, Colorado, Wyoming, and New Mexico. None of them centered on Castle Valley, however, which remained at the fringes of several bands. The Pahvant Utes and the San Pitch (or San Pete) bands throve west of Castle Valley; the Uintah and the Tumpanawach (Timpanogos) Utes lived largely to the north. To the southeast lived the Weeminuche, and, just north of them and due east of Castle Valley, the Uncompahgre.[14] Many other bands lay scattered throughout this vast area. In prehistoric times the Ute bands cycled leisurely through their seasonal homes, but their lives changed with Spanish contact. According to Ute historian Clifford Duncan, the "most important effect Spaniards had on Ute life was to introduce them to the horse. The Ute bands in southern Colorado and southeastern Utah were the first to obtain horses. The more northern Ute groups acquired them later in the seventeenth and eighteenth centuries."[15] Horses increasingly allowed skilled Ute riders to sweep into Castle Valley, deepening the Old Spanish Trail.

Despite their unfamiliarity with the Castle Valley portion of the Old Spanish Trail itself, the Spanish had also made sporadic forays into nearby Ute lands. They craved Ute-processed furs, and, most important, slaves, used largely as servants in Santa Fe. In return, the Utes sought cattle hides, a few imported goods, and prized Spanish horses. This trade was patently illegal. Spain had outlawed the slave trade in 1589 and commercial contact with the Utes in 1778, but commerce nonetheless continued.[16] Therefore, by 1805 an acculturated Ute known to the Spanish as Manuel Mestas was able to negotiate the return of Spanish livestock stolen by the Comanches and later won in battle by the Tumpanawach Utes. He probably traveled through Castle Valley to broker the deal, and his example of intercultural cooperation prefigured one of the valley's later hallmarks.[17] Others may have chanced over the local segment of the Old Spanish Trail. Records are inconclusive, but perhaps Spanish citizens Mauricio Arze, Lagos Garcia, and their party rushed eastward along its length, fleeing murderous San Pitch Utes in 1813. Bearing twelve slaves, they reached the Colorado River and safety—but went to trial in Santa Fe for their illegal goods.[18]

Mountain men next pressed toward Castle Valley, driven by the Arikara Wars further north and by continuing depletion of the beaver. Anecdotal records mention Utah forays by William Becknell and Etienne Provost of Taos in 1823–1824, and a British Hudson Bay Company brigade led by Peter Skene Ogden arrived to the north in 1825.[19] Legendary American trapper Jedediah Smith came a year later and probably even visited Castle

Valley. As he recorded in his journal:

> . . .having learned that the valley was verry barren and Rocky I did not ven-
> ture into it. The country is here extremely rough little appearance of Indi-
> ans and game quite scarce a few Mt Sheep and Antelope. after traveling in
> this direction 2 days the country looked so unpromising that I determined
> to strike westward to a low place in the Mountain and cross over.[20]

Other trappers known to have been nearby included James Ohio and Syl-
vester Pattie in 1828; William Wolfskill, Ewing Young, and William Huddart
(or Heddest), who trapped and ran pack trains, and William (or Julian)
Pope and Isaac Slover, who brought their Mexican wives and children over
the Old Spanish Trail in 1837. At the same time, mountain men Antoine
Robidoux and Dennis Julien ran a trading post to the northeast on the
Green River, leaving names scrawled on rocks: near future town of Green
River, "D. Julien, Mai 1836"; farther north, on the Roan Cliffs, "A. Robidoux,
1837," and "Julien" again by Ivie Creek, west of Castle Valley.[21]

All of these adventurers had arrived in lands now controlled by Mexico, which had won independence from Spain in 1821. Free of Spanish
mercantilism, Mexico revamped its trade policies and opted for direct
trade between New Mexico and California. The first two official Mexican
trade caravans rolled along the Old Spanish Trail in 1830 and 1831, the
wooden wheels of their *caretas* creaking through the valley's vastness. The
Utes reacted to this increasing traffic through their lands by demanding
tribute, so Mexican traders formed ever larger and better-armed caravans
in an attempt to travel unmolested. Undaunted, Utes decided to get prized
Mexican horses at their source. By the 1830s, Utes began riding through
Castle Valley all the way to California. In cooperation with mountain men
Thomas "Pegleg" Smith and the African American James Beckwourth
(who knew the route), Ute leader Wakara (also known as Walker) and
his band of Tumpanawach Utes raided all along the Old Spanish Trail.[22]
By the 1840s, Utes appeared at ranchos near San Bernardino, California,
"with bells and gaudy trappings," painted faces, "buckskin shirts, leggings,
and moccasins, beautifully marked with beads and porcupine quills [and]
with sometimes a single feather in their hair."[23] Reaching San Bernardino
itself in 1845, Wakara, with forty of his men and their families, traded
peacefully. Then, suddenly, the men rode whooping into the local herds,
swirling red and blue blankets over their heads, cutting out hundreds of
animals. Galloping north over California's Cajon Pass, they drove the herd
east across the Mojave Desert, riding hundreds of miles more until they
crossed the Wasatch Plateau and entered Castle Valley. No one would follow them there. Inevitably, some of the horses escaped and, instinctively
finding good water, spread out in the San Rafael Swell and foaled future
generations. Meanwhile, Ute raids in California became so frequent that

the route through the Mojave and over Cajon Pass became locally known as Walker's Trail.[24]

Outside events soon pushed a new breed of men through Castle Valley. Just three years after Wakara's first daring raid, in 1848, Orville C. Pratt, former lawyer and politician, became the first United States official to record his impressions of the area. Following government orders, he went west to Santa Fe and then took the Old Spanish Trail to California for a confidential meeting with the United States Consul in Monterey.[25] Escorted by sixteen experienced guides who provided basic security, Pratt (much given to exclamations) noted on September 21, 1848, "The country continues . . . sandy, hilly & utterly barren. Water is also scarce, & if there is no mineral wealth in these mountains I can hardly conceive of what earthly use a large proportion of this country was designed for!" Two days later bad weather stopped his party on Ivie Creek, with "a terrific hail storm . . . [and hail] as large as hens eggs!"[26] Pratt then passed out of Castle Valley up over the Wasatch Plateau and on toward California, suffering worn-out boots, blistered, feet, and a body "alive with vermin!"[27] But at Rancho Cucamonga on October 23, he cheered at "the first news of the discovery of gold. . . . It seems incredible. . . . But, they insist here it is true."[28] Like thousands of others he headed north, following the stories first noted in the January 1848 entry of former Mormon Battalion member Azariah Smith: "This week, Mon. the 24th [date inserted later] Mr. Marshall found some pieces of (as we all suppose) Gold. . . ."[29]

How did Mormon Battalion veterans get to Sutter's Mill? Put briefly, they had first walked all the way from Iowa to California in 1846–1847 to fight Mexico for the United States. Meanwhile, their friends, neighbors, and families were fleeing westward to escape the very country for which they fought. A fuller explanation involves the religious tempest of America's early nineteenth century. The LDS Church itself grew out of the great Protestant revival known as the Second Great Awakening, which swept western New York's Burned-Over District, home of young Vermont native Joseph Smith.[30] Smith's revelations in the 1820s led to publication of the *Book of Mormon* in 1830, and the foundation of the church he headed as both President and living Prophet.[31] Considering themselves "the chosen" over their gentile (non-Mormon) neighbors, Mormons heeded Smith's preaching, including the directive that "whosoever belongeth to my church need not fear. . . . But . . .they who do not fear me, neither keep my commandments . . . it is they that I will disturb, and cause to tremble and shake to the center."[32] The animosity expressed here met its equal in their non-Mormon neighbors, spawning violence on both sides. The Saints, outnumbered, fled westward—first to Ohio's Western Reserve, then to Missouri, then to Nauvoo, Illinois. As historian Klaus Hansen observed, "By 1844 . . . it had become all too obvious that Mormonism, because of its fundamental antipluralist nature, would come into conflict with a pluralistic American society."[33] (Decades later, exactly the same tension would forever make Castle Valley distinctive within Mormon Utah.) When an angry mob soon killed Joseph Smith and his brother Hiram at the jail in Carthage, Illinois, they exacerbated the split and created lasting martyrs for millennial Mormonism. Despite a host of uncertainties, most of Smith's former adherents decided to follow the Quorum of the Twelve Apostles, the second layer of LDS Church authority, and its president, Smith's fellow Vermonter, Brigham Young.[34] In May 1845, the Smiths' accused murderers were acquitted, and the Mormons no longer felt safe in Illinois.[35]

While tensions escalated, LDS leaders studied travelers' reports of the West, including California.[36] The October 1845 general conference (a semi-annual meeting to which all church members are invited) unanimously voted to move westward—but where?[37] A few reconnoitering parties set out: Sam Brannan slipped out of New York Harbor with a few volunteer Mormon families on February 4, 1846, on the ship *Brooklyn*, "with a flag hoisted bearing as a blind the word 'Oregon.'"[38] He later insisted, "The plans of the Mormon Church. . . . embraced an overland journey of the main body under the leadership of President Brigham Young, whose ultimate destination was announced to be California, . . . [following] the voyage of a smaller number of an advance corps [Brannan's group] by the way of Cape Horn to Upper California."[39] Another expedition, the so-called Mississippi Saints, got as far west as Pueblo, Colorado.[40] Seemingly independently, Mormon Thomas Rhoades also headed overland, allegedly "en route to the hunting grounds of California."[41] He may have been hunting, all right, but not for furry animals. According to his family history, "Thomas was made captain [in a typical LDS organization] over a group of families."[42] His group of about forty people included his wife, Elizabeth Foster Rhoades; their fourteen surviving children, some with spouses, offspring, and in-laws; Mormon widow Lavina Murphy and her seven children, two sons-in-law, and three grandchildren, a party guaranteed to scare the animals. The family traveled part way in the company of the infamous Donner Party, preceding them over the Sierra and into the Sacramento Valley in 1846 after allegedly scouting the way west for the LDS Church.[43]

By the time the Brannan and Rhoades parties arrived in California, the international situation had deteriorated. On May 13, 1846, the United States declared war on Mexico. American victory was a foregone conclusion. No longer could Mexican territory, specifically California, be a safe haven for the Saints, but the main body of the faithful still had to move westward, away from the states and their anti-Mormon powers. Therefore, in 1846, LDS leaders issued a church call for 500 men who would fight for the United States in the Mormon Battalion and donate their enlistment money to pay for the church's travel westward. The Battalion members marched all the way to California, cutting a new road and observing the territory along the way.[44] They sensibly avoided the Old Spanish Trail and Castle Valley in preference for a southern route.

The Battalion mustered out at San Diego on July 16, 1847. The men scattered, some reenlisting, others heading over the Sierra to find their families until they received orders to return to California so they would not come east empty-handed. Some sought work at Sutter's Fort, including journal-keeper Azariah Smith and shoemaker Orlando Mead, who would later help colonize Castle Valley.[45] American emigrants had begun gathering near the fort, so Swiss entrepreneur Johan Sutter decided to construct a sawmill to provide planks for houses, preferred by the Americans over traditional California adobes. He sent his carpenter, John Marshall, east on the American River (aptly named) with eight former Battalion members and a contingent of Indians under the supervision of Peter and Elizabeth Wimmer.[46] In short order, in the brand new millrace, the men discovered gold.

The timing was perfect. Fighting between the United States and Mexico had ceased, and the Treaty of Guadalupe-Hidalgo was signed in February 1848, before the golden secret leaked out. In April, Kit Carson galloped east along the Castle Valley corridor, carrying Sam Brannan's April 1, 1848, *California Star* in his saddlebags which announced the gold discovery to all the world.[47] Soon an estimated fifty thousand souls wandered the Mother Lode. Families were the rule in the mines, including the Rhoades brothers, who had lost but one brother-in-law in the war against Mexico. Unfortunately, matriarch Elizabeth Foster Rhoades had then succumbed to illness and was buried in an unmarked grave somewhere near Benecia, when the man who promised to erect a marker absconded with the money Rhoades had given him for the purpose. She left behind a host of children, including eleven-year old Caleb, future Castle Valley colonizer.[48] Members of the Rhoades family joined Battalion members (including Orlando Mead) some twenty-five miles down river from Sutter's mill on a huge, unclaimed sandbar, soon known as the fabulously rich Mormon Island, one of the richest placer (loose gold) deposits in world history.[49] In one week alone the Rhoadeses amassed $17,000. Their total take has never been recorded.[50]

While Americans fought Mexicans, the LDS Church under Brigham Young had established themselves in the Salt Lake Basin in 1847. In the fall of 1848, Young commanded the California Saints to "gather to Zion" and bring their gold to the LDS Church.[51] Thomas Rhoades, accompanied by Caleb, a younger sister, and two grandchildren, became the richest Mormon to comply.[52] When Thomas reached Utah, he deposited $10,826 in the gold dust accounts maintained by Brigham Young, leaving a remainder of $6,174 for himself.[53] In exchange for the sacks of gold, one of which allegedly weighed sixty pounds, Young "allowed him to withdraw from the tithing office all the food supplies necessary. He also received a herd of cattle in consideration for the gold dust" and subsequently married five wives in polygamy.[54] President Young also made a cautionary example of him in 1850, referring to "Father Rhoades" as "the wealthiest man who came from the [California] mines . . . with $17,000, [but] could he buy the possessions I had made in one year? It will not begin to do it. . . . and again, look at the widows that have been made, and see the bones that lie bleaching and scattered over the prairies."[55] Nonetheless, Brigham Young wished to control California under reliable LDS authorities, having broken with Sam Brannan, the original leader of the Saints there. Mormon wagon trains rolled westward in 1849.[56] That November 3 another train, organized by two merchants from Missouri, hired some Mormon drivers, including Edwin Pettit, his brother-in-law, David Seely, and David's younger brother, Justus Wellington Seely, father of future Castle Valley colonizers, Orange, Sarah, and Justus Wellington II. On this particular trip, Orange and Sarah were left behind in Salt Lake with their mother, Clarissa Jane Wilcox Seely, who delivered Justus Wellington II (or Wink) during his father's absence.[57] Thus, Castle Valley's main pioneer leaders—Caleb Rhoades and Orange Seely—were together at the Salt Lake fort that winter, though no one has recorded if they met.

Even before the wagon trains set out, LDS authorities had formulated a new Utah government. In the spring of 1849, they created the state of Deseret, headed by the same men who controlled the LDS Church, a genuine theocracy. On paper at least, Deseret embraced an area from western Colorado into northwestern New Mexico, to Arizona north of the Gila River, California east of the Sierra and south of the Tehachapis, as well as parts of Oregon, Idaho, and Wyoming. The U.S. Congress, on the other hand, established in 1850 the territory of Utah, encompassing a much smaller area: all of present-day Utah, western Colorado, and most of Nevada. These dual governments began a contest over who governed, how much territory, and for what purposes. The rivalry between national and theocratic authority would develop into an overt LDS American contest that would affect Castle Valley settlement more than two decades later.[58]

To make matters worse, in 1852 the LDS Church publicly announced plural marriage (one man, several wives) as a tenet of its faith. Although practiced in private for probably two decades, this public announcement doomed the Saints' repeated requests for statehood. Nonetheless, they tried: by memorial in 1852, 1853, 1854, and, finally, with a constitutional convention in 1856–1857.[59] In the other states of the Union, plural marriage constituted bigamy, a criminal offense. But since states regulated marriage, admitting Utah to the Union would protect this "peculiar institution." Consequently, Congress had no intention of granting Utah statehood until its leaders outlawed polygamy, an unlikely event in light of Utah's theocratic government, also anathema to America at large. Thus, battle lines became drawn around these two, interlocking issues.

While politicians fretted briefly about the Mormons, the whole nation thrilled to the excitement of California gold. Hundreds of thousands of foreigners raced to the gold fields: men (and a few women) from Mexico and Chile; Ireland and Australia; Russia, China, France, and Great Britain. Americans from the East went, too—and had to sail around the Horn (three months) or ride muleback across the Central American isthmus (quicker, but malarial) or take a wagon train across the country (four to six months). Not only did foreigners pose a threat to U.S. control, but the nation needed California gold to coin money in those pre-paper days. The country needed a railroad. Congress heartily agreed, but the precise route across the continent became a political firestorm. Every powerful American politician wanted the eastern terminus in his own state or section, so his constituents could be nearest the gold arriving at the end of the line.[60]

One of the loudest promoters of his favorite route was Senator Thomas Hart Benton of Missouri, the father-in-law of explorer John C. Fremont. Benton supported building along a line that ran directly west from St. Louis (in his home state, of course) to San Francisco Bay—which took it right through the Castle Valley corridor.[61] At a St. Louis railroad convention in 1849, Senator Benton eloquently proclaimed:

> Let us beseech the national legislature to build a great road upon the great national line which unites Europe and Asia—the line which will find on our continent the Bay of San Francisco at one end, St. Louis in the middle, the National metropolis [Washington, D.C.] and great commercial emporium at the other end.

In case anyone missed his point he concluded, "There is the East—there is India."[62] Suddenly, Castle Valley—located, by chance, at roughly the same latitude as St. Louis and Sacramento—was on a line that would girdle the world. This route, of course, existed only in Senator Benton's imagination until proper surveys could be made. Even then, actual construction began only after the Civil War had eliminated from Congress the powerful Southern bloc, who favored a New Orleans terminus. In the meantime, several men jockeyed for positions on the all-important survey parties, now that science, not politics, would allegedly decide the route.

On March 2, 1853, Congress finally passed a Pacific Railroad Bill to fund speedy railroad surveys, with reports due—in dizzying haste—by January 1854. Among the four routes under study, Senator Benton particularly championed that along the 38th parallel, and favored his son-in-law as the head of the expedition. Instead, the nod went to Lt. John Williams Gunnison who had previously served in Utah in the 1850 Stansbury expedition, which mapped the Great Salt Lake. Fremont, who had had his own western experiences, attracted private financial backers.[63] Another government expedition under the direction of E. F. Beale, newly-appointed Superintendent of Indian Affairs for California (to deal with other problems caused by the flood of gold-seekers), set off first along the 38th parallel route in July 1853. Beale's party, all traveling horseback, simply followed the well-worn Old Spanish Trail through Castle Valley. His diarist and artist, Gwin Harris Heap, left a succinct description: "The trail led us over low hills much cut up by dry and rocky ravines, and on our right were sandstone bluffs. Vegetation was scanty, principally dwarf cedars, artemisia, and cactus, and occasionally patches of gramma grass. We found no water from camp to camp."[64] Gunnison's more elaborate expedition included experts to make scientific observations and lots of equipment. Hauling their supplies in wagons, his men had to cut a wider road clear across the continent. Dr. James Schiel, the party's physician, looked west at Castle Valley in early October 1853, just before they crossed the Green River. He pronounced it "a wild and unproductive country . . . [where nothing is] likely to diminish the gloom of this view."[65] After crossing the river, they veered off the Old Spanish Trail and headed north, seeking watering spots for their teams. They reportedly reached the Price River near the present site of Wellington, then turned southwest to meet the original route again near Huntington Creek, creating the northern route, or the Gunnison cut-off, of the Old Spanish Trail.[66] Exploring as they went, some men proffered "specimens of coal . . . from the hills near the camp," according to the expedition's chronicler, Lt. E. G. Beckwith. "Capt. Gunnison and Dr. Schiel . . . [differed] in opinion as to its quality."[67] That mineral, then so drab compared to California gold, would eventually become Castle Valley's main economic support.

The Gunnison party pressed on across this inhospitable terrain, fearing Indian attacks.[68] The Utes had reason for hostility. They had been trading with New Mexicans, Californians, and mountain men for decades, some of them following the seasonal route that took them from Utah to California and back. Recently, Mormon colonists had taken choice lands, especially near Utah Lake, northwest of Castle Valley. To support themselves, the Utes aggressively pursued more trade, offering the most readily-available commodity: slaves. The disapproving Saints then tried to stamp out the sale of humans (although they encouraged the indenture of Indian children to suitable Mormons). In 1851 and 1852, judicial and legislative actions effectively cut off New Mexicans from the Utes, strangling the Ute market for slaves.[69] Each band then sought its own economic solution. The Northern Utes—the Tumpanawach—hardened their stance toward interlopers. In July 1853, near Utah Lake, a Mormon killed a Ute and wounded two others in an altercation over trade. This event sparked the Walker War (named for Wakara) and sparked a series of Indian raids on whites that lasted until May 1854.[70] According to a recent study, Wakara's "limited goals in the series of raids he directed . . . were simply to obtain Mormon cattle to feed his people and to force the Mormons into perpetually purchasing his Paiute captives."[71] The Southern Utes (including the Weeminuche), meanwhile, stayed peaceful. Schiel noted the very friendly Indians at their camp on the Green River.[72] He called them "a cheerful tribe. . . . A piece of bread with

some bacon made them dance with delight." The joy over food was under-
standable, considering that, as he noted, they lived "in an absolutely sterile
country. There could be no thought of any subsistence by the hunt, for
one can travel for weeks without finding any game besides a pair of lonely
jackdaws [ravens], or a few contented lizards, which seem to represent the
animal life here. It is a country where, according to the statement of a famous mountaineer, Kit Carson, 'not a wolf could make a living.'"[73] West of
the Wasatch Plateau, the Pahvant, San Pitch, and other Utes were also being driven to hunger and desperation by Mormons who had taken up their
traditional hunting lands, killed game, and replaced camping sites with
farms.[74] There, the legacy of mounting Ute displacement, coupled with
American hostility, broke upon the Gunnison Party. Just before Gunnison's
arrival, in the fractious fall of 1853, a California-bound emigrant company
had refused food to hungry, ragged Utes and had tried to disarm them.
When one Ute struggled and wounded an American, the emigrants fired
indiscriminately on the Indians, killing several, including Mareer, an old
chief. The emigrant train left immediately, fearing retaliation.[75] The un-
knowing Gunnison party was the next group of whites to come through the
area. On October 6, 1853, angry Utes, including Mareer's son, killed Gunnison and seven of his men in revenge.[76] The expedition's second-in-com-
mand, Lieutenant Beckwith, completed the survey, but Gunnison's death
prompted a rumor of Mormon involvement—helping to prevent annexa-
tion of Deseret to the United States.

Meanwhile, only a week or two before Gunnison's murder, back in
Missouri, John Fremont had belatedly launched his own attempt to map
Benton's pet railroad route to the West. To illustrate his forthcoming report, he engaged the services of a young, Jewish artist and photographer,
Solomon Nunes Carvalho, whose reminiscences give the best view of this
expedition. They started out so late that, by the time they reached the
snowy lands by the Colorado River, they were killing their horses for food
and taking an oath against cannibalism. Struggling further west, before
crossing the Green, Carvalho noted "Capt. Gunnison's wagon trail was still
plainly visible," although they chose not to use it. The Utes in the vicinity
traded them grass seed, their only remaining food, and Carvalho (who had
already eaten his pony) parted with virtually everything but his daguerreo-
type boxes in trade. He concluded that he owed his subsequent survival to
"the sustaining properties of this cereal." Once across the Green, the city-
bred Carvalho lagged behind with a badly frozen foot in a "desert waste
of eternal snow." Prepared to die but revived by memories of his wife and
children, he painfully caught up with the group, who went on to complete
their journey.[77] Later, back in Washington, Gunnison's survey, despite the
political maneuvers of Beale and Fremont, officially put to rest Benton's
unrealistic image of "a great central path to the Pacific."[78] Castle Valley
would not be the chosen corridor from the East Coast to India until the

late twentieth century, with the completion of Interstate Highway 70, far too late to pacify Benton.

Meanwhile, this parade of federal surveyors put the Saints on notice that their protective isolation would soon end. Before the gentile juggernaut arrived, Mormons had to hold by colonization as much of Deseret as possible.[79] Consequently, in 1851 Brigham Young sent out San Bernardino colonists, a group of families headed by twenty men including David and Wellington Seely. Future Castle Valley colonizer Orange Seely, then an eight-year-old, later remembered planting "Olive trees and grapes for Ordinance purposes. I saw the town of San Bernardino surveyed and lots drawn." His family built the first sawmill in the nearby mountains, and David Seely took over the colony's leadership from Apostle Charles C. Rich—all good examples of pioneering for future Castle Valley colonizers Orange, Sarah, and Wink.[80]

While San Bernardino Saints built homes from planks cut by the newly-erected sawmill, another Mormon group headed toward what is now southeastern Utah. Called to found one of five Indian missions established between 1854–1856, their selection signaled a change in LDS Indian policy generated by the end of the Walker War. Forty-one male missionaries gathered in the spring of 1855, including John Lowry, Jr., whose family would later have a major impact on Utah's Indian relations and on Castle Valley. In May, the party crossed the Wasatch Plateau, through Joe's Valley and down Cottonwood Canyon to the Castle Valley floor, following a Ute guide. They found ancient Indian rock art and "stone coal" (Castle Valley's future wealth) near the mouth of Cottonwood Canyon; located sandstone pockets over a hundred feet below their trail through the San Rafael Swell and painfully drew up water, quart by quart for their stock; crossed Gunnison's trail, and made their way as best they could along the "Spanish trail . . . [traveling] over a good country for a road without water," a poor compliment indeed.[81] Building a stone fort, the Elk Mountain Mission, near the site of present-day Moab, the missionaries enjoyed some initial successes until, after five months, several local Utes turned murderously on them, driving the survivors back to the settlements. Thus ended this first official Mormon foray across Castle Valley, doing nothing to expand Zion nor to improve impressions of the area.[82]

While the Saints spread out, the federal government also intensified its attempt to control this distant territory with a host of new appointees in 1855. A new federal surveyor-general attempted to finalize land titles by U.S. law, while the Saints feared dispossession. LDS bishops allocated Utah lands to their followers by drawing lots for townsites and farming fields, holding waters and forests in common under the direction of powerful church leaders. While Mormons saw this process as benefiting the Saints's general welfare, non-Mormons, shut out entirely, regarded this system as a monopolistic, theocratic impediment to American free enterprise.[83] As America pushed westward, this potential conflict festered, unresolved by conflicting judicial systems. Federal judges tried fruitlessly to establish their authority as church members avoided their courts in favor of local, probate courts staffed entirely by Saints. A series of natural disasters in 1855–1856 helped prompt the LDS Church to launch the Reformation, in which Saints consecrated all worldly goods (especially land) to Brigham Young as trustee-in-trust. While greater America recoiled at this new evidence of an un-American theocracy loose in Utah, the Reformation's other aspects—the view of Adam as a god, rebaptism for all Saints, and a reaffirmation of the holiness of polygamy— did nothing to calm their fears. As charismatic LDS Apostle Jedediah Grant avidly preached blood atonement—the spilling of guilty blood to the point of murder—fearful federal officials fled the territory.[84]

Concurrently, John C. Fremont, running for President in 1856 on the Republican ticket (a brand new party) promised to stamp out the "dual relics of barbarism, slavery and polygamy." Slavery remained respectable, especially in the South, a district particularly hostile to Mormon polygamists as shown by the 1857 murder there of beloved Apostle Parley P. Pratt. He had just married another plural wife (his twelfth) who had left her estranged husband but had not divorced him. The aggrieved man killed Pratt, spawning a Mormon outcry for blood atonement.[85] Nationally, when Democrat James Buchanan won the Presidency, he co-opted Fremont's rhetoric against the more politically acceptable target of polygamy and launched the bloodless Utah War that sent federal troops into Utah in 1857–1858.[86] The Saints completely abandoned their San Bernardino colony, a movement begun before the army's approach.[87] Under these tense conditions, on September 11, 1857, Mormons led the massacre of approximately one hundred California-bound travelers at the southern Utah grazing ground called Mountain Meadows.[88] Twenty years later, John D. Lee died by firing squad as the scapegoat for this atrocity, while his son, George, joined the outlaw element in Castle Valley, as later events would reveal. Meanwhile, the well-disciplined U.S. Army took up residence in the Salt Lake area for the next three years, bringing an end to the fervor of the Reformation.[89]

This series of events had a direct effect on a future Castle Valley leader. As the San Bernardino colony broke up, most of the Seely family left in a wagon train on December 24, 1857. They departed without Mary Pettit Seely and her children, except for eldest son, David, who had chosen to accompany his father, David, Sr., back to Utah. As son David later reported: "She said that she had walked as far as she intended to walk when she came to California, having come from Long Island, to Illinois, to Utah, and then to California"—even farther than the Mormon Battalion.[90] The return trip was especially exciting for David's cousins, children Orange, Sarah, Wink, and their four other siblings. When the group camped near the site of the Mountain Meadows Massacre, the boys found the remains of some of the slaughtered. "The graves had been shallow, and the wild animals had dug up the bodies. One of the boys took a skeleton and thrust it into the wagon opening, and terrified the girls. Another boy found a gold watch."[91] The Seely train had a dangerously dry crossing, but their wagons rolled into Pleasant Grove, Sanpete County, in April 1858.[92] When they arrived in Utah in the fading light of the Reformation, Brigham Young probably counseled David, Sr., to enter polygamy, since Mormon commitment to plural marriage had intensified throughout the 1850s as objections to it grew.[93] At any rate, as son David reported, "father and Brigham Young had a heated argument, and finally Brigham Young told David Seeley [Sr.] to go back to California."[94] In later years, David, Sr.'s brother, Justus Wellington, who stayed in Utah, would, like Thomas Rhoades, also take plural wives, forever committing him to a life in Mormon Zion.[95] All the children brought back from a California childhood would thus be on hand when Castle Valley needed colonizers.

The Reformation had also brought changes in Indian-white relations through the consecration movement, in which the faithful dedicated all possessions to Brigham Young as LDS Church trustee-in-trust. Sanpete County, the Seelys' new home, recorded 197 land deeds of consecration, including one from Ute chief Walker's brother and successor, Aropeen (Arapeen, Arapine) who had converted to Mormonism. Since the Utes did not recognize private property, Aropeen deeded all of his tribe's holdings: the "portion of land and country known as Sanpete County together with all timber and material on the same" as well as enumerated livestock, guns, and tools to Young.[96] The LDS Church also commanded that Justus Wellington Seely and one of his brothers give the Utes their farm at Indianola, Sanpete County, in exchange.[97] Perhaps this mutual church involvement helped foster the bond which grew between the Seelys and the Utes, which would become so obvious when both groups later moved to (or through) Castle Valley.

Before anyone took further notice of the Castle Valley corridor, however, the whole nation had to weather the Civil War. With the South out of Congress in the short-lived Confederacy, the remnant U.S. Congress in 1862 passed three acts of tremendous significance to the West: the Homestead Act, the first Pacific Railroad Bill (followed by another in 1864), and the Morrill Anti-Bigamy Act. The first law allowed a claimant to obtain 160 acres for only the $10 filing fee, if he (or she, in the case of a widow) lived on the land for five years and made specified improvements. The second provided federal finding and generous land grants to corporations building a transcontinental railroad. The last statute outlawed what it called bigamy (including polygamy), disincorporated the LDS Church as an organization that supported plural marriage, and limited the holdings of any charitable organization (meaning, the LDS Church) to $50,000 in real property.[98] However, the Morrill Act proved unenforceable because Mormons consistently filled both grand and petit juries in Utah. The government ignored its defects, preoccupied with war.

Fighting on eastern battlefields had drawn Union soldiers out of Utah, where they had been garrisoned since 1858. All over the West, natives took the opportunity of the departing blue-coats to attack interlopers on their lands. President Lincoln, short of troops, first asked the Mormons to guard the mails before assigning antagonistic Colonel Patrick Edward Connor and the California Volunteers to guard Utah. Connor established Camp (later Fort) Douglas on the bench east of Salt Lake City and spent most of his efforts killing Indians, including approximately 250 Shoshoni on Bear River, and harrying Utes in the mountains just north of Castle Valley.[99] After 1868, three years after the war ended, the Utes were increasingly confined to reservations by federal troops, who now took the side of land-hungry Saints. According to a recent study, "Inviting the army to take charge of checking raids and pushing Indians onto reservations opened a new era for Mormon expansion."[100]

Spreading Mormon settlements had already destroyed Ute lands in Sanpete County, and Utes retaliated by capturing Mormon stock, driving the captured animals eastward into Castle Valley. Tensions exploded in April 1865 as Ute-speaking John Lowry, one of the former Elk Mountain missionaries, got into a serious tussle with Black Hawk and with Jake Arapeen, a son of the man who had consecrated the tribe's lands to the LDS Church. Within twenty-four hours, Black Hawk's Utes were driving off Mormon cattle and killing all the herders they found, the beginning of the Black Hawk War.[101] Orange Seely took command of a Sanpete cavalry unit, pursuing the Utes and their stolen stock into Castle Valley all the way to the Green River. Finding no Indians there, they retraced their steps as far as Cottonwood Creek, seriously short of provisions. Seely wrote, "We go[t] as far as [present-day] Castle Dale and . . . were soon met with provisions at the head of Rock Canyon. After this it did not take long before I reach[ed] home tired and happy to get back.[102] The provisions that saved them came from mule packers carrying some strong-smelling, homemade cheese. According to a later local history, "The Indians were coming and when they smelled the cheese they went away and did not dare to come near."[103]

Cheese, of course, was not a permanent deterrent. Soldiers were. The Black Hawk War dribbled to an end with a treaty in 1872, but Ute raiders continued driving livestock to New Mexican markets, this time from Sanpete County rather than California, pursued by Mormons down the Castle Valley corridor. Increasingly, the Utes were joined by Navajo, Paiute, Apache, Hopi, Shoshoni, and white rustlers as the resistance grew from Brown's Hole, Wyoming, into Arizona and New Mexico. To counteract this growing lawlessness, soldiers came back throughout the West. Some entered Castle Valley following the Old Spanish Trail westward from Colorado to the Green River crossing (where the Seely party had abandoned pursuit), then across the Castle Valley plains to the north, following the Price (then called the White) River. As the men proceeded upstream, they discovered that the Price River Canyon was too steep to be a practicable pass. They returned to the valley and retraced their steps eastward to the first passable canyon cutting north into the heights, now called Soldier Canyon—the final route of the Midland Trail. Somewhere in this vicinity, several of their party died and were buried in an unmarked grave. The area is now called Soldier Summit. The bodies have never been found.[104]

While the Civil War created the last major opportunity for Indian resistance, it more significantly decided once and for all whether states or the federal government would be supreme. The South, of course, preferred state supremacy, as did the Mormons with Utah's peculiar marriage practices and theocratic government. But the North won. In the political climate of the 1870s, when the full force of the national government sought to control rebellious states, actions in Utah Territory gained the limelight. Non-Mormons pushed for more rights and property. As a territory, Utah remained (allegedly) entirely under federal legal control. Therefore, confrontations could only increase until Utah could become one of the states in the Union. It could never become a state, however, while its leaders embraced theocracy and polygamy.

This growing clash also played out on the personal level. For example, non-Mormon Dr. J. King Robinson, taking advantage of Utah's cloudy land titles, tried to build a number of businesses in Salt Lake City. When Mormons disputed his claims to the mineral springs just north of Salt Lake City, he hired attorney Robert N. Baskin—another non-Mormon arrival of 1865—to defend his claims. The stakes were high: if Robinson won his suit, he would overturn most land titles in Utah.[105] Baskin could do little to help Robinson, however, when unidentified hoodlums began intimidating the doctor and wrecking his property. Called out one dark night allegedly to see a patient, Robinson was shot and knifed to death, and his case died with him. The murderers were never caught; Mormon lawlessness became a national scandal, and Baskin, viewing the mutilated body of his dead client and friend, vowed to empower federal authorities to bring justice in Utah.[106] The Saints had just made a most dedicated enemy—at least until the rise of riches in Castle Valley coal.

A receptive Congress also reacted. As the Robinson murder and other Utah violence gained national attention, Congress proposed the Wade Bill of 1866 and the Cragin Bill of 1867 to limit severely the authority of the LDS Church. Both bills failed.[107] Infuriated, Baskin tried the local approach. In 1869–1870 he helped organize Utah's Liberal Party, which also attracted General Patrick Edward Connor, an active participant in its convention. The Liberals foundered on the rock of excommunicated Mormons who joined the party but clung to their polygamous wives, a practice the Liberals opposed. Nonetheless, they fielded a slate of candidates, forcing devout Saints to organize the People's Party.[108] LDS leaders had always insisted that more than one political candidate contradicted the divinely inspired political order. Righteous Saints exercised their freedom by unanimously sustaining their leaders' decisions and by voting by acclamation for the proffered candidates. Or, as the *Deseret News* later put it, "One policy, one ticket, one ballot for all. 'Whatever is more or less than this cometh of evil.'"[109] In adopting a party system, the Saints slowly swung toward the American mainstream.

By this time, the Mormons' separate Zion faced a host of other new pressures as well. Most important, in the post-war years two mighty railroads swung toward Utah as hammers rang on steel across the Sierra Nevada and on the cold, harsh plains of the Midwest. California's Central Pacific (CP) struggled eastward; the Union Pacific (UP) nosed westward, and the nation waited expectantly for the fulfillment of its Manifest Destiny. LDS leaders, recognizing that geographic barriers were about to fall, in 1867 created the School of the Prophets, a communal endeavor based on earlier models such as the Law of Consecration and Stewardship of 1831 and the Mormon Reformation of 1856–1857.[110] The School began shaping economic policy by directing Mormon involvement in the Union Pacific Railroad and fostering cooperative industries to build farm machinery, wagons, and furniture, to spin silk, weave wool, and to construct local branch railroads. Most important, in 1868 its leaders founded Zions Cooperative Mercantile Institution (ZCMI) to handle wholesaling and to manage "foreign" imports.[111] One division developed strategies to preserve Mormon land claims. Another touted ways to bring LDS converts to Zion to counteract the anticipated wave of non-Mormon voters.[112]

In direct contrast to the Mormons' threatened view of the transcontinental, the rest of the nation celebrated its promise. As political jockeying delayed the driving of the Golden Spike to unite the two lines, cities all over America readied for celebration. Early in May 1869, telegraphers in New York, Washington, Chicago, New Orleans, and a host of other cities waited eagerly for news coming through the Western Union's Omaha office. The nation, now wired in one huge electrical circuit, seemed to exhale with one breath as a lone telegrapher at Promontory, Utah, tapped out, "Done." Fire alarms rang, church bells thundered, cannons boomed, and parades formed spontaneously (the one in Chicago stretching seven miles long). The event had all the joy and patriotism of a universally-favored war, without the fears of oncoming suffering, death, and destruction. Back in Utah, Brigham Young did not attend the festivities.[113]

The Union Pacific continued maneuvering for economic advantage after it entered Utah in 1869. In 1872, as the UP moved toward acquisition of the Mormon-built Utah Central Railroad between Salt Lake City and the transcontinental to the north, Brigham Young worked out an arrangement to benefit his church. The UP was allowed to buy up the Utah Central through controlling its stock, leading to a railroad stranglehold on Salt Lake City and a monopoly on the coal trade (so important for home heating and industry)

Cowboys continued to round up wild horses on the San Rafael Swell for three quarters of a century, seeking the herds among Castle Valley's fantastic rock formations and rare watering holes. Courtesy of Emery County Archives.

from the UP mines in Wyoming. The UP soon acquired other Utah railroads, monopolizing access to growing hard rock mines but guaranteeing its Mormon partners a powerful advocate in Washington.[114] Cementing the relationship, John Sharp, who had represented Brigham Young at the Golden Spike ceremony and who had helped found local railroads, gained a position on the UP board in 1875, which he held to the end of this life.[115]

Meanwhile, as officials drove the Golden Spike home, Utah came under study by one of America's greatest explorers, the one-armed Civil War veteran John Wesley Powell. He led two exploration parties in 1869 and 1871 down previously uncharted waterways from Green River, Wyoming, through the Grand Canyon of the Colorado, floating along Castle Valley's eastern flank. For once, viewed from the river, the area's beauty triumphed over its aridness: the "long narrow valley with mesas and buttes . . . [reaching to] a stupendous line of cliffs 2,000 or 3,000 feet high . . . of many colors. . . . called the Book Cliffs."[116] He and his men left copious records noting Ute camps, desolate canyons, azure mountains and occasional wildlife. Some of his findings, published in 1879 as *Report on the Lands of the Arid Region of the United States*, noted: "The largest body of arable land within the drainage basin of the San Rafael is in Castle Valley, a long, narrow depression lying between the eastern escarpment of the Wasatch Plateau and the San Rafael Swell. . . . No permanent settlements have been made in the valley, but it is used as a winter herding ground for stock owned by the settlers in other portions of Utah."[117]

By the time Powell's report issued, some of its comments were out-of-date. Human impact had transformed Castle Valley in the eight-year interim between Powell's last exploration and his published report. Federal surveyors had completed mapping most of the Castle Valley corridor; Brigham Young had issued his last settlement call to populate it a week before he died, and clusters of settlers had begun wresting homes from its inhospitable lands. More significantly for the future of this natural passageway, the juggernaut of industry, embodied in a newly-chartered railroad, was on its way. Reluctant partners of church and state, communitarian and capitalistic, old and new, had begun their final dance within this "last frontier."

# 2

# The Significance of the Frontier,
# 1870–1882

*The whole region was essentially a territory primeval and . . . a railroad project*
*under such conditions was fraught with the utmost difficulty. Returns on investment*
*were, because of the sparsely settled region, very problematical to say the least.*[1]
— ARTHUR RIDGEWAY, DENVER AND RIO GRANDE RAILROAD

What was the significance of a primeval frontier? Frederick Jackson Turner, the seminal western historian, decided the very existence of an American frontier, progressively "civilized," created our national democracy. He imagined an orderly parade of types striding westward from the Appalachians, bringing "the process of civilization, marching single file . . . the Indian, the fur trader and hunter, the cattle raiser, the pioneer farmer."[2] Like so much else in Castle Valley, local facts did not quite fit the theoretical pattern. By the time Turner's parade reached Utah's last frontier, the cowboys had gotten somewhat out of line and came at roughly the same time as—if not a year or two before—the hunter and trapper. They rode over the Wasatch Plateau and down through the Book Cliffs, driving restless livestock literally to greener pastures.

By the mid-1800s, several small herds of mustangs, descended from those which had escaped from generations of Spanish and Mexican horse traders, roamed the Swell. The animals drank from the San Rafael, the Muddy, and the countless little washes and springs that bubbled up in their season. They foraged on bunch grasses and brush that grew in lush, shaded corners among the broken rocks.[3] Shortly after the end of the Black Hawk War in 1872, ranchers moved their herds into Castle Valley. The men often stayed to capture more horses; some became settlers. In very short order the railroad followed, bringing American industry to what had so recently been "a territory primeval."[4]

Castle Valley's white settlement began with independent herders around 1875, part of a long American tradition. Throughout the American West from 1866–1886, legendary cattle trails spread from Texas northward to the extending railroad end-of-track pushing ever westward.[5] When trailing ended in the late nineteenth century, ranching operations had spread over the entire United States, following the ebb of native peoples and the diminishing grasses trampled underfoot by expanding white settlement. American cowboys used techniques drawn from throughout the globe, including Spanish transhumance: moving animals seasonally to different climate zones. Texas provided Utah with the word "cowboy" (rather than the "buckaroo" used in Nevada) and the acceptance of absentee owners in the raising of open-range cattle. Ideas from the British Isles (by way of the midwestern U.S.) included raising sheep as well as cattle, another common local practice.[6]

Well-known stockmen from Sanpete County, familiar with all these ways, arrived in 1874 or 1875 as individual entrepreneurs. They included Leander Lemmon, James McHadden, Knuck Woodward, Bill Gentry, Alfred Starr, the Neatherys, and the Swasey brothers: Joe, Rod, Charlie, and Sid.[7] Michael Molen—who had a town named after him—came with his herds about 1875.[8] They drove their stock east, down the wooded canyons cut by flowing streams that usually dried up in gulches sprinkled with alkali (still called "Utah summer snow"). They moved from canyons cut by Huntington Creek all the way south to Ivie Creek and out onto the Castle Valley plain. In the north, the Whitmores trailed their herds down through the Book Cliffs to Grassy Trail Creek in 1878.[9]

The Swaseys were reputedly the first to push their own horses up on the Swell. Their independent natures mirrored the romantic vision of the cowboy, so inaccurate for the other youths who rode the cattle drives as wage workers for big-time ranchers.[10] Nonetheless, they certainly were young when they came: in 1875 Charles was twenty-four; Sid, twenty-two; Rod, sixteen, and Joe, fourteen–years-old.[11] Their lives in Castle Valley, to some extent, fit American romance. For example, Sid and Charley bet seventy-five head of cattle that Sid's handsome saddle horse couldn't jump across a spectacular gorge in the San Rafael Swell. Here, the San Rafael River cuts down fifty-eight feet through the limestone, leaving a canyon about fourteen feet wide with sheer rock walls. Taking a long run, Sid made it, won the cows, and the spot has been called "Sid's Leap" ever since.[12] At home in the Swell, the Swaseys later gave other names to its striking features, including Joe's Office (the San Rafael Knob), Sid's Mountain, and the rock formation, Joe and His Dog.[13]

The federal government, too, wished to explore this last frontier. After the Powell surveys of 1869 and 1871, two more government parties mapped the area. First came Lt. George M. Wheeler, commander of the Army's western geographical surveys from 1871–1878, allegedly chasing "the prewar glories and fame of Captain John C. Fremont."[14] His Wheeler Survey traversed Castle Valley in 1873 roughly along Gunnison's route. Two members of his party noted some of the local coal-bearing strata.[15] The second surveyor, A. D. Ferron, was a Utah man with a contract from the federal government. In July and August 1873, his party surveyed the far southern end of Castle Valley and, in three ways, left his name on the land.[16] First, perhaps tired of the hot, lonely work, one of his team said, "If you will let us duck you in this creek, you can have it."[17] He did, and his name went on the map as "Ferron's Creek" (later without the possessive "s"). A town founded on its banks in 1878 bears the same name, as well as nearby Ferron Mountain.[18] After their efforts, claimants could rely on federal law to acquire Castle Valley lands—if they wanted to.

According to historian Frederick Jackson Turner, movement west was a crucial step in American history, and the "growth of nationalism and the evolution of American political institutions were dependent on the advance of the frontier."[19] Nonetheless, at the time, Washington ignored Wheeler's work as a duplication of that of more well-connected surveyors John Wesley Powell and Clarence King. Ferron's survey escaped official notice. Powell indeed had an impact, albeit a negative one in a nation still reeling from the devastation of the wide-spread Panic of 1873. Powell observed that a 160–acre farm, allowed under the 1862 Homestead Act, provided insufficient land to sustain a farming family throughout most of the arid West. "Powell had swept aside hopeful fantasies about the West," wrote historian David Wrobel, and "his report helped spark a land reform movement . . . . In 1879 a Public Land Commission was created for the purpose of apportioning the remaining lands in a more rational manner."[20] More cynically, historian William Goetzmann suggested that Powell's report pandered to western ranchers in Congress, making it less than "a straightforward scientific report."[21]

All the same, the existence of federal surveys marked a clear intention to claim the wilds of Utah. Saints, needing new grazing for their expanding herds and homes for their growing number of children, took another look at Castle Valley. First, Sanpete Mormons formed cooperatives and hired men to manage their livestock. They began with the Northern Sanpete Co-operative Institution in 1867, formalized in 1871 with a constitution and registered brands.[22] When the School of the Prophets initiated the United Order of Enoch in 1874 (mandating pooling resources, sharing labor, and eating together), Sanpete Mormons adopted this system for managing their herds.[23] In 1875, they leased their sheep to responsible men rather than hire employees. Orange Seely became the first lessee, charged with herding "sheep for three years and pay[ing] to the different owners annually one and a half (1 ½) pounds of wool for each sheep and at the end of three years deliver (13) thirteen sheep for every eight received."[24] He or others also leased cattle and perhaps pigs, although these contracts have not survived.

In the winter of 1875–1876, Seely and about a dozen other men from the Mount Pleasant and Fairview United Orders drove over 1,500 head of sheep and 1,400 head of horned stock and eight yoke of cattle (probably oxen) east over the Wasatch Plateau all the way to Castle Valley. Those with him included his younger brother, Justus Wellington II (Wink) Seely; their cousin, David Randolph Seely, and two Indian pig-herders named Aub (English name Joseph) and Piggy. Aaron Oman cut the road for the two ox-drawn wagons as the herds laboriously struggled fourteen days to cross the forty miles into Castle Valley.[25]

Most of the Sanpete United Order group wintered together in a 20 x 30–foot dugout built by the two Seely brothers about one mile west of present-day Castle Dale.[26] David Seely, however, got separated from the group and spent winter in the open, taking "my bed and food with me on a pack mule, and camped where night overtook me." By early spring, he cut a startling (and probably smelly) figure, having donned roughly-sewn flour sacks in place of his worn-out pants and a cap of coyote skin, an animal he had killed himself but probably had not had time to tan. As the snow started to thaw on the Wasatch Plateau, he decided he could get out, and, still without any of the rest of his party, "went by the Salina Canyon. . . . It took me three days to get home." Coming down into the settlements, David self-consciously tried to avoid others, sending the sisters of his first host into gales of laughter and frightening his wife, who slammed the cabin door in his face. After an argument, she finally recognized David and let him in.[27] He soon learned that the United Order was dissolving, as most Utah Orders did in 1875 (although some in Sanpete County endured a year or two longer).[28] David Seely reminded the unraveling institution of his four-year herding contract, and was bought out with the excess unbranded animals, some "170 head of cattle, [and] 300 head of sheep," which he figured "paid up for all the hardship."[29]

Living on the land as Seely had, independent trappers also entered the area. A handful of memories descend to us, including a local historian's note that "some time after 1877 and before the first settlers came, Nathan Galloway shipped furs on a raft down the Price River." Alleged by some to be the first navigator of the Colorado River (although the historical record notes a complete voyage by him from Wyoming to the Needles only in 1896–1897), Galloway "built a large dugout near the present location of Wellington and used it as a storehouse for his furs and also as his headquarters."[30] Other known trappers included "James Bean, T. H. Auphand, W. Wilcox and Tom Creek," who found a great variety of peltry, including "beaver, bear, fox, panther, bobcats, timber wolf, and mountain lions," according to old-timers' recollections recorded by a local schoolgirl.[31]

Independent ranchers arrived in Castle Valley simultaneously with the others. For example, around 1875 Samuel Gilson established his ranch on

Ivie Creek. Like so many others, as a boy of fourteen, Gilson had joined his brother in the 1849 California gold rush, then had tried ranching in Nevada, where they claimed an entire valley (named for themselves), with a Wells Fargo station.[32] In 1871, the Gilson brothers decided to drive their herds for sale in Kansas and got as far as Utah's Sevier Valley, just south of Sanpete, where they stayed until 1875. Like so many others, they then drove their stock east over the Wasatch Plateau, starting their new ranch on the Castle Valley side.[33] Farther north, the adventurous Swaseys moved permanently to Castle Valley, as did cattlemen William Gentry and Alfred Starr. Leander Lemmon, Pete Grant, and Reuben Miller brought sheep in from California. Miller and his brothers, James and Melvin, subsequently founded the largest stock raising company in Castle Valley's history.[34] Lemmon meanwhile partnered with James McHadden to develop the area along Huntington Creek, each filing a claim on 160 recently-surveyed acres from the federal government and digging an irrigation ditch at the mouth of Huntington Canyon (known as the McHadden Ditch, although he subsequently left the area).[35] Lemmon eventually prospered; by 1897 he had an elegant brick residence worth $3,500, which endured into the twenty-first century as "among the finest surviving examples of nineteenth-century . . . residential architecture."[36]

Stockmen came slightly later along the north side of the Price River. The two Whitmore brothers, James (or "Tobe") and George, began running some of Castle Valley's largest cattle herds in an area called Sunnyside in the Book Cliffs, giving their name to the canyon just above it. They originally hailed from Texas, and had grown up in Salt Lake City and then in southern Utah, immersed in their father's cattle business. After he was killed by a Navajo raiding party near Pipe Springs, Arizona, early in 1866, their mother brought the family back to Salt Lake City.[37] Trailing their animals eastward from Sanpete County in 1878–1879, they established the northern Castle Valley livestock industry.[38]

Departing even further from historian Turner's list of romantic western types, local industrial development also began in the mid-1870s. In the winter of 1875–1876, John Nelson and Abram Taylor wintered in the Wasatch Mountains northwest of Castle Valley to hold coal land for its claimants, giving the area the name Winter Quarters.[39] In 1876, merchant Milan Packard of Springville, Utah County (north of Sanpete), organized the Pleasant Valley Coal Company together with some Sanpete and Utah County men. They hired others to cut a wagon road south of Springville and up Spanish Fork Canyon to the coal deposit and to survey a nearby townsite. George Matson, one of their employees, later remembered driving the mine's No. 1 tunnel, loading the coal in sacks, and packing it out by mule to wagons for the trip to Springville where it sold for $4.00 or $5.00 a ton. The round trip took four days and could not be made in the winter (when coal was most needed) because of deep snow. In June 1877, fifteen other men hiked north to Pleasant Valley from their new coal mine in Huntington Canyon and dug additional coal from No. 1. An early winter compelled them to stay until February 1878. All these transportation difficulties convinced Milan Packard to build a narrow gauge railroad in 1879, following the route of his wagon road. Lacking specie, Packard paid both sub-contractors and workmen with calico out of his store, hence his line got the name Calico Road. Officially called the Utah and Pleasant Valley Railroad, it stretched between Springville and Thistle Junction in Utah County, then ran in a series of switch-backs up to the Pleasant Valley town of Scofield, named for railroad president Charles W. Scofield. Spurs then led to the Winter Quarters mines.[40] While his industrial enterprise fit well with greater America's concurrent Industrial Revolution, it served notice that Castle Valley, despite its recent settlement, did not represent a typical western frontier.

Far away, the pace of life quickened with events that would soon come crashing over Castle Valley's protective walls. In the 1870s and 1880s, John D. Rockefeller, the oil magnate, was inventing the trust, a corporate structure designed to control all aspects of an industry. He soon achieved true vertical integration in oil, meaning that he controlled every step of the industry, from wells, to transportation, to refining, to retailing.[41] Soon, many other businessmen would try to copy his success in every branch of industry—including Castle Valley coal. Meanwhile, Congress floundered, scarred by the 1872 Credit Mobilier railroad scandal and the so-called Salary Grab Act of 1873. Resulting instability caused the national Panic of 1873, thoroughly discrediting the ruling Republican Party while stimulating the cooperative United Order of Enoch back in Utah. Belatedly seeking railroad reforms, Congress impaneled the Poland Committee, chaired by upright Representative Luke Poland of Vermont.[42] His reforming zeal soon turned to other causes, including Mormon polygamy, sponsoring the act signed into law on June 23, 1874. The Poland Act, largely written by Utah's Liberal Party founder Robert Baskin, strengthened federal authority over district courts, granted further powers to the U.S. marshal and U.S. attorney, established a new jury selection process designed to ensure non-Mormon as well as Mormon participation, and granted the right of appeal of any polygamy case to the U.S. Supreme Court.[43] Thus began the effective enforcement of federal laws against the LDS Church.

Besides, Brigham Young, who had led the LDS Church into the far West, planted it deeply in Utah soil, and nurtured it for thirty years, was nearing the end of his life. He sent an exploratory party east from Sanpete County in the summer of 1877 to identify viable townsites near potential farmland. Its members, Elias Cox, Benjamin Jones, John Cox, Elam Cheney, and Jefferson Tidwell (who had married Sarah Seely), would later become Castle Valley settlers.[44] When they returned to Sanpete, they "gave a splendid report of the country bordering the three streams in the upper valley, but suggested it would be hard to control the waters."[45] Putting this matter in its best light, on August 22, 1877, Brigham Young issued his last settlement call in a document that read, in part: "There are numbers of brethren in Sanpete County, who have not an abundant supply of water for their land, who would, no doubt, be happy to remove to a valley where the water is abundant and the soil good. We should like to have at least fifty families locate in Castle Valley this fall."[46] Then, the printed document was apparently posted. Ever since, in friendly rivalry, two versions of the Sanpeters' response have been repeated on either side of the Wasatch Plateau. In Castle Valley, people claim that those who could read showed their religious devotion by going. Sanpete residents say that the literate saw Castle Valley as the destination and stayed put. One week after issuing this call, Brigham Young died. Again, settlers on either side of the Wasatch Plateau expressed divided opinions: either the Prophet's earthly work was finally done (the Castle Valley version) or he had just made his most serious mistake and needed to be "called home" (the Sanpete view).

Despite this pronouncement, no one rushed to settle Castle Valley. A month later, the interim church government repeated the call. Church authorities selected Christian Grice Larsen, a Danish convert and former bishop of Spring City, to head the Castle Valley Mission, but, for a while, he stayed put. Instead, Orange Seely became Castle Valley's first resident ecclesiastical leader.[47] In November 1877, he dutifully led a party of men to scout the best townsites in the part of Castle Valley they knew best, along Cottonwood Creek.[48] The men made preliminary homestead choices (relying on federal, not church law) and Erastus Curtis built a log cabin, the first in Castle Valley. His sons, Erastus, Jr. and William, spent the winter of 1877–1878 there while their father went back to Sanpete County for his two wives and other children and eight other men. Seely spent the winter in the old herders' dugout with six other men, hunting and trapping a host of animals including thirteen wolves in a single night.[49]

Another 1877 group of pioneering Saints led by preliminary explorers Elias Cox, Elam Cheney, Jr., and Benjamin Jones, simply picked up and moved. Bringing family members (some of them polygamous), they traveled northeast to Thistle, then down Soldier Canyon, cutting a new road east of the old Gunnison trail and across the Price River. As much as possible, they tried to follow the land's contours, naming sites along their way: Sagebrush Bench, bumpy Washboard Flat, and Poison Spring Bench (for the horrible alkali water there). As they crested the last hills northeast of their chosen site on Huntington Creek, they saw below a flock of sheep tended by two lonely herders, Warren and Marion Brady (nineteen and twelve, respectively). As the boys dashed to the river to see who the settlers were, Rosannah Brady Jones, married to Cox's nephew, was astonished to spot her two little brothers. Elam Cheney rode back to Fairview to lead more settlers, and the women brought their spinning wheels, knowing that they could get wool to spin.[50] Like the other settlers before them, they strung

Orange Seely, leader of the settlement party called by the LDS Church, poses with his initially reluctant wife, Hannah Olsson Seely. They eventually prospered in Castle Valley. Courtesy of Emery County Archives.

out along the creeks where they could get farms started instead of founding the traditional, organized town touted as the hallmark of LDS settlement in every other area.[51]

To the south, on Cottonwood Creek, families arrived only in 1878, and late in the year at that. Wink Seely felt pressured to take up the land he had claimed for his homestead before another man settled it, so packed up his very pregnant wife and a special nurse to make the ten-day trip. After a week of jolting over the Wasatch Plateau, Anna Eliza Reynolds Seely went into labor a few days short of the settlement. Healthy little Clara, their first daughter and third child, was born in Cottonwood Canyon. Both mother and baby survived, and that December, Wink made a special trip to Salt Lake City to file a formal homestead application.[52] His older brother, Orange, despite his initial leadership role, was one of the last to come that fall. He may have tarried in Mount Pleasant to comfort his wife, Hanna Ols-son Seely, a Swedish immigrant. Like many other European converts, she had already crossed an ocean and most of a continent, learned a new language and adapted to a new culture and religion, which may have seemed like quite enough. By 1878, they had nine children and a lovely home, two city lots and nine acres of farmland which she hated to leave. In October Hanna had a trying, two-week journey across the Wasatch Plateau and when she arrived in Castle Valley saw nothing but a straight stretch of road between Wink's dugout and their own log home.[53] She said, "Damn the man who would bring a woman to such a God forsaken country!" She had never sworn before.[54] Likewise, Danish immigrant Ellen Anderson Miller, the wife of fellow Dane, Neils Peter Miller, was equally disillusioned. When Neils pulled up their wagon in front of his dugout on Cottonwood Creek in the summer of 1878, Ellen moaned, "Has it now come to this, that I have to live under the ground?" Neils rose to the occasion and by Christmas of 1879 they had the largest house in the area—15 x 21 feet (with a dirt floor)—and consequently hosted many local dances.[55]

To sustain their farms, settlers inaugurated irrigation systems on Castle Valley's thin perennial waterways. Men began the Huntington North Ditch in 1877, followed by the Avery Ditch that later reached the new town of Lawrence.[56] Another ditch tapped Ferron Creek beginning in 1878. Its handful of founders—Larsens, Petersons, Taylors, and Wrigleys—had arrived in November 1877, grew a little wheat, and were joined by others in 1878. That fall, all of the women went home to Sanpete except Ann Singleton Wrigley. She was a plural wife, and decided she would rather stay in Castle Valley with her small children (the oldest, Clara, aged five) than go back with her husband to fetch his other wife.[57] He (and his other wife) returned with a group the following spring. The men tried to cut an irrigation ditch, but had only one plow, a pick, and two shovels. They jerry-rigged a new plow from a forked cedar stump weighed down with a big rock pulled by two oxen. The wind blew steadily; animal feed grew two long miles up the canyon; their ditch silted in and had to be re-dug; the only local material they could find for a dam was prickly pears.[58] Ellen Larsen, the wife of J. F. Larsen, remembered regularly collecting buckets full of fish trapped in the canal's muddy pools and sodden debris after the annual spring flood.[59]

Meanwhile, Jefferson Tidwell, belatedly following Brigham Young's call, led his oldest son, William Jefferson, and fourteen others to an area along the Price River in 1879. They dug cellars for shelter from summer's relentless heat and raised some grain. Although some wanted to call this new place Jefferson, either Tidwell or his wife, Sarah Seely Tidwell, recommended that it be named Wellington, after her brother, also known as Wink. In the fall, the community stored the harvest for the next spring's planting, dammed the river preliminary to irrigation work, and went home to Sanpete County for the winter. The following spring, much of their hard

Jefferson Tidwell and Sarah Seely Tidwell, founders of Wellington, named the town after Sarah's brother, Justus Wellington (Wink) Seely. Courtesy of Western Mining and Railroad Museum.

work washed away in the annual flood—just as the men had predicted after their 1876 reconnoitering expedition.[60]

While all these people struggled to establish themselves, residents sought a federal mail route—their first overt governmental action, prompted more by painful isolation than an attempt at American democracy. The Post Office granted their petition in 1878, establishing a star mail route along the Gunnison Trail from Salina, Utah, to Ouray, Colorado. At that time, Wilsonville was the only so-called settlement on the 250–mile trail through Castle Valley. It owed its establishment largely to two sizable families who had chosen the same area: the Wilson brothers (George, Nick, Chris, Davis, Silas, and Sylvester, who became the mail carrier) and the Swaseys (Charles Swasey, Sr. and his siblings Rodney, Joseph, Frank, Dudley, Lena, and Hannah Rose).[61] Settlers scattered farther west along Huntington and Cottonwood Creeks had to travel to Wilsonville to get their mail, a tiring and tedious process. The following year a committee petitioned the Post Office Department for another post office at what they called Castle Vale on Cottonwood Creek, about five miles west of Wilsonville. The government granted their petition effective June 1, 1879, but changed the name of the site to Castle Dale. Store-keeper John K. Reid became the first postmaster, but for almost five months he still had to go to Wilsonville and sort out the mail for his jurisdiction. A town started to cluster near his store, and the growing ascendancy of Castle Dale over Wilsonville led to the mail route's rerouting. By 1880, the mail route, in addition to serving Wilsonville, wound through a series of new towns with post offices: at Ferron, then to previously established Castle Dale, then to Huntington, and on across the gullied, alkali miles to Blake, over on the Green River.[62]

Blake and many other Castle Valley towns had been settled in that general land rush of 1878. Always rather isolated from the rest of the settlements, it grew on the banks of the Green River at the site of the only significant ford for miles, in use since prehistoric times. Established initially under the leadership of Thomas Farrer, his sons, and a handful of others, the town had had a distinctive beginning. Farrer, allegedly of English landed gentry, was not motivated by the church call but instead "wanted to get as far away from civilization as possible and there is little doubt that Greenriver [as Blake was later known] in those days filled the bill; the only person here being Mr. Blake who used this crossing as a station on the mail route from Salina to La Sal [further southeast]."[63] In 1879, J. T. Farrer opened a general store in Blake; a year later, Thomas Farrer became the postmaster. Others arrived, and in 1880, like every other Castle Valley community, seventeen of Blake's citizens formed an informal group called the Blake City Water Ditch Company. They installed a brush and rock wing dam on the Green River, and paid each man who brought a team of either horses or oxen $2.50 a day for labor. Thus, the town hung on, until a brand new railroad would put it on the map of spreading commerce.[64]

Meanwhile, other Mormons had arrived farther north. Led by Caleb Rhoades, who had learned boyhood pioneering skills in the California gold rush, settlers outside the church call had come south down the Price River Canyon. After his California sojourn, Rhoades had worked as a prospector, trapper, and boarding house owner in a western Utah mining town, working there with his wife, the former Malinda Powell. Around 1875, Rhoades had returned unexpectedly from hunting and discovered his wife with Joseph Gammage, which eventually led to divorce. Malinda and Gammage then married and took Caleb's three surviving children to live with them in distant Green River. Despite this, Caleb remained on good terms with his former brothers-in-law, Abraham Powell (Malinda's younger brother) and Frederick Empire Grames, who had married Malinda's sister. In the winter of 1877–1878, the forty-one-year-old Rhoades and nineteen-year-old Abraham Powell explored along the Price River, and Powell left behind a cabin he built when they went back to Salem, Utah County, that spring.[65] Meanwhile, bachelor James Davis Gay had arrived in January 1878, and became the only settler in Castle Valley's northern reaches when Rhoades and Powell left.[66] Powell never made it back to Castle Valley; he died after being mauled by a bear late in 1878. "In the early part of 1879 Caleb Rhodes [sic], Frederick Empire Grames, and Charles Grames left Salem and made their way over to the North west corner of what was then known as Castle Valley and made their abode on the Price river, arriving on the 21st day of January 1879," reported Ernest Horsley, one of Rhoades's later neighbors and friends.[67]

Shortly thereafter, the Powells came. According to Horsley's reckoning, March brought William Z. Warren, Robert A. Powell of Salem (another of Malinda's brothers) and William Davis, among others.[68] A Powell sister came, too: Martha Ellen Powell Grames, the wife of Frederick E. Grames, to join her husband.[69] Another Grames brother, Alfred, came about the same time.[70] John Amon Powell, who had been on the ill-fated bear hunt, came on April 1 with his wife, Sarah Jane Plumb Powell. "She was the first woman on the river," wrote Horsley, "but Martha E. Grames who came June 6 always disputed this."[71] This tiny handful of individuals spread out along the Price River, each family finding a likely spot. As the earth began to thaw, they and others took the first step in founding a farming settlement—surveying irrigation ditches. Fred Grames, a talented jack-of-all-trades, made the level from a coal oil can with a small lamp chimney placed at each end to allow the surveyor to look over the top of the water, balanced on a tripod of cottonwood sticks. "[W]ith this instrument the Rhoades ditch (Pioneer No. 1) was surveyed for about two and a half miles," wrote Ernest Horsley, as was "the Fred Grames ditch (Pioneer No. 2) for almost the same distance."[72] A touchy instrument, this home-made level could only be "used well when [the] wind [was] not blowing too hard . . .,"[73] a rare day in the chilly Castle Valley springtime. In short, while these northern Castle Valley settlers all belonged to the LDS Church, they acted like typical pioneer Americans, traveling with family, choosing sites by individual taste, not clustered in the confines of a typical Mormon town nor led by any ecclesiastical authorities. They thus added flexibility to what would become the most distinctive corner of a highly distinctive state.

In many ways, the individualistic nature of at least some Castle Valley settlements was hardly surprising, as all these tiny clusters of humanity lived virtually isolated from one another, forced apart by an inhospitable environment. People got on as best they could, while few others rushed to fill up the spaces between the far-flung dwellings. As if to underscore the residents' isolation, the weather soon turned particularly nasty. The winters of 1877–1878 and 1878–1879 had been mild, allowing easy travel and town-building. Then drought and cold arrived. According to Ernest Horsley, in September 1879 the Price River got "so low [it] could be stepped over in many places."[74] Next came the grasshoppers. Ferron's John Lemmon made a hurried trip to Manti to buy chickens to eat the 'hoppers; by the time he got back, all the insects had left, gorged on the community's crop. Livestock fared no better. Lemmon and John Duncan had earlier driven over 2,000 head of cattle from Sevier Valley. In the winter of 1879–1880, all of them died.[75]

Others' plans also foundered in Castle Valley's climate swings. Along Cottonwood Creek, a new company of settlers had arrived in mid-1879, including the Jewkes family: Samuel and his sons and a daughter-in-law. Earlier that year, the Jewkes men "had formed a sort of united order copartnership before removing to Castle Valley," and eagerly awaited parts for a grist mill being hauled over from Fountain Green, Sanpete County. The machinery had to be dismantled, which took time, and it was November before the struggling ox teams could cross the Wasatch Plateau, now under two feet of snow. These burr mills used horsepower for grinding, but only three "teams were able to pull the sweepstakes for the mill . . . [and they] were kept busy chopping grain, which was used for man and beast."[76] More ominously, as the winter progressed, the snow deepened throughout Utah.

During that terrible winter, the people remaining in Castle Valley felt absolutely cut off. Along Cottonwood Creek, "no one could be found to volunteer to haul Christmas goods, even at 10 cents a pound for freight from Manti."[77] Finally, four local merchants started out, abandoning their wagon on the east side of the Wasatch Plateau to struggle up Salina Canyon through eight-foot drifts. They bought goods and came back, leading three pack horses, one of which tumbled off a fifty-yard-high ledge spilling the group's small keg of liquor. The men arduously dug out the horse, readjusted the pack, and then ate some of the liquor-sodden snow. Instead of revitalizing, it numbed them, so they force-marched on to their wagon and made it back to Castle Valley with Christmas treats and kerosene to light the chilly dwellings all along Cottonwood Creek.[78]

Despite this brief holiday respite, the weather did not let up. As 1880 began, Castle Valley settlers began to run out of flour. Someone managed to get word of impending starvation back to Manti in late April, when, despite "deep snow and drifts, 6,500 pounds of flour were brought back [to Castle Valley] and distributed." Even then, as a local history put it, "Hunger was not unknown."[79] Pioneers on Huntington Creek, probably using the road they had cut coming in from the north, raided the cache of grain and goods that other Saints had left on the Price River at Wellington. When the Tidwell party returned in the spring of 1880, after spending that horrible winter in Sanpete County, they not only found their dam washed out but their seed and other foodstuffs eaten. They scattered along the Price River, relying on hunting to eat. Fortunately, game remained plentiful in the nearby Book Cliffs to the north, so the men took a wagon up Whitmore Canyon and came back with one hundred twenty deer. Jefferson Tidwell hung them in his granary, and all the local settlers could help themselves.[80]

Hunters going out for food had to pick their way through a veritable boneyard. Cattleman Dan Parker, interviewed sixty years after the fact, recalled, "The winter of 1879 and 80 was a tough one. . . . I saw horses and cows standing up, dead, and frozen stiff as icicles."[81] The valleys of the Price River, Huntington, Cottonwood, Ferron, and Muddy creeks gave off the stench of death as the thawing carcasses of cattle and horses rotted in the sun.[82] In newly-settled Lawrence, residents had had no feed for their livestock, so had turned them loose in the foothills. By spring, only one team and a heifer had survived.[83] Still, hope returned. As one man remembered, "The next spring the grass came back so thick it would drag your stirrups."[84]

The harsh winter had also weakened Castle Valley's ties to Sanpete County. In real terms of travel time and difficulty, the distance "back home" had seemed greater than ever. Consequently, a three-man committee—Emanuel Bagley, Elias Cox, and John K. Reid—carried a petition with 316 signatures to the territorial legislature requesting the creation of Castle County. Opposing the measure, Warren Peacock arrived with a petition signed by twenty-six others. Supporting the majority, the territorial legislature granted Castle Valley political autonomy in 1880. Rejecting the requested name, however, the legislature opted for Emery County after the outgoing territorial governor, George W. Emery. Popular for his fair treatment of Mormons during his 1875–1880 tenure, this graduate of Dartmouth College and former law partner of Benjamin Butler (later a presidential candidate) was then in Washington, seeking re-appointment. Instead, Congress replaced Emery with Eli H. Murray, a man far more hostile to the Saints, in a move indicative of shifting national attitudes toward Utah.[85]

This shift resulted largely from the *Reynolds* case, billed by historian Edward Leo Lyman as "a turning point in the history of the territory."[86] The case had begun in 1874 when George Reynolds, Brigham Young's secretary, agreed to be the defendant in a test case intended by the Saints to overturn the 1862 Morrill Anti-Bigamy Act. Reynolds's second wife willingly provided testimony convicting him. Although his first conviction was overturned on a technicality, the second case went to the Supreme Court. In January 1879, the unanimous decision firmly established polygamy as a federal offense.[87] While Congress studied a host of anti-polygamy bills (none successful), and President Rutherford B. Hayes asked Congress to deny citizenship to Utah residents until they renounced plural marriage, privately federal officials offered leniency to the Saints if they would renounce this illegal practice.[88] President Hayes, in particular, courted national support. He had won the presidency in the confused election of 1876, when the national electorate (including Utah Territory), fed up with Republican scandals, seemingly selected his Democratic opponent. An extra-constitutional committee shifted twenty disputed electoral votes, however, electing Hayes by a one-vote margin. In 1880, Hayes visited Utah on one of his several railroad tours designed to strengthen the presidential office. Although Governor Murray apparently sought to isolate the President from the Saints, even positive contact would have made little difference. Back in Washington, the political ball was already rolling. Once Hayes returned to Washington, he joined a growing number of federal officials who supported denying the right to vote, sit on juries, and hold office to polygamists and to those who supported the practice, meaning all members of the LDS Church.[89] Under these circumstances, Castle Valley's remoteness took on a new appeal.

These threatening circumstances prompted further formal organization for Utah's last frontier. Completing Emery County's creation, Utah's legislature named Castle Dale as the county seat and appointed three men (also LDS leaders) as county selectmen, Elias Cox, Jasper Petersen and William Taylor, who, in turn, appointed other county officials until elections could take place the following August. That same month, LDS Apostles Erastus Snow, Brigham Young, Jr., Francis Lyman, and Sanpete Stake President Canute Peterson, came into Castle Valley. They rendezvoused at Wilsonville on August 23 and shortly thereafter held an LDS conference at Wink Seely's homestead, choosing the same initial selectmen as bishops of the local wards.[90] Privately, Lyman recorded his views of Castle Valley: "the more of such land a man possessed himself of, the poorer he would be." He also objected to the scattered nature of the settlement on Cottonwood Creek, with every man "located upon his quarter section," in accordance with U.S. homestead laws. But, in an open letter published in Salt Lake City's Mormon newspaper, the *Deseret News*, Lyman wrote, "the grass that once was plentiful has vanished before the flocks and herds that have pastured in this region. Good water, good land, and fine climate are inviting the industrious husbandmen to come and make desirable homes for good Latter-day Saints."[91] After traversing Castle Valley and crossing the Green

River, Lyman wrote another open letter to the *Deseret News.* He recounted the counsel given the brethren along Cottonwood Creek that they gather in towns. This directive had resulted in the establishment of two townsites (originally called Lower and Upper Castle Dale) in place of their scattered farms. First, the authorities had approved the site of (Lower) Castle Dale, chosen by Orange Seely, the leading resident (who had just been released as bishop). Further upstream, they had told settlers to cluster on John Reid's townsite, where Reid maintained the (Upper) Castle Dale post office in his store. But they named Reid's town Orangeville, after Orange Seely, who lived downstream in Castle Dale, where the post office was not. (Yes, this arrangement is confusing, but it has lasted to the present.) Then Lyman recounted how he and his party went on to Green River City (Blake). Lyman noted "a large tract of country on each side of the river for miles up and down, covered with cottonwood forests and good land beside to make homes and farms for 100 men 'chock full of a day's work.'" He also mentioned "rich coal mines within 15 miles," possibly the first LDS Church recognition of Book Cliffs coal, which would play such a significant role in the history of Castle Valley.[92]

That coal certainly interested William Jackson Palmer, a Civil War veteran with strong commercial ambitions. In 1870, he had incorporated a new Colorado railroad, the Denver and Rio Grande Railway Company (D&RG). As its name suggested, it began at Denver and originally headed toward the Rio Grande River, thence to El Paso, with an eventual intention of reaching the Pacific. These plans faltered when a rival line, the irrepressible Atchison, Topeka, and Santa Fe (AT&SF or Santa Fe), won rights to the single passageway south through Raton Pass in 1878. Two months later, the AT&SF tried to strangle its rival on the westward path through Colorado's Royal Gorge, but this time the Rio Grande won in the courts. This result freed Palmer's line, feisty but financially troubled, to build westward, into Utah.[93] This altercation also represented just a fraction of the struggle between giant, national corporations, particularly railroads, which would help shape transportation struggles in Castle Valley.

In short order, the Rio Grande was hiring all the men it could get to press on before railroad rivals drove it further toward the wall. It had to build quickly to secure coveted routes, so between the fall of 1879 and the spring of 1881, the railroad shipped thousands of laborers to its scattered grading camps strung along the newly-chosen route in Colorado and Utah. According to its construction manager, the Rio Grande was paying the highest wages ever offered for railroad work in Colorado. For a while, agents even advanced fares to workers, many of whom quickly deserted, causing losses of over $30,000 in 1880 alone. Negotiations with Utah Mormons led to a promise of 2,000 laborers for that fall, 300 of whom promised to bring their own teams.[94] Among these was seventeen-year-old George Storrs, who persuaded his education-loving father that working on the D&RG in

Colorado offered a better future than study at Brigham Young Academy. Traveling with a friend, he drove his wagon through Castle Valley in 1880:

> We went through Spanish Fork Canyon through what is now known as Colton, then through Emmas Park down to what is now Price. At that time there was one house in Price. There was no town of Helper, and no railroads through that country.[95]

He correctly assessed the empty landscape: in 1880 only 556 settlers lived along the entire Castle Valley corridor.[96] Storrs, later a coal boss in the area (he would even have a town named for him), then jolted on to help lay the steel tentacles driving westward toward Utah's last lonely region.

Other men also answered the call for men and teams. Contractors Joseph Smith Black and his brother, William, hired 75 teams with drivers to grade twenty-five miles of roadbed along the proposed route, initially intended to head up coal-bearing Salina Canyon to the west of Castle Valley. In the 1800s, railroads and coal were inextricably linked. Trains needed coal, especially where wood was scarce, such as across barren Castle Valley. Symbiotically, commercial coal development needed railroads, since coal sold by the ton, and vast quantities had to be moved to market to realize a profit. Therefore, the Rio Grande's original route roughly followed the southern branch of the Old Spanish Trail, entering Castle Valley's east side near the 39th parallel at Blake, on the Green River, and exiting the valley through Salina Canyon on the west, cutting through the tiny southern settlements.[97] During the spring and summer of 1880, the Blacks' men and teams cut fifteen miles of roadbed within Castle Valley itself, moving out of the valley to Thompson's Springs, forty miles east of Green River, to continue working there as fall came. At the same time, in order to connect with the heart of Utah at Salt Lake City, the D&RG's chief construction engineer, M. T. Burgess, surveyed an additional route north up Price Canyon, following the path the Rhoades Party had taken when it came south to colonize. Joseph Black went along with Burgess to survey the Price Canyon route while the teams he had hired worked tirelessly to the southwest.[98]

Suddenly, with their camps and teams moved and thousands of dollars of supplies on hand, the Blacks received word that the head office had decided to halt all construction. The front office was debating a change of route. Officials had just learned that the Union Pacific, through the Utah Central Railroad, was maneuvering to monopolize the valuable Winter Quarters coal deposits. The D&RG therefore hastily made overtures to Milan Packard and associates, founders of the Pleasant Valley Coal Company. Pleasant Valley coal, when tested by Rio Grande geologists, proved more accessible and of higher quality than the deposits in Salina Canyon. These northern coal beds were also on a direct line to the Salt Lake City market.

D&RG officials promptly contemplated rerouting their road.[99] While corporate arrangements hung fire, further construction had to wait.

Consequently, in a December 1880 meeting at the mouth of Price Canyon, Chief Engineer Burgess reluctantly asked the Blacks to discharge all their teamsters. Stunned, the Blacks pointed out that they had just moved the work camps and had bought thousands of dollars of unused supplies. Without the railroad contract, they were ruined. Burgess sympathized but said their only appeal lay with the railroad's chief officer, General Dodge, due in Salt Lake City the following day. Since some forty snowy miles lay between Price Canyon's mouth and the nearest train connection to Salt Lake, there was no hope.[100]

With everything at stake, Joseph Black decided to ride. While he drank a bracing cup of coffee, William saddled their best horse, Prince, for the long trip. They started up the intervening 7,500 foot pass, the road sometimes three to four feet deep in drifted snow. "It was bitter cold," Black remembered. "At daybreak I gained the summit . . . 9 miles from the station." Prince seemed to understand the urgency of his forced, all-night ride and he "flew over ravines, rocks, and hollows . . . [as] the cold morning almost pierced me to the marrow." Still two miles short of the station, Black heard the whistle of the approaching train. Urging Prince to his utmost, they clattered in just as the train began pulling away. "The horse was as wet as he could be. I threw the lines to the proprietor . . . and said, 'Take good care of Prince.'" Jumping on the very last of the cars, an exhausted Joseph Black rode on to Salt Lake City.[101]

Black got his interview with General Dodge, who listened attentively and then referred him to another official, George Goss. Black demanded ten thousand dollars in damages for the broken contract, as well as the right to return to work with some of the teams. Goss noted that the railroad would not need to build on the grade for at least one year, and began to figure. The men both remained silent for half an hour, accompanied only by the scratch of Goss's pencil. Finally, Goss raised his head and said, "'Mr. Black, you should not have it.'

"'Well,' said . . .[Black], 'money is power; what will you do?'

"He answered, 'I will give you $9,994 and you can go back with 20 teams.'"[102]

As Black soon learned, rather than pay damages which might make the railroad liable for payments every time it altered its route, Goss had changed the initial rate of pay. He raised the amount due for scraper work already performed from fifteen cents to twenty cents a yard and so on throughout the old contract. Goss also agreed to a payment of $3,000 for the immediate emergency, giving Black a check for that amount. Joseph Black quickly telegraphed his brother, William. Their fortunes were saved.[103]

The two arranged to continue grading the railroad route at a much-reduced pace.[104] Where the line would ultimately go through Castle Valley remained unclear. Railroad officials now seemed to favor turning the route northward, toward the larger towns along the Wasatch Front which would provide a healthy market for its services. In order to climb the heights out of Castle Valley, however, the railroad needed a local supply of coal, such as it had already located in Salina Canyon. Thus, grading slowly continued along the line toward Salina Canyon in southern Castle Valley, as railroad officials pondered where to build. Meanwhile, M. T. Burgess, who bore direct responsibility for the decision, teamed with a company geologist, Ellis Clark, Jr., who traveled along the Book Cliffs in an attempt to locate more convenient coal deposits near the Price River grade.

A few locals had preceded Clark and found what he was seeking. The first now known was Charles P. Johnson, who had originally built the first log cabin in Muddy (later the town of Emery) in 1879 and then moved north and helped dig the Price River Pioneer Ditch No. 2 alongside Fred Grames, John Amon Powell, and others. In March 1881, Johnson brought his family to northern Castle Valley and, in the words of Ernest Horsley, "dug the first coal at Castle Gate which he used to sharpen everyone's boots with during [the] 1881–1882 RR construction. A man named Black took up the claim afterwards."[105] In fact, both the Black brothers, William and Joseph, acquired areas of the infant Castle Gate mine, as did engineers Mellen and Kerr.[106] When geologist Clark encountered this known coal outcropping, he sent a long, technical description to D&RG President William Jackson Palmer incorporating pen-and-ink drawings of the coal horizons (vertical cross-sections). The best outcrops, he concluded, were at the juncture of the Price River and Willow Creek, about eight miles north of the Rhoades party's settlement. He added, "None of the coal beds are large, [this observation later proved inaccurate] but their value to this company depends upon their close location to the line of railroad at a point (the heavy Price River Grade) where extra locomotive power will be required." He then recommended prompt purchase of the earlier locations for just under $5,000, "thus saving the additional ten dollars an acre which it will cost from the Government after the rails have been laid."[107]

While the railroad's front office continued deliberating, peripatetic Samuel Gilson stepped in with his own route proposal. Although he still had a ranch on Ivie Creek, mining had never really left his blood. He had recently been exploring for minerals in the Uintah Basin, the valley northeast of the West Tavaputs Plateau, behind the Book Cliffs.[108] In this remote area, he made the astounding discovery of an extremely rare hydrocarbon, then known only in Palestine, near the Dead Sea. As the Utah Land Board noted a few years later, "[I]t was mined by the Arabs and carried on the backs of camels, to the Suez Canal, whence it was shipped to all parts of the world . . . [to be used for] Asphaltum carriage varnishes . . . [bringing] about $160. per ton, in our markets."[109] This brittle, black, tarry-looking substance had a brilliant luster, softened with the heat of the body, and stuck easily. Water-insoluble, it could only be removed by liberal application of coal oil.[110] With typical bravado, Gilson called the stuff "gilsonite" and actively sought railroad access to tap this rare substance. As Gilson well knew, only two major canyons cut through the Book Cliffs. Rivaling the passageway down the Price River Canyon used by the Rhoades party and now under active consideration by the railroad was the Soldier Canyon trail that Huntington settlers had taken. If the railroad could be diverted up Soldier Canyon, it would pass much closer to Gilson's discoveries, allowing him easier access to the markets of Utah, Colorado, and beyond. Gilson consequently made up a story about the prohibitive steepness of the Price River grade to lure the line his way. Burgess, ignorant of Gilson's true motives, studied the terrain and disagreed.[111]

By the end of 1881, Burgess was forced to make a final recommendation about the proposed railroad route. Choosing the Price River Canyon in his final report, he concurrently voiced his own misgivings about the earlier plan to follow the Old Spanish Trail across southern Castle Valley to Salina Canyon. Fewer than 800 people resided along that route, he noted, and most of the country was "barren and unsettled. . . . East of Castle Valley Junction [now Price]," he added, only 150 resided at Blake City (now Green River). How many customers—and how much freight—could the railroad attract in this sparsely-populated region?[112]

Even after receiving his considered decision, corporate headquarters dallied. Their apparent indecisiveness had other, stronger roots: competition with other carriers, the sort of contest which had destroyed the Rio Grande's original building plans in Colorado. This time the major opponent was the Union Pacific; the major target, the Pleasant Valley mines. Believing that the Castle Gate area offered only a small coal field, the Rio Grande needed to acquire more fuel for its locomotives. The Union Pacific, which already held a small mine in Pleasant Valley, could potentially stymie acquisitions there if it knew the Rio Grande's final choice of route. Consequently, Rio Grande officials acted quickly and quietly to sew up Pleasant Valley coal lands. This purchase required a new corporation in keeping with Utah territorial law, which stipulated that all incorporators must be Utah residents. Consequently, Colorado resident and Rio Grande President William Jackson Palmer rounded up some Utah friends and paid their expenses to acquire the Utah and Pleasant Valley Railroad and its associated mines.[113] As soon as they could, some other Rio Grande-affiliated officials formed new Utah corporations, the Denver and Rio Grande Western Railway Company (the Western or the D&RGW) and the Rio Grande Western Construction Company, the latter with a built-in life of twenty years.[114] Soon, the railroad was secretly running the Winter Quarters coal mines, which remained under the public ownership of the Pleasant Valley Coal Company (PVCC), now owned by Palmer's Utah friends. The railroad legally cemented its ownership on June 14, 1882, when the Pleasant Valley

properties fell under foreclosure and were immediately snapped up by the
Rio Grande Western Construction Company (not the railroad, an interesting wrinkle with important legal ramifications later on).[115] Only then did the
Rio Grande publicly announce its final railroad route decision—the Price
River Canyon—which would allow it easy access to the "newly-acquired"
Pleasant Valley mines. Officials finally abandoned the more southerly route
along the Old Spanish Trail, losing an investment worth some $217,470,
including not only the railroad grade but several stone structures such as
a lime kiln constructed to provide building materials.[116] The magnitude of
this investment created the false hope, expressed as late as 1898, that "some
day, no doubt in the not very distant future, [southern] Castle valley will be
the main thoroughfare across the continent."[117] It never was.

While railroad building commenced toward Castle Valley from both
ends of the route, most folks along the newly-selected right-of-way enjoyed
the prospect of connection with the outside world. At least one recent
settler in northern Castle Valley, however, seemed to find most contact
disagreeable. He was Teancum Pratt, a son of the late Parley P. Pratt and
thoroughly devout Mormon, who kept the only known local diary (not
reminiscences) of his day. He had arrived at the mouth of Gordon Creek
in mid-1880, but found the area occupied by "hunters, trappers & bachelors & raveheads & did not welcome any settler. So I had a very tough
time of it & had to leave that location & moved up to what is now Helper,
at that time a lonely wilderness & commenced anew in 1881." At Helper,
Pratt complained, "The Price River was unfortunate in getting its first settlers. They were not of the honest kind who will pull together and sacrifice
for each other."[118] He nonetheless settled in with his two wives, Anne Eliza
Mead and Sarah Elizabeth Ewell, concurrent with the arrival of railroad
grading crews.[119] To protect his farm from acquisition by the railroad, Pratt
promptly filed homestead papers on his Helper property in October 1881.
He was closely followed by his wives' families: Sarah Mead, the mother of
his first wife, and Francis M. Ewell, who, with the rest of his family, had
homesteaded just south of Pratt, initially giving his name to a town that
would later become Spring Glen.[120]

Like everyone else in Castle Valley, Pratt worried about water for his
farm. On June 8, 1882, Pratt worked on his "levee hoping to finish it before
any heavy rains come, so it will catch the floods." Farming was exhausting,
and the whole family pitched in: "Sister Mead & Amanda planted some
white beans & finished planting corn. . . . I also finished plowing & took the
plow home to Ewells. Today was [second wife] Sarahs birthday she forgot it
till night. She is 22 years old." A few days later, men carrying their blankets
passed through Pratt's homestead, heading north from Colorado. They
were part of a growing number of transients complaining of "hard times
in the mining camps . . . general[l]y hungry wanting to buy provisions,"
of which Pratt had little to sell. "The children were hungry & so were we

A railroad worker on the D&RGW allegedly took this photograph in 1883 of the first dwelling in what is now Helper. Teancum Pratt and his two wives, Annie Eliza Mead and Sarah Elizabeth Ewell, raised a large family and wrested a living out of this inhospitable terrain. *Courtesy of Albert and William Fossatt.*

all," he added, although his successful hunting brought some meat. In July 1882, the desperate Pratt left his farm in his ox-drawn wagon, seeking cash employment on the railroad. He found no work. As Pratt glumly headed down the steep Price River Canyon, he saw the sky suddenly darken and a tempest begin, with "such thunder [as] I never heard before, it was a continual roar for I should think over half an hour." The river rose in moments to a raging "flood that carried away thousands of ties for the D.&R.G.R.R. Co. The oldest flood marks of the river banks were buried" and all the brand new railroad bridges washed away. When the flood subsided, Pratt tried to ford the river where the bridges had stood. At the second ford, "my cattle shied off down the stream & I lost control of them in the flood . . . & to save my self I plunged in & swam to shore." Luckily, he was able to scramble back on the wagon to draw out the tongue bolt, "thus liberating the oxen and saving their lives." The exhausted man and beasts spent that night with an old Irish miner at the new Castle Gate coal mine near Price Canyon's mouth. When they reached home, Pratt was delighted to find that the levee around his garden had held, even though the flood reached the very top, but he lost: "one wheel, a chain, 1 sack salt, my molds for my gun with some primer & powder & nine days time on the trip."[121] His families still went hungry.

The Rio Grande not only lost bridges, ties, and a prepared railroad grade in that great flood, it faced economic disaster. A year earlier, the

Colorado line had deferred a dividend payment, and in August 1882 it reorganized under conditions very favorable to Utah, shifting the whole system's axis "to an east-west position," according to the railroad's leading historian.[122] Abandoning its original drive to New Mexico and the Pacific, Rio Grande owners now depended on Utah riches to recoup the fortunes of the entire system. Consequently, the railroad began, even before its completion, to seek wealth along the Castle Valley corridor. It thus quickly transformed the area into what historian Carlos Schwantes called a "wage-workers' frontier." This concept, for him, "was a child of the steel rail." Claimed Schwantes, "Pioneer residents of the classic West [whatever that was] probably remained unaware of the wageworkers' frontier, or were at least untroubled by it."[123] Not so in Castle Valley. Industry, embodied by the D&RGW, inundated the area just as the first, struggling settlements took hold, putting development on fast-forward and compressing the time need-ed for significant, historical change.

With the coming of the Western, northern Castle Valley prospered. Struggling farmers no longer had to rely on scratching out a living in alka-line soil. The influx of railroad pay, much of it passing through the hands of the Black brothers, immediately shifted northern Castle Valley from barter to a cash economy. Prices soared. "Oats sold for five dollars and wheat for three dollars per hundred pounds. Onions found a ready cash market at ten cents, and cabbage 8 cents a pounds [sic], eggs 30 cents a dozen, butter 40 cents, potatoes 5 cents and carrots 3 ½ cents a pound," all in cold, hard coin.[124] Greater Utah eagerly anticipated similar economic blessings when a completed D&RGW would offer some allegedly stiff competition to the monopolistic Union Pacific.[125] With mutually rosy expectations of dropping prices for Utah residents and eager customers for the railroad, construction continued.

Spurred by accelerating change, the LDS Church decided to cement more firmly Castle Valley to the realm of the faithful. Consequently, in August 1882, Apostles Erastus Snow and John Henry Smith traveled south-ward, spending the first night with Pratt's father-in-law, Francis Ewell. Pratt piously recorded that he "felt greatly encouraged & strengthened by the visit," after hearing Snow praise "the climate & country & [he] spoke of its facilities showing that we have a very good land to make homes in. . . . He gave much good counsel," Pratt added, "& promised to have a ward organized & to send us some missionary settlers & a bishop."[126] Snow and Smith then moved down the Price River to the area occupied by the Powells, Grameses, Rhoades, and others. The Apostles pointed out the best future townsite (officially established as Price in 1892),[127] which would also be the optimum terminus of the irrigation ditch residents were still doggedly dig-ging. (The importance of this work had multiplied since the drought of the month previous, when water was so scarce that Gordon Creek ran dry and its settlers had to bring water from Caleb Rhoades's brackish spring.)[128] The authorities chose high ground to keep the new town from floods, but the townsite consequently lay a long way from the nearest canal. Residents had to haul Price River water by the bucketful to store in home-side barrels for culinary and agricultural uses. When it was first dumped in, the muddy water took time to settle, but the process could be speeded by adding prickly pears. Ignoring any inconveniences, Snow further prophesied "that the town established there would become the largest in this section and would be the metropolis of eastern Utah."[129] Without creating a formal church organization, Snow and Smith continued to the south.

Arriving at the southern Emery County settlements, the Apostles responded warmly to those who had conscientiously maintained church ties. At a meeting in the old bowery on the Wink Seely residence, Snow and Smith partially organized the Emery Stake of Zion, a larger, umbrella organization designed to encompass several wards. They set aside Christian G. Larsen as president, Orange Seely as first counselor, and Rasmus Justesen as second counselor. Snow also named two wards (the equivalent of parishes) along Cottonwood Creek at Orangeville and Castle Dale. The Apostles also organized the women. They set apart Anne Ungerman Larsen, a childless plural wife of the stake president, to head the Relief Society, the LDS organization for women.[130] In addition, Stake officials also oversaw wards (or potential wards) at Huntington, Ferron, and Price. The following November 20, Stake President Larsen and his counselors visited the Price area and formally organized its ward with George Frandsen as bishop. Frandsen shortly had to return to Mount Pleasant, from which he had just been called, leaving his counselors to oversee the welfare of some 215 hardy souls, the entire population in the Price area by December 31, 1882. In the next couple of years, Stake officials formed two other wards at Emery (originally Muddy Creek) and Molen.[131]

Commercially, Castle Valley towns also enjoyed increasing progress. For example, transportation over to Sanpete Valley improved in 1882 when the territory granted $150 to cut a road up over the southern end of the Wasatch Plateau from Ferron. Abe Conover supervised the roadbuilding, and paid his men in cash: fifty cents a day.[132] Nearby, Harrison Fugate opened a small coal mine at the mouth of Ferron Canyon, later run as a cooperative by Mike Molen.[133] Near the northern edge of the Wasatch Plateau, a sawmill on Huntington Creek produced boards for a cluster of new houses on the townsite and a 40 x 60–foot meeting house. The community all pitched in to build the latter, bringing finished doors and windows over from Sanpete County.[134] Further south at Castle Dale, Wink Seely built the first lumber home in 1886, followed by a brick house (still standing) three years later.[135] Thanks to his brother, Orange, and others, Castle Dale got a horse-powered thresher in 1882, a $700 machine for which the company had to pay an additional $83.80 in freighting and miscellaneous expenses.[136] Even with an improved road to Sanpete County, when freight changes amounted to over ten percent of the total expense, no wonder the area craved a railroad. Like the rest of rapidly industrializing America, however, Castle Valley residents had no idea of the many, varied changes it would bring.

3

# The Railroad and the Raids,
# 1882–1890

*Then came 1890 & after 8 years of dread & worry I was arrested for U.C. [unlaw-*
*ful cohabitation] . . . . I was at Sarah's & in the night the deps [deputies] came*
*to Annies & she misled them as to my whereabouts, but they left a paper [scrip] for*
*my [railroad] fare in case I chose to come of my own accord & stand trial. So after*
*counselling together, I went & waived examination . . . then giving bonds for my*
*appearance, I returned home.*[1]

—TEANCUM PRATT, POLYGAMIST

Pratt's legal problems arose from new federal laws, spawned in a new national era. According to historian John Garraty, from 1877–1890 "American civilization underwent a basic transformation." This change included "greatly expanded reliance by individuals upon group activities" and "Industrialization with its accompanying side effects—speedy transportation and communication, specialization, [and] urbanization."[2] In Congress, Republican and Democratic control see-sawed with dizzying speed. College professor and future U.S. President Woodrow Wilson claimed, "a man who has served a dozen terms in Congress is a curiosity."[3] Historian Matthew Josephson added, "a slight movement of public opinion, the smallest turn of a screw . . . [would] effect victory for one side or the other."[4] In the host of murky political battles over the tariff, civil service reform, currency inflation, race relations, and control of monopolies, politicians naturally targeted sure-fire issues—like polygamy.

Led by reforming Republican Senator George F. Edmunds of Vermont, "the iceberg of the Senate," Congressmen passed the new anti-Mormon Edmunds Act in 1882.[5] A contemporary observer explained its background:

While Congress pays the [Utah Territorial] legislative expenses, amounting to $20,000 per session, the Legislature defiantly refuses to comply
with the laws which its members are sworn to support. . . . Neither seduc-
tion, adultery, nor incest find penalty of recognition in its legal code. . . .
Twenty-eight of the thirty-six members of the present Legislature of Utah
are reported as having from two to seven wives each. While the Government of the United States is paying these men their mileage and *per diem*
as lawmakers in Utah, those guilty of the same offense outside of Utah
are leading the lives of felons in convict cells. . . . For thirty years have the
Mormons been trusted to correct these [and other enumerated] evils and
put themselves in harmony with the balance of civilized mankind. This
they have refused to do.[6]

Consequently, the Edmunds Act stiffened penalties against the Saints, im-
posing a fine of up to $400 and a prison term of up to five years for anyone
found guilty of newly entering polygamy and a new misdemeanor, unlawful cohabitation, for men with long-standing plural wives (like Pratt). "Cohabs" could face a fine of $300, a six-month prison term, or both. The bill
also regulated jury membership, allowed for amnesty, legitimized children
of earlier plural marriages, and denied the vote and the right to hold office to polygamists and their wives. Lastly, the Edmunds Act established
the Utah Commission to run elections.[7] In reaction, LDS leader Daniel H.
Wells rushed to Washington with the Utah constitution and a request for
statehood. Congress ignored him.[8] At this point, Teancum Pratt began to
worry.

As outside forces sought to overwhelm Castle Valley's historic isolation,
anxiety must have spread widely throughout the area. Plural families lived
in virtually every settlement. The first settlers along the Price River, for example, included polygamist John Amon Powell, brother of Caleb Rhoades's
dead exploration partner, Abe Powell. John had arrived on April 1, 1879,
with his wife, Sarah Jane Shields Plumb Powell, originally a sister-wife to
Hannah Matilda Snyder, whom John had married ten years earlier. Hannah
died in December 1877, leaving Sarah to care for her six children as well as
Sarah's own increasing brood. Three years after their arrival in Castle Valley, John married 19-year-old Rosaltha Allred. Sarah claimed Abe Powell's
land, which she later sold, moving his cabin on to her own parcel.[9] Additionally, Orangeville's first settler, Erastus Curtis, was a polygamist, as was
Stake President Christian Grice Larsen, now resident in Castle Dale. Larsen
eventually provided each of his four wives with her own substantial home,
built by the talented local mason, Henning Olsen Ungerman. Ungerman,
who later dropped his last name to achieve anonymity, had three wives of his
own, begetting nineteen children and acting as step-father to twelve more.
His family relations faltered, however, when one of his stepsons became a
deputy marshal and made several unsuccessful attempts to arrest him.[10]

Helper's first settler, schoolteacher, farmer, and later coal mine owner, Teancum Pratt worked hard to develop his Castle Valley lands but never prospered. Courtesy of Western Mining and Railroad Museum.

Several more polygamists lived in Huntington, including original settlers and brothers Elias and Jehu Cox, Jr., two of seven polygamists within
their sizable extended family. Several other men had two wives, including
Danish immigrant Jens Neilson, who had arrived in America with one wife,
Anne Christine Hansen, and, in Utah, married Karen Dortha Mikkelson
(or Tay). In the spring of 1881, Jens and Tay had made a dugout home
along Huntington Creek; then he went back to get his first wife, Christine.
As the story goes, "When he arrived with his other wife the two women lived
in the dugout and locked him out making him sleep in his wagon box until
he had dug another dugout for Christine."[11] Likewise, John Leasil Brasher
took two wives: first, Eliza Cheshire, and second, Ann Buttler. They had answered the call to settle Randolph (in northern Utah), where both families
befriended those of William Howard, an Irish immigrant and LDS convert
with three wives. According to a local historian, "When he [Howard] was released from this [settlement] mission in June 1880, he was advised to move
to Castle Valley in east central Utah. He took their advice."[12]

So those families came, as did other polygamists to the various other
area towns. Just exactly who advised them to settle Castle Valley has never
been specified, but LDS leaders may have wanted to get polygamists as far
out of sight as possible, making Castle Valley a first-rate choice. Protected
for a time by its remoteness, polygamous Pratt just kept his head down and
kept working his farm. On February 20, 1883, he offhandedly reported, "I
grubbed my land below the garden & at about 11 oclock Mr. Gillett agent
of the D.&R.G.R.R. called & settled with me for my land which the Co had
crossed with the [rail]Road. The weather is very spring like, the ice is melt-
ing out of the river."[13] Sandwiched in between the farm and weather reports, Pratt had just noted a major step for the entire Castle Valley corridor.
The land he sold Gillett would later become a railroad division point—the
official break in the line, housing train crews and railroad workers—and,
consequently, a major Castle Valley settlement.

Almost inevitably, railroads became the new engine powering an increasingly wide-spread industrial machine. According to historian Samuel
Hays, "Americans in all walks of life visualized the economic progress that
cheap transportation could set in motion."[14] The Rio Grande system was but
a single wave in a spring tide, described by historian Robert Weibe: "three
more transcontinentals [in addition to the Union Pacific]—the Southern
Pacific, the Northern Pacific, and the Atchison, Topeka, and Santa Fe—
were completed at two-year intervals in the early eighties. A fourth, the
Great Northern . . . [meant that] together the four lines gave the sudden
impression of an integrated country."[15] That tide, and all that came with it,
had almost breached Castle Valley's ramparts.

In the spring of 1883, the gap between the outside world and Castle
Valley shrank with the slap of the last iron rails on wooden crossties. Then,
the spring floods came again. Big trees rode the water's crest down the

Green River and caught on the bridge piling by the town. Railroad workers dumped a trainload of rock on the bridge, hoping it would hold. The floodwater backed up until it measured twelve feet higher on the north side of the bridge than on the south side. The bridge collapsed with a roar. Another flood crest surged down Price Canyon, ripping out a sizable section of track, then pushed east down the Price River. For the first time, the dam at Wellington stood fast. Once the flood subsided, the Western Construction Company's weary track crews went back to work. Hurriedly, Orangeville's John K. Reid negotiated transportation for a waiting load of farm equipment stalled in the heights at Pleasant Valley Junction. He needed it in Price (then called Castle Valley Junction), where he could load it in wagons, haul it south to his store, and have it ready for spring planting now that the ground was wet and soft. Only after he agreed to assume all responsibility should the tracks fail again would the D&RGW allow its construction engine to haul its first load of Emery County farm machinery down the steep Price Canyon grade. Luckily, this time the hastily-reconstructed track held.[16] After further repairs, the first full train all the way from Ogden pulled into Price a few weeks later. In April, track was completed further east to Desert Switch, just west of the town of Green River (Blake or Greenriver, as it was called earlier).[17] The railroad through the Castle Valley corridor was almost done.

Before the two lines joined, Green River had mushroomed into a classic end of track town: a typical, western hell on wheels. According to a local history, "While the railroad was going through, Greenriver was one of the wildest of boom towns. There were killings and fights, drunken bouts, women of more comeliness than character."[18] For example, a fellow named Jack Cook rode into town, proposing to start a boneyard of buffalo bones brought in by train from the prairie, bones which he intended to grind and sell locally for fertilizer. He and Frank Ganes started airing their differences in the saloon, and Frank shot him dead.[19] This rough element remained a problem until the completion of the railroad. Then, many of the rowdies began to drift away as Green River became the Rio Grande's first Castle Valley division point, and a much more civilized place.

Aside from the immediate significance of Cook's sudden demise, his plans for a boneyard pointed up another major change stealing over the American West. Ecological disaster was stalking the Great Plains. As described by historian Ralph Andrist, by the late nineteenth century the buffalo there had come under heavy pressure from "meat-suppliers for railroad work gangs, so-called sportsmen, killers for commercial butcher firms, wanton killers who shot into herds for no reason other than the momentary excitement of seeing one of the great beasts stagger and drop . . . . The Indians did their part . . . [sometimes] killing a buffalo for nothing but the tongue . . . [or] stampeding a buffalo herd over a cliff, when one was handy, killing far more animals than could possibly be used." Cows were the choice target because of their superior meat. "Then, in 1871 . . . [a] method of tanning buffalo hide to produce excellent leather was developed." One entrepreneur amassed an order for three thousand hides at $3.50 each, and the buffalo was doomed.[20] Herds that had numbered in the millions shrank to a few hundred, opening the prairies for America's great cattle culture.

The rising tide of change that marked the late nineteenth century even swept into Castle Valley. All along the valley corridor, isolation ended in April 1883 as George Goss, the same man who had treated Joseph Black so charitably after his desperate ride to Salt Lake City, drove another golden spike at Desert Switch to join the two ends of the D&RGW. Celebrants toasted the glorious event with a barrel of beer provided by Goss and a whole load of the beverage brought in by Tom Farrer. According to a local history, "The first passenger train ran [on] April 23, 1883, with Mr. Jim Beal as engineer. Round trip tickets to Salt Lake were sold on July 4th that year and cost $15.15, just half the regular fare."[21]

Green River particularly felt the railroad's impact as the corporation encouraged growth of a respectable town for its division point, although this transformation was not always without problems. In the words of Joseph T. Farrer, "When the railroad came to Greenriver, it went across our land and never paid a cent for it. They tried to jump my brother's claim, got a man to contest his right, but the proof was too strong and after several years we finally won out."[22] On the other hand, Joe Gammage, another local resident, found advantages in the railroad's arrival. The engineer who was surveying the line had boarded with him and his wife, the former Malinda Powell, who had previously been married to Caleb Rhoades. The engineer had advised Joe to buy ground north of the tracks, land viewed by the founding Farrers as worthless "blue 'dobe." Joe did as suggested and shortly thereafter was able to sell the railroad forty acres on which to build a station and the elegant Palmer House, named for the line's president, William Jackson Palmer. The railroad could then offer the public rooms and meals, and could remove the old boarding car previously run by George Goss for the convenience of the construction crews.[23]

Not all the crew stayed in the boarding car, of course. The Chinese were segregated. Not only did they make a little over half the white wage ($1.10 a day as opposed to $2.00), they were provided no accommodations at all. They were forced to dig their own dugouts on Reservoir Hill, where it became the "favorite pastime of the town kids . . . to stuff rags or paper down the stove pipes [sticking up out of the hill] then hide until the Chinamen got smoked out," according to a local history. "Roaring and cursing to right the damage they chased the kids if they were close enough. It was fraught with enough danger, the youngsters hoped, to be exciting."[24] This petty harassment by children echoed far more serious adult violence. Throughout nineteenth-century America, the Chinese suffered from increasing discrimination. In the 1850s, California imposed a selectively enforced

Foreign Miners' Tax to drive Chinese from the gold fields. Later, labor agitated for Chinese exclusion as industrialists, beginning with the Central Pacific Railroad, hired cheaper Chinese laborers over other workers. Consequently, in May 1882 (two months after the anti-Mormon Edmunds Act), Congress passed the Chinese Exclusion Act, stopping Chinese immigration for ten years. This racially-based restriction—the first limitation on immigration to the U.S.—became permanent under President Theodore Roosevelt in 1902.[25] Meanwhile, in 1883, the Rio Grande's Pleasant Valley Coal Company introduced Chinese labor in the heights above Castle Valley. They cut the portal of the Mud Creek Mine with picks, by hand: "as beautiful a piece of work as one could wish to see in a coal mine . . . The sides are perfectly straight to a certain height and the roof is semi-arched. . . . [T]his entry will stand indefinitely," opined a local historian.[26] Later that year, echoing growing American racism, an angry mob attacked the Chinese at Pleasant Valley, herded them into a boxcar, locked all the doors and pushed it down the track. The car gained momentum on the grade below the mine and rolled uncontrollably for about ten miles before coming to a halt just short of the steep Price River Canyon where it would surely have overturned. The Chinese broke out of the car and scattered.[27]

By this time, the Chinese were fearfully fleeing for their lives all over the West. The worst atrocities occurred in September 1885 at Rock Springs, Wyoming. English-speaking miners had recently organized a union and gone on strike. The Union Pacific Coal Company retaliated by bringing in Chinese strikebreakers who worked for half the white wage. Enraged, a mob of white miners set fire to the company shacks designated "Chinatown." Fifteen Chinese were wounded and twenty-eight killed, some of whom burned alive in their houses.[28] Although the Wyoming massacre led to official diplomatic exchanges and President Cleveland's denunciation of the "outrage upon law and treaty engagements . . . committed by a lawless mob . . . ,"[29] the murderers escaped all punishment.

Despite all the prejudice and poor conditions, the Chinese did fine work. In addition to the Mud Creek Mine portal, they built the piers for the railroad bridge across the Green River, replacing the structure lost in the 1883 flood. They made them wide enough so that the bridge could still be used when the railroad switched from narrow gauge to standard gauge in 1890. They built them strong enough that they were still standing in 1949.[30] One Chinese man, known only as Tom, was renowned around Helper as a former railroad builder who was rewarded by the railroad for "having saved the rights of the company" in an unremembered plot. "[R]eputed to have been Mayor of Hongkong earlier in his life, he was given a lifetime job as mail carrier and he treasured his position as a sacred trust. About 1918 he went back to China and little was known of him thereafter."[31] Except for occasional elusive workers like Tom, however, after the railroad's completion few Chinese remained in Castle Valley.

Just weeks after the Green River celebrations, railroad festivities moved north. Between May 1–15, 1883, trains ran through Price on a test basis.[32] The men of the construction crew who had spent months muscling ties and rails onto the hard-packed roadbed fully appreciated the settlers' struggle to hack out farms on this frontier. Consequently, "just before the regular train service was established, the construction train gathered up all the settlers they could along the [Price] river, and took them for a free excursion down to about Mounds [about fifteen miles] and back, to the great delight of all."[33] On May 17, 1883, the first regular train service began between Grand Junction, Colorado, and Ogden, Utah, the full extent of the Western's line. In short order, the earlier-established Castle Valley Junction was superseded by Price as a regular stop.[34] A train from the west came daily around 5 pm, and the one from the east at 11 pm, unless held up by more "freshets" (or flooding) along the line.[35]

The local Indians (probably Utes in from the Uinta Basin) were also fascinated by the railroad. According to Ernest Horsley, who watched the scene, they "used to come in, stand far off and watch the movement of the train. The thing that bothered them was when the train backed up how the cars could pull the engine back. They could understand the engines pulling the car."[36] Not all Utes were so incredulous, however. At least one Ute family—Joe and Rose Montus and their children—helped pioneer Wellington in 1883.[37] Although their previous residence is unknown, their arrival at that time may well have been related to the departure of the respected Indian agent, John J. Critchlow, from the Uinta Basin Ute reservation northeast of Castle Valley that same year. Designated as Utah's Ute homeland since the Civil War, the reservation suffered from the usual litany of unratified treaties, short rations, broken promises, and white encroachment that characterized the rest of the American West. Furthermore, the government expected male Utes to become farmers, contrary to the native tradition that men hunted and raced horses while women farmed and gathered wild plants. The situation worsened with the infamous clash between Colorado Utes and their Indian agent, Nathan C. Meeker, in 1879. With tensions high, the reservation Utes invited the Critchlow family and other agency employees to join them in the mountains where they withdrew for safety—an almost unprecedented expression of confidence in a federal Indian agent. Meeker's high-handedness and the subsequent slaughter then led to the forced removal of Colorado's eastern bands onto the ever-more-crowded Utah reservation in the early 1880s.[38] In short, with all these difficulties, Castle Valley may have seemed to the Montuses like an improvement over reservation life.

After helping to pioneer Wellington, the Montus family left town for the reservation around 1890. Their probable motive was to take up their land allotment granted under the 1880 Ute Agreement and the federal Dawes Severalty (General Allotment) Act of 1887, an action that would finally bring them U.S. citizenship.[39] Furthermore, the government had begun enforcing Ute settlement on the reservation when "trespassing miners discovered valuable Gilsonite (asphaltum) deposits on the Uintah and Ouray reservations in 1886 and 1888."[40] Sam Gilson's secret had come out, leading to considerable confusion on the Ute Reservation. The Utes, understandably upset by trespassers on their severely-shrunken ancestral lands, had become increasingly hostile, particularly after the massacre of Utah Utes in Colorado in the summer of 1886. Determined to hang on to the valuable gilsonite deposits, corporate owners sought special legislation in Congress which ultimately resulted in "the Strip," a mineral-rich area (and later, a center for vice), being carved out of the reservation in 1888. This 7,000–acre land transfer brought the Utes only twenty dollars an acre, but yielded gilsonite originally sold on the American market for $120 per ton. Under these circumstances, while citizenship and residence near other Utes held its attractions, Rose Montus, Joe's wife, clearly recognized the reservation's many deficiencies. At the time of the move to the Basin she was pregnant and feared for the life of her weakest child, Ben, should she die. She allegedly exhorted a promise from Wellington neighbor, Josephine Zundle, that Ben would be cared for if necessary. Just as Rose feared, the birth of her baby brought her death. The Zundles raised Ben, who married into the community and fathered two children with his locally-reared wife.[41]

In most cases, however, Utes and Castle Valley settlers kept each other at a distance. One early report noted that Utes came through Castle Valley "to beg food, and sometimes demanding food with threats."[42] Not only did many settlers fear Indians, contact with white settlers had left the Utes with a host of realistic worries which were sometimes utilized against them. For example, Lydia Jane Metcalf Price, living in Scofield about the turn of the century, decided to trick unwanted, begging Indians into leaving. When some came to request food, they noticed a slaughtered pig on the back porch. When they asked what it was, "I told them a dead man. They asked me what he died of and I told them smallpox," she remembered. "The next day there wasn't an Indian left in Scofield."[43]

Despite this general underlying tension, some Castle Valley settlers enjoyed cooperative relationships with the Utes. For example, Sunnyside's Ernest Stevenson recalled, "Once an Indian named Gray Wolf brought about 15 or more horses to sell [from the Uinta Basin reservation]. I helped him with the horses and sales. When he left, he gave me his dog, Keno."[44] In a similar, friendly vein, Molen resident Lucy Hansen Nielsen, born in 1889, remembered some Indians who stopped by her house in the mid-1890s. "It was near dinner time so the Indians stayed. Daddy helped unload the horses and fed them oats, hay, and water. I stood near ma, hiding under her apron. The chief caught me peeking and pulled me to him . . . and said, 'Cat's got her tongue.' Then he took a strand of beads off his neck and put it on mine." She kept those beads all her life.[45] For decades after settlement,

Utes played fleeting roles in traditional community celebrations. As historian Frederick Hoxie noted, given that "Indians were indigenous to America, and their fate was inevitably linked to the progress of American civilization[,] . . . [i]t should not surprise us . . . that Indians generally had a prominent place in patriotic celebrations and ceremonies."[46] His statement could easily apply to Castle Valley, where Eva Westover Conover, a native of Huntington, described one of the Twenty-fourth of July parades in her hometown sometime before the First World War. Utes, she wrote, came "all painted in their war-paint, faces streaked with black, red, and white; stripped to the waist, brown as bears," armed with bows and arrows. "Now and then, they would let out an Indian war-cry. . . . And one or two would break away from their formation and race up along and beside other floats, gesturing with their bows and threatening."[47] Orange Seely, who died in 1918, always got the Indians to come for these parades based on their mutual friendships. He also welcomed all the Utes traveling through the Castle Dale area to camp under a large cottonwood tree on his property. Both he and his brother, Wink, reportedly spoke Ute and opened their homes as "free wayside hotels," entertaining, as well as white travelers, "the friendly Indians when they were passing by."[48] The Utes reciprocated this hospitality. After the completion of the railroad, Orange and Wink went to Thistle Junction to catch a train. The Utes encamped there "welcomed them like long-lost brothers" and invited them to dinner—cricket-stuffed sausages—which they gamely sampled until their train arrived.[49]

Throughout Castle Valley, business picked up with the rhythm of the railroad schedule. The Price area in northern Castle Valley was particularly affected. For example, Joseph Birch quickly established the Railroad Eating Place for workers and passengers alike. An English convert, he had arrived in Price in September 1882 with his wives, Dorothy Chambers Birch and Mary Elizabeth Sylvester Birch, and several of their children, including Dorothy's daughter, Isabella, married to Henry G. Bryner. Birch turned in forty acres of land for the Price townsite after it was selected by the LDS Apostles.[50] Concurrently, community leaders pitched in to build a meeting hall on the Price townsite, allegedly the largest building in Castle Valley. It was dedicated on Sunday, April 13, 1883, and a dancing party a few days later brought out "no dancing pumps, but the strong stogies [boots] helped smooth off a great many slivers and rough places [on the new floor]. . . . Only four sets could be danced at once, and no one missed when their number was called."[51] The spirit of celebration persisted into May. For the 1883 May Day festivities in northern Castle Valley, Henry Babcock of Spring Glen made a supreme sacrifice. His favorite watchdog had just died, and, as Ernest Horsley noted:

> . . . he felt very badly, but the pioneer habit was to use everything. So he
> removed the dog's hide, freed it from the hair and stretched and cured

A D&RGW locomotive steams past the Castle Gate rock in Price Canyon, the northern gateway to Castle Valley. The arrival of the railroad forever changed life in the valley. Courtesy of Western Mining and Railroad Museum.

the hide by an Indian process. He trimmed up an empty nail keg he had received from a gang of railroad carpenters, stretched the dog hide on its end and made a drum. He joined the May Day orchestra and was a "howling" success.[52]

The crew and passengers of a Rio Grande train were able to join the May first celebration since yet another washout had marooned the train at Price. They watched the afternoon children's dance at the new meeting house (Horsley noted that "the slivers . . . [were] pretty well rubbed down. The children were nearly all barefoot, of necessity") and bought out all the oranges at Joseph Birch's railroad restaurant as presents for the young dancers. (That glorious luxury could only have come on the railroad, since Castle Valley's frosty winter climate kills orange trees.) That night, all the adults danced, and "at midnight the train whistle announced the washouts had been repaired, the orchestra struck up 'Home Sweet Home' and the day was over."[53]

This community-passenger party resulted from some of the late-nineteenth century hallmarks described by historian John Garraty: improved transportation and communication (which brought the railroad guests), and, in a small way, urbanization, since Price was large enough to have a railroad stop and a community hall. Like the rest of contemporary America, in the 1880s and 1890s, Castle Valley also formed its own organizations, often centered on music, theater, and pageantry. For example, at Castle Dale, Samuel R. Jewkes gathered local music talent in 1883 and formed a brass band which made its first appearance on election day that year.[54] Every town had its own gatherings. Some staged bow dances, in which men chose their evening's partners by blindly selecting an envelope and matching the bow inside to the one pinned on the woman's dress. Together they could dance quadrilles, polkas, schottisches, or even the pologamy waltz, in which one man danced with two women. "It was a special waltz called with words to the music, similar to the quadrill[e]," recalled Molen's Lucy Hansen Nielsen. "It was fun to watch but I was too little to dance it." She also remembered the musicians: George Biddlecomb, who played violin and "was firm with his foot stomp to help us Primary children to keep time."[55] Several towns enjoyed "spelling bees, quilting bees, candy pulls, popcorn parties, corn husking parties, home dramatics, traveling theater, traveling circus, fairs and jubilees."[56] More formally, each growing town soon supported its own thespian group: the Orangeville Dramatic Association, Huntington Dramatic Club, and Ferron Dramatic Club.[57] Townspeople watched their relatives and neighbors in such offerings as *The Red Light*, a temperance play staged in Price in 1885 accompanied by a three-piece orchestra and followed by several short sketches. The main production began as the curtain, inexplicably painted with a pig, rose before a crowd seated on chairs, benches, and spring wagon seats in the all-purpose log building used for church, school, opera house, and courthouse.[58] Holidays, too, especially the Fourth and Twenty-fourth of July, promoted pageantry. One Twenty-fourth of July, Molen made a grand parade of "the pioneers of 1847, Handcart companies, Indians, Brigham Young, etc. . . . As everybody was in the parade, there were no spectators."[59]

While these growing settlements formed their own associations, they increasingly received goods and outside news from the newly-completed railroad. Castle Valley communications swung to a north-south axis as the old star mail route down Salina Canyon and east over the Old Spanish Trail was abandoned. Wilsonville, Castle Valley's original post office site, died a slow death. In Price, Fred Grames opened a store stocked with the inventory of the departing railroad grading camp's commissary: bacon, tea, coffee, tobacco, sugar, overalls, stogie shoes, and spools of thread. Some three months later, regular mail service began on the railroad, so on August 30, 1883, Fred and his brother Albert opened a U.S. Post Office in the back of the store. Fred served as postmaster and Albert as mail carrier and chief clerk for a munificent twelve dollars a month. They handled the mail not only for northern Castle Valley but also for the southern towns of Cleveland, Huntington, Castle Dale, Orangeville, Ferron, Molen, and Muddy, regardless of weather.[60] "Those horses," remembered James Gardner, "when they'd get to Huntington, their tails would just be one solid pack of mud, right from their backbone right to the tip. The road was so muddy and sloppy, you know. They'd have, sometimes, four head of horses . . . just the same . . . covered with mud."[61] Mail pouches arrived on the train every day except Sunday, connecting Castle Valley to the entire world with only slight delays.[62]

While the railroad brought luxury goods and mail to many remote areas, it also allowed non-Mormon residents (and voters) access to still-theocratic Utah.[63] At least non-Mormon Ovando James Hollister took this view, and authored a sizable booklet, *The Resources and Attractions of Utah*, for sale at the Denver Exposition of 1882. He enthused over Utah's people, climate, soil, agriculture, mineral wealth, railroads, and so on, concluding with the declaration:

> A few years will inevitably bring a majority of the people to the support of the new order of things, when Utah can safely be admitted as a State. Polygamy will gradually withdraw into the past, and a freed people will require their church to confine the use of its machinery to spiritual concerns, leaving politics and business to their natural development.[64]

The LDS Church intended no such withdrawal and countered by trying to spread the Saints more widely throughout Utah. Consequently, in the fall of 1884, church historian Andrew Jenson rode 127 miles south on the D&RGW with Apostles Joseph F. Smith and Erastus Snow all the way to Price, where settlers still strung out for 14 miles along the river, owing to "a little land difficulty" on the chosen townsite. Their party then took a "25 mile moonlight ride over a broken and uneven county to Huntington, at present the largest settlement in the valley" (although the settlers there were still also "considerably scattered"). Then they moved on to Castle Dale for the quarterly conference, subsequently visiting Orangeville before returning to Price.[65] There, they organized a local Quorum of the Seventies with Teancum Pratt proud to be admitted as one of their number, although he grumbled about the choices for Quorum president and local bishop.[66] The Apostles, meanwhile, joined by their wives, continued on an extended railroad trip to LDS stakes in Colorado, Arizona, and California before returning to Salt Lake City. Jenson returned immediately to Salt Lake City, where he published a letter in the church-affiliated *Deseret News* lauding Castle Valley's "room for thousands of thrifty Latter-day Saints, who are invited to come and cast their lot there among a truly good and God fearing people." He stressed the valley's productive soil and promising future, offering "good homes on very easy terms." He added, "In view of the hard times and the scarcity of labor this season and [with so] . . . many people without homes of their own in our older towns, I would earnestly recommend that such of our brethren who are not afraid to take hold with a will and labor patiently and hard for a few years to subdue a new country should turn their attention to Castle Valley."[67]

While Castle Valley residents very surely labored patiently in their challenging surroundings, their local railroad faced problems of its own. The first of these was to turn a profit, not an easy task in the frenzied capitalistic world of the later 1800s. To reassure jittery investors, the D&RGW issued its first annual report in 1883, trumpeting its access to Utah's resources, including those near Castle Valley. "For more than one-half of its length it [the railroad] lies within comparatively easy reach of coal, the best of which, the 'Pleasant Valley deposit,' is a 10 feet seam of excellent coal, without a particle of slate," it declared.[68] The invitation to extractive industry was unmistakable, particularly since in 1884, coal surpassed wood as the fuel of choice in the United States.[69] Despite access to such resources, construction had siphoned off tremendous amounts of capital. Furthermore, when the D&RGW reached Ogden in 1883, the UP dropped its freight rates between there and the Missouri River from $3.00 per ton to only twenty-five cents. The Rio Grande system had to match this in a growing rate war.[70]

The Rio Grande lost money, but Utah residents cheered. More specifically, the rate war permitted cut-rate import prices on heavy farm machinery, much to the benefit of the latest LDS cooperative venture, the Cooperative Wagon and Machine Company (later, through a merger, the Consolidated Wagon and Machine Company), organized in 1883. This new venture was one of many that had flowered as locally-based United Orders failed. In response, LDS leaders in 1878 had formed a centralized organization, Zion's Central Board of Trade. It sponsored "cooperative marketing, cooperative buying, [and] the development of new industries" such as wagons, farm implements, iron, sugar, silk, and wool.[71] This church-sponsored venture thus helped steer communitarian Utah toward unavoidable capitalism brought by America's railroads. Furthermore, in 1882, LDS President John Taylor explicitly endorsed free enterprise, stressing the importance of putting "our own business people in the place of outsiders."[72]

Many Castle Valley residents agreed and opened their own businesses. For example, David Williams and sons, residents of Winter Quarters, moved to Price, bought out Fred E. Grames and built a large mercantile building. Locals such as Sam Hill and Owen Smith with Charley Barnes went to Bear Creek Canyon and nearby Deer Creek, respectively, to open hillside wagon mines. These little caves earned their name because most were only wide enough to admit a single, horse-drawn wagon, into which the exposed coal could be shoveled and then hauled to town.[73] In later years, James Gardner remembered when his father, Albert Clifton Gardner, partnered with Erin Howard and Ulysses and Sam Grange to open a wagon mine above Huntington, in Cedar Creek Canyon. In the winters, the only time coal was in demand, the four men took turns staying up at the mine. Gardner remembered lying in his bed in the one-room family cabin on a winter morning:

Freighters gather at Price in the late 1800s, when the town became Castle Valley's communications hub. The photographer carefully included all the local means of communication: the wagons and teams, the telegraph pole, and the railroad tracks (foreground). Photo from the author's collection.

"[I]t was still dark; you could hear the wagon wheels . . . crinkling on the snow . . . the wagon boxes rattle . . . trying to beat the other guy out of town to get up to the mine first so he could get served first . . . They'd start [up] that way before daylight . . . and they'd get back late in the evening." Customers took run-of-mine coal, meaning, any size they could get, and if it were too big to lift into the wagon, they would have to break it themselves with a pick.[74] In another stab at private enterprise, in 1889, naturalized Scot John Thompson Rowley utilized his earlier experience as a charcoal burner to erect twelve beehive kilns near the new railroad track. His Blue Cut Charcoal Company soon provided charcoal for gold and silver smelters from Utah to Nevada.[75]

Thanks to the railroad, Price grew, particularly after 1886, when the army established Fort Duchesne to manage the Utes in the Uinta Basin. The soldiers guarding the fort included two companies of the Ninth Cavalry, one of the units of the famed Buffalo Soldiers. Those in residence totaled some 584 African Americans, plus their dependents. They all disembarked at Price and the soldiers mounted their horses, also shipped by rail, to ride the ninety miles of newly built road to the fort. Supplies and families followed in wagons. The military had just completed this new wagon road up Soldier Creek Canyon to a height of over 7,300 feet, then down to the northeast along Nine Mile Canyon and north through Gate Canyon into the Uinta Basin. During their fifteen-year tenure at Fort Duchesne, the Buffalo Soldiers were joined by Lts. John Alexander and Charles Young, two of only three African Americans then graduated from West Point.[76] Along the same route, the soldiers soon strung a telegraph wire, destined for long service in Nine Mile Canyon.

This new military presence confirmed Price as the regional communications center, bringing prosperity and problems. The post and the Utes needed all sorts of supplies, so the local freighting industry flourished. Price constructed freighting yards and a campground. Nearby, "two or three saloons furnished some of the trouble stuff," according to Ernest Horsley.[77] Agents gathered freight, mail, and produce at the Price railhead and stored it in warehouses, if necessary, awaiting the arrival of freight wagons. Men from most neighboring farms took turns making the roughly two-week trip, usually hauling two-ton loads (including, initially, water in huge barrels and feed for the horses). A twice-weekly stage service, established in 1888, was upgraded to a daily run a year later.[78] Gilsonite, the black, sticky mineral named for Sam Gilson, also traveled out of the Uinta Basin on the huge freight wagons. Bert Seaboldt, manager of construction for the D&RGW, located claims to the mineral on Ute Reservation lands in January 1886, just months before the troops arrived. Once the Army had constructed that good road, Seaboldt and associates began taking out tons of gilsonite, all of it illegally, until the corporate consortium which took over their claims convinced Congress to remove the gilsonite-bearing strip from reservation lands. In 1888 alone, freighters hauled 3,000 tons of gilsonite to the railhead in Price, where it sold for $80 per ton.[79]

With this increasing traffic, local teamsters simply could not meet the demand. The Army consequently bid out its freight contract "to an eastern firm named Mulholland, Shaw, and Winston. Other freighting outfits came, [including] John B. Milburn," Horsley noted. Locals stopped work on the canal in favor of more lucrative freighting, but in the fall when the Mulholland company teams stood idle, they "made a contract with the board of directors of the Price Water Co. to make the canal through the Rock cuts for $9,000." As a result, after a carload of lumber for flumes arrived in January 1888, work rushed forward on the canal, and "about the forepart of May water flowed onto the [Price] townsite eastward" at a total cost of $20,000.[80] The old days of the shaky water level and hand-dug canals had been superseded in Price by a more convenient, capitalistic arrangement.

While the new Rio Grande Western generally stimulated Castle Valley development, privately, it was slipping into economic rigor mortis. Frequent washouts and high water along the line—including in Price Canyon—had seriously disrupted traffic. Checking the books for 1883, the first year of operation, railroad accountants discovered that the whole D&RG system had made a net profit of only $3,741 or $12.25 per mile of track. The railroad canceled dividends. Major investors blamed Palmer and forced a change of management that split governance of the Utah and Colorado lines. Other strife mushroomed until Colorado's angry new Rio Grande president ordered one mile of track pulled up just east of the Colorado line, splitting the system in two. Profits plummeted. After a subsequent reorganization, receivership, a strike by the Knights of Labor, and inter-company lawsuits, in 1886 the whole sad episode ended. The lease agreement between the two lines was dissolved as Colorado's Denver and Rio Grande Railway was sold at auction to long-time investors who renamed it the Denver and Rio Grande Railroad Company and retired its debts. The Colorado line gained a new president, Edward T. Jeffrey, who promised cooperation with the Western, which was released from receivership and remained under Palmer's control.[81] As the network recovered, in 1887 railroad workers began building over two dozen frame houses on Pratt's old homestead (acquired by the Western in 1883), in anticipation of creating a freight terminal there.[82] The 1887 D&RGW's annual report claimed slow but steady growth in hauling Utah's mining and agriculture output, handling metals worth $7,630,000 and shipping Utah produce largely to Kansas.[83] The line seemed to be prospering.

At the same time, the railroad faced a new, untested obstacle, the federal Interstate Commerce Act of 1887. Just days after its approval, Congress passed the Edmunds-Tucker Act, supported by perennial lobbyist Robert Baskin. The latter act's various sections dissolved the LDS Church, its emigration company, and the Nauvoo Legion; confiscated all church property in excess of $50,000; abolished Utah women's suffrage; disinherited all children of plural marriages, and prescribed an anti-polygamy test oath for voters, political candidates, and prospective jury members. It also further empowered numerous federal officers, revised authority over territorial schools, required that all marriages be certified in probate courts, and wiped out existing election districts.[84]

This new legislation marked the crescendo of a rising tide against Mormonism, beginning with use of the 1882 Edmunds Act to deny practicing polygamist George Q. Cannon his seat in the U.S. House.[85] Then, Rudger Clawson, convicted in the nation's first anti-polygamy trial under the Edmunds Act, had his conviction upheld by the U.S. Supreme Court in March 1885 and had served a heavy double sentence for polygamy and unlawful cohabitation. Courts began prosecutions of other prominent Saints, including George Q. Cannon and Lorenzo Snow.[86] Federal marshals and their deputies flocked to Utah in what the Saints called the Raids, and polygamists, including LDS President John Taylor, went underground. Others fled to Mexico and Canada, away from the reach of U.S. law.[87] Some polygamists even sought refuge in remote Castle Valley, including the two families of Henry Ammon Fowler. He had married Mary Susannah Fackrell, herself the daughter of a polygamous union, in Orderville in 1880, and had taken a second wife some six or seven years later. When the raids began, Fowler moved both his families to Huntington, where his sister and brother-in-law already resided, claiming "I thought I had a better chance of getting a farm and home there."[88] Life in Castle Valley, though, remained as difficult as ever. Susannah Fowler moved her five children (all under eight years of age) into a two-room cabin with a sod roof that leaked whenever it rained hard.[89] Teancum Pratt, too, found little solace in his isolated farm. In 1886 he confided in his diary his fears of "expected raids from the U.S. Marshalls. These have not been very happy years for me," he added. "I have lived in the wilderness with my families & had seemingly no friends & naught but poverty."[90]

Deputy U.S. marshals, including gilsonite discoverer Sam Gilson, fanned out throughout Utah. A sensational report, published in 1916 by Mormon Apostle Orson Whitney gave this dramatic account of the anti-polygamist searches:

> Paid informers, both men and women, were put to work to ferret out cases of polygamy. . . . [They] insinuated themselves into private dwellings. . . . At night dark forms could be seen prowling about the premises of peaceable citizens, peering into windows or watching for the opening of doors. . . . Some of the hirelings were bold enough, or indecent enough, to thrust themselves into sick-rooms and women's bed-chambers, rousing the occupants from slumber by pulling the bedclothes off them. Houses were broken into by deputy marshals armed with axes.[91]

This view, published about twenty years after the fact, was quickly rebutted by Robert Baskin, of the other end of the political spectrum, who quoted the United States District Attorney, Charles S. Varian:

> The historian [Whitney] gives no particulars—and it is certain that he would have given names, dates, and details, if he were able to do so. Such conduct on the part of government officers would have been generally denounced . . . and promptly punished—had there been occasion.[92]

The courts had specifically declined to make sexual intercourse the test for cohabitation, requiring only that a man live in the house of more than one wife, so bedroom raids were unnecessary. The federal hunt for polygamists was real enough, however. The Saints' task consisted of avoiding any contact with deputies, since, in that honest era, a man confronted with accusations about his polygamous lifestyle (such as Pratt), would own up and face his punishment.[93]

During this cat-and-mouse game, deputies stood out in Mormon communities, or so learned Henry Mathis late in 1889 when he drove his spanking new buggy (bought on eight months' credit, no money down) home from Price to St. George, in far southwest Utah, to get married. He stopped in Ferron to spend the night with a friend, Joe Stevens. "People, seeing us drive into town in a buggy thought we were marshals after 'cohabs'. . . . The people kept Stevens awake nearly all night coming to inquire if we were 'deps,'" Mathis later wrote.[94] After his marriage and a few weeks of visiting, early in 1890 Mathis packed up his wife, the former Mary DeFriez, in his fancy buggy and headed back toward Price. Two memorable events marked their journey. First, on the west side of Salina Canyon, in the town of Salina, the proprietress of their hotel "was very jubilant and dancing around. . . . The Liberals had won the election [in Salt Lake City] and elected a mayor and council over the People's Party," he reported. After remarking that the Saints supported the People's Party and non-Mormons the Liberals, he added, "this was a great victory for the Liberals to win Salt Lake City. . . . a victory they had been working for for years."[95] Although the election had been badly marred by subterfuges if not outright fraud, after the Liberal success, non-Mormon businesses poured into Utah's capital. Land prices soared up to 700 percent, valuations increased 400 percent, and taxpayers wailed.[96] American capitalism had indeed arrived in the formerly communal Zion.

The morning after hearing of the Liberals' success, Henry and Mary Mathis started up snowy Salina Canyon, "the only road [to Castle Valley] that was kept open through the mountains in the winter." It was a poor road, taking more than a day to cross, and the Mathises, knowing no hotels stood along the way, anticipated they might have to sleep under the frosty sky or in the freezing buggy. At the top, Henry remembered that ex-U.S. Marshal E. A. Ireland had a ranch nearby and decided to drive over to request accommodations. Ireland had served as chief U.S. marshal in Utah Territory from the beginning of the Raids until 1886, when he was replaced by Marshal Frank H. Dyer. During his tenure, he had earned the Saints's hatred, not only for arresting the polygamous, but for his prison policies. His restrictions included requiring striped suits like common criminals for Mormon cohabs, insisting that they be clean-shaven (emphatically not the fashion), and establishing a photographic Rogues Gallery of criminals in pairs, which sometimes coupled Saints with horse thieves, murderers, and other felons.[97] After his resignation, Ireland had bought a ranch in the heights west of Castle Valley. While his cowboys lived in log cabins, Mathis noted, " Mr. Ireland had quite nice quarters. I informed him we had our lunch but needed a bed. He readily vacated his room and turned it over to us." The Mathises slept comfortably, and in the morning, "When I asked him what the bill was, he said, 'Nothing at all.' That seemed really nice to come from a man that nearly all the people of Utah had hated so. . . . He and his deputies had been hunting out all the men that had plural wives and bringing them into court. Of course, they were just doing their duty in enforcing the law. He was a real gentleman to us."[98]

Irrigating Castle Valley meant long hours for men and teams. Here, a crew works to bring water from Muddy Creek to the area that became Moore. Courtesy of Emery County Archives.

The next night brought the Mathises to the Muddy River, where they found shelter with Casper Christensen, the LDS Bishop. A Danish immigrant, Christensen had first entered Castle Valley in the 1870s with his livestock, and begun digging the local canal in 1881. He became Muddy's (later Emery's) first postmaster in 1882 and bishop a year later. After all this hard work, he took farming very seriously, even when a U.S. postal inspector appeared on a surprise inspection. Keeping the official waiting, Christensen continued irrigating. When he finally came to the house, the self-important postal employee scolded him, saying, "'Do you know who I am? I am a United States Postal Inspector.' Christensen replied, 'Do you know who I am? I am the Bishop of Muddy Creek.'" As reported by historian Edward Geary, "Even today, when someone gets to bragging about his own importance, some of the old people in Emery will say, 'I am the Bishop of Muddy Creek.'"[99]

Clearly, a diverse set of people now encountered each other along the Castle Valley corridor. Some of them found new grounds for cooperation. For example, in 1888, government surveyor A. D. Ferron had called at the home of Teancum Pratt to inform him of a coming coal boom. In an action not then illegal, Ferron sought to take advantage of Pratt's knowledge of the nearby mountains, so proposed that Pratt "show him where the best lands were probably situated & he would work up the Boom & look after purchases for our joint locations while I should work the claims & receive wages for my labor, he being responsible for same."[100] Looking after his own interests, Pratt noted, "In 1888 . . . I was able to forsee sufficiently to locate the proper coal lands so that I earned $1,300.00 prospecting, & also earned a team & wagon & mower & rake. . . ."[101]

The U.S. marshals finally came, too. First, in 1888, they rounded up O. J. Anderson of Castle Dale who had married sisters Kathinka and Nathalia Wilberg. He received a $50 fine and 120 days in jail.[102] Early in 1890, they found Teancum Pratt. He noted, "At this time I was in good financial circumstances having prospered & having plenty of the necessaries, fields, fruits, teams, vehicles, implements & stock & was nearly out of debt."[103] While he waited for his trial, he went to cut wood on contract and severely broke his left lower leg. Less than a month later, he and his second wife, Sarah Ewell Pratt, took the train to court in Provo. Pratt limped in on crutches, pled guilty, and hoped for leniency. But, he reported, "[I] received the full sentence & fine & costs, all the law allowed."[104]

Prison life, somewhat altered under Marshal Dyer, intrigued Pratt. The prison surgeon cared for his leg and hospitalized him for a couple of months. Pratt liked the hospital fare and found the room comfortable, "but the inmates were awful wicked men."[105] Prisoners who could work had more privileges than Pratt, although all had to wear prison garb. Nonetheless, Pratt joined the prison choir, composed largely of Saints. "As they were short of bass," he reported, "I was quite at home."[106] He also enjoyed playing checkers, chess, quoits, and other games, and took advantage of classes in bookkeeping and mathematics. He noted many of the inmates "were happy & very jolly fellows & seemed to be glad to be where they were, but would never admit such was the case; I fully believe in the principle of hard labor for convicts & lawbreakers & I say it is a great injustice for society to keep prisoners as they are kept at the Utah penitentiary."[107] For his own part, he added, "The prison is not severe upon the Brethren. They are out at work in the fields & go to town on errands for the prison & inside the yards they rest & visit & are permitted many pleasures & privileges. I was permitted free access to the library & read much including Young's Night thoughts."[108]

Pratt left the penitentiary in August, 1890, a pivotal year across America. That year's census results, as mapped by historian Frederick Jackson Turner, showed no more line of westward-marching settlement along the frontier, long the divider between civilization and wilderness. Instead, islands of settlement peppered a West where the Native Americans had never been counted (or the outcome would have consistently appeared quite different). Utah had certainly grown in population and diversity; the 1890 census showed that 44 percent were not Mormon, especially miners and railroad workers, of which a goodly number ranged along the Castle Valley corridor.[109] Additionally, the federal government exercised increased political power nationwide. Not only did the Supreme Court enhance federal control over Utah Territory, as noted, but Congress also took a new, ultimately more far-reaching step to limit Big Business. Although the Interstate Commerce Act, aimed at controlling the railroads, had made the first move in that direction in 1887, the far more significant Sherman Anti-Trust Act passed in 1890 with only a single dissenting vote in all of Congress. It made any combination in restraint of trade a federal offense and permitted a private individual who was injured by a person or corporation in violation of this act to sue.[110] Although for years the act lacked teeth, subsequent amendments would directly affect a growing number of Castle Valley businessmen, particularly in the mines and railroad.

This growing federal power forced numerous changes throughout Utah. In 1888, territorial representatives had passed laws to regularize their own procedures, conforming as nearly as possible to federal law. The legislature adopted voluminous statutes regulating railroad corporations, irrigation companies, church incorporation, the Perpetual Emigration Fund Company, water rights, courts, and attorneys (previously forbidden by Mormon custom); defining prohibited incestuous relationships (for the first time); establishing a full criminal code, and so on, most of which had earlier been managed under Ordinances passed by the state of Deseret, not by law in compliance with national requirements. It also forbade marriages "When there is a husband or wife living, from whom the person marrying has not been divorced [that is, it outlawed polygamous unions]," but it added, "Marriages solemnized in any other country [such as Mexico or

Canada], State or Territory, if valid and solemnized, are valid here," meaning, one could marry plural wives in another jurisdiction.[111] In addition, the LDS Church sued the federal government in the Supreme Court to restore its corporate body and to regain its property. In May 1890, the church lost.[112] A few months later, on September 24, the President and Prophet of the LDS Church, Wilford Woodruff, announced a revelation that seemed to put the practice of polygamy permanently to rest. His announcement read, in part:

> Inasmuch as the laws enacted by Congress forbidding plural marriages, which laws have been pronounced constitutional by the court of last resort, I hereby declare my intention to submit to those laws, and to use my influence with the members of the Church over which I preside to have them do likewise. . . . And I now publicly declare that my advice to the Latter-day Saints is to refrain from contracting any marriage forbidden by the law of the land.[113]

The Saints, meeting at their semi-annual conference in October, upheld this directive by unanimous vote. Yet the so-called Woodruff Manifesto, stressing President Woodruff's "influence," offering his "advice," and concerned specifically with the laws of *this* land, fell short of a command and had a confusing effect on his followers. Some Saints immediately abandoned plural wives, who had to shift for themselves as best they could.[114] Most polygamists clung to their families; several men persisted in polygamous relations and even contracted new plural marriages both within and outside the United States.[115] Consequently, the specter of Mormon polygamy would last well into the future.

Throughout Utah, the Woodruff Manifesto did not automatically end the practice of plural marriage, nor arrests for it. Yet the number of convictions dwindled from a high in 1889 of 6 convictions for polygamy and 294 for unlawful cohabitation. In 1890, although 10 men earned polygamy convictions, only 101 (including Pratt) went to prison as cohabs. The numbers dropped to 3 and 72, respectively, in 1891, and zero and 37 in 1892. After that, although accusations continued, no more were convicted.[116] As the raids dwindled, Castle Valley, no longer so isolated, could get back to the business of community-building.

4

# Cowboys and Industry, 1890–1899

*When No. 2 [engine] pulled out [from Castle Gate] for Helper, the paymaster
and deputy crossed over the tracks to the Wasatch company's store . . . and were
just about to carry the treasure [sacks of gold and silver] up . . . to the P. V. Coal
company's offices, when a rough looking individual, evidently "Butch" Cassidy,
stepped in front of Mr. Carpenter [the paymaster] and exclaimed, "drop them sacks
and hold up your hands."*

—*Eastern Utah Advocate*, 22 APRIL 1897

Historian Walter Nugent claimed, "The transformation of America
from the frontier rural society of the eighteenth and nineteenth century to the metropolitan society of the twentieth was the major change in
American history."[1] Castle Valley, too, made this all-American change, but
modern industry crowded in side-by-side with vestiges of the old frontier.
The area reached its glory days in the late nineteenth century, as residents
tamed the land, formed lasting institutions, and made a comfortable living
from farming, stockraising, mines, and railroads. Growing prosperity also
attracted outlaws, among them Butch Cassidy, whose mine payroll robbery
was the largest haul in Castle Valley history. Meanwhile, other law-abiding,
hard-working souls pursued less glamorous options.

One of these was Teancum Pratt. He discovered the money-making
"probability of my place being made the R.R. Division point" while he was
still in prison and worried that he was "only partially secure in my land or
have only secured part of it."[2] In fact, the imprisoned Pratt proved up, and
his father-in-law, Frances Ewell, patented adjacent land on September 2,
1890.[3] They were thus in the enviable position described by nineteenth-
century economist Henry George to obtain the unearned increment on
rising land values when railroads crossed their land. On August 7, 1891,
the local paper reported, "Messrs Pratt and Ewell of Helper, were in town

Tuesday. They say that the surveyors are laying off side tracks and yards for the railroad division at that place. With proper handling a good town can be made there."[4] Fanny Ewell, Teancum's mother-in-law, actually *earned* her additional income by taking in boarders both during railroad construction and in 1890–1891 when the track was being standard-gauged.[5]

The D&RGW had decided to move its division point—the official crew rest stop between sections of the line—west from Green River. It began by constructing a fifteen-stall roundhouse of sandstone from nearby ledges, allegedly "the best building stone in the territory."[6] In 1892, the *Salt Lake Tribune* reported the addition of "a new depot, with reading-room for the employees, and minor buildings," the origins of the new town of Helper, named after the engines added there to haul heavy trains up the steep Price Canyon.[7] Standard-gauging of the entire Rio Grande system meant that tracks were being widened from their original three-foot narrow gauge to the standard four feet eight-and-a-half inches. This change allowed railroad cars to be shunted to other lines throughout the country. The Western justified spending $60,000 on this shift by capturing a part of the Denver-to-Ogden trade that used to go on the Union Pacific.[8] Making Helper the new division point put the union station of the eastern and western sections of the Rio Grande system squarely on Castle Valley's north-south axis, although Green River, far to the east, shrank proportionately.

Much of the financing for the Rio Grande Western's unprecedented development came from coal. Utah's production had first topped 300,000 tons in 1890, and by 1892 the Western's Pleasant Valley Coal Company (PVCC), combining Winter Quarters and Castle Gate tonnage, produced almost two-thirds of the coal mined in Utah Territory.[9] The Winter Quarters mine in Pleasant Valley dated back to the old days of Milan Packard and his Calico Road; Castle Gate mine development had progressed rapidly since geologist Ellis Clark noted the high-quality coal at the mouth of Price Canyon. The town of Castle Gate, named after a towering rock formation just up the canyon, had been established near the mines in 1887 by the PVCC, arm of the D&RGW. By 1890, the Castle Gate mines employed about 150 men who lived in company houses, shopped at the company-owned Wasatch Store, and needed a school for their children. Some worked at eighty beehive-shaped coke ovens, used to reduce coal through controlled burning to coke, a coal derivative demanded by smelters all over the West.[10]

Nineteenth century coal mines normally offered only seasonal, wintertime employment. Castle Gate, however, because of the coke ovens, employed miners year-round. Coke pulling—a hard, sweaty job—remained the same for decades, as described by a later worker: "The ovens were connected on the outside with a straight brick wall," wrote Paul Turner, and inside each looked like a beehive ten feet high and ten across. A train ran across the top of the ovens to dump eight tons of coal into each oven through a small round opening in the top. The heat inside the oven immediately ignited it.

Coke ovens under construction at Sunnyside, around 1900, provided year-round work for local men, and, increasingly, immigrants from southern and eastern Europe. Courtesy of Western
Mining and Railroad Museum.

"At the front of each oven was an opening about the size of two kitchen cabinet doors. These were bricked up for the coal inside to be burned and taken
down when the coke [reduced to five tons] was ready." A road ran in front
of the ovens, its other edge bounded by the top of a ten-foot-high rock wall,
below which stretched another set of tracks, parallel to the bank of coke
ovens. When the coke had burned, it had to be pulled and loaded into the
waiting railroad cars on the track opposite the ovens. To do this, the operator unbricked the door, sprayed the hot coke with water for ten minutes (using a twelve foot pipe), hooked the steaming coke with a beaver tail paddle
(its handle also twelve feet long) and dragged the coke, load by load, out to
the road. Then he had to shovel the hot coke into a wheelbarrow, wheel it
across the road, up a plank to the top of the railroad car (sticking up about
three feet above the level of the road), and dump it in. Practiced men could
pull two ovens a day. Fifteen-year-old Turner, pulling coke as a summer job
with his fourteen-year-old brother, remembered "we lost the wheelbarrow
into the half-filled railroad car and spent twenty minutes getting it out of
the still hot coke inside; . . . I got the hair above my forehead singed badly
by getting too close to that hot oven; . . . I don't remember ever working that
hard and sweating that much in the fifty years since then."[11]

Coke-making relied on coal, hand-dug from the earth in dangerous conditions. According to long-time mining man A. Philip Cederlof, a miner's

job went something like this: first, he would put on warm clothes (coal mines are consistently cold and often wet), take up his lunchbucket and head to the mine portal. From there, he walked (or sometimes rode a man trip—a line of cars pulled by a horse, mule, or later, an engine) hundreds of yards—even miles—down the mine tunnel to his assigned room at the face, where a vein of coal lay exposed. He may have carried a few sharpened picks to put with others in his locked box inside his coal-walled room. Earlier, he had shored up the roof with wooden poles, each with another small wedge of wood jammed in between its top and the mine ceiling. If the roof started to cave in, the poles would twist, the wedges would shoot out, and he would run for his life. Seeing everything in place, the miner started work. A patient, burly man might undercut the coal "by hand with a pick. The miner would lie on his side [in the coal dust] . . . and pick away at the coal, until by the time he was finished, his hands were nearly frozen to the pick handle." Many a miner, frustrated with this slow, laborious work, would instead try "shooting off the solid." Using a hand auger, he drilled holes (as few as possible), filled them with black powder "sweetened up in many cases with dynamite," then inserted "'squibs' . . . little waxed paper affairs, with a little powder twisted up inside." He lit them and ran. (Later, a separate shot firer did this one job all along the face. As Cederlof noted, "There was a heavy turn-over in shot firers.") After the smoke cleared, the miner returned, aided only by his cap's flickering light, originally "an oil can with a spout and wick." Later came the carbide lamp—still an open flame—and then the safety measure of routing fresh air through the mines to ventilate the black dust and smoke.[12]

The miner then began hand-loading the loosened coal into a mine cart, using a "scoop shovel [or] coal fork; we had big, wide coal forks," remembered James Gardner, who shoveled it up by the hour, breaking up too-large lumps with his pick.[13] The cars "had to be 'chinked' up. They couldn't afford to let a car go out that didn't carry all it would hold." The miner put his tag on the car so he would get credit for the coal once it was outside and weighed. Running on a track the miner had previously laid himself, the cars were pulled by a mule whose driver got around to all the rooms as best he could. "Often the men pushed the cars out of the room if the mule driver wasn't handy. The mules were kept in underground barns and once in the mine, they didn't come out until they were hauled out." Steam hoists hauled loaded cars up steep underground slopes.[14]

Once the car left the mine, a company checkweighman weighed the coal, checked the tag, and noted which miner got paid for its contents, deducting some weight (up to one-third) for the rock inevitably mixed in. The coal was then dumped on a conveyor belt headed for the top of a tipple, a huge, multi-storied warehouse-like structure. As it flowed on the belt past the boney-pickers, (usually boys), they would pick out the rock, or boney. The tipple's multiple, floor-sized shaking screens then sorted the coal into lump (largest), nut (medium), and slack (almost dust) through a series of holes of decreasing size, a process which covered the whole coal camp in a fine mist of dust. (Today, more sizes have been defined.) Cederlof added, "There was no workman's compensation. If a man got hurt, he had to sue— or take what he was offered. When business was rushing, the mine worked on Sundays and on all but the major holidays. Shopping was done at the company store and 'scrip' was extensively used."[15]

Castle Gate, with its mine tunnels and bank of ovens, was something of a showplace and went well beyond these primitive mining methods. As territorial mine inspector Robert Forrester noted in his 1892 report, "Altogether this is a mine in which no expense is spared to provide for the safety of the workers, and methods are in daily use here [i.e., coal dust dampened and all explosives fired electrically], which are not found in any other part of the mining world."[16] These innovations, keeping the coal dust down to help prevent black lung (the dust was not then thought to be explosive) and firing all shots by electric charges while the men were out of the mine, were truly technological advances of which Castle Valley could be proud. (Later came the addition of a fireboss, a certified expert who had to supervise the shooting and declare the mine safe before the miners could go in, as well as trouble-shoot inside the mine. Firebosses, for example, burned out pockets of flammable methane gas.) These improvements, however, had only come as the result of an explosion in 1890, in which three men lost their lives.[17]

This commercial development of Castle Valley's fine, thick coal seams, allowed potential coal production to outstrip the available workforce. The 1890 census counted only 5,076 people in all of Castle Valley, most of whom, even if they worked the mines in the winter, went back to their farms when spring came.[18] The LDS Church again promoted the area in an 1890 article, stressing "towns and villages . . . [with] the appearance of comfort and prosperity." Then came the hook: "More settlers, however, are needed and anyone in need of a home who is not afraid to face the hardships and dangers of a new country will be made hartily [sic] welcome by the people of Castle Valley."[19] The juxtaposition of "comfort and prosperity" with "hardships and dangers" may have been truthful, but it was hardly calculated to attract many takers.

Local communities, therefore, grew mostly through natural increase. In a very practical sense, Castle Valley population growth depended on reliable nursing and the successful birthing of children. The southern communities had weathered their most serious setback in the fall of 1886, when the "black canker" (diphtheria) hit southern towns. An epidemic swept through the area, killing twenty-seven people in Huntington alone, thirteen dying between Christmas and New Year's Day.[20] Molen, about halfway between Huntington and Muddy Creek, also suffered severely, and the John Duncan family lost four children within hours of each other. Under the pressure of mounting deaths, the Warren Peacocks had to lay their two little girls in a single grave. Coffin-maker Hans C. Hansen planed rough lumber by hand and made white cloth covers, fighting frustration as well as grief when no more fabric was to be had.[21] All over, women nursed the sick. In Huntington, Sally Wimmer, Mary Jane Hill, "Aunt Jane" Woodward, and Mary E. Westover entered house after house. When disease won out, Esther Grange and Adelia McElprang arrived to wash and lay out the dead and measure them for burial clothes. Before returning home, they had to sequester themselves in some unheated shed or outbuilding, wash thoroughly and change clothes in an attempt to prevent the spread of disease—all in the freezing temperatures of a Castle Valley winter. Huntington's Peter Johnson and his son, James Peter, worked with several other men making coffins literally night and day, despite the loss of the family's youngest child, Ulalia. The disease reoccurred for the next several years, but never with such fatal consequences as that first, awful winter.[22]

People also needed their teeth fixed. Orange Seely first pulled aching teeth, just because no one else would do it. Dr. Paul Christensen, Castle Dale's first trained dentist, arrived in 1894 and relieved him of this duty. Christensen practiced dentistry for forty-four years, despite local residents' frequent inability to pay. In 1901, for example, Christensen complained that people should not think less of his dental abilities just because he also did carpentry and fixed clocks and watches to make a living. As the population increased, other dentists eventually arrived, some riding a circuit. For example, in 1908, Dr. I. S. Kirkwood placed a notice in the paper that he would soon be visiting all Emery County towns: "I was so busy and rushed with work that I was unable to meet my previous appointments."[23]

With so many young pioneer families in the area, midwives also remained in demand. Mary Davis Biddlecomb fulfilled that role from Wilsonville to the head of Ferron Canyon. As the wage earner for her family, she charged $2.50 for a confinement case, tending the mother and baby for ten days; $5 if she did all the housework, too. Of course, if people could not pay, she worked for nothing, also providing what they needed. In this way, she safely delivered an estimated 450 to 500 babies and lost a total of four patients. Orangeville's Sophia Lewis Jewkes practiced homeopathic medicine, and once rode all the way to Ferron in a lumber wagon to care for patients there. Ferron residents also received help from Eliza Lake Stringham of Molen. She used sagebrush to make tea to bathe frozen feet; milkweed for dropsy, spring tonic, and a blood purifier; wormwood tea for tonic, and "humbug oil" on everything from a bee sting to a diphtheria-swollen throat. In Castle Dale, Annie Catherine Rasmussen ("Grandmother Rasmussen"), a Danish convert who arrived in 1879, utilized her own knowledge of local herbs and bushes and her no-nonsense personality to treat the sick. By the time she died in 1946 at the age of 102, she had aided countless patients and assisted with a total of 464 births, for the first twenty-five years without

Dr. Ellis Reynolds Shipp (in the center in black), graduated from the Women's Medical College in Philadelphia. She then spent a lifetime training other women in medicine, including her Castle Valley class, here showing off their diplomas. Courtesy of Emery County Archives.

the aid of a doctor.[24] The LDS Church also assisted local women with mid-wifery training. In 1905, famed doctor Ellis Shipp, a polygamous wife sent East for medical training by Brigham Young, arrived in Huntington to provide a three-month course. The Relief Society paid the fees of those who wished to attend; students had to buy their own books. Huntington's Margaret Ellen Black Rowley, or Maggie, convinced her husband to let her use some of the money from his wheat sale. Although nineteen women started, only eight finished the course, including Maggie Rowley. They some-times studied together in each others' homes, and, at the end of the course, took a wagon together to Price and then the train to Salt Lake City. After three days of tests by the State Board of Examiners on Obstetrics (which all of them passed), they returned to a skeptical county where women objected to midwives who had received theoretical training but had no real practice. When Roselle Brinkerhoff went into labor, the usual midwife, Aunt Jane Woodward, was not in town. Rowley, accompanied by two other Huntington graduates for moral support, went to tend the birth. "During the hard labor Sis. Brinkerhoff kept saying, 'Oh, Maggie, I didn't want you a bit, not a bit, but keep it up, you are doing fine.'" After this success, Rowley continued with her midwifery practice, including delivering a neighbor's baby while in labor with her own tenth child.[25]

Castle Valley also attracted immigrants, a story replicated all over America. The overall population in the continental United States grew from over thirty-nine million in 1870, to over fifty million in 1880, to almost sixty-three million in 1890, an additional twenty-three million people in just twenty years, or over a million a year. Of these, the population of the foreign-born increased from five-and-a-half million to over six-and-a-half million to over nine million during the same period.[26] Some, like Grandmother Rasmussen, were LDS converts. Plenty of others came from the British Isles. Soon, however, industrial work gangs from far-flung nations would change the rural complexion of Castle Valley.

Growth also prompted administrative readjustments. In 1892, the Emery County Court approved the official organization of Price Town. James (Tobe) Whitmore became the first Price town president. Then, Price tried to get the county seat away from Castle Dale. This drive failed, and Castle Dale confirmed its legal preeminence by building a fine brick courthouse at a cost of about $5,000. The sessions of the Seventh Judicial District Court met there for years.[27] Early in 1894, the northern section responded with petitions to carve a new county out of northern Emery County. Canvassers visited the towns of Wellington, Price, Spring Glen, Helper, and Castle Gate, Scofield and Winter Quarters (at Pleasant Valley), and Minnie Maud (up Nine Mile Canyon in the Book Cliffs), getting almost unanimous signatures. In February, the Territorial Legislature approved the petition and Carbon County was born, named for its leading resource, coal. Helper put up a good fight, but Price became the county seat. This first major political split along the Castle Valley corridor brought some distress to southerly, truncated Emery County, since it lost population and considerable tax revenues based on railroad mileage, businesses, and livestock herds then proliferating to the north.[28]

This county division also institutionalized a rural-urban split. In the industrializing northern portion, residents sometimes characterized their more southern neighbors as backward "hayseeds." Southerners fought back, in part, with music. In 1895, Thomas L. Hardee, a Welshman, organized a choral group from Huntington and Cleveland. They challenged the Scofield Welsh Singers at the 1896 singing competition, known as *Eisteddfod* in Wales. Working with a group of mixed ethnicity, but principally Danes, Professor Hardee practiced a number of selections until the June competition, when his determined Castle Valley Choir traveled up in the mountains of Pleasant Valley and camped out under the trees. When the Scofield Welsh Choir and the largely Danish Castle Valley Choir went head to head on the stage set up in the D&RGW roundhouse, the judges chose the lowlanders. As reported by a local historian, "The cheering was long and loud, not only from the 'hayseeds' but the people of Scofield as well."[29] In the following program, triumphant Hannah M. Johnson sang "There Is No Hayseed In My Hair," and brought down the house. The Castle Valley Choir entered another Eisteddfod in 1898 in Salt Lake City, where they won no awards, but earned the honor of singing at the General Conference of the LDS Church.[30]

Although most immigrants to Castle Valley came from humble origins, at least one new local resident exemplified a significant new trend in America's industrialization: an unusually heavy reliance on foreign capital.[31] Like much of the American West, Castle Valley had attracted a member of the English nobility.[32] In the late 1880s, Lord Lewis A. Scott Elliot, an aristocrat apparently invited to leave England, bought from an unnamed trapper his squatter's rights to a dugout at Big Springs, one mile south of the D&RGW tracks and about twelve miles east of the strung-out settlement of Wellington. Tapping his family's wealth, Elliot next acquired uncounted head of horses and cattle, an estimated 30,000 head of sheep, and acreage that provided thousands of tons of hay. He left the dugout for a fourteen-room rambling house, where he reportedly brought his wife and lavishly entertained the foreign visitors that occasionally visited the ranch. For his guests' amusement, according to local report, "he had live grouse and quail shipped in and turned loose in the sage brush to provide his guests with suitable hunting." For additional targets, he also introduced rabbits, widely regarded as pests because they ate desperately-needed crops. "There are those still living who can forgive Lord Elliott everything but that," the report continued. Fortunately, either his guests' marksmanship or Castle Valley's persistently inhospitable climate made short work of the bunnies.[33]

Like many of those already resident in Castle Valley, Lord Elliot soon realized that ranchers did not prosper nearly as quickly as coal developers. He filed for a coal certificate in April 1890, choosing 160 acres on lands essentially comprising his Big Springs Ranch.[34] He also ran a barbed wire fence around his lands, and, in so doing, ran strands diagonally across a parcel still claimed by the nation. The federal government, offended at this fencing of its public domain, sued him in 1891.[35] Since Utah was not yet a state, the case became complicated. Although the land in question technically belonged to the federal government, once Utah achieved statehood, it would become state land. In pondering their decision, the judges referred to "Vast tracts of public lands . . . fenced with barbed wire by wealthy cattle owners," the essence of the West's violent range wars.[36] This was Castle Valley, however. The property was uncontested. Elliot won the right to keep his fence up, but he left his Big Springs Ranch in 1894, moving on to other climes and eventual paralysis in an elephant accident in Ceylon in 1906.[37]

Plenty of other people stuck with ranching. For example, Scotsman Alexander McPherson and his nephew, Jim, moved their cattle herd into Woodside, northwest of Green River in the fall of 1885. They trailed the animals out the next spring, returning to winter their herds at the mouth of Florence Creek on the Green River a few years later. After Alexander drowned in the Green, Jim fenced their summer range and bred pure Hereford cattle, introducing the breed to the region.[38] As John H. Pace recalled, after years of mixed-breed cattle he, too, turned to Herefords, "the best for the[se] ranges. . . . Herefords are better rustlers for feed [and] . . .

they stand the vagaries of the climate better."[39] The Whitmores, established in the Book Cliffs north of the Price River since 1879, combined cattle with banking. Tobe established Price's First National Bank, while brother George started a bank in Nephi, Sanpete County.[40] Both grazed their herds in Castle Valley, following an annual cycle. The animals wintered "down in Big Springs country [Lord Elliott's ranch], this side of Sunnyside, and up in Clark's Valley," where the grass grew especially high. "As late as, oh I guess in the 1920's," Rolla West remembered, "on a wet year, I saw grass . . .[up to the] belly of a horse. Not thick grass, desert grass . . . a bunch here and there." From there, he continued, "in the spring they'd trail them down Nine Mile and Myton and by Vernal [in the Unita Basin] up on the Diamond Mountain." Originally they had trailed them "clear over to Cheyenne [Wyoming], the end of the [Union Pacific] Railroad. Then as the railroad moved west and trailing down to Rock Springs was the closest station, and they trailed them . . . [there to] ship them to the market."[41] Alternately, drovers pushed the cattle overland to Denver, where the agents for the pooled Castle Valley stock would receive their payment in gold. Their saddlebags bulged with this yearly income as they made the long ride back—a round trip which could take a man up to three months.[42]

This wealth, on the hoof and in the saddlebags, tempted the dishonest. Allegedly, the Whitmores came to Castle Valley in part because they "liked to be where there was plenty of action . . . clearing out the . . . bad men who had ruled before their coming."[43] Whether they sought it or not, the Whitmores certainly had trouble, particularly with Joe Walker. He claimed that the Whitmores owed him a long-standing debt contracted by their father, allegedly also Walker's uncle, back in Texas. The Whitmores insisted that Walker was no relation and that they owed him nothing. Lingering nearby, Walker did odd jobs around Castle Valley, including a stint at the Huntington sawmill. He started raiding Whitmore stock, got into a shoot-em-up in Price in the summer of 1895, and finally joined up with outlaws camped out in the desert southeast of Castle Valley at the infamous Robber's Roost.[44] After that, he apparently spent some time as a hired hand on Jim McPherson's ranch on the Green River (now a favorite river runner stop).[45] In 1897, he again took a predatory interest in Whitmore horses. With the help of Clarence L. ("Gunplay") Maxwell, another local troublemaker, Walker stole several head from the Whitmore stable and drove them south from Price into the rough lands of eastern Emery County. Maxwell apparently backed out of the deal, and may have even returned to Price to inform the Whitmores. Tobe joined the posse, headed by Carbon County Sheriff C. W. Allred. Further south, Emery County Sheriff Azariah Tuttle joined, not only to chase Walker, but to find George Lee, a son of John D. Lee, the Mountain Meadows Massacre scapegoat, said also to be a member of the Robber's Roost gang. About fifty-five miles east of Orangeville, Tuttle was able to arrest Lee, sending him back to town under guard. Later, the posse found Walker and both sides started shooting. Walker's bullet caught Tuttle in the right thigh, crippling him. While the others went for help, Tuttle lay behind a big rock, suffering acutely as the sun climbed higher. In that odd frontier camaraderie that exists in desolate places, Tuttle finally asked Walker to bring him some water. The outlaw agreed, and Tuttle allowed him to go. After thirty-six hours, the posse returned, but Tuttle remained lame for life.[46] Walker's luck ran out in May 1898, after he beat up the Whitmore foreman and Tobe's son. This time, the posse found him and a companion sleeping on the eastern side of the Green River and shot them to death before they could rise. The posse returned with twenty-four "above average" horses taken with the outlaws and divided up the $250 reward for Joe Walker, earning $20.80 each.[47]

Far less attractive to outlaws, sheep also did well in Castle Valley's tricky climate. By 1890, one million sheep roamed Utah, including sizable herds belonging to Sanpete County's John H. Seely, brother of Castle Valley pioneers Orange and Wink Seely and Sarah Seely Tidwell.[48] John Seely began in the sheep business in 1885 when he took over management of the Sanpete co-op herd (once ranged in Castle Valley) from his older brother, Orange. By 1888, John had his own herd, and in 1890 he returned to California, his birthplace, for purebred stock. (He had been born in San Bernardino when the Seely family helped found the LDS colony there.) He bought 140 head of purebred Rambouillet sheep at Los Angeles and drove them back to Utah. Subsequent California forays in 1892, 1898, and 1899 solidified John H. Seely's status as the introducer of purebred sheep to Utah and the owner of the first Utah flock accepted for registration in the *American Rambouillet Record.*[49]

Many Castle Valley sheepmen improved their stock through the Seely bloodline. For example, as the paper reported, "John H. Seely sold 135 Rambouillet bucks to Crawford & Peacock of Emery; J. W. Seely sold thirty head of the same kind of animals to Sam Singleton of Ferron," and whole herds of sheep changed hands up and down Castle Valley and over the Wasatch Plateau.[50] Breeding Rambouillet rams to common range ewes gave superb results: an eventual weight increase of from 100 to 130 pounds, and a finer clip which increased in average weight from 5.5 pounds in 1892 to 9.0 pounds by 1921.[51] Wink Seely was among those who ran large herds of sheep on the San Rafael Desert, many of them herded by Wink's son, William. Out there on the range, William occupied himself with reading, and sought new books whenever he came into town to get supplies. He decided that what he and other sheepmen needed was a desert lending library. William found a small, dry cave to store his books, and other passing herders would borrow what they wanted and leave their own books and magazines, amassing quite a variety. The location of this library has been lost; it remains one of the more engaging mysteries along the Castle Valley corridor.[52]

Herders practiced transhumance, still used today. In the spring, animals began foraging high in the mountains, fattening on thick grass. As autumn snows threatened, sheepherders drove their stock down on the desert. The seasonal shepherding cycle climaxed at the spring shearing. Lucy Hansen Nielsen remembered the cluster of camp houses and the thousands of sheep sheared at the desert corral southeast of Molen, her home town. "During sheepshearing spring work, the herds were shorn on their way from the east winter locations to the west mountains [the Wasatch Plateau] summer range," she recalled. "The big wool sacks were deeper than a man was tall. It hung in a frame, open at the top so a man could jump down into it. As fleece was tossed into it, the man would press it into the corners at the bottom and then . . . stomp them tight until the bag was full. It was then released from the frame, carefully laid on the ground, the top was sewn together and then rolled to where it would be loaded on to the wagon." The men worked all day except for the midday break, alternately standing and stooping, bending and kneeling, all the time turning each sheep and clipping off its fleece with hand shears. Meanwhile, aided by a special gang of men brought in to feed the crowds, the women built big wood fires and cooked. The shearers ate in shifts, nearly all day long, "Water for the kitchen and drinking was hauled in a wagon with three fifty gallon wood barrels every day," she added. The dishes never seemed to get done. Buyers came down from Price, and then the "big sacks of tightly stomped wool were loaded on covered wagons like bales of hay and hauled to Price to the railroad."[53]

Sheepmen built another shearing corral next to the railroad at Mounds, about twenty miles east of Price along the D&RGW line. Most of the year, the waterless site remained unoccupied. At shearing time, a railroad employee and his wife took up residence, supplied with water from a huge tank-car pulled up to the siding. The shearing corral, funded by stockholders including Wallace Lowry, was a big barn-like structure where clippers hung from rotating metal shafts which ran the length of the building. Professional sheep-shearers removed the fleeces, released the sheep into an outside pen, and sent the wool along a conveyor belt to the wool sacks. The wool-tromper still manually performed his work, but then the filled sacks, each branded with the owner's mark, went by machine to the warehouse or directly into the railroad cars. Over one hundred thousand sheep sometimes passed through the Mounds corral in the two months of sheep-shearing season.[54]

The sheep industry also connected Castle Valley permanently with global markets. Local wool prices responded to the wool clip in Australia and New Zealand; sales could be made to Boston, to St. Louis, to Kansas City, to Denver. Castle Valley sheepmen tied together ranching activities from Nevada to Montana to California. President Cleveland's Dingley Tariff protected wool, allowing the price to rise until the 1920s. Hired herders—who

Honore Dusserre, the dean of French and French Basque sheepmen, kneels in front of his flock. By the time this photo was taken (c. 1925), he had spent over three decades breeding sheep and helping other immigrants get started in the business. Courtesy of DeNae Dusserre Johns.

often became owners—came from Argentina, Mexico, and, especially the Pyrenees, from predominately Basque, but also Spanish and French stock. Many of the men, as well as the sheep, came along the Castle Valley corridor from California, driving prize flocks for hundreds of miles.[55] Their names rang with European rhythms: Moynier, Dusserre, Jeanselme, Neugier, Eselle, Ramband, Leautaud, Lavigne. Some later owners started out as herder-partners of Wallace Lowry, including Auguste Aubert, William Etchebaine, Pierre Etchevery, the Mecham brothers, A. E. Pace, Dan Oman, J. C. Jensen, Edward Christiansen, and a host of others.[56] Old-timers interviewed in 1940 remembered that "Felix Dusserre's father started in 1892 to raise sheep and brought 12,000 head here from California in 1896." One also mentioned, "Pete Moynier started to work as a herder in 1898 and in 1903 he bought a 1,000 head of sheep."[57] It could have been earlier: "in 1894, Neugier, Eselle, Ramband and others trailed their herds from Bakersfield [California] to Price, a distance of more than seven hundred miles."[58] No matter. By 1900 the sheep had arrived by the thousands.

Running cattle and sheep in the same isolated area caused predictable conflicts. Sheep, if not properly managed, will eat grass right down to the roots, leaving nothing on which cattle can graze. Much of the land used by both beasts then belonged to the United States, and could be claimed by any stockman who used it. According to an old-timer, cowmen down at Buckhorn Draw, east of Castle Dale, conscientiously pushed their animals through the area in fall and winter to save the good grass for spring. Then came "a tramp sheep outfit with about three thousand head . . . on their way to the lower desert. They stayed in the canyon, where they had no herding to do, and moved along slowly, cleaning out all the feed."[59] Sheepmen were the invaders, to be treated accordingly. Although Castle Valley experienced only a handful of the grisly incidents of America's range wars, local killings extended into the early 1900s.[60] Then, "Winn Thompson, a cattleman from Green River, called the [Wallace] Lowry home at three o'clock one morning to say that some drunken cow hands had found two [sheep]herders on the range," reported son Walker Lowry. The cowboys had "bound them securely with ropes, locked them inside a log cabin, and gleefully burned the cabin to the ground."[61] Wallace Lowry rushed to Green River to protect his foreign-born herders from further violence. Green River citizens, strongly anti-sheep, released the guilty cowhands, reasoning that "the boys were drunk and didn't know what they were doing."[62]

While violence sought personal targets, a faltering economy could hurt everyone at once. Like the rest of America, all of Castle Valley suffered as the Panic of 1893 began in February with the failure of the Philadelphia & Reading Railroad. Investors dumped over a million of its shares in only seven hours, bankrupting the line. Then, the National Cordage Company (the rope trust) failed. The Panic snowballed. Banks called in loans and balked at giving new ones. Businesses, lacking capital, closed their doors. Workers thrown out of their jobs bought fewer and fewer consumer goods, weakening other industries. Farmers could not ship their harvests nor purchase the materials and machinery they needed for the next season. The price of silver collapsed. Railroads that had freighted goods and ore went under. The Erie, the Northern Pacific, the Santa Fe, and the once-mighty Union Pacific all went bankrupt—a total of sixty-five railroads across the nation. The whole Rio Grande system remained remarkably healthy except for the fall of the Rio Grande Southern. But it was an exception. Right and left, people demanded gold for their stocks, bonds, and greenbacks, causing a drain on the U.S. Treasury. Thanks to the Sherman Silver Purchase Act of

1890, the federal government would buy silver (with gold) but not coin it. Everywhere, suddenly, any investment meant gold, and there was simply not enough to be had. While Congress myopically fiddled with the tariff, on April 22, 1893, the national gold reserve fell to below $100,000,000, long considered the rock-bottom amount necessary to shore up America's confidence in her currency. By the end of the year, an estimated three million people were out of work.[63]

The Panic soon reached most Castle Valley residents. Only Caleb Rhoades had gold. Rhoades claimed he could pay the national debt in 1893 if only he could get permission to work his Uinta Basin mine, on the Ute reservation. The Utes threatened to kill anyone who came on their land except Rhoades, who, like his father before him, had maintained a privileged relationship. Although Rhoades returned on occasion with his saddlebags full of gold dust and nuggets, the reservation stayed closed. Most of Rhoades's heavy gold stayed where it was.[64] Much more typically, in January 1893, Teancum Pratt complained of the expense of maintaining two separate households, in compliance with the Edmunds-Tucker Act. His second wife, Sarah, in Salt Lake City, with "her children in school & my children numbering 13 living, robust, hearty souls & eat & wear; so my only course must be to live by faith."[65] By June, he had moved Sarah back to Castle Valley over Annie's objections.[66] His Helper property was of little assistance. Although he held "700 lots, have only sold some 30 yet . . . [as] cash is hard to get."[67]

Complaints like Pratt's mushroomed throughout the country. Congress met in special session and repealed the Sherman Silver Purchase Act with a law effective November 1. The economy did not recover. In Massillon, Ohio, the next spring, visionary Jacob Coxey began assembling an army of the unemployed to march on Washington, D.C., to demand that the federal government provide public works jobs for the hungry workers. Out in California, Charles Kelley recruited his own Industrial Army of 600 men, including not-yet-famous Jack London and William "Big Bill" Haywood. From Los Angeles came 800 men more, all determined to join with Coxey by riding the railroads East, sure that the lines would help them. Sometimes conductors let them ride; more often, railroad owners refused, afraid, like the rest of the elite, of the "dangerous classes." Then, these industrial armies snuck aboard anyway, some of the men assuming precarious positions under the cars, truly riding the rails. Some 1,200 men reached Utah Territory on April 13; six days later, another newly-recruited company of the unemployed joined them in Salt Lake City, where five soup kitchens had opened the previous December to feed the hungry. In towns and cities all across the nation, equally disillusioned citizens offered them free food, free shelter, and frequent encouragement. To continue their trip, when the Union Pacific balked, a company of the Industrial Army stole a UP train at Lehi, Utah, and drove it eastward.[68]

Henry Mathis watched the men pass through Price on the Western and summarized their fate: "When they got to Washington, they were treated very coolly. The officials simply told them to 'Keep off the Grass.'" For that, Coxey was arrested and jailed, his followers scattered by mounted police. A sympathetic legislator read Coxey's "Address of Protest" to Congress, demanding the right of all citizens to petition for the redress of grievances. It continued, "Up these steps the lobbyists of trusts and corporations have passed unchallenged on their way to committee rooms, access to which we, the representatives of the toiling wealth-producers, have been denied."[69] His views on the power of lobbyists had long been recognized by the LDS Church, perpetually seeking statehood. They would soon press the advantages secured by their own use of a railroad lobby to a successful conclusion.

In the meantime, not all of Coxey's Army made it as far as the nation's capital. They dropped out along the way, as energy and enthusiasm flagged. When the California recruits reached Castle Valley, a few stayed in Price, including a brickmason named Mr. Simon. He built two houses for polygamist John Amon Powell, who got the money to pay him by selling some cows. Henry Mathis swapped two cows to the owner of the brickyard between Spring Glen and Helper, getting enough bricks to build himself a home on Price townsite. Simon worked so fast that Mathis joined with a Mr. Schuler, his hired man, to keep up with mixing mortar and throwing up bricks. As Mathis remembered, "Schuler and I were able to keep the mason going, but I had to work very hard and push Schuler up some. I got Old Man [Frantz] Grundvig from Wellington to do the carpenter work." Mathis set up all night tending a fire to dry out the interior plaster in the freezing weather, although "it was not entirely successful as part of the plaster fell off and had to be replastered. However, we . . . spent our first winter in town." This outcome delighted his new wife, Sarah Macfarlane Mathis, whom he had married after the death in childbirth of Mary DeFriez Mathis in 1891. Sarah had felt lonely and discouraged out on the farm, and the move to town, with new neighbors and activities, cheered her. Luckily, too, the farm provided wheat, pigs, and a cow, with hay enough to cover the store bill, his only assets "to pull through the Democratic Grover Cleveland administration. These were hard times. We had plenty of bread, milk, meat and potatoes to eat, but groceries were almost out of the question."[70]

Other towns, also cash-poor but more remote from the bustle of railroad entrepot or division point, lacked the same pervasive cash economy and sometimes-skilled drifters that came to Price and Helper. Consequently, citizens continued in the LDS cooperative movement, largely abandoned in the rest of Utah. For example, Wellington development flowered in 1892 with construction of a meeting house, largely done by donation "as there was very little money in circulation. Fred Hansen, being one of the very few men [along with Lehi Jessen] who had a job which paid cash, contributed the money to purchase doors and windows." The meeting house's milled lumber was hauled all the way from the Seely Mill at Gordon Creek, not far from Pratt's homestead at Helper. At the same time, a cooperative store was set up in the home of E. E. Branch which lasted until 1899—right through the Panic.[71] Huntington established its own two-room cooperative store the same year as Wellington's.[72] One of the most successful cooperative efforts, the Huntington Flour Mill, began when local residents formed a nominal corporation in 1893. It was reorganized in 1895, with the Panic still in effect. Mill construction began a year later. Originally powered by a small steam engine provided by Bishop Charles Pulsipher, the mill shortly sported a Pelton undershot wheel eight feet in diameter which was set six feet into the ground in Huntington Creek to increase the force of water flowing under it. People came from all over Castle Valley to use it, those from a distance initially enjoying a two-to-three-day camping trip while they waited for their grain to be milled. As fall progressed, the ditch would become clogged with leaves, and in winter the shallow creek froze up, halting milling entirely. Despite these deficiencies, in 1898 the mill produced fifty barrels of flour and continued in operation for almost a century.[73]

Castle Valley women also shared the cooperative impulse and started a silk industry. As far back as 1866, President Brigham Young had directed Mormon missionaries in France to obtain mulberry seed, resulting in over 100,000 trees spread throughout the territory. Silkworm eggs had been introduced, and one young man was set aside as a special "silk missionary" to teach processing techniques.[74] Three decades later, in 1896, sericulture reached Castle Valley. Lucy Hansen Nielsen remembered when her mother, Mary L. M. Hansen, "acquired some silkworms. It was funny to see the long lumber table covered with worms. Screen wire formed an edging all around. Newspapers covered the bottom of the cage. The worms ate the tender green leaves of mulberry trees . . . [hurrying] like chickens . . . to the fresh leaves from the skeletons of the leaves fed the day before." Her task, "to feed the crawling, hungry livestock" resulted in smelly worms about four inches long that had originally hatched from eggs about one-eighth-inch across. "Square pieces of paper then was twisted into cone shaped scoops and laid before the worms which crawled into them and with a movement of the head waving from side to side they built a round, oblong cacoon [sic]."[75] At Huntington, Bishop Peter Johnson brought mulberry trees from Salt Lake City and Miss Pearl Daily arrived for a six-month stay to teach sericulture.[76] As a local historian explained, "Miss Daily taught our women how to gather the cocoons, dip them in hot water, find the end of the silken thread, unwind it onto spools. . . . Then the process of spinning and weaving silken fabrics followed. . . . done at Salt Lake City under the direction of . . . [the] superintendent of the silk industry project." Although Chris Anderson (known as Blind Chris, to differentiate him from others of the same name) assumed local leadership of the silk project when Daily returned to Salt Lake City, the industry failed in Huntington just as it had long before in the rest of Utah. The trees, still remaining in the late 1940s, were its last legacy.[77]

Some of the cooperative efforts served more than one purpose, as was certainly true of the Emery Stake Academy: a sectarian institution with religious as well as educational priorities. At the urging of LDS President Wilford Woodruff, a committee met in 1889 to plan a Mormon school at Castle Dale. Justus Wellington (Wink) Seely became president of the Emery Stake Board of Education; local women raised funds by donating a chicken or its cash equivalent. On February 12, 1890, the school opened with twenty-one students. By 1892, the principal, Alexander Jameson, earned a yearly salary of $750, but in 1893–1894 he and all the school teachers had to serve as voluntary LDS missionaries, due to the national Panic. In its grip, the Academy had to close for two years. It reopened in 1896 and by 1899 offered courses to eighty-five pupils housed in a brand new three-story brick building, a structure first discussed ten years earlier.[78]

By the time the Emery Stake Academy reopened, a whole kaleidoscope of changes had transformed Utah. The most significant events culminated with statehood in 1896. According to Joseph Rawlins, elected Utah's non-voting delegate to the House of Representatives in 1892, his troubles in promoting statehood started in the House Committee on Territories headed by friendly Gen. Joseph Wheeler of Alabama, a former Confederate. Wheeler and Rawlins each submitted a Utah Statehood bill, but that of Rawlins contained more liberal land provisions and was adopted in committee. When President Cleveland, spurred by the Panic, called a special session to consider repeal of the Sherman Silver Purchase Act, Rawlins brought the statehood bill to the House. Republicans began a vicious, anti-Mormon filibuster. Rawlins countered their arguments, saying that "deplorable atrocities, such as the Mountain Meadows Massacre, had been committed in the past, [but] I asserted that the present generation of Utahns was not accountable for them. As well blame the Senator from Wyoming for the massacre of Chinamen at Rock Springs." He then assured his listeners that polygamy, another of the sticking points, had been abandoned. "The House immediately passed the Bill," wrote Rawlins, "and then it went to the Senate."[79]

There, the bill stalled into 1894. Rawlins speculated that promises that Utah would become Republican (it eventually did) brought the bill to a vote.[80] However, there was more to this story: Utah's lobbyists had secretly been hard at work behind the scenes. Three key men, identified in a later memo only as "Clara, Tobias, and Clio" (probably James Clarkson, Isaac Trumbo, and Hiram B. Clawson, respectively) had met with a long list of Congressmen, brokering votes for other pressing issues in trade for Utah statehood support. The end result, the Utah Enabling Act, became law on July 16, 1894, allowing the creation of a Utah state constitutional convention but delaying statehood itself to 1896.[81] When the Enabling Act finally passed, Clarkson sent LDS Church President Woodruff a 33–page, typed letter outlining years of dedicated lobbying, the people involved, and the many debts incurred. Brigham Young's son-in-law, Hiram Clawson, the much-trusted original superintendent of ZCMI and former manager of Young's private business, added his own memo. Clarkson closed with the recognition that the statehood fight had made Utah's resources "known to all the intelligent people of the republic . . . and this information will bring to you speedily and in vast volume the capital necessary to develop your natural wealth."[82] Clawson put the matter more bluntly: "All men in public affairs keep books. They render no service without expecting return."[83]

Statehood was finally only a constitution away. In November 1894, voters selected 107 delegates to the state constitutional convention, representing a cross-section of Utah's males. They met on March 4, 1895, to begin their work. With the national economy still reeling, men competed for the convention's salaried secretarial and clerical positions. Delegates passionately advocated either side of some of the most controversial issues: woman suffrage (it passed), and the formation of corporations, balancing growth and development with fear of trusts.[84] This concern was well-placed. In 1895, Big Business had triumphed when the Supreme Court found that E. C. Knight and Company, which refined ninety percent of America's sugar, was not a trust because it only manufactured, but did not sell, the sugar.[85] Consequently, businesses could continue their free-wheeling operations virtually unmolested—although Utah tried, in its constitution, to restrain them.[86]

Utah's constitutional delegates addressed other thorny issues. They created a new court system, eliminating the Mormon-dominated probate courts and supported non-sectarian education for Utah's booming school-age population. High schools, however, lacked state funding until 1906. Labor won minimal protection. Private property rights to existing water infrastructure were confirmed, and prohibition, a potentially divisive issue, was tabled. In May, the delegates signed the lengthy document, each with his own pen—a ready-made momento. In November 1895, Utah approved the constitution by better than four-to-one. On January 4, 1896, President Cleveland signed the Utah statehood proclamation, and celebrations erupted all over the new state.[87]

Castle Valley joined in. Ernest Horsley reported that when the statehood proclamation came over the wires at 10 a.m., church bells tolled, men shouted "Hurrah" and fired their guns in the air, and "the old wagon thimble cannon [was] loaded to capacity and bang she went." The band played patriotic tunes. That night, the community met for a big party at the meeting house "that lasted until morning. Some rejoiced too much and had to be kicked out."[88] LDS Church property, previously consigned to trustees-in-trust to protect it from the federal government under the

Edmunds-Tucker Act, was transferred back to local bishops. In November, Utah's voters, including women, elected new state officials and chose Democrat/Populist William Jennings Bryan over Republican William McKinley for U.S. President by a vote of over two-to-one.[89] Their choice made little difference, however, as McKinley swept into office, heading a pro-business regime.

As the economy recovered, locals opened their own coal mines along the well-known veins in the heights surrounding Castle Valley. Throughout the late 1890s, Utah's State Coal Mine Inspector noted a number of small mines stringing south to north along the Wasatch Plateau, swinging east along the Book Cliffs, and ending just north of Green River, where Thomas Farrer had an opening. In the Pleasant Valley area, side-by-side with larger developments, other small mines proliferated.[90] By the late 1890s, demand for coke, in particular, had soared. Coking coal, sold to smelters throughout the West, made more money than any other sort, and the PVCC held a virtual monopoly. All of it was roasted in huge ovens erected at Castle Gate. Hundreds of men gathered there, some to work on the railroad or to mine coal, others to tend the coke ovens. Castle Gate alone almost doubled its tonnage between 1896–1897, making it the largest mine in the state.[91] In 1897, the PVCC experienced its first, brief industrial disturbance. A walk-out at the new Sunnyside developments elicited a short notice in the Castle Valley paper: "The coal miners['s] strike will not be a failure in one respect," it said. "It furnishes fresh material on which to blame the delay in the return of prosperity."[92]

The local economy had rapidly sprouted national links, and, across America, statistics remained grim. Unemployment registered fifteen percent in 1897, dropping to a still-disturbing ten percent by 1899.[93] Among the other farmers turned mine developers was Helper's Teancum Pratt. Ever struggling to make ends meet, he had finally achieved some prosperity with his coal mine in Sowbelly Canyon above Helper. He entered the business in 1895, reporting, "We have been talking up the coal business in the ward. We are subject to heavy extortion by [the] R.R. Co & so learning that the Sowbelly canon was vacant I lost no time but took my last money . . . to file on some claims." Four brothers-in-law helped him. By 1896, they had developed the mine and were selling coal in town. Pratt finally bought out the others in 1897–1898 and "made a good living with the mine."[94] Specifically, he received permission from the railroad superintendent to supply new company houses in Helper with coal. He made enough money to send "4 of my children to Provo academy & one daughter Helen Grace for the whole school year."[95] By October 1899, he noted, "my business is now swelled beyond my capacity." He hired a neighbor to drive the coal wagon and went to Castle Gate to learn more coal-mining techniques: "how to use a bar for prying off coal & how to make effectual crank for machine also how to undermine it seem like fun almost." But by early December the ever-pious Pratt admitted, "We are not very good church attenders these days, it being so far & us being so unkempt."[96]

Pratt's dilemma of balancing capitalism with religion reverberated to the very top of his church. In the Panic of 1893, Apostle Heber J. Grant had secured eastern credit that carried Utah's two main banks, Zion's and the State Bank of Utah, through the ensuing, long-lasting depression. But by 1896, LDS President Woodruff privately lamented, "Unless the Lord opens the way in a marvelous manner, it looks as though we should never pay our debts."[97] Practical economic adjustment, not divine providence, provided the solution. In the 1890s, the previously-communal LDS Church and its leaders either originated or invested in a number of capitalistic industries, including the Utah Sugar Company (later Utah-Idaho Sugar Company) and the Intermountain Salt Company, later consolidated with the Inland Crystal Salt Company. The salt company ran a subsidiary, the pleasure-palace Saltair Pavilion, under private, non-Mormon sub-contractors. Saltair even stayed open on Sundays and served liquor, but it made money. As historian Leonard Arrington noted, one of the significant differences between these later enterprises and earlier efforts to "build the kingdom of Zion" was their for-profit nature, which could even supersede established religious values such as abstinence and Sunday closings.[98]

As the LDS Church took tentative steps to allow a small measure of American capitalism into the rest of well-regulated Utah, Castle Valley bore the full brunt of unbridled, capitalistic skullduggery. Industry—in the form of a growing monopoly—became ever more entrenched in this barely-settled region. First, at Pleasant Valley, the PVCC monopolized all the commercial mines after Union Pacific permanently closed down there in 1897.[99] It already owned Castle Gate, with its first-class safety measures and glowing banks of coke ovens. Then came the battle for Sunnyside, which solidified the industrial future of the Castle Valley corridor.

Out in the eastern Book Cliffs in Whitmore Canyon, the Western, through geologist Robert Forrester, competed with Salt Lake entrepreneur George T. Holladay, his Tidwell associates, and a host of others to secure the best coking coal in Utah. First Forrester tried unsuccessfully to bribe Holladay to give up his extensive Sunnyside claims, which he had disingenuiously filed with Tidwell under the lenient federal law governing hard rock mining as far back as 1890.[100] Then the Rio Grande tried threats. Going to the Salt Lake office to complain, Holladay was wooed away with a free railroad pass to the West Coast where he could ship out for the Klondike gold rush of 1897–1898. He got only as far as Portland when he realized his mistake and rushed back to Castle Valley into a Sunnyside gunfight with another would-be coal developer, Robert Kirker.[101] Holladay later testified, "Kirker and his men came out of the cabin I had built and swore and cursed me," firing warning shots over the unarmed Holladay's head. "I tried to get my father's Winchester away from him," he added with certain

Branding day at Grove Farm brought out all available hands to protect the rancher's cattle from rustlers. Courtesy of Emery County Archives (Lemon Collection).

braggadocio, and "jumped off my horse and they all ran into the house like rats into a hole."[102] He then confronted Kirker with a legal suit for forcible entry, filed by the Holladay Coal Company—a fascinating association uniting devout Saints from Tidwell-Seely clan, anti-Mormon lobbyist Robert N. Baskin and fellow Liberals, and Holladay's immediate family members.[103] In 1899, Utah's Supreme Court Judge Henry H. Rolapp (later a Castle Valley coal developer) granted Holladay "the highest form of possession" and the legal maximum acreage under the strict federal coal land laws: 640 acres. Unfortunately, this award constituted a much reduced amount from the area Holladay had actually claimed and was insufficient for a commercial mine.[104] After winning this limited claim to Utah's richest coal land, Holladay agreed to sell his parcel to the Rio Grande system for an alleged $22,000.[105] The railroad now had a complete monopoly not only on rail transportation through Castle Valley, but on all its commercial mines.

Even before it officially acquired Sunnyside, the railroad's mines were rich, and everybody knew it. Hardened drifters, looking for the main chance, crossed Castle Valley on the Outlaw Trail, described by sometime Price mayor Rolla West. It started in Montana or Wyoming, coming south through the Ute reservation in the Unita Basin then through "Nine Mile [Canyon] and over to Price and down to Green River, and [to] the Robber's Roost stops down from Green River and on southeast across the river at Hite

in the early days." Riding through the sparsely-settled area, outlaws sometimes rounded up unbranded calves (or "slicks") or rustled cattle whose
brands could be altered with a running iron, building bankrolls through
economies of scale in stolen beef. "I understand they got $10 a head, but
they had a lot of cattle," recalled West. "And then they got to robbing trains
and robbing banks . . . [because] there was more money in it."[106]

Butch Cassidy (formerly Robert Leroy Parker of Circleville, Utah) soon
staged one of the most daring robberies in the American West. Accounts
differ as to where he spent the winter of 1896–1897, but all agree that he
was one of two men who met the Castle Gate payroll train that Wednesday
in April 1897. The 12 o'clock train, the paper noted, had delivered the
payroll to Castle Gate: "two sacks of silver, one of $1,000, one of $860, one
sack of gold containing $7,000, and a satchel holding the rolls and checks
for another thousand dollars, in all $9,860." E. L. Carpenter, the paymas-
ter, and a deputy clerk picked up the money-filled baggage and carried it
about fifty yards to the steps of the company store while the train pulled
out and about one hundred men stood around, waiting for their pay. In
an instant, a "rough looking individual" shoved a gun in Carpenter's face
and demanded the sacks. Eyewitnesses described the outlaws: "one about
25 years of age and the other as middle age. The younger man wore a
black hat, blue coat, and goggles, while the man who held Mr. Carpenter
up had on a light slouch hat, denham [sic] overalls and brown coat. Both
men were sun-browned and appeared more like cowboys or common ho-
boes than desperate highwaymen."[107] But the guns showed their intentions.
Carpenter dropped his sacks and raised his hands, while deputy clerk T. W.
Lewis dashed into the company store with one sack of silver, alerting other
company men whose shots went wild. The two robbers slung the bags of
gold and silver coin over their saddles, mounted up and bolted, firing shots
overhead, pausing at the south end of Castle Gate just long enough to cut
the telegraph wires. They soon dropped the heavy silver but kept the gold,
heading up Gordon Creek to mislead the posse, swinging abruptly south to
Cleveland, then to Black Dragon Canyon in the San Rafael Swell and on to
Robber's Roost.[108]

Paymaster Carpenter, in a new industrial twist, hopped a locomotive
and went steaming down the tracks toward Price, where Castle Valley's first
telephone line had been installed just the year before. Strung out for thirty-
five miles south of Price, it reached one phone each in Huntington, Castle
Dale, Emery, and Ferron.[109] Carpenter got a call through before the outlaws,
coming out on the road in Emery County, cut the wires. Carbon's Sheriff
Gus Donant, and Emery's Sheriff Azariah Tuttle, with a good description of
the robbers and their horses, organized posses and rode after them. Down
on the Swell, men from Castle Dale and Huntington mistook each other for
the outlaws and started shooting; luckily, the only casualty was a gray mare.
A week after the heist, the paper opined that the outlaws "are now as safe

Imagine a much larger crowd of miners, standing in front of this Castle Gate store, waiting for their pay, the day that Butch Cassidy and his Robbers Roost gang stole the payroll. This photo was taken about the time of the robbery. Courtesy of Western Mining and Railroad Museum.

as though they had been swallowed up by the earth and thus the Carpenter holdup will probably end."[110] And so it did, except that the following July, a special officer of the PVCC demanded that Carbon County's Board of Commissioners remove Donant for his incompetence in failing to capture the robbers. Utah Fuel lawyer Mark Braffet supported the sheriff, but Donant was nonetheless defeated in the subsequent election.[111]

After this heist and get-away, fears of outlaw activity flourished throughout Castle Valley. In March 1898, rumors spread that outlaws from the Robber's Roost, recently seen around Price, were planning to steal the $30,000 Ute annuity coming in on the D&RGW. The Ninth Cavalry—the famed Buffalo Soldiers—rode down from the Basin and met the train first in Helper, then again at Price, and escorted the Indian agent with the payroll safely back to the fort. While viewed locally as an asset, these African-American soldiers faced special problems of prejudice in the larger society, exemplified by the then-recent 1896 Supreme Court decision in *Plessey v. Ferguson* that made "separate but equal" (really, inherently *un*equal) the law of the land.[112]

Despite stiffening racial prejudice elsewhere, all of Price turned out a month later to honor two companies of the Ninth Cavalry who rode down from Ft. Duchesne to ship out on the D&RGW after the U.S. battleship *Maine* blew up and sank in Havana Harbor. Cuba belonged to Spain, and

Congress had just declared the Spanish-American War. The new state of Utah not only lost the Buffalo Soldiers but also filled her volunteer quota, including four men recruited at Price. Back East, young Theodore Roosevelt resigned his government post (as Under-Secretary of the Navy) to assemble his Rough Riders to fight in Cuba. On May 1, U.S. Commodore George Dewey crushed the Spanish fleet in the Philippines, prying America's new Pacific colony from Spanish hands. People celebrated Dewey's conquest with sheet music, prose, poetry, and a new holiday on May 1. Rivaling the Dewey fervor, people lionized the voyage of the great battleship *Oregon* around Cape Horn to join the Cuban conflict. Its commander, former Confederate General Joseph "Fighting Joe" Wheeler (also former House member and friend of Utah's Joseph Rawlins), forgot where he was for a moment, yelling, "We've got the damn Yankees on the run!" After 113 days of fighting on Pacific and Caribbean fronts, the Spanish-American War was over. The D&RGW, hauling war-bound freight and troops, made more money than ever. Castle Valley towns like Price and Huntington even post-poned beloved Pioneer Day celebrations until July 25 to hold the *Maine* Martyr Memorial services on July 24. In December, after the war ended, the post commander, headed out for Ft. Duchesne, presented the Price district school with an American flag.[113]

This patriotic interlude hardly stopped business as usual for local law-breakers. On May 28, 1898, Gunplay Maxwell and an accomplice held up the Springville Bank, located in Utah County to the north of Castle Val-ley. They botched their get-away and the posse quickly caught them. While awaiting trial, Maxwell turned his famous ingenuity to making a mock pistol out of a match box, soap, twine, and tinfoil. He planned to scare the deputy who brought his meals and thus make an escape. Another prisoner spilled the plan to Sheriff George Storrs, now a much-esteemed peace officer. (Storrs had begun his career as a seventeen-year-old railroad grader for the D&RG in Colorado, passing through northern Castle Valley when only one house stood on the flat.) Thus frustrated, Maxwell turned to writing. He penned a book, now lost, illustrated with his own sketches, denying any as-sociation with the Robber's Roost gang and airing grievances about officials who allegedly owed him for protecting their gilsonite claims. At Maxwell's trial, Tobe Whitmore swore to seeing over $1,600 in gold taken from Max-well, the proceeds of the robbery. Sheriff Storrs testified that Maxwell had confessed. The defense produced no witnesses, but objected to the jury of only eight men, the entire panel selected for the term by jury commission-ers. The under-sized jury found Maxwell guilty and the judge sentenced him to eighteen years in the state penitentiary. Maxwell appealed, and a subsequent U.S. Supreme Court decision upheld the legality of a felony conviction brought by only eight men.[114] Maxwell, having exhausted his le-gal remedies, then tried a prison break with a real weapon he constructed "with only an iron bedstead and a box of matches as his material." Wardens confiscated his unfinished mini-cannon, which worked as well as a standard rifle when they tried detonating it.[115] After this, Maxwell stayed put—for a while.

Despite these law-and-order successes, an 1898 history apologetically noted that "The San Rafael mountains [sic—Swell] have long been regarded as a safe retreat for thieves and outlaws, and Emery county has been shunned because of the existence of the famous 'Robber's Roost'" (in fact, located in more southerly Wayne County).[116] In Price, the *Eastern Utah Advocate* reported at the end of December 1899 that "There is every indication that the Robber's Roosters have resumed business at the old stand. Stock is again missing from the range, and there are suspicious characters in the bad lands."[117] The Castle Valley corridor had earned a new, unsavory reputation, based on its gunmen rather than its geography. Soon, these men would get mixed up in its major industry: coal.

# PART II
# NEW PEOPLE, NEW WAYS

# 5

# Industrial Revolution, 1899–1905

*Between 4:30 and 5 o'clock in the morning I . . . saw about forty-five deputies. They*
*descended upon the sleeping tent colony, dragged the miners out of their beds . . .*
*[without time] to put on their clothes. Shaking with cold, followed by the shrieks and*
*wails of their wives and children, beaten along the road by guns, they were driven*
*like cattle. . . . Two days after this raid was made, the stone that held my door was*
*suddenly pushed in. A fellow jumped into the room, stuck a gun under my jaw and*
*told me to tell him where he could get $3000 of the miners' money or he would blow*
*out my brains.*[1]

—MOTHER MARY HARRIS JONES, UNION ORGANIZER

As the twentieth century arrived, America's Industrial Revolution
boomed. According to historian Samuel Hays, all of American history
from 1885–1914 was a simple reaction to industrial growth.[2] Certainly, Castle Valley fit this model, as coal mining grew in importance. Farmers still
struggled to get enough water to raise their crops, and stockmen still tended their flourishing herds, but coal became king. As a handmaiden industry for smelters spewing metals, for locomotives hauling goods nationwide,
and for home heating, coal danced to tunes whistled elsewhere. Increasingly, so did Castle Valley's residents. Their daily lives changed as metals,
smelted with coke from coal, were shaped into marvelous new inventions
such as sewing machines, electric irons, and the delicate filaments inside
light bulbs. Like the rest of the nation, Castle Valley residents wanted these
material goods, even if local miners sometimes paid the ultimate price in
fueling America's industry.

The Denver and Rio Grande Western and its Pleasant Valley Coal Company, Castle Valley's leading industrial complex, made important strides just
as the nineteenth century ended. In August 1899, the PVCC opened a new
mine, Clear Creek, just south of Winter Quarters. Miners there earned sixty

cents a ton for screened coal—a good price at the time.[3] Those good wages contrasted with problems at the oldest Scofield mine, Winter Quarters No. 1, where in January 1898, coal wagon drivers had struck based on the new eight-hour law. "The drivers came out dissatisfied with going in and out of the mine on their own time," wrote Gomer Thomas, the state coal mine inspector. "They demanded 25 cents of advance per day, or go in and out of the mine on the company's time." After one day out, he wrote, "They decided that they would go in on the company's time and come out on their own time."[4] This low-key, civilized negotiation marked the virtual end of gentlemanly agreement in Castle Valley's industrial disputes.

Industry became institutionalized with Sunnyside's inauguration in November 1899. Robert Forrester had opened the mines there "in shape to ship coal in less time than any other mine in the West," bragged Coal Mine Inspector Thomas. "By the middle of November the mine was producing 500 tons per day."[5] At the beginning of that month, Forrester proudly accompanied D&RGW president William Jackson Palmer and his official party as they steamed up the recently-completed Sunnyside spur to view the workings.[6] Eleven days after Palmer's visit, the Sunnyside labor force struck, angered at a reduction in pay. Once Palmer had departed, Forrester had replaced the set daily wage of $2.75 and $3 with "tonnage prices, which is five cents lower than Castle Gate and ten cents under the Scofield scale," reported a Salt Lake newspaper. "The men also claim there are no accommodations there which makes the work further undesirable."[7]

The company responded by importing foreigners, most of whom could not speak English and were unfamiliar with workers' rights. The Price paper, for example, reported in November 1899, "About fifteen to twenty Italians have arrived in town, presumably to work in the mines here at Castle Gate or at Sunnyside."[8] Castle Gate's new Italians formed the nucleus of Castle Valley's first Catholic Church, St. Anthony's, a small frame building erected in 1897 that lasted ten years before burning down. Other nationalities came, too, such as John Vuksinick from Slovenia (then part of the empire of Austria-Hungary, making him an Austrian, in local parlance). He had worked his way across this country, first in Pennsylvania, then in Minnesota, then to California where a Slovenian agricultural colony failed due to the perfidy of the priest in charge. With nowhere else to go, he and his wife, Mary Kokal Vuksinick, also came to Sunnyside in 1899. Numbers of foreign-born residents rose from over six million in 1880 to over nine million in 1890 to some 10,300,000 by the turn of the century. In ensuing decades, it would only rise.[9]

More foreigners came and began the slow process of cultural accommodation. Up at Pleasant Valley, the PVCC imported Finns. Driven out of their sub-Arctic homeland by the suppression of their Russian overlords, many Finns—particularly males subject to conscription in the Russian army—came to America. By 1900, over 200 of them lived in Pleasant Valley, which somewhat resembled their northerly home. The company segregated them into "Finn Town" or upper camp, at Winter Quarters, where they were considered non-white for their foreignness, not their appearance. Together with their neighbors, they prepared to celebrate their first patriotic American holiday, Dewey Day on May 1 in honor of the Admiral's recent, glorious victory in the Philippines (the same as May Day, an old European holiday). Other residents, such as the Robert Farish family, must have particularly enjoyed the commemoration; they had named their youngest daughter, born July 8, 1898, Manilla Dewey Farish. Therefore, when an explosion echoed down Pleasant Valley about 10:25 that morning, people thought the party had started early.[10]

Slowly, people realized that Winter Quarters No. 4 had exploded. At the portal, explosive winds carried young Jack Wilson eight hundred-twenty feet into a gulch. A huge splinter stuck through his abdomen, and the fall crushed the back of his skull. He survived, permanently disabled; his coal-mining brothers, James, Willie, and Alexander, did not. Flames roared through No. 4, raising deadly afterdamp (poisonous gases) that spread relentlessly into No. 1 where the two mines connected at the back. Men started running, some of them right into the No. 4 fire, the shorter way out from the back of No. 1. The burning coal glowed all around the trapped miners; flames ate the wooden ceiling props, and crashing rock and coal dust completely blinded them. Fifteen-year-old Tom Pugh heard the explosion and seized his cap in his teeth to keep his nostrils covered while he ran a mile and a half in complete darkness to the portal of No. 1, where he fainted. He survived; his father died in the mine. Young Willie Davis tried to do the same, but dropped his cap when he stopped to help an older man trapped in the rubble. He was later found dead, his arms locked around the older man's waist.[11]

Immediately, rescue crews tried to scramble over the thick tangle of timbers and a dead horse blocking the entrance to No. 4, but were driven back by the rising gasses. Time and again rescuers forced their way into the mine only to be stopped by the afterdamp. Robert Forrester succumbed on two consecutive tries and almost died. Finally inside, rescuers unrolled yards and yards of canvas and burlap brattice cloth to block off selected passageways, directing the fresh air to one portion at a time. Teams brought the first man to the surface: John Kirton, first believed to be Harry Betterson, so burnt that he was unrecognizable. He died in agony a day later. Mine cars began rolling out of No. 1 piled high with the dead, up to twelve in a car. Superintendent Thomas Parmley found the body of his brother, William, the No. 4 foreman, deep inside where the fire had been worst. Only William knew where each of his men had been stationed; with him died the chance of finding them all.[12]

In the midst of the horror, miracles still happened. The first afternoon, six horses galloped out of No. 1 still in their harnesses and frolicked down

Castle Gate superintendent Frank Cameron, Winter Quarters superintendent Thomas Parmley, and Clear Creek superintendent H. B. Williams confer outside the wrecked entrance to Winter Quarters #4 mine as rescue work continues underground after the dreadful explosion of May 1, 1900. Courtesy of Western Mining and Railroad Museum.

the hill to the stable. Two men were found three and a half hours after the explosion in the depths of No. 1, unaware of the disaster.[13] Soon, hope for further survivors dwindled. As one rescue team member later described the scene inside the tunnels: "When a man was caught by the full force of the explosion he was hurled against the wall or floor . . . [like] . . . a piece of dough against the wall." He added, fighting the urge to "just cry my heart out, [that] when the last body is out of the mine you will see more of us break down . . . very soon."[14] Once sixty-six men at a time lay ready for iden- tification. That job fell to boyish, twenty-three-year old Clarence Nix, the store clerk. He had passed out the monthly scrip to each miner and knew them all. He passed down the rows of bodies covered by burlap brattice cloth dragged in from the company store. The legs of grown men stuck out to the knees; dead boys revealed only their feet. Uncovering their faces, he eventually identified over two hundred corpses, the last found on August 9. The Finns maintained that some of their men were never recovered.[15]

Help poured in as Scofield prepared for Utah's largest mass burial ever. Piles of dirt rose on the hillside as dozens of men dug graves in the hard, cold ground. Coffins came from as far away as Denver. Salt Lake schoolchil- dren donated flowers which dignitaries tied into bouquets as they rode down on the Pleasant Valley train, its progress watched by silent crowds all along the route. At the spur by the Scofield cemetery, grieving survivors accepted the flowers for funerals conducted by a variety of clergymen, including a Finnish Lutheran pastor brought in from Rock Springs, Wyoming. Nearby coal camps sent money. So did San Francisco. The LDS Church donated $2,500; the Catholic bishop of Utah welcomed all fatherless children into Salt Lake City's St. Ann's Orphanage. President McKinley cabled his condolences and forwarded expressions of sympathy from the President of France. Food poured in from Salt Lake City, and the Pleasant Valley Coal Company wiped out all the miner's debts for April. The PVCC also gave $500 to the family of each man killed, amounting to a total of $100,000. The D&RGW transported mourning family members free of charge.[16]

Castle Valley lost more than coal miners that day; it lost a wide array of local talent. Carbon County Commissioner John James, among the first to be found, died in the embrace of his son, George. The dead Evans brothers, Richard and David, had survived an 1882 coal mine explosion in Abercarn, Wales, and had come to Castle Dale, forming a prize-winning orchestra with their parents and brothers. Thomas Farrish, an experienced coal miner from Cleveland, Utah, also died—along with six other farmer-miners from his tiny hometown.[17] This story of loss repeated over and over throughout Castle Valley, the rest of Utah, and the world.

What had happened? Some people scapegoated the Finns, those strange newcomers who had refused (except one) to help search for the dead. In his annual mine report, Inspector Thomas identified no human agent, but stressed his new realization that coal dust itself had proven flammable, not just the gasses previously considered dangerous.[18] In the local communities, some said the company was at fault. Others claimed "it was one of those things over which no man has control, and for which no man or men should be held responsible."[19] A subsequent grand jury inquest exonerated the PVCC and all individuals involved. Although many of the victims' survivors sued, the company always won. For years, all Pleasant Valley businesses closed on May 1 to honor the dead. The only practical result of the explosion came in 1901, when the Utah state legislature passed reforming safety laws that mandated sprinkling mines with water to settle coal dust, maintaining sufficient ventilation, and limiting the amount of explosives brought into a mine. None could be stored there.[20]

The 200 dead miners had to be replaced, so the PVCC tried recruiting up and down the Castle Valley corridor. Among those who responded were Teancum Pratt and his eighteen-year-old son, Joseph. Pratt's earlier, tenuous prosperity had evaporated in the hard winter of 1899–1900 and the following dry spring and hot summer. His coal sales simply could not keep pace with the needs of his devastated farms. In the fall of 1900, after the men went off to the reopened Winter Quarters mine, Annie Mead Pratt took up her husband's diary: "it was a hard winnter & not much snow, & the water went back on us so we lost all our crop of corn & potatos, & a very nice garden. We seen the crops burn up . . . our means were gone & nothing to live on. . . . So Teancum thought it would be best to go to Scofield & work in the mines for the winnter so we could go on the farm in the spring. But the Lord willed it otherwise. . . ."[21] On September 8, 1900, Pratt was dead.

Joe had to tell his mother about how the side of the mine room where his father had been working had caved in and how Teancum was crushed against the coal car he had been loading. Death was instantaneous.[22] Pratt was buried in the Scofield cemetery, so recently expanded by the victims of the explosion. As the local newspaper noted in his obituary, "He once owned Helper townsite, but fortune never smiled upon him for any length of time and his large family is now left in poor circumstances."[23] Pratt's name also appeared on the State Coal Mine Inspector's long list of fatalities and injuries for Winter Quarters in 1900. Aside from the roughly 200 killed in the explosion, nine other fatalities and sixty-three serious injuries occurred in Utah's mines that year. Of these, the bulk came at Winter Quarters, indicating that the inexperienced replacements faired badly.[24]

At the corporate level, the Rio Grande system simultaneously weathered a hushed, rocky adjustment. For one thing, the national government took a renewed interest in the legal disposition of its land. In July 1900, government surveyors completed the official survey of the Book Cliffs around Sunnyside, allowing the Western to regularize its shady ownership, which it did through the newly-created Utah Fuel Company. Through a series of complicated legal maneuvers involving corporate giants and two investment banks, Utah Fuel acquired the PVCC and the Western Construction Company. Then, the Rio Grande Western Railway turned around and bought the Utah Fuel Company, further hiding its corporate machinations. Within weeks, the D&RGW itself reorganized. Edward Jeffrey, president of Colorado's Rio Grande, also became head of the Western, ousting founder William Jackson Palmer once and for all. At the same time, the Gould brothers, George, Frank, and Howard (heirs of the late communications magnate Jay Gould) and Union Pacific owner E. H. Harriman took their seats on the board of the now virtually-consolidated Rio Grande system.[25] As a result, Castle Valley's most lucrative coal mines and its entire railroad network were now cemented to one of the nation's largest trusts, guaranteeing their accelerated exploitation.

Capitalists branched out into another speculative local investment: oil. John D. Rockefeller of the Standard Oil trust, the refiner of over ninety-five percent of America's oil (as well as holder of wells, pipelines, railroads, and vast fleets of ships) was already worth over $100 million. Plenty of others wanted to copy his success. So Castle Valley oil companies blossomed, at least on paper. Charles Swasey filed on oil locations, selling some to Mrs. Agnes D. Ireland, widow of the late Marshal Ireland. Others came from far and near, including A. J. Lee, freighter and developer; merchant Louis Lowenstein, one of the Jewish pioneers of Utah; Joseph R. Sharp, superintendent of the Utah Fuel Company; Dr. Andrew W. Dowd, Utah Fuel physician;

Heber M. Wells and James H. Moyle, Utah governor and future governor, respectively; LDS leader George Romney, Sr.; Utah's hard-rock mining developer Senator Thomas Kearns, and Wyoming's Senator and railroad promoter Clarence Don Clark, and others. They formed corporations with exotic names, like the Baku Oil Company, (after the capital of oil-bearing Azerbaijan, on the banks of the Caspian Sea), holding almost 10,000 acres in Emery's Green River field and Carbon's Colton field, which had yet to sink a well. The more down-to-earth New York-Utah Oil and Mining Company held 35,000 acres in five counties, including Carbon and Emery, and planned to set up two rigs to start drilling in early 1902. By then, Utah's deepest well, on the San Rafael Swell, went down 1,240 feet. Investments poured in. As late as 1913, Royal Swasey was still pumping oil on the San Rafael Desert, writing to his sweetheart of the seven oil rigs still doggedly, though not very profitably, at work.[26]

Some of these capitalists made other, more practical investments in Castle Valley. For example, in 1901, Dr. Andrew Dowd teamed with Utah Fuel geologist Robert Forrester; Truman Ketchum, a special agent on the D&RGW, and a "tough gun," English immigrant Tom Dilly, to form the Patmos Head Land and Cattle Company on Lord Elliott's old Big Spring Ranch. A year or two later, Dilly killed a man over a range controversy, went to trial, but was not convicted (some said due to his powerful associates). That fall, he agreed to accompany a huge herd of local stock to market, rode off on the train with the animals, and never returned. Superintendent Joseph R. Sharp subsequently bought out the ranch and turned it into a dairy. During World War I, Price's Lee Bryner, a pneumonia victim, met a nurse named Miss Dilly in an English hospital. Through her, he learned of her father, Tom, who asked after several of his old Utah acquaintances. Selling the cattle, he had prospered, returned to his native land, and settled down, apparently with no regrets.[27]

Forrester did better with another of his local investments. Together with G. W. Laing he formed the Gardenia Land and Water Company to develop an area just east of Ferron in southwestern Emery County, traditionally known as Poverty Flat. A few families had already settled there, including the Prices. They used to drive their wagon to Ferron down a dugway of blue clay, which, after a storm, would stick so firmly to the wagon wheels that it had to be shoveled off every two rotations. The new entrepreneurs quickly renamed the area Independence Flat, and the new town Rochester, after the hometown of their associate, M. B. Whitney, new head of what in August 1906 became the Emery County Land and Water Company. Not all went smoothly. As the Price family historian reported, "A Mr. Lang [sic] came to Rochester in a smart looking surrey with a fringe on top and talked the farmers into consolidating their water into a company, and they would each benefit with more water. But they were actually receiving less and were forced to sell their holdings because they didn't have enough water."[28] The families who stayed benefited from consolidation of other properties. By 1930, the Rochester precinct contained twenty-one farms with a total of 10,140 acres, far more than the typical amount in Mormon Utah.[29] Under a new arrangement—non-Mormon agricultural development—Castle Valley had continued to diversify.

Changes also marked the nation at large, sometimes tragically. On September 6, 1901, a disaffected anarchist fired two shots, point-blank, into President McKinley, who was visiting the Pan American Exposition at Buffalo, New York. Doctors immediately removed one bullet but decided against using the new, untested X-ray machine on display at the exposition to locate the second. McKinley died eight days later of its poisons. Young Vice President Theodore Roosevelt became President. He spearheaded reforms that would usher in America's Progressive Era, a time marked by a reliance on experts, general optimism, and a firm belief in progress.[30] Roosevelt, having briefly ranched out on the Little Missouri, knew and loved the "great grazing lands of the West . . . [in] the arid belt," which he described as "one vast stretch of grazing country, with only here and there spots of farm-land."[31] He made common cause with Francis J. Newlands, then U.S. senator from bone-dry Nevada. Newlands, elected to the House for the first time in 1892, rose after a tough fight to the Senate. In 1902 he sponsored the Newlands National Reclamation Act to authorize federal construction of reservoirs and highline canals funded through the sale of newly-irrigated public lands in the arid states.[32]

This legislation built on previous federal involvement, begun with the first National Irrigation Congress held in Salt Lake City in 1891. There, delegates had demanded state control over local irrigation, a suggestion rejected by the federal government. In 1894, Congress had passed the Carey Act to provide some federal funding for western water projects.[33] Under its auspices, Castle Valley boosters had excitedly hatched unfulfilled schemes to divert the Green River, to dam the lower San Rafael River, or to bring water from the Wasatch Plateau to the lands between Huntington and Price. Huntington's Don C. Robbins tried, prematurely, to promote a reservoir in Joe's Valley, high on the Wasatch Plateau west of his town, not only for irrigation but to generate electricity for a proposed new railroad connecting the Emery County towns with Price. Meanwhile, the Carey Act, implemented largely in Wyoming, proved ineffective.[34] States simply could not afford large scale irrigation projects, even though land, once reclaimed, could be sold to recoup building expenditures. Consequently, Castle Valley residents soon joined other westerners in seeking help under the new 1902 Newlands Reclamation Act. A local irrigation convention met in 1902 and petitioned for federal assistance to reclaim 50,000 acres of dry, alkaline Emery County.[35]

Castle Valley certainly qualified as arid land, and its settlers had a long history of dealing with water problems. For example, the old Emery county town of Kingsville had been long dependent on an 1896 canal that had carried water from Ferron Creek. When its lands became alkaline, Stake President Reuben G. Miller instructed the local bishop, Hyrum Nelson, to pick a new site. Bishop Nelson, twice plagued with broken singletree clips on his wagon, decided to stay at the spot he had reached and chose a site about two miles to the west. While some questioned his choice, most people loaded their tiny log houses on wheels and moved. As local residents later explained: "They probably took the wagon box off the wagon and spread the wheels out enough [on the reach poles] to fit the length of the house, put the house on the wheels with the reach poles connecting the wheels, hooked up the team and dragged the house up to the present site."[36] In 1904, Apostle Rudger Clawson (who had served his prison term but clung to polygamy, for which he was later ousted from the Quorum), arrived to organize the ward. In his honor, people called their new town Clawson "from a visitor of a few hours, who, so far as is known, never returned."[37] Further north, the arid valley flatlands seemed to offer new settlement possibilities, if only they could be irrigated. Thomas Wells had moved his family six miles east of Cleveland to optimistically-named Desert Lake in 1888. Soon, members of the Powell, Wells, Thayne, Winder, and Marsing families and others had started work on an 500–foot earthen dam to create a 300–acre reservoir for irrigation, dependent on an extension of the Cleveland Canal. Their Desert Lake Reservoir and Irrigation Company, incorporated in 1892, went bust when the dam broke four years later, almost drowning some of the residents. When the community lacked the money to raise a new dam, the LDS Church provided a thousand dollars. With this, Cleveland folks also extended the Huntington North Ditch to serve their town, since the water from Cleveland had begun to go alkaline.[38]

No matter where one settled, irrigated farming would drop the water table while the ever-present alkali rose, eating into adobe structures and causing changes in vegetation. As the alkali swamp spread to Desert Lake, Manassa Blackburn, its school teacher, moved to land about six miles away and founded Victor in 1896. Although the new town soon sported a school, church, post office and store, it was gone before World War I due to lack of water and ever-encroaching sand dunes.[39] Just a few miles to the north, in 1904, a group of men moved from increasingly swampy, alkali Cleveland to another unoccupied portion of Castle Valley about four miles away. They helped build the Eagle Extension Ditch from the Cleveland Canal to their new homesites. In 1912, the town held a meeting to choose a name and, allegedly, only four men attended: Messieurs Erickson, Larsen, Mortensen, and Oviatt. Using the first letter of each of their names, the town was christened "Elmo."[40] This time, their town did not fall victim to an alkali swamp.

Some water problems originated with Castle Valley's increased stock-raising. Expanding sheep herds typically befouled the watershed over which they ranged. Recognizing this fact, in 1892 the Utah Territorial Legislature had passed a law prohibiting sheep from watersheds within seven miles of a city in an attempt to keep the water unpolluted. Castle Valley's notorious Mule Case of 1901 brought the problem home. When a sheepherder's pack mules fell to their death from a ledge above Huntington Creek, the rotting carcasses made a nasty impact on Huntington's water supply downstream. The mules' owner, a young sheepherder, pleaded guilty and was fined $5 and costs of $21. The local newspaper noted, "The people of Huntington, as well as other towns, are growing weary of drinking filth from the sheep and stock on the headwaters of our streams."[41] Petitions for state and federal aid in protecting watersheds poured out of Emery County towns, starting the shift to new power structures to solve local problems.[42]

Simultaneous with the Mule Case, the first dispute over rights to Castle Valley's flowing water reached local courts. Cottonwood Creek, just a few miles south of Huntington Creek, had long supplied Orangeville and Castle Dale through a series of ditches. Town residents and independent users had formed a succession of canal companies, including the Blue Cut Canal, the Star, Mammoth, Clipper, and Great Western. By the turn of the century, the water supply could no longer meet the demand. Therefore, in May 1901, a "friendly" lawsuit by the Blue Cut against the rest of the companies (with other individual users on each side) led to a binding settlement. Court-appointed referees (and LDS leaders)—Emery Stake president Reuben G. Miller and Apostles John Henry Smith and Anthon H. Lund—recommended the application of the established doctrine of prior use (first in time, first in right) to non-Mormon Judge Jacob Johnson of Spring City. In the twentieth-century spirit of Mormon-gentile cooperation, on February 2, 1902, the judge promulgated the Johnson Decree, stipulating that senior users (those who had entered on Cottonwood Creek before 1884) received first-class rights; second-class rights devolved on those who had entered since that year. The Great Western Canal Company, begun in 1884 but not yet completed, was granted both second- and third-class rights due to the tremendous investment already sunk into its construction.[43] The Johnson Decree by no means settled all dissension; neither did it adequately provide for local needs. By August 1902, Castle Dale townsite ditches ran dry, to the desperation of farmers on the newer canals. The stockholders of the Blue Cut and Clipper companies allowed some of their water to flow into the Mammoth and Great Western canals, permitting a harvest. Canal consolidation followed. In April 1903, all of the previous litigants became united in the Cottonwood Creek Consolidated Irrigation Company except for the Blue Cut, which thereby protected its generous first-class rights.[44]

Meanwhile, as Castle Valley residents waited to hear about their request for help under the Newlands Reclamation Act, they hedged their bets by also applying to the state for aid. In April 1903, state representative Joseph E. Johnson presented the State Land Board with Huntington's petition for

$30,000 to build a reservoir on Buckhorn Flat. The land board rejected this request after calculating the cost at over ten times the suggested amount.[45] The federal government seemed more supportive when, the following September, the National Irrigation Congress met in Ogden. Senator Newlands himself addressed the delegates and stressed the importance of federal-state cooperation. Perhaps aware of Utah's theocratic history, he proudly noted that the Secretary of the Interior had the right to nominate all candidates for Nevada state engineer. This federal supremacy over public lands and state personnel not only represented, for Newlands, the efficiency of the federal bureaucracy, but addressed his concurrent concerns about the power of monopolies. If the federal government controlled the water, he thought, the trusts would not.[46] How well this latter message played in a land where all community resources were once held by the LDS Church can only be imagined. As far as actual water works were concerned, Castle Valley profited little. In fact, a 1904 report by the Department of Agriculture noted that roughly thirty percent of Emery County farmland had recently been abandoned.[47] Perhaps because of these difficulties, in February 1904, Castle Valley farmers invited two professors from Utah State Agricultural College to Orangeville to lecture on farming techniques. They suggested means for dealing with the pervasive local alkali, and encouraged farmers to report on their successes, which often came as a surprise to their neighbors who had been too busy farming their own places to share techniques. As a result of this meeting, the first farmers' association in Castle Valley was formed.[48]

Local attempts at improving Castle Valley fit well with another of President Roosevelt's crusades: to give diminishing federal lands to homeseekers rather than see them fall to monopolies. To meet this goal, Roosevelt established the second Public Lands Commission in October 1903 with wealthy, civic-minded Gifford Pinchot as its secretary. Pinchot had made a unprecedented professional career in forestry and realized that the activities of railroad companies, mines, sawmills, and town building augured a short life for remaining stands of trees. He instead favored conservation for use, a policy he consistently implemented after Roosevelt had appointed him Chief Forester at the head of the newly-created Forest Service in 1901.[49]

Two years later, the Forest Service entered Castle Valley. In 1903, the federal government set aside the Manti National Forest on the Wasatch Plateau, creating a host of repercussions along the Castle Valley corridor. First, rangers began enforcing stock regulation. For decades, seasonal traffic between Castle Valley's nearby highlands and the San Rafael characterized cattle raising. For example, Jim Liddell, who got into cattle ranching in 1901, described his yearly cycle to an interviewer in 1940. "He wintered his cattle down in the lowlands around here [Price] and at Woodside, and . . . in the spring as soon as snow was nearly gone the ranchers would have a spring round up to collect the cattle and then drive those that they didn't sell up to the mountains." Liddell grazed his herds in Whitmore Canyon, letting them "graze up into the mountain right behind the snow. In the fall, around October, the ranchers would get together and stage another round-up." Then, they drove the herds down low again for winter grazing, and to count their "calf crop." Beef bound for market was loaded at Woodside and sold in Denver.[50] Preston Nutter, one of Carbon County's most prosperous cattlemen, ranged even more widely. He had started out in Colorado in the 1880s, built up herds on the Arizona Strip, and moved into Nine Mile Canyon in the West Tavaputs Plateau at the northern border of Carbon County in the late 1890s. His ranch headquarters lay to the north in Duchesne County, but he owned range lands stretching south into Castle Valley's high hinterlands.[51] His far-flung operation, devoted solely to stockraising, was the exception in Castle Valley.

This approach, leaving the herds to fend for themselves between spring and fall round-ups—the Texas method—and was initially incomprehensible to more communitarian Utah farmer-ranchers, according to Clair C. Andersen, who later compiled Castle Valley's grazing notes. Mormons "first resented it, then tried to understand it, and finally, by increasing their own herds, to compete by ranging in the same manner." As a result, "the Mormon livestock industry emerged from a subsistence basis into the diversified-irrigated farm-ranch that prevails today."[52] Much as he described, Emery's Lew Peterson began working Durham shorthorn cattle for the Ireland Land and Cattle Company in 1885 and saved enough money to start his own business, adding a few cattle (probably unbranded mavericks) to his herd every year, in the locally-accepted fashion. About May 15 he would drive the cattle on to their summer range in the Manti National Forest; in the winter they ran on the east San Rafael Desert. His 200–acre ranch adjoined both ranges, "with his ranch on the dividing line," where he fed calves during heavy snows. He raised his own silage and hay and shipped steers—mostly two-year-olds—out of Price bound for Denver, as did most Emery County ranchers.[53] Other cattlemen also alternated their stock between winter farmsteads and public lands for summer range. For example, James Allred of Cleveland ran his cattle south of town in the winter but moved his stock to his homestead in the Park, in the Book Cliffs north of Wellington, as the weather warmed.[54]

All those who had freely used the Wasatch Plateau for summer grazing suddenly encountered federal regulations. Larger stockmen now had to share the range with smaller outfits, and number of head was limited to the carrying capacity of the range. Stock raisers of Huntington, Cottonwood Creek, Emery, and Ferron reacted by forming local livestock associations to improve range conditions through constructing bridges, making trails, maintaining water troughs, and acting as herders, all to improve the quality of their cattle. The federal government continued extending its control over local lands with the creation of the La Sal National Forest near Moab in 1906, combining it a year later with the Manti Forest covering the Wasatch Plateau west of Castle Valley, and with the Monticello Forest Reserve far to the south to become the Manti-La Sal National Forest.[55]

While creation of the Manti National Forest stimulated improvement of the livestock industry, it hampered other forest endeavors. Associate Chief Albert F. Potter, taking an informal survey prior to the forest's formal designation, noted in his diary, "Met. Mr. [Sam] Singleton, merchant of Ferron" who spoke of the "great hardship" as forest personnel shut down sawmills that summer. The settlers were so far from a railroad that they could not get timber, Singleton asserted, so some people could not build. Locals would not object to limited grazing on the Forest, Potter noted, if "the settlers can [still] get the mature timber."[56] But everyone realized that, after federal designation, operators could no longer cut where they pleased. Even with limitations, local sawmills persisted. The last on the mountain was removed in the 1960s; as late as 1991 one sawmill still remained in Fairview Canyon west of Castle Valley.[57]

Likewise, Castle Valley's dairy industry suffered with the forest's establishment. Amos and Almira Stevens had begun the first dairy in 1882 on Ferron Creek with a herd of red Durham cattle which they had grazed on Ferron Mountain during the summer. They sold their butter and cheese as far away as Grand Junction, Colorado, sometimes tapping daughter Elmira to drive one of their huge freight wagons. Deprived of free mountain grazing, the Stevens family struggled to maintain the industry, transferring it to Ferron's Creamery Co-op from 1905–1913. It later passed to a series of corporations, surviving well into the twentieth century.[58]

On the other hand, the Forest Service provided much-needed jobs for a few Castle Valley residents. One of the area's first forest rangers was a home-grown boy, George Westover. He had reconnoitered Castle Valley for his Dixie-dwelling family in 1888 and moved there around 1890. Every spring, he had typically sheared sheep for his neighbors, usually in the mountains that bounded it to the north—in the Park near Soldier Summit, near the railroad junction at Colton, or by the mining town of Scofield. Consequently, he knew many of the lands falling under federal forest conservation.[59] His outdoor life included driving stagecoach from Price to Fort Duchesne in the early 1890s, when once he saved his frozen feet and calves from frostbite (and amputation) only by sticking them through a hole cut in the icy crust of a mountain creek, an old freighter cure. His toughness and experience made him an ideal choice for ranger's assistant when the forest was first created. After several years the head ranger retired, and recommended George Westover as his successor, following the obligatory federal tests. George passed the oral test brilliantly. Like so many boys of his generation, however, his full outdoor life had left him time for only about three years of schooling. He failed the written test, and the ranger post went to another.[60]

Without the income from employment on the forest, Westover went back to freighting and working with his team, later involving his whole family. Daughter Roxie Westover Nelson remembered going from Huntington to Price after a load of coal. "We left home at 4 in the morning so we would get there before the other wagons and be one of the first to be loaded." Her father let her drive: "such an honor," she remembered. On another occasion, "we camped overnight at a wagon campground and stayed all night under the wagon in a pile of quilts. The next day poppa unloaded the freight and loaded up another and we went back home."[61] The freighting industry had long helped unite Castle Valley's towns. As far back as the 1890s, Ferron settlers such as Chris Nelson and C. R. Killpack had willingly driven their teams and wagons on the six- to nine-day round trip to the mines at Sunnyside to sell surplus crops, meat, eggs, butter, and cheese. They often returned with freight brought in on the railroad. After more than two decades of fighting shifting sands, insects, and frequent home fires (at least one Ferron home burned down each year until the late 1930s), the mines provided what looked to them like a bonanza.[62]

Keeping the farmer-peddlers happy, local mines had recently expanded. In early 1902, one hundred new workers built a bank of Sunnyside coke ovens whose output fueled the growing Utah smelter industry. Many Emery County farmers peppered this workforce, joining the ranks of labor with their teams to earn ready cash.[63] Others, however, were Italian laborers who had just experienced the rise of industrialization in the northern part of their new nation. By the beginning of July, fifty of the two hundred planned ovens were in operation, signaling an expanding market for coal and a consequent need for more labor.[64] Some of those who arrived came from previous jobs in the eastern United States, where President Roosevelt—in an action "absolutely without precedent"—had arbitrated Pennsylvania's coal strike of 1902. When the union and the owners there had failed to reach a settlement and fuel ran low, the President had forced the parties to the bargaining table, gaining miners higher wages.[65] This success spurred the United Mine Workers of America (UMWA) to try organizing the West.

On November 9, 1903, Castle Valley's miners, many of them Italians, Finns, and Austrians (mostly South Slavs from Austria-Hungary), voted to strike. They demanded an end to the scrip system, in which the company gave men paper redeemable at full value only at the high-priced company store, or at a twenty percent discount at private businesses elsewhere. Strikers also sought accurate weighing scales, the right to choose their own check-weighman, enforcement of Utah's eight-hour day for miners, a pay increase, and recognition of the UMWA. The November timing offered the best chance of success because it cut off much-needed winter fuel. Italian organizer Charles Demolli arrived in Castle Valley and addressed his countrymen (generally blamed for the strike) in their native tongue. At the company's request, Governor Heber M. Wells sent in the Mormon-led National Guard.[66]

While the Guard and the strikers warily eyed each other across picket lines, Utah Fuel needed strike-breakers to keep its mines going. Although LDS President Joseph F. Smith carefully avoided any public, partisan announcement in favor of the coal companies, he supported the efforts of Bishop John Potter of Sunnyside and of Brigham Gould to recruit strike-breaking miners from among Emery County Mormons. When these efforts succeeded, the First Presidency sent a congratulatory letter to the Utah Fuel Company.[67] Orange Seely campaigned against the strike, prompting the Castle Dale City Council to pass a resolution denouncing it. Seely went so far as to deliver an anti-strike sermon in the LDS Church at Castle Gate, after which an irate Mormon striker struck him on the head with a revolver, causing a wound that was deep but not serious.[68] National guardsmen remained generally neutral, not necessarily harboring ethnic prejudices, although they objected to the union.[69]

The strike dragged on into 1904. Miners were evicted from their camp housing in early January and retreated to tent colonies set up nearby. When no riots occurred, the National Guard withdrew at the end of the month. Arrests of union leaders continued, and in April 1904, the UMWA brought in Mother Jones. The legendary Mary Harris Jones, a long-time union organizer despite her grandmotherly appearance, came to Castle Valley from Colorado, where she had been organizing other striking miners. She roomed with an Italian family in Helper until local officials claimed that she had been exposed to smallpox and sought to isolate her in the hastily-constructed Helper pest house. It mysteriously burned down that night. Jones relocated to the strikers' tent colony, where she stayed with another Italian family. Allegedly quarantined, she kept on meeting with miners and their families, keeping up their spirits. Coal company officials appealed to Governor Wells to redeploy the National Guard. He declined. Next, they turned to local government for enforcement. The Carbon County sheriff organized a posse of approximately forty-five men to raid the colony of strikers protecting Mother Jones. She had been tipped off by the postmaster that a raid was coming and got the men to bury their guns to avoid bloodshed. Thus defenseless, 120 Italian miners were dragged from their beds before 5 a.m. and herded, shivering in their night clothes, down the road to the nearest rail spur. Gunmen shoved them into a box car to run them down to the Price jail.[70] When the jail proved too small for this sizable crowd, company employees threw up a bullpen, surrounded by a high fence and watched by company guards, to house the strikers. Just after the strikers' round-up, a ruffian broke into Mother Jones's room, shoved a gun in her face, and demanded the $3,000 he thought she had. Unafraid, she turned her pocket inside out and showed him all her wealth: fifty cents. He left. She later found out he was a sworn Carbon County deputy and former bank robber, Gunplay Maxwell.[71]

Striking miners, mostly Italians, wait at the bullpen in Price under the watchful eye of rifle-toting guards. In the foreground, far left, stands Gunplay Maxwell; just right of him is Mark Braffet. Courtesy of Western Mining and Railroad Museum.

Maxwell, released from prison when the governor commuted his sentence (allegedly for helping stem a prison break), had become Mark Braffet's bodyguard. A photograph captured the unpopular Utah Fuel attorney and Maxwell at the bullpen, cradling shotguns as they guarded union men, including Charles Demolli.[72] The bullpen remained a semi-permanent Price structure as the strikers' trials dragged on into May.

That month, Mother Jones left Castle Valley. The Western cheerfully transported her for free, glad to get the trouble-maker out of town. She went to Salt Lake City to attend the concurrent conventions of the Utah Federation of Labor and the Western Federation of Miners (WFM), then considering a merger. Organized in 1893 in Butte, Montana, on the heels of a bitter strike in Coeur d'Alene, Idaho, the WFM had led subsequent strikes in Cripple Creek and Leadville, Colorado, in 1894 and 1896, respectively; another in Coeur d'Alene in 1899 and in Telluride, Colorado, in 1901. The WFM had bonded with the Socialists around 1902, which worried Samuel Gompers, head of the American Federation of Labor (AFL), founded in 1886. Friction between the AFL, the United Mine Workers, and the WFM increased as all three competed for western membership.[73] Only the UMWA remained active in Castle Valley.

As spring brought warmth and the usual flood-waters along the Castle Valley corridor, many of the recently-recruited Emery County strikebreakers went home to their farms. Suddenly, more miners were needed, and the solution had not changed. Orange Seely toured southern Utah bearing testimonials about good mining wages and safe working conditions, (both issues in dispute during the strike). While recruiting at Richfield (outside

Castle Valley), Seely had to counter the rumor that coal companies demanded 3,000 pounds of coal to a ton, mirroring the strikers' demands for their own check-weighman. Seely's appeals evidently brought fewer men than needed, for coal companies soon employed more foreigners. Although the State Coal Mine Inspector did not yet record ethnicities of miners, his 1904 report did show that Carbon County (more heavily ethnic) had gained forty miners over 1903 (raising the total workforce from 1927 to 1967), while Emery County (persistently Mormon) had lost thirteen of its twenty-eight coal miners. These new foreign miners were generally contracted by English-speaking bosses of their own nationality, some of whom demanded a kick-back from every paycheck to insure that the miner kept his job—the source of a later union grievance, especially by the Greeks. Other nationalities arrived in smaller numbers. Japanese labor contractor Daigoro Hashimoto recruited only eight in 1904, including their leader, Kotaro Nakagawa. Japanese presence in Castle Valley dated back to May 1901, when they had replaced Italian D&RGW section hands for a savings of twenty-five cents an hour. In 1903–1904, strike-breaking recruits also included a few African Americans, widening the ethnic diversity in northern Castle Valley.[74]

Ultimately, the recruitment drive and harassment of strikers brought success to the coal companies. By late July, the strike was winding down. Management wanted any remaining strikers out of town, so about twenty armed guards, duly deputized by the county, rounded up the men left in the tent colony and marched them up to what was known as the dead line. Finally, in November, the UMWA sent $7,000 to a Price bank to defray departure expenses of the final, striking miners who had been blacklisted by the coal companies and would never again work in Castle Valley (at least not under their own names).[75] The strike had been lost, but a new, polyglot population now settled down along the Castle Valley corridor.

Blacklisted Italians who could not get back on the mine payrolls turned to farming, the only other occupation most of them knew. As a contemporary observed, "They have cleared off the land that has been considered of no value whatever, removed tons of boulders and rock, and [are] turning over the soil until they had actually got it to bearing crops."[76] Among them was James Rolando, a northern Italian from the Castle Gate mine, who first settled farmland in Spring Glen (right next to Teancum Pratt's old homestead) in 1903.[77] He became the leader for his countrymen who settled nearby, including the Martellos, Formentos, Clericos, and Marchellos, all from the same town, near Forno. Pete Clerico later recalled that his father, Battista, had relied on Rolando: "He was pretty sharp, you know. . . . He knew the law and what was going on."[78] Southern Italians, a distinctive group (divided from their northern brethren by differences at home) also arrived in the persons of the Saccomanno Family, who were the first immigrants to pay off their Spring Glen farmstead.[79] Pete Saccomanno had arrived in Utah in the mid-1890s from Grimaldi, Calabria, in southern Italy, with his brother-in-law, Antonio Jachetta. They first worked on the railroad, then ran a produce store in Salt Lake City, and by 1905 Saccomanno had money to put down on a farm in Spring Glen. Pete's brothers, Frank and Riley (originally Raffaele), joined him and acquired the farm when Pete went back to Italy. In 1907, Jachetta became "managing director of the Utah-Italian Bank and . . . Italian vice consul in Salt Lake City."[80] His bank helped immigrants send money home to Italy while he facilitated communications between those at home and those remaining in America. Together, they thus created a stable, unique Utah enclave: non-Mormon, ethnic farmers.[81]

The end of the strike also brought other ramifications. Labor's defeat had exposed the weakness of the American Labor Union or ALU (especially in Colorado) and led the WFM to initiate collaborative conferences, like the one Mother Jones attended in Salt Lake City.[82] Similar meetings followed, culminating in Chicago in 1905, when WFM leader "Big Bill" Haywood joined Socialists and other labor leaders to form "one big union." Its leaders decided to organize unskilled, industrial workers in competition with the more elite craft unions and "wage unrelenting class war against the capitalists until the existing system of society and government was overthrown."[83] These militants called themselves the Industrial Workers of the World, soon known as the IWW or Wobblies.[84] The Western Federation of Miners became the mining department of the IWW, and headed to Goldfield, Nevada, to organize miners there.[85] Meanwhile, Gunplay Maxwell, no longer Mark Braffet's bodyguard, got involved in local mining ventures, some of them with Braffet. When he could not get transportation for his ozokerite (a black mineral wax used for the new Edison records) and saturated the local demand for "Maxwellrite," his newly-invented, ozokerite-based shoe polish, he, too, fled to Goldfield.[86] There, as Thomas Bliss, he provided perjured testimony to convict two key union organizers of murder, effectively sabotaging the union effort. As the union failed in Goldfield, Maxwell seemingly just slipped away.[87]

The corporations that hired gunmen like Maxwell felt compelled to use any means to power as mergers increased and corporate competition intensified. The stakes also rose. In 1904, the national wealth reached over $108 billion.[88] Fueling some of this growth, in 1905, Utah mines (mostly around Castle Valley) produced the greatest amount of coal per man in the entire United States, according to the USGS.[89] Under this pressure, the railroad system that owned all the commercial mines and sped freight into the national network split asunder. Although Edward H. Harriman of the Union Pacific and George Gould of the Rio Grande had originally shared seats on the Rio Grande board, Gould was secretly planning a new transcontinental line in direct competition with the venerable UP. Since 1902, through a series of front men, Gould had built or acquired short lines running east over California's Sierra and west from Denver, aiming toward a connection with the Rio Grande main line at Ogden, Utah. While a suspicious Harriman sometimes queried Gould about his intentions, Gould consistently denied any involvement. This dissembling ended in early 1904, when major investment firms, one of them headed by George's brother, Edwin, stepped out of the shadows and joined the backers of the recently-incorporated Western Pacific Railway Company (WP). By the end of April 1905, Harriman had resigned from the D&RG board, and Gould had drawn up the infamous Contract B between his publicly-adopted new line, the Western Pacific, and his old Rio Grande system. On June 8, 1905, the Rio Grande board ratified this agreement, which, in broadest terms, made the D&RG and D&RGW liable for the interest on the WP's bonds and on the building costs to complete it, should there be over-runs. (There were many, often due to corporate machinations.)[90] While the Utah Construction Company pressed on with WP construction, reaching full completion only by 1910, the UP retaliated by closing the so-called Ogden gateway to Rio Grande traffic in 1905. In essence, this action meant that the Rio Grande could no longer transship its goods—including Castle Valley coal—to the UP line at Ogden. Long-time railroad man Fred Voll remembered the specifics: "Poor little old Rio Grande," he reminisced. "They had to . . . use a part of the switch track with the Union Pacific on it. . . . . [T]he Rio Grande built as far as they could one night, and the next night they went back to finish the job and there was a couple of flat cars and a switch engine hooked to them and the UP shoved [them] off the end of the track!"[91] The feisty Rio Grande Western, once heralded as the financial savior of Castle Valley, was sliding into commercial impotency.

In further homage to a passing age, Caleb Rhoades, the pioneer founder of Carbon County, died on June 2, 1905. In a sense, his death was symbolic. He had founded Carbon County some twenty-five years earlier with a handful of devoted Saints willing to strike out into what was then uninhabited wilderness. Partly for this effort, he had been honored as one of Utah's Mormon pioneers, receiving, as his friend wrote, "the Gold Pioneer Medal 1847–1897 of which he was very proud," despite the fact that he had been pioneering in California in 1847.[92] His obituary mentioned his early life, his subsequent service to Castle Valley and the Price LDS Ward, and his efforts as "the first man to survey water from the Price river through what is known as Pioneer Water Company No. 2 canal," when Castle Valley's all-important irrigation depended on physical strength and cooperative effort. Now, large-scale federal irrigation projects engulfed the nation. So did trusts. His obituary further referred to the machinations of the "asphalt trust"—the interlocking St. Louis Gilsonite Company and the Gilson Asphaltum Company—that had allegedly prevented Rhoades from proving up on his "fabulously rich [gold] mine on the [Uintah Ute] reserve."[93] These Basin lands actually opened to entry on October 1, 1905, but the Rhoades mine has never been found.[94] He had hidden it well from greedy capitalists, who rapidly sucked up natural and human resources nationwide. Castle Valley's

Caleb and Sidsie Rhoades pose for a portrait in the last years of Caleb's life. By then, the settlement he founded had grown to a modern town. Courtesy of Western Mining and Railroad Museum.

physical isolation proved an insufficient barrier to the thrust of new ideas generated by this humming outside activity. Its continuing remoteness, however, meant that newly-introduced foreigners and descendants of old settlers would have to find mutual ways to deal with rising national conflicts.

# 6

# Moving in Together, 1905–1909

*We landed in New York by boat. . . . they always kind of look you over and they give*
*you a vaccination. . . . then we went directly by wooden train to Sunnyside. . . .*
*[T]hey had the coke ovens, you know, where they burn the coal into coke and a lot of*
*flame [rose high] . . . and my mother . . . said to me, "It looks like we came to hell."*[1]
— Anna Marolt Tolich, Slovenian immigrant

Industrial America often startled newcomers, who embodied the high tide of American immigration—a total of roughly nine million new arrivals from 1901–1910.[2] Many, like the Slovenian Marolt family, had come from green, flower-filled rural districts and had rarely seen a factory or mine. The Marolts settled down in coal-blackened Sunnyside and learned the rhythm of an isolated company town, while around them, older, independent settlements enjoyed private telephones, better roads, and expanding markets. Thrown together in this still-isolated valley, its spectrum of residents seemed to reflect historian Robert Wiebe's vision of early twentieth-century America: an original "society of island communities" swept up in an urban-industrial river where "men [and women] were now separated more by skill and occupation" than by geography.[3] Castle Valley residents tried to maintain their community balance in the oncoming rush of further industrialization, immigration, and active Progressive reform.

To some extent, modern technology helped break down geographical barriers, whether for good or ill. Many technological changes slid easily into place, grafted on previous successes. For example, Justus Wellington (Wink) Seely spearheaded innovations in his hometown, Castle Dale. Since 1893, he had owned the Eagle Flouring Mill with his brother, Orange, and became sole owner in 1899. He then converted the mill by pulling out the old burrs and putting in a set of rollers for more efficient milling. In 1904, he added a big boiler to help power a new electric light plant, the

Justus Wellington Seely, or Wink, appears as the progressive gentleman he was. By the turn of the century, when this photo was taken, he had helped establish many of the improvements in his home town, Castle Dale. Courtesy of Emery County Archives.

first electrification on the eastern side of the Wasatch Plateau. By 1909, his plant had metamorphosed into the Electric Power and Milling Company to supply both Orangeville and Castle Dale with lights and power and to operate the first purely municipal telephone. Seely had also provided his sturdy brick house with electrical wiring (the second man in Castle Dale to do so, after his brother, William), and his wife, Mary Jorgenson Seely, owned the first electric iron in town.[4] In 1918, he even installed an indoor bathroom, including the second bathtub brought to Castle Dale. When Seely strung the telephone line between the mill and his house, he made two immediate impacts. First, his wife could finally plan the size of her dinners. The Seely brothers had long been in the habit of bringing mill customers home to eat. Now, Wink could call Mary to let her know how many people to expect. Second, his children had a new diversion. They prepared recitations to say over the phone, with one child at the mill and one at home. Neighbors found the new invention just as attractive; some would call the mill just to hear a voice coming over the wire.[5]

At nearby Huntington, the new miller, Olaf W. Sandberg, also turned to electricity. Sandberg, a child of Swedish LDS converts, had emigrated with his family in 1878 at age two, making an eleven-week steamship crossing and arriving in Utah by train once they had been cleared through Ellis Island. Starting at age fourteen he had learned his craft by apprenticeship, growing up in Washington County, Utah, then milling in Idaho, Oregon, and Sanpete County, Utah. While visiting the Bryner family, his wife's relatives, in Price, he heard that the Huntington mill was for sale. In an increasingly typical technological mix, after Sandberg bought this mill, the family crossed over Salina Canyon in their Studebaker; a friend brought their belongings with horse and wagon. Sandberg immediately made changes in Castle Valley agriculture. At the time, local residents raised"two-crop" wheat from seeds planted in the spring. When little of it grew, farmers would irrigate their fields to encourage a second crop. Appalled by its poor quality, Sandberg shipped in two carloads of hard wheat, picked it up with his wagon at the Price depot, and gave it to local farmers as seed for fall planting. After that, he had almost more work than he could handle.[6] His son, Willard Sandberg, who succeeded him as miller, remembered, "He went to Utah Power and Light. And I think he had to pay $2,500 to have them put a line . . . about two blocks. And he had to sign a guarantee of so much power usage a year. He had to buy the wiring, and he had to buy the transformers." After that, he could mill year-round. The old Pelton wheel, which had run the mill through water power in the fall, winter (afternoons only, when the creek melted), and spring, was buried in the wheelhouse where it stood.[7]

Today, the profound impact of now-commonplace innovations like electricity and the telephone can hardly be imagined. Electricity, harnessed back in 1879 when Thomas Edison invented the incandescent light bulb, changed the way America lived. No longer did the rhythm of life depend on sunrise, sunset, and the flickering kerosene lamp or hearthfire. Communities became locked into a single power system, as Utah Power and Light Company (UP&L), incorporated in 1912, stretched throughout parts of Utah. As early local companies formed, they passed many expenses on to the consumer, just as UP&L had charged Sandberg to wire his mill. By the early 1900s, builders nationwide generally charged $12 to wire new homes, with an additional fee of $2.50 per outlet (explaining why older homes generally have but a single outlet in each room). Homeowners electrifying existing buildings could select a payment plan that stretched out for as long as two years. For decades, installations remained primitive. To run appliances, for example, residents typically had to unscrew a light bulb hanging from a ceiling wire, put a plug in its place, and then plug in the apparatus they wished to use. To provide the copper wire needed for all these connections, copper mines and smelters expanded, and needed more coke (such as that from Castle Valley). Households lost their self-sufficiency as people came to depend on an electrical system and a far-away generator for their power. Of course, in isolated Castle Valley, this benefit sometimes took a long time coming. Ranches outside of Ferron and along Miller Creek finally got electric power through the Rural Electric Committee in the 1940s.[8]

The telephone, too, connected a widening circle of people. When Alexander Graham Bell first patented the device in 1876, he modestly billed it as "an improvement on the telegraph." Soon, however, his invention fostered a stunning infrastructure of its own, including the first central telephone exchange (serving twenty-one subscribers in New Haven, Connecticut, in 1878); the invention of switchboards, the replacement of the original rowdy male operators (who sometimes used rude language) by more mannerly females, the first publication of telephone books, and the proliferation of hundreds of thousands of independent local exchanges, like the one in Castle Dale. By 1900, Americans owned 1.3 million telephones and would acquire 12 million more by 1920. Castle Valley's connections, like those elsewhere, were originally do-it-yourself efforts. In 1907, the U.S. Bureau of Commerce and Labor counted over 17,000 separate, private, rural circuits all of which relied on ringing the operator to get a connection. This system gradually faded as the Bell System started buying up competitors, beginning in 1908, and replaced the "hello girls" with machinery, continuing its growth even after a Justice Department challenge to its monopoly in 1913.[9]

On the other hand, despite the telephone's rapid proliferation nationwide, parts of Castle Valley remained unconnected. This convenience did not reach Lawrence, east of Huntington, until 1952, when thirty-six families could pay the $25 necessary for installation. Well into the 1980s, families in Nine Mile Canyon, northeast of Wellington, had to ring the Salt Lake City operator to make a connection. Using an old hand-crank phone, a caller could ring the operator, give her the number, hang up while the operator made the connection, and pick up again when the phone rang. Since all Nine Mile ranches were on a single party line, each subscriber had a characteristic ring: two short, or three long, or some other combination. Whether they listened in on their neighbors' calls was pretty much up to them. The telephone line itself remained the old telegraph line strung in 1886–1887 by the Ninth Cavalry at Fort Duchesne on metal poles, installed after the first wooden ones had been cut down, allegedly by Indians for firewood. Yet as Wellington's Tom McCourt wrote, "[A]nyone with common sense could see that telegraph poles would have made much better building material for settlers than firewood for Indians. Firewood was plentiful. . . . long, straight fence poles and roof beams were in short supply."[10]

In Price, telephone connections began early under the leadership of Reuben G. Miller, Emery Stake President and local entrepreneur. Born to an enterprising family, Reuben G. built upon the cattle and sheep empire originated by his father and uncles in the late 1800s. Like so many other Mormon stockmen, the Miller brothers had come into Castle Valley around 1880. They apparently forged a deal with the Whitmores that the Millers would run their stock south of the Price River, while the Whitmore animals grazed north of it. By the twentieth century, the Millers operated in a huge area along the western edge of Castle Valley. A political activist, Reuben G. Miller became a county official upon the creation of Carbon County in 1894, joined the first Utah state senate in 1896, and represented Carbon County in the state house of representatives beginning in 1898. He helped build up Castle Valley after becoming Emery Stake president in 1899, fostering the reopening of Castle Dale's Emery Stake Academy after its forced closure in the Panic of 1893. In Price, where he lived, he and his family became the major stockholders in the Price Cooperative Mercantile Institution and joined Tobe Whitmore in setting up the First National Bank in Price, both in 1901. In 1902–1903, Miller served one term as Price Town President, purchasing a site for a reservoir, another parcel for town expansion northward, and establishing an official freighters' campground southwest of town. He simultaneously served on the Price school board, and from 1905–1910, actively promoted the Eastern Utah Telephone Company. His son, J. Rex Miller, later managed the telephone company, which linked the three exchanges (with over 750 stations, or subscribers) at Price, Helper, and Scofield to the Mountain States Telephone line at Vernal. In 1919, the company got permission to extend a line to Green River, allowing the previously-separate Green River Valley Telephone Company's subscribers to call long distance to Denver and the East.[11]

Despite his public progressivism, Miller's life reflected private contradictions. Rolla West remembered that Miller "had quite a little telephone company and [was] doing good, but he forgot about the [Woodruff] Manifesto, and got away from home over in Emery County, and he married another woman and got another family."[12] Specifically, he took his first plural wife, Martha ("Mattie") Nelson, in 1903, and she bore his daughter a year later. Broadening the reach of "the principle," he apparently encouraged, participated, or acquiesced in the plural marriage of G. F. Hickman, principal of the Emery Stake Academy, to one of the teachers, Chloe Palmer, in 1910. Miller continued in polygamy even after the death of his plural wife in 1912. A year later, with his first wife still living, he married a third woman, Emma Crossland (or Emma Mills). This time, the LDS Church excommunicated him, marking a new public response to an old practice.[13] As historian Edward Geary wrote, "In spite of the church's formal renunciation of polygamy in 1890, the period from 1900 to 1910 brought a rash of clandestine plural marriages with the tacit approval (if not the active encouragement) of some church leaders. . . . More than one plural marriage took place in Emery County during this period."[14]

In many ways, Miller had simply stayed in step with his church, as America discovered to its horror when the Utah legislature elected LDS Apostle Reed Smoot to the U.S. Senate in 1903. Smoot's political opponents remembered the outcome just four years earlier, when polygamous Democrat Brigham H. Roberts had been denied his seat in the U.S. House of Representatives since his second wife had recently borne twins.[15] Exercising its constitutional privilege to vet its own members, the Senate impaneled a Committee on Privileges and Elections to investigate Smoot. They soon heard LDS President Joseph F. Smith testify that he indeed had five wives and had continued living with all of them since the 1890 Woodruff Manifesto. Americans were shocked out of their complacent, monogamous presumptions—that the LDS Church had ordered the abandonment of polygamy before statehood. The *New York Times* correctly observed that "the law of the land is not obeyed in good faith" by the LDS Church and that "Smoot is also a representative of that institution."[16] That truth, however, did not make Smoot a polygamist. He was not. Nonetheless, in the 1904 Utah election campaign, the losing Democrats condemned polygamy; the triumphant Republicans (Smoot's party) ignored it, and the anti-Mormon American party (a resuscitated Liberal Party) took Salt Lake City. When in 1906 the Senate's Committee on Privileges and Elections voted seven to five to unseat Smoot, the issue then went to the Senate as a whole. But the political tide had begun to turn. Smoot's Republicans triumphed in Utah elections in 1906, entrenching the Federal Bunch, a Republican political machine which functioned smoothly until 1916. On February 20, 1907, the Senate voted 42 to 28 to expel Smoot, falling well short of the two-thirds (59) needed for his expulsion.[17] After the vote, one senator remarked, "I don't see why we can't get along just as well with a polygamist who doesn't polyg as we do with a lot of monogamists who don't monog."[18] Privately, Smoot lobbied his fellow Apostles to end polygamy. As the first generation of Mormon leaders passed away, the LDS Church finally came more into line with American expectations and the issue of Mormon plural marriage faded from the national press. Smoot himself went on to a long senatorial service with significant national ramifications.

Smoot joined a Congress heavily caught up in its own turmoil, complicated by the president's push for Progressive reforms. Republican Theodore Roosevelt had won the presidency in his own right in 1904, emboldening his reform efforts. A few months prior to the election, Roosevelt's second Public Lands Commission had issued a partial report on national land fraud, augmented in February 1905. Both findings went directly to the President, since Congress, especially the Senate, harbored far too many "friends of business." For example, Wyoming's Senator, Clarence Don Clark, was the brother of Dyer O. Clark, manager of the Union Pacific Coal Company and heavily involved in western coal land fraud. In those days, when state legislatures elected U.S. Senators, Clark had essentially purchased his seat with a handful of well-placed bribes. The same could be said of so many others that contemporary journalist David Graham Phillips wrote of "The Treason of the Senate" in his 1906 series of muckraking articles for *Cosmopolitan* magazine.[19] Therefore, President Roosevelt took the public lands report to Congress himself and recommended, among other measures, that it pass a coal land leasing law and halt all sales of the coal-bearing public domain. Congress stalled, demanding a study. Fresh from a judicial victory over the trusts in the 1904 *Northern Securities Case,* Roosevelt used his executive power to send special investigators from the Department of Justice to identify land fraud throughout the West—including Utah.[20]

While this sparring rattled Congress, a slew of capitalists descended on Castle Valley coalfields in the summer of 1905. Utah Fuel geologist Robert Forrester continued lining up false claimants (dummies) to expand the Western's coal land holdings, working just ahead of federal surveyor Joseph Taff of the Geological Survey (USGS) who, with his crew, meticulously mapped coal-bearing sections and falsely-claimed "grazing" lands on the valley's heights.[21] Simultaneously, the paper reported plans of the San Pedro, Los Angeles, and Salt Lake Railroad (usually called the San Pedro) to build a line west over the Wasatch Plateau and north through the Castle Valley corridor in direct competition with the Rio Grande. "It goes without saying," the article noted, "that the Gould interests, who heretofore have practically had a monopoly on Utah coal, will fight the new project to a standstill."[22] In just one example of local corporate machinations, Huntington Canyon became a tensely-watched battleground. Emery County surveyor William J. Tidwell, secretly working for the Rio Grande, kept up a barrage of reports to his bosses. He described the comings and goings of Huntington's George M. Miller and his partner, banker George C. Whitmore of Nephi (brother of Tobe Whitmore of Price). They jockeyed for coal land position with Don C. Robbins, a long-time Emery County mining man, and his associates: members of the Filer, Senior, and Freed families. Whitmore, Tidwell reported, held an option for $250,000, payable if the San Pedro successfully developed Huntington Canyon coal.[23] The UP was also trying to bribe its way into the good graces of the Miller-Whitmore-San Pedro partnership by placing "$10,000 to Miller's credit on condition that he could get or would agree in writing to get titles to the land which he has not yet got." Miller then proposed to buy Robbins out for $10,000 or jump his claims. Appalled, Whitmore tried to break the partnership. Robbins, meanwhile, refused to sell, and "had men go over to his claims . . . to keep possession or kill Miller's men." Tidwell added, "I have Miller watched."[24] Meanwhile, Walter Filer, son-in-law of Charles M. Freed, unilaterally offered to sell his group's claims to the Union Pacific Railroad for $75 an acre, a price between the $15 per acre they had paid for "grazing" land and its

real $300 per acre value.[25] In the end, despite all this maneuvering, the
San Pedro never built into Castle Valley and the Union Pacific stayed out
of Huntington Canyon coal. A major stumbling-block to their success came
when President Roosevelt abruptly withdrew all available public lands from
entry beginning in mid-1906. In Utah, thousands of acres suddenly became
unavailable.[26]

Before the withdrawal, new developers actually managed to open a
mine. In 1902, twenty-three-year-old Arthur A. Sweet had entered the coal
game by filing an individual claim for land near Sunnyside. Chased off by
Rio Grande gunmen, he eventually sold out to the railroad's agents.[27] Four
years later, he was back in company with his brothers Frederick, C. N., and
William, armed with new knowledge of local terrain. Spring Glen resident
Heber J. Stowell had located a coal outcropping in the ledge above his
home in 1904 and told Price's W. H. Lawley. Lawley contacted neighbor
Henry Wade, who relayed the information to his son-in-law, Arthur Sweet.
After a brief false start, most of these men cooperated in the well-named Independent Coal and Coke Company (IC&C), meaning they had their own
financing, independent of any railroad. They added as secretary and treasurer newly-arrived Spring Glen homesteader, Lucius H. Curtis, who had
obtained more of the rocky cliffside using the federal Timber and Stone
Act, swearing he intended to sell building stone at Helper (surrounded by
its own prodigiously rocky slopes). By 1907, the IC&C had bought the Price
Trading Company's Aberdeen Mine above Spring Glen and had founded
its own town and mines called Kenilworth, allegedly because the three high,
adjacent cliffs resembled the three towers of Scotland's Kenilworth Castle.
The IC&C shortly began shipping coal in direct competition with the Rio
Grande mines (and, thanks to the scrutiny of ongoing federal investigations, using the D&RGW tracks). The new coal company also condemned a
railroad right-of-way through Spring Glen for its spur line, the Kenilworth
and Helper Railroad Company, and purchased a Shay engine to pull cars
up the steep mountain grade. It hired a doctor for the rising company town
and attracted a polyglot assortment of laborers: Greeks from the Western's
section gang at Helper, Italians earlier blacklisted from the mines, and locals previously employed in other lines of work.[28]

Throughout the United States, growth meant jobs and jobs attracted
immigrants. Over a million arrived in 1905 for the very first time. Although
Utah found it necessary to establish a Bureau of Immigration in 1911, hundreds had arrived in Castle Valley well before that. The Japanese, for example, brought in to work the coal in the strike of 1903–1904, replaced
striking "dining room girls" at the Rio Grande Hotel in Helper three years
later. Their availability as strike-breakers diminished as the pressure of West
Coast politicians led to the 1907 "Gentleman's Agreement," made formal
by the Root-Takahira Agreement in 1908. Japanese laborers could no longer enter the U.S.[29] Other nationalities kept coming. Plenty of other single
men made this trip, sometimes accompanied—or later followed—by wives
and families. In 1905, the State Coal Mine Inspector made his first report of

These Greek immigrant coal miners (Michael Kontas on the right) posed for their picture, show-ing off all the tools of their trade: their lunch buckets, shovel, drill, and miner's caps with at-tached lights. They would send this picture home to relatives (often illiterate) to show that they were working and prospering in far-away America. Courtesy of Western Mining and Railroad Museum.

miners' "Nationalities," listed here from the largest to the smallest groups: Americans (including all white, native English-speakers, including British citizens), Austrians, Italians, Finns, Greeks, Germans, Japanese, Negroes (who weren't considered Americans), Swedes, Slavs, and Mexicans, with no numbers given for Spanish and Chinese.[30] By 1908, Carbon County had almost one thousand Italian residents (the most of any Utah county), with northern Italians outnumbering their southern brethren by two to one. The paper felt compelled to add: "among them are very many good citizens, in fact they predominate."[31]

Nonetheless, Helen Barboglio Leavitt, the child of an Italian immigrant, remembered that her father helped found the *Stella D'America* lodge "as a protection against the prejudices of other Utahns in the area. It provided small loans to its members in good standing, and aided them with the courts in getting their citizenship."[32] Stella D'America, founded in Castle Gate in 1898 (and moved to Helper in 1903 during the strike) served the northern Italians, separated from their southern brethren by problems at home. Another lodge, Principe Di Napoli, probably originated among southern Italians, but fused with Stella D'America in the strike of 1903. Men joined, paid regular dues, and espoused loyalty to America and American ideals.[33] In the absence of any kind of state or national insurance, lodges provided the best guarantee of a decent burial (often photographed, with an open coffin, to reassure families back home of the presence of a priest and mourners) and basic provision for widows and fatherless children.

People known locally as Austrians also had specific lodges for each of their ethnic groups. Slovenians often joined the Western Slavonic Lodge, or the rival *Slovenska Narodna Poporna Jednota* (Slovene National Benefit Society or SNPJ). In 1909, John Juvan helped found SNPJ Lodge 32 at Winter Quarters, which later established off-shoot lodges. Serbs had the Serb National Federation; Croatians organized the Croatian Fraternal Union. In Sunnyside, disabled miner Tony Krissman swore in new members of the Croatian Fraternal Union, some as young as five-year-old Anna Marolt.[34]

Krissman had arrived in America with his disability, one of the very few immigrants ever to enter the States that way. He had his left leg severed below the knee, and apparently got through immigration thanks to relatives in Colorado who sent affidavits that he would not become a public charge. He moved to Sunnyside in 1905, where people saw him every day, carrying his picks into the mine. Soon, his wife joined him. Later they sent for their six children, who traveled with their grandmother across the Atlantic. Ellis Island was a whole new world to eleven-year-old Mary Krissman Topolovec. Officials separated women and men. Mary's brothers had all their belongings, including her grandmother's sack with whiskey in it. Afraid at the separation, the girls kept crying until an interpreter asked them the trouble. He took them up on a balcony rimming the grand entrance hall to look for their brothers. The girls spotted them, selling Grandma's liquor

South Slav men and boys, dressed in their finest, pose at Sunnyside, holding items that show their prosperity (bottles of liquor, a parrot, a rifle, and an accordian). Those identified are (sitting in front, left to right), John Russ, Joe Petronel (with parrot), unknown [with rifle] and Frank Zupon Sr. with the accordian. Behind Petronel stands Leonard Mahorich. The man standing on the far left was known locally as "Mustacher," carved gravestones, and went back to Yugoslavia around 1913. The man on the right holding the bottle is John Vuksinick, who helped open Sunnyside in 1898. At the rear, second from right, is Frank Mezek. Photo courtesy of Western Mining and Railroad Museum.

and circling an old African American to see if, as they had been told on the boat over, he really had a tail. The family was reunited, but still had to wait on the island for nineteen days until trains rolled to Sunnyside and back, carrying affidavits from Tony and Anna Verzuh Krissman assuring the support of these dependents.[35]

Others also came through Ellis Island, including Rose Katalin Brajkovich from Croatia. She remembered that all the women on her ship were forced to strip en masse, and had their clothes bundled up, labeled with their names, and sent out for fumigation. Brajkovich had previously always kept both clean and modest, wearing her petticoat to wash her dress, then changing into her dress to wash her petticoat. But one old Italian lady on the ship had been discovered with lice, she said, so she and many others had to suffer this embarrassment.[36] Mary Zagar Dupin also made the trip through Ellis Island after emigrating from Slovenia in 1910. While the family waited for processing, her mother got her a banana—a new, unfamiliar fruit—and cut it in slices. Mary pointed out that others had peeled theirs first. "Yes," said her mother, "they peel pears and apples, too, and that's extravagant" and made her eat it with the peel on. Mary did not eat a second banana for a long, long time.[37]

Immigrants and Americans learned to get along. For example, Slovenian Martin Millarich moved from Kenilworth to Spring Glen late in 1907 and built a saloon, getting a county license a year later.[38] Millarich's daughter remembered that "[LDS] Bishop [John] Rowley [told her father] . . . that the Mormons didn't approve of his having a tavern there." Her father replied, "'You know, Mr. Rowley, the road out front runs right past this place, & the door swings open & shut for whoever wishes to enter, but I do not go out into the street & grab people by the arm & force them to come in.' He had no problems after that."[39] Often more acculturated children became go-betweens, easing their parents' transition. For example, Marie Auphand Fidell, who immigrated from France in 1901, often had to translate for her mother. "We all got along even if my mother couldn't speak very much," she later remembered. "All the people got along really good."[40]

To a point, that is. While Kenilworth was under construction, for example, the IC&C tolerated peddler-farmers such as the Saccomannos, established in Spring Glen since 1903, who alternated selling farm produce with mining at Kenilworth. In 1909, however, when Spring Glen neighbors James Rolando and Martin Millarich raised over a hundred dollars by subscription and begun to improve the road between Spring Glen and the now-established camp of Kenilworth, the company objected. Officials wished to confine miners to trading at the company store and obtained an injunction forbidding peddlers from entering its camp. Helper's John Diamanti, a Greek immigrant, sued. The local newspaper editorialized that the injunction "should be strongly resented by every citizen in and around the camp, and for that matter . . . by every citizen of the state and nation, because it [the injunction] . . . strikes at the very root of our democratic institutions." The court agreed; the injunction was lifted, and peddling continued.[41] Northern Italians John Marchello and Gabriella Clerico, Spring Glen neighbors, each had their regular customers among the coal camps. Marchello, raised on an Italian farm, had returned to farming in 1912 when he developed severe asthma and could no longer work in the mines. "He peddled . . . up Spring Canyon to Standardville, Latuda, and to Kenilworth," remembered his son, Martin, who had accompanied him until he was old enough to go to school. John peddled daily, loading his small buggy with "a dozen bunches of carrots, a dozen bunches of beets, a box of live chickens, two to three boxes of peppers, some cucumbers, or whatever was available." He also sold his second crop of hay in Latuda, to feed the mine's horses and mules. "Sometimes our wagon would be on one side of the street, and the Clerico's—or someone else's—on the other," Marchello added.[42] Despite old-country traditions that sequestered mothers and daughters in the home, Gabriella Clerico defied the norm. She had joined her coal-miner husband, Battista, in America after cooking for a rich family in northern Italy, near Turin. Consequently, she could make delicious butter and cheese for sale. She also peddled cherries, apples, pears, apricots, and peaches, grown in the

An unidentified Italian fruit peddler poses with his team, wagon, and children, all of which represented his wealth. Children very commonly accompanied their parents on peddling trips after helping to harvest and pack foodstuffs for sale. Courtesy of Western Mining and Railroad Museum.

relatively sheltered valley of Spring Glen where the family had planted an orchard after a mine accident disabled Battista, driving them back to the soil. They also raised a garden and bred rabbits, remembered her youngest son, Pete, who frequently accompanied her on her twice-weekly trips, mostly to Helper, Spring Glen, and Castle Gate. The IC&C remained disturbed by this seasonal traffic, and, in 1912, again tried to shut out peddlers. The suit, this time decided in Salt Lake City, overturned the coal camp's prohibition on peddling.[43]

As the American economy expanded in the early 1900s, other entrepreneurs saw different money-making visions in Castle Valley. Frank Cook and E. T. Merritt took a hard look at Green River and saw a future farming paradise. Merritt, originally attracted by the 1901 oil boom, realized that a lot of disappointed people could not afford the expensive orchard land then for sale in western Colorado and decided to attract them further west. He began buying up area ranches in 1904. By 1906, he and Cook had formed the Cook and Merritt Land Company and the Green River Land and Townsite Company.[44] To provide water to the expanded townsite, Cook took a spot on the board of the newly-incorporated Green River Canal Company in 1904, which had acquired the holdings of older irrigation associations. Doing his own part for irrigation, Merritt orchestrated what became known as "the forty-two foot lift" of the old dam, facilitating efforts to draw

Men trying to figure out how to float the Undine, gone aground on her maiden trip from Green River toward Moab. Courtesy of Marriott Library Special Collections, University of Utah.

irrigation water from the river up to the townsite on the bluffs above with giant water wheels (some of which remained well into the 1970s). In good Progressive fashion, Merritt left a place in the new dam for an electrical power plant to be installed later, a plant actually constructed in 1914. The dam itself, completed late in 1906, was only six weeks old when the annual spring ice breakup on the Green River took it out. Undaunted, engineer George Thurman headed up the rebuilding project after stipulating that he be given complete charge and a free hand. Under his direction, the dam rose again and Thurman remained as director, and then president, of the Green River Canal Company for over forty years.[45]

Starting out from the revitalized town, no longer a rowdy end-of-track, Capt. Frank Summerill, in 1901, had launched the steamboat *Undine*, a combination freighter and pleasure craft, which lasted a year before foundering. In 1905, Capt. H. T. Yokey built the two-deck sternwheeler, *Cliff Dweller*, and tried to cruise to Moab (site of the old Elk Mountain Mission) on the Colorado above its confluence with the Green River. His craft ran out of fuel before it completed the voyage. Once coal arrived to fire its boilers, the boat chugged back to Green River where it was rebuilt and rechristened *The City of Moab*. It again failed to reach its destination and was eventually moved to the Great Salt Lake for other pleasure excursions.[46]

Thus, very early in its history, Castle Valley residents experienced the romance of wilderness, an impulse just taking hold in the eastern United States. The notion of wilderness as romantic originated with some early mountain men, grew with the writings of Henry David Thoreau, and even inspired scientific observer John Wesley Powell in some of his lyrical descriptions of Castle Valley's azure cliffs and remote grandeur. By the turn of the century, as cities and farms covered the remotest corners of the West, appreciation of unspoiled nature had become more widespread. The hunter-friendly Boone and Crockett Club, founded by Theodore Roosevelt in 1888, espoused a hairy-chested philosophy which turned city slickers into robust sportsmen through taming supposedly savage nature. The Sierra Club, formed four years later, wanted to preserve nature untamed. Locally, Castle Valley's widespread practice of Eastering down on the San Rafael Desert to celebrate the end of winter's cabin fever was well-established by 1910 and persists into the twenty-first century.[47] In short, as the Progressive Era wore on, the general public increasingly experienced the wild outdoors (perhaps even with a sail down the Green River).

Transportation improved in other ways. Cars were coming. As early as 1902, Congress had debated the first specific proposal for federally funded highways, though it was tabled. That same year, private parties founded the American Automobile Association, which cooperated with the National Grange in holding a Good Roads Conventions five years later. Meanwhile, Castle Valley residents struggled and finally succeeded in improving local roads and bridges. By the early 1900s, Emery County was putting every spare cent into roads and bridges, bettering connections to the towns along the skirts of the Wasatch Plateau all the way from Emery to Price, east over the Green River, and across the San Rafael River. When rains and floods in September 1909 washed out every bridge on the Emery-Price road except the one at Huntington, Emery County floated its first bonds to fund steel bridges. Out at Green River, townswomen passed a petition requesting a new bridge and feted the investigating state politicians with songs, banners, and a banquet at the Palmer House. The state then provided Green River with $35,000 of the $45,000 it cost to replace the old ferry with a reliable steel bridge.[48]

This robust town, a magnet for state funding, grew from "the land boom of 1905–08," Green River resident Una Gillies remembered, when "hundreds of people from the Middle West came here hoping to make a fortune in peaches."[49] The first peach orchards along the Green had dried up when the dam went in 1907, but Merritt, undaunted, platted a grand townsite, selling land all over the country, including a lot for a livery stable to former outlaw Matt Warner (now gone straight). In August 1906, R. M. Eldred and Frank Cook had opened a new bank. Farmers tried planting melons, building on the hard-won knowledge of John F. ("Melon") Brown that Green River's soils and climate were particularly ideal for cantaloupes. In the fall of 1907, Green River settlers had marketed more than ten thousand crates of cantaloupes in Denver and Chicago, and celebrated its first annual Melon Day a year later. Also in 1907, the town had inaugurated its own local telephone system. In October 1906, a group had gathered at the swanky Palmer House, formed a Presbyterian church building committee, and committed to raising $2,500 for a church building. Green River Townsite Company donated the land and townsfolk celebrated the church dedication a year later.[50]

The Presbyterians had entered the Castle Valley mission field in 1905, starting at Ferron. The town was thriving, due in part to newly planted apple orchards, and more so due to its famous peaches, grown commercially ever since John Lemon hauled in 2,500 trees from Grand Junction around 1900. Rev. J. G. MacGillivray, the head of Presbyterian Sunday Schools throughout Utah, led rousing revivals in a gospel tent near the orchards that summer. By then, greater Utah had accepted Presbyterians as respectable after a rough beginning. They had entered Utah with the transcontinental railroad, but the earliest pastors had faced harassment and the Saints who aided these gentiles suffered stiff LDS discipline. By 1905, however, the LDS *Deseret News* was complimenting Presbyterian education in Salt Lake City. Consequently, before he left Ferron, MacGillivray selected a local site for a combined church and school and raised $1,000 towards construction. He reported his activities to the Women's Board of Home Missions, which, in the late 1890s, had assumed responsibility for Presbyterian education— one of those national reforms that saw women's moral influence spreading from home to the public sphere. The Board approved his efforts, reporting in its 1906 minutes that "Emery county . . . is virgin territory for missionary enterprise. . . . The communities are Mormon through and through but are generally of a more liberal type. A petition has been signed in Ferron by fifty persons—some of them Mormons—asking that we enter permanently in that town."[51] The Presbyterians had chosen an auspicious time, for Ferron had begun to prosper, inaugurating its famous Peach Days that same year, now said to be the oldest continuous celebration in Utah. After a few false starts, MacGillivray became pastor at the Ferron Church and taught classics and mathematics at the Forsythe Memorial Chapel School House, completed in 1911. He and three other teachers taught over one hundred students, making the Presbyterian school, for a time, the largest in Emery County. His successor dedicated a separate church building in 1914, which hosted services until the American Legion bought the building in 1942.[52]

Harmony did not necessarily accompany growth. In 1900, Utah Fuel had installed at Sunnyside new mine pumps, fans, pipelines, and water tanks and improved mining apparatus, housing, and community buildings. A year later the company added 100 more cottages, complete with electric lights and running water. It also built a church, school, hospital, boarding house, and company store for its town, whose population had now reached 1,500.[53] All of this development took water. The company had been drawing all it needed for Sunnyside from two wells by Grassy Trail Creek which ran right through the town. Water trouble had begun in 1902 when rancher

George C. Whitmore sued the Utah Fuel and the Rio Grande Western Railway over their wells. He claimed that so much sub-surface water now flowed into Sunnyside that some of the springs on Whitmore's range were going dry. He won all rights to the water, which did not stop Utah Fuel. Whitmore sued again in 1905, and legal testimony grew to over 1,500 pages as the case dragged on and on. The same year, the coal company condemned lands for a reservoir, tunnel, and pipeline at Range Creek, just east of Grassy Trail Creek. In the second contest Whitmore won judgment for $12,500 for water illegally taken. Meanwhile, the company set up a pumping station at Range Creek and hired a married couple to tend it. A string of pack mules traversed the trail daily in summer, as the couple stocked provisions to keep them going when winter snow drifts—often ten to twenty feet high—cut them off completely except for a telephone connected to the pump house in Sunnyside. Next, Utah Fuel, now supplied with water from Range Creek, sued Whitmore and associates in 1909, trying to get back the water from Grassy Trail Creek. This litigation continued until 1920, outliving George Whitmore by three years. Unsuccessful in the courts, in 1921, the Utah Fuel Company finally got a private bill through Congress which allowed it a water supply for Sunnyside, allegedly partly for conserving the water and timber on these lands.[54]

In one way or another, local developments prospered, and the national economy hummed along nicely. Through most of 1907, prices rose on nails, flour, shoes, pianos, and everything imaginable.[55] In early fall, an Indiana banker claimed, "We could not if we would stop this onward march of progress, we might as well try to stop the ebb and flow of the ocean tide."[56] Wages rose more slowly, but they rose. In Castle Valley coal mines, each man made from $8–$10 per shift. Utah got more "American" miners (a category which included all native English-speakers, including citizens of the British Isles) as the Wyoming coal mines decreased their hours. The racially-biased *Advocate,* very much in step with the times, reported that for the first time in twenty-five years the mines would be fully staffed, as whites replaced so-called coolie labor.[57]

Then, disaster hit. The great New York banks had overextended themselves in keeping up with nation-wide speculation, like the oil, coal, railroad, and irrigation projects that dotted Castle Valley. By mid-October 1907, banks froze assets, tightened credit, and some closed their doors. Another Panic had begun. Roosevelt's secretary of the treasury cooperated with J. P. Morgan in switching millions of dollars in Treasury funds from one bank to another to keep them open. The president also issued $150 million in Treasury certificates and bonds, putting more paper in circulation to cover over-extended reserves. Congress considered a currency bill based on railroad and municipal bonds, finally passing a much-watered-down version. By December 1907, Castle Valley residents could read in the local newspaper the salient points of President Roosevelt's up-beat message to Congress: business was fundamentally sound; an emergency currency was needed; trust-busting should continue; the federal government needed to regulate strikes and lockouts; irrigation must expand; the government should protect the small landholder; the nation needed a Bureau of Mines, and the armed forces should be expanded.[58] Despite this public optimism, Roosevelt wrote privately of the Panic that "the damage actually done was great, and the damage threatened was incalculable," predictably crediting the federal government with holding off its worst effects.[59]

As in the rest of America, the Panic wreaked havoc in Castle Valley, but it did so selectively. Its impact showed clearly which of Castle Valley's industries connected with other businesses, and in what ways. The railroad mines, largely dedicated to producing coke for the Smelter Trust, felt the weight of plant shut-downs across the West. In early fall 1907, copper smelters closed at Butte and Anaconda, which, in turn, snuffed out 250 Castle Gate coke ovens and then reached out to Sunnyside. The PVCC and Utah Fuel laid off miners and sold their coal within the state. Joyfully, coal retailers, for once, met all their orders and stockpiled coal for what they hoped would be a coming boom. It never materialized. By November, the Panic had hit Utah. The railroad mines began paying partly in cash, partly in checks, while the D&RGW itself gave only checks to its workers.[60] By early 1908, the Rio Grande's coal mines had reduced coal prices for the very first time and were turning away two or three men for every job the company filled. The railroad mines worked only four days a week in January 1908, dropping in February to six or seven days for the entire month. George Gould, head of the Rio Grande system and other lines, was accused of sheer meanness as he yanked twenty-five years' worth of labor advances from his striking shopmen at Denver and Salt Lake City. By the end of the Panic he had earned the name, "The Sick Man of Wall Street" as his railroad empire crumbled.[61]

When the hard-pressed Rio Grande would only take cash in payment for shipping sheep, the wool trade suffered and the railroad lost money. Wool had previously been a big money-maker, since the sheep industry had flourished in Castle Valley since the 1870s. By the early 1900s, traditional LDS sheepmen like Karl Seely of Castle Dale wintered six thousand head of sheep and one hundred head of cattle on the San Rafael Desert and drove them to the Manti National Forest in summer. Immigrant sheepmen also swelled the wool trade, just as other foreigners had increased mining production. Frenchman Honore Dusserre, dean of the local French and French Basque sheepmen, had begun raising sheep in Castle Valley in 1892 and brought an additional twelve thousand head from California in 1896. Like every other local stockman, he moved his herds seasonally, driving his sheep over 175 miles from winter pasture on the San Rafael Desert to summer pasture in Whitmore Canyon, Scofield, and at Beaver, about 20 miles northwest of Price. He helped a lot of other sheepmen get started, especially fellow countrymen. For example, Honore (Henry) and Pierre (Pete)

Moynier also left California for Price, traveling from Bakersfield in 1898. First working as herders (possibly for Dusserre), they saved up enough money to go into business for themselves in 1903. By 1910, they had purchased a sizable home in Price (now eligible for the National Register of Historic Places). Samson Iriart, originally a member of the Basque Colony at Tehachipi in the mountains south of California's great Central Valley, had migrated to Price between 1909 and 1911, where he tried his hand at the sheep business. Although he was back in Tehachipi by 1920, his relative, Bernard Iriart, Sr., remained in the wool business in Castle Valley virtually until his death in 1980. Likewise, Basque Gratien Echibarne brought a large herd to Clark's Valley, northeast of Wellington, in 1910. He actually filed on the land in 1916, and became one of the main promoters of a little town called Kiz, after the first woman to reside there: Kiziah Dimick, the wife of settler Ephriam Dimick.[62]

Most of the sheepmen, native-born Mormons and foreign immigrants alike, joined together at corrals along the railroad for the annual spring shearing. As Seely told a later interviewer, "The shearing is done at the Mounds shearing corrals, at Mounds, Emery Co., Utah. The shearers work for the corral at so much per head doing all the herds that shear there."[63] Since owners had to pay the shearers cash at the corral, and pay the railroad cash to haul the fleece, and only then receive their own payment in cash upon sale, the sheep wore thicker coats in 1908.

Banks also struggled. Salt Lake banks started issuing certificates to be redeemed later at face value, and allowed depositors to withdraw only $200 per week, later down to $100. In December, the bank at Green River, largely dependent on railroad trade, closed after only sixteen months of service. Before its demise, it paid all depositors in full.[64] With this exception, little changed at Castle Valley banks since "it has never been the policy of the banking institutions of this section of the state, because of local conditions [meaning outlaws], to carry very great sums of cash in their vaults, people generally preferring exchange," claimed the local paper.[65] Rolla West told a story illustrating this point. Banker Tobe Whitmore allegedly enjoyed Price's big poker games, and one night he ran short of funds, so went to borrow money from his bank's vault. Fellow card-player and sometime outlaw Matt Warner stuck with Whitmore, removing cash at the same rate as Tobe himself. Not one to risk being shot, Whitmore let Warner take the money. When the game ended, Whitmore slung his big overcoat over his arm and took the next train to Salt Lake City. Within a few days, Price residents spied a large package at the depot, sent from Salt Lake City and addressed to the First National Bank. Inside was a time vault, which no one could open once the timer was set. It was the first of its kind in Castle Valley.[66]

Within a few months after the first downturn, coal prices started recovering. Since some mines had closed down, the scarcity of coal drove up its price, prompting a Chicago investor to note, "Since the great coal shortage last fall in the West, no doubt there has been a great effort on the part of capitalists . . . to open up new coal fields . . . [for] commercial channels."[67] Kenilworth fit this mold, blossoming as the Sweets pushed development regardless of the economic downturn. In 1907, a hundred miners struck over unequal work on their three shifts. They remained peaceable, and the company offered them "almost anything to return to work."[68] Huntington's George Westover, unsuccessful in his Forest Service exam, hired out with his team to help construct the town, and earned the respect of the foreman when he uncharacteristically refused to move a big rock which the unobservant superior had asked him to drag downhill, over the top of his horses. By June 1908, the Sweets' Independent Coal and Coke Company employed 150 men to run the mine at its fullest capacity. Three months later, over 200 men worked the IC&C mines, putting out about 600 tons daily, still below the amount needed to fill orders. Tom Haycock, son of a Mormon farmer in Spring Glen, got the job of engineer on the Shay engine and ran many a fast coal train down the steep mountain grade to connect with the Rio Grande.[69]

The D&RGW remained the mainstay of Castle Valley transportation. By 1900, the Price depot ranked third in Utah (after Salt Lake and Ogden) in volume of commerce handled, and by 1913 only Salt Lake City outranked it. This visible wealth attracted notorious floaters who gathered in Price to eye the depot and relax in the town's well-developed Outlaw Section. Saloons and bawdy houses stretched along the boardwalk from the old depot (which burned down in 1910) to the old courthouse where the county maintained a jail and sheds for freighters.[70] After the Uinta Basin opened for white settlement in 1905, traffic from Price initially increased, despite the construction of a railroad from Mack, Colorado, to the Basin's gilsonite mines the same year. Expansion of these mines helped freighters to resume a two-way haul: freight in, gilsonite out. However, a new policy shortly developed that each freighter could only carry for a single supplier. As half-empty wagons pulled over the pass, Armour and Company and the Cudahy Packing Company led the defection to the new railroad as primary supply line to the Uinta Basin, cutting into the freighting business at Price.[71]

Locally, tensions mounted. In 1905, Carbon County Commissioners hired a new deputy sheriff to help arrest the displaced bums riding in on the Rio Grande. John U. Bryner had previously worked as Price town marshal, crossing swords in that capacity with former Klondike miner and freighter John Millburn, who ran the Oasis Saloon in the outlaw section. On Saturday night, October 7, as the lawman was escorting a drifter to jail, the inebriated Millburn stood outside his saloon, threatened the men, and fired off some shots. Bryner shot him dead.[72] A coroner's jury ruled it justifiable homicide, but at least one local citizen viewed Millburn as a harmless, habitual drunk, and the deputy as a sober, deliberate shooter. "It was good shooting. You could cover the holes . . . with the brim of your hat," he said.[73] Rolla West, who knew Bryner well, said the killing bothered him for the rest of his life.[74]

The law of the gun remained a necessity in still-isolated, robust, thriving Castle Valley. The D&RGW, however, took some responsibility for civilizing its division point at Helper. Millionaire M. C. Peabody, on the Rio Grande board of directors, reportedly funded the construction of the Helper Railroad YMCA, dedicated in 1906. The *Advocate* editorialized, "Since the erection of the Young Men's Christian [A]ssociation building at Helper, that town has had a steady and substantial growth, people feeling that there is now a permanency to the place that did not exist before."[75] Civic-minded individuals also took the initiative. One major contributor, Louis Lowenstein, a Jewish immigrant from Latvia, had originally come from Salt Lake to Castle Valley seeking oil. He opened his Helper store that same year with a dance for two hundred people held on the upper floor of his regal Lowenstein Building, built of stone from a quarry near where Mother Jones had been imprisoned. His family and that of his sister, the Steins, together with Morris Glassman, who had stores in Castle Dale and Huntington, formed part of the small local Jewish mercantile community. His two nephews, Ben and Sam Stein, managed his two stores in Helper and Price. They remained stalwarts of Castle Valley until they moved to California in 1939, selling the building which still stands on Helper's historic Main Street.[76]

The kind of permanence Lowenstein Mercantile and other buildings represented stemmed, in large part, from the earlier designation of Helper as the railroad division point. Railroad officials lived at the "Y," including Julius Sheppard, who served as its secretary and "became one of the best known and beloved characters along the entire system."[77] In addition, in the 1890s, the D&RGW had built a chapel near their station in Helper, heated by railroad steam and furnished with the aid of the "Inter-denominational Sunday School," remembered Marion M. Robinson, the wife of Kenilworth's doctor. "[S]everal denominations held services there," she added, the Catholics, LDS, Methodists, and Episcopalians broke off to found their own churches around the time of World War I.[78]

As Castle Valley towns became more settled, free-wheeling frontier development still characterized the coal mine industry. With Kenilworth still under construction, the Sweets moved southwest to land they had claimed earlier on the Black Hawk vein at the border of Emery and Carbon Counties. To work it, they incorporated the Consolidated Fuel Company in 1908 and formed the town of Hiawatha. They also proposed the ultimate challenge to the D&RGW: "a railroad to connect with the Denver & Rio Grande at or near Price and Helper."[79] Moroni Heiner and associates founded the mine and town of Mohrland nearby, its name based on the initials of the principal investors: James H. *M*ays, Walter C. *O*rem, *H*einer, and Windsor V. *R*ice (perhaps copying the town of Elmo in this regard). In July 1909 they officially incorporated the Castle Valley Coal Company, and in

Louis Lowenstein built the large building on the left in 1906 for an estimated $7000 to house a mercantile store on the first floor and a hall for dances and lodge meetings above it. "Uncle" Bert Martin also showed silent films in the second-floor hall. This photo, taken around 1930, recorded the view of Helper's Main Street a few years before the Lowensteins moved away. The building, however, still stands. Courtesy of Western Mining and Railroad Museum.

August, formed the Castle Valley Railroad, a spur to extend from the Mohrland Mine to Hiawatha. Heiner also became part owner in the Sweets' new Southern Utah Railroad, and ultimately his company (by then known as the Southern Utah and Castle Valley) owned the rails all the way to Helper.[80] The D&RGW, severely weakened by the Panic of 1907, made its own adjustments. First, as noted, it came to terms with its sister line in Colorado, resulting in an official merger mirroring earlier, informal arrangements. Then George Gould, the new head of both lines, dealt with Union Pacific's E. H. Harriman to reopen the Ogden Gateway for transshipment from the Rio Grande to the UP and Oregon Short Line.[81] As a result of all these developments, coal from the Castle Valley corridor now flowed all over the Pacific Northwest.

These transformations proved a powerful stimulus to more commercial mines in the cliffs ringing Castle Valley. Laudatory articles in Orem's *Weekly Bulletin* and the prestigious *Salt Lake Mining Review* fanned development fever.[82] Consequently, new enterprises popped up like mushrooms after rain. Moroni Heiner's relative, Daniel Heiner, attracted backing from Ogden capitalists M. S. Browning (famous for his rifle works), H. H. Rolapp (judge in the *Holladay v. Kirker* suit), and David Eccles (Utah's first millionaire) to create the Black Hawk Coal Company and open a mine between

Hiawatha and Mohrland.[83] In a speculative mood, Henry Wade, associated with the Sweets at Kenilworth, even planned "a railroad from Wellington to the town of Emery in Emery county," thence over Salina Pass to the San Pedro, though it was never built.[84]

This mine development increasingly depended on contract, immigrant labor. Company policy typically segregated ethnic groups within the towns, in part to discourage the cooperation which would foster unions. For example, in 1908, Kenilworth carpenters constructed three nationality houses (bachelors' boarding houses), providing separate quarters for Japanese, Greeks, and one other group (probably Italians).[85] Kenilworth also added a saloon in early April and the company store in November, just as the mines started winter production. With an increased workforce, Kenilworth's monthly payroll jumped from $12,000 to $35,000 in the winter of 1908–1909, money sent up to the mine in cash. The company sought to recoup most of it through rents, the saloon and the store—if no one stole it first.[86]

That exact idea occurred to Gunplay Maxwell. After his union-busting at Goldfield, Maxwell had returned to Helper where he had suffered a broken right collarbone in a drunken shootout. He healed up and ricocheted back and forth among Utah, California, and Nevada, getting in trouble all along the way. In 1908, he tried to rob the Kenilworth payroll. Edward Johnstone, the new county deputy and coal camp marshal, foiled the attempt.[87] On August 23, 1909, Maxwell again showed up in Price, "'sore on himself' and everybody else," as the paper put it. Drunk, he ran into Johnstone in a bar and insisted that the deputy go drinking with him. The two stepped out on the street, arguing. Maxwell drew his gun and fired, his bullet cutting through Johnstone's shirt at the waist. Johnstone shot three times. Maxwell died on Price Main Street in a pool of blood.[88] His funeral preparations revealed a problem not in evidence in the 1907 shoot-out at Helper: opium addiction. "His left arm from the wrist to the shoulder and around as far as he could reach was punctured with a hypodermic syringe," said the paper, "while in his pockets was found a quantity of gum opium."[89] In later years, locals speculated that Maxwell's death had more to do with the commercial rivalry between the IC&C that employed Johnstone and the Utah Fuel Company itself than with any addiction.[90] Keeping mum on commercial conflicts, Utah Fuel attorney Mark Braffet eulogized his former bodyguard as "a bad man, but a good servant."[91] The conditions surrounding Maxwell's death would soon mushroom, as corporate rivalry moved not only men but mines, political parties, and civic-minded women in an escalating conflict.

# 7

# Facing Off, 1910–1919

*I had a little reckless spirit of adventure yet . . . so that night we went . . . to a
recruiting station and joined the Army. . . . They shipped me to New York . . . and
there was His Majesty's steamship the Baltic, White Star Liner, transformed into a
troop carrier. . . . I asked how many they had aboard, and they said 5,000, and I
said, Gee whiz, the whole town of Price could get on this ship.*[1]
—ROLLA WEST, CARPENTER AND WORLD WAR I VETERAN

World War I, also called the Great War (for its size, not its glory), eventually brought an end to America's Progressive Era optimism. Before
the reform spirit died on bloody, distant battlefields, Castle Valley developed the national hallmarks of progressivism: town-building boosterism;
anti-vice crusades in warring newspapers; and, most of all, political reform
as commercial rivalry between the railroad mines and independents soon
came to a head in politics. In his introduction to *The Progressive Movement*,
historian Richard Hofstadter spoke of a diversity of "issues, and the diversity
of social classes and social interests that were at play in the political system."
He added, "This promise of social progress was not to be realized by sitting and praying, but by using the active powers—by the exposure of evils
through the spreading of information and the exhortation of the citizenry;
by using the possibilities inherent in the ballot to find new and vigorous
popular leaders; in short, the revivification of democracy."[2] Put less elegant-
ly, as civic-minded citizens and crusading journalists exposed abuses, more
people voted for leaders who could clean up the mess.

Women, long involved in combating abuse, wanted to be part of this
reforming electorate. In Utah, where women already had the vote, they
actively sought elective office. For example, plural wife Kathinka Wilberg
Anderson was elected Emery County Recorder in 1900, the first woman to
hold Castle Valley office in her own right. English immigrant and Demo-

crat Sarah Ann Stevenson Fullmer stayed busy in politics after pioneering Orangeville alone with her children while her husband, John Solomon Fullmer, remained in Sanpete County with his other two wives. Sarah Fullmer served as a Democratic Party delegate, and was twice elected school trustee. She also became president of the Women's Suffrage Association of Emery County in an attempt to help win the vote for other women nation-wide.[3] With the same goal in mind, members of LDS Relief Societies in 1909 passed around a "Woman Suffrage Petition to Congress." Clear instructions included a requirement that each signatory give his or her own full name so the gender of the signer could be readily determined. Each signer also had to enter an occupation, and women who received wages for housework in the homes of others were directed to sign as "housekeepers as distinguished from homemakers," their non-salaried counterparts.[4] All of the petitions from Utah—where, of course, women had voted for years—were pasted to-gether, then joined to others from each state to form a monster petition with over 404,000 names. President of the National American Woman Suffrage Union, Carrie Chapman Catt of New York, formally presented it to Congress in the spring of 1910, arguing that, if the nation's women could vote, they would help clean up the political mess. Fearing just exactly that, Congress-men—many of them elected by corrupt political machines—took no action.[5] Nationally, votes for women would have to wait another decade.

Despite this setback, a host of other reforms swept Castle Valley in the Progressive Era. As Price resident W. Frank Olson later wrote, "Disraeli once said that there is no gambling like politics. . . . Yet there is something about a political fight that exhilarates, and I could not keep away." Elected as Price mayor in 1910 (beating Tobe Whitmore by a mere fifteen votes), Olson started instituting improvements. He organized a county band (build-ing on a long tradition) that won first place in the state-wide competition. Price had no electric lights, so he pushed a bond election to pay for them. When Whitmore called him into his office to confer on the bond proposal, Olson expected a verbal thrashing. "'Olson, I admire your enthusiasm, and your spirit of progress, and I think Price is ready for electric lights. I am for you and we'll put it over,'" said Tobe. The bond passed, and the lighting system was readied for the Fourth of July. "[W]hen the switch was thrown, lights flooded the business houses and homes. It was a thrilling sight. We tried not to think about the bonded indebtedness," Olson added. Others did, however, and plans for an improved reservoir subsequently failed.[6]

Other improvements did succeed in Castle Valley. In 1910, a tongue-in-cheek newspaper article warned Emery County residents of the dangers of houseflies, suggesting that if eating every night in a restaurant were not practical, they might install wire screens so that "all the flies of the neigh-borhood may collect inside, and then the family can go out and have an undisturbed repast in the back yard."[7] More seriously, in 1913, Price city health officer Dr. A. C. Sorensen warned residents to kill flies and clean up garbage to prevent disease from spreading. That summer, he had already treated two cases of typhoid fever, one of scarlet fever, and several of whooping cough and warned mothers "that especial [sic] care should be taken not to let the babies drink the hydrant water before it is boiled," to avoid cases of cholera infantum.[8] Rolla West, a skilled carpenter, also remembered that summer. "That year we made more window screens than any other time in the history of Price, I guess. . . . [E]verybody wanted screens, because the flies were terrible."[9] Other local, progressive improvements also targeted the young. Huntington's Fern Young, a domestic science teacher, organized Castle Valley's first local school lunch system in 1917. She told students to bring their own sandwiches, bowls, and spoons and fed them additional soup, cocoa, or chocolate, all for two cents a day, often paid in farm produce.[10]

Locally, civic minded women and men could also stay informed about various problems and reforms. Crusading journalists known as Muckrakers published well-researched articles about a host of widespread ills. These nationally-syndicated investigators included Ida Tarbell, chronicler of the seamy side of Standard Oil trust; David Graham Phillips, who revealed which U.S. Senators had sold out to Big Business, and Lincoln Steffens, who exposed self-serving city bosses all around America.[11] All across the nation, partisan newspapers—over 2,600 of them—also fought acrimonious political duels. Castle Valley had its share of controversy after 1910, when the area acquired a new newspaper, the *Carbon County News.* Its owners sympathized with the independent coal operators rather than the Utah Fuel/Rio Grande trust, which had won the support of the venerable *Eastern Utah Advocate,* founded in 1891. Rounding out the picture, the less partisan *Emery County Progress* had been around since 1900, and continues to serve Castle Valley today.[12] Thus, in the heat of Progressive Era politics, the news would be reported from two distinctly different angles.

The watershed 1912 election revealed a case in point. Just before the election, *News* editor W. C. Benfer wrote in response to a complaint of political bias, "I have sold space . . . to the republicans, (Taft wing), the democrats, the socialists and the progressives (Roosevelt republicans) . . . Might as well accuse the News of 'catering' to the Utah Fuel company or the Independent Coal & Coke company, for both these concerns buy space in the News to express their views."[13] Thus succinctly, Benfer outlined the major gladiators in the ring.

Nationally, the presidential election of 1912 offered a host of twists and surprises, echoed by Castle Valley's complicated political contests. When incumbent President William Howard Taft won the Republican nomination, ex-President Theodore Roosevelt, who allegedly "roared like a bull moose," advanced his own candidacy through the Bull Moose Party. Roosevelt had earlier broken with Taft, previously Roosevelt's hand-picked successor. However, in 1909, *Collier's* magazine published muckraking articles revealing that Alaskan coal lands were being gobbled up by the Guggenheim syndicate (part of the Smelter Trust), allegedly with Taft's knowledge. While President Taft was never convincingly implicated, the rift with Roosevelt remained permanent.[14] Consequently, in 1912, after Taft got the Republican nomination, the Progressive Party jettisoned their dedicated leader, Robert M. LaFollette, and nominated Roosevelt instead. "Reform Republicans" backed the Progressives, guaranteeing a split in the Republican vote.[15]

Locally, Progressives also organized. Theodore Roosevelt contacted the state Progressive Party, headed by Moroni Heiner, a Castle Valley coal developer, who had also served as state dairy and food commissioner, and had helped in the passage of Utah's pure food law.[16] Roosevelt later thanked Heiner for "the good [organizing] work which you and other friends did in Utah."[17] In Castle Valley, W. F. Olson, together with C. H. Stevenson, Joseph R. Sharp, and William Hamilton of Helper, began "organizing a new political party in Carbon County to be known as the Bull Moose Party."[18]

The Socialists also became energized, building on an organization founded nationally and locally in 1901. Nationally, the Socialists nominated Eugene V. Debs in his fourth run for president. Debs had begun as a trade unionist and, in 1893, organized the American Railway Union. He had led it into a heated strike against the Pullman Palace Car Company in 1894, which only ended when Democratic President Cleveland, over the objections of the Governor of Illinois, ordered federal troops into Chicago. Debs's involvement led to a six-month jail sentence, his first, and stimulated his involvement in the Socialist Party.[19]

Castle Valley Socialists also had a long track record, with particular strength in Emery County. There, the party philosophy made a lot of sense to people nurtured in the old LDS communal tradition (as it did to many others elsewhere in Utah). Socialists had run their first Emery County slate in 1904, subsequently staying active in Castle Dale, Ferron, Cleveland, and Huntington. They ran their first Carbon County ticket in 1910, and even elected a justice of the peace and constable in Cleveland that year. In 1911, Socialists made significant gains in other Utah towns. In 1912, an Emery County native, William A. Jameson, ran on the Socialist ticket for Carbon County sheriff. Jameson, a 1901 graduate of the Emery Stake Academy where his father had been principal, had a varied career. He had become a licensed boiler maker, worked in Old Mexico, and returned to Castle Valley to live in Helper where he served as the financial secretary of the Socialist Party of Carbon County.[20] Describing Jameson's opponents, Helper's Socialists (in the *News*) characterized the Republican nominee for sheriff, Thomas Burge, as a "gun thug who acted as a scab herder during the [1903–1904] D&RG strike" and the Democratic candidate, T. F. Kelter, as a man who "allowed the coal corporations to guard the trains going into the coal camps, depriving citizens of their right to free speech and free assembly."[21]

These public accusations highlighted the growing political split between the Rio Grande syndicate and the independent coal mine operators. The setting for this division began around the turn of the century, as Congress tried to rein in the nation's railroads. A series of anti-railroad legislation—the Interstate Commerce Act (1887), the Sherman Anti-Trust Act (1890), the Elkins Act (1903)—culminated in the Hepburn Act of 1906, the first anti-railroad act with teeth. It mandated that railroads could not carry coal mined by their own companies beginning May 1, 1908.[22] Like many other corporations, Utah Fuel now mined coal in violation of federal law, although enforcement appeared problematic. Consequently, the Justice Department began trying to separate the railroad from its coal lands in another way, charging that these holdings had been obtained by fraud.[23] For consistency (and, hopefully, to gain a workable legal precedent), federal attorneys filed similar cases against some of Castle Valley's independent coal operators. Specifically, in January 1907 the federal government also indicted Arthur A. Sweet, Castle Valley's first independent, for fraudulently obtaining coal lands on the Black Hawk vein, along the Wasatch Plateau at the border with Emery County.[24] This suit finally reached the Supreme Court in 1914 (although ownership of the land remained in question until 1921).[25] Similar cases against independent developers Stanley B. Milner and Sam Gilson lasted even longer (until 1932, by which time the surviving case was known as *Utah v. United States*).[26]

In this contentious atmosphere, Utah Fuel fought back. Fighting its federal indictments with all its considerable monetary power, the railroad syndicate managed to escape from most coal land fraud indictments in 1909 when President Taft directed frustrated Justice Department attorneys to forge some out-of-court settlements.[27] Taking advantage of its superior legal position, the Utah Fuel/Rio Grande monopoly then sought to strengthen its political hold over the area surrounding its coal fields. "In view of the settlement with the Government," a long letter began, Utah Fuel in 1909 made its attorney, Mark Braffet, Carbon County's political boss.[28] He was charged with managing elections to make sure Utah Fuel miners—dependent on company goodwill for employment—voted the "right" ticket. For example, in 1910, the *News* printed a "Letter from Scofield" stating, "The good people of Scofield are tired of politics as conducted in Carbon county, and are ready for an Independent ticket . . . While we believe the Utah Fuel Company ought to have representation, the people here are extremely tired of Utah Fuel company interference in politics."[29] This vaguely-stated political meddling became concrete when, just before the election, Utah Fuel raised miners' wages throughout their camps, attempting to sir up a wave of good will.[30] A mixed result ensued, as Republicans and Democrats split local offices.[31]

By 1912, local political strife had become entwined with events on the national level. First, the possibility of a Democratic victory posed a real threat to Utah Fuel. The national Democratic Party, enjoying the possibility of a presidential victory due to the split in Republican votes, had nominated Woodrow Wilson, earlier president of Princeton University and governor of New Jersey (a state known as the Mother of Trusts). In the national media circus, although incumbent President Taft remained on the ballot, the 1912 Presidential election really came down to a contest between Progressive Roosevelt and Democrat Wilson. Both men targeted Big Business. Campaigning on his "New Nationalism" platform, Roosevelt demanded federal control of the trusts. Wilson went even further. His "New Freedom" contrasted the power of the trusts with the growing weakness of corporate employees. "American industry is not free, as once it was free," Wilson claimed, "because the laws of this country do not prevent the strong from crushing the weak."[32] Therefore, if elected, Wilson intended to dismember monopolies. Startled by the unpleasant possibility of Wilson as president, the Rio Grande sought and achieved the last of several out-of-court settlements on pending federal cases in advance of the 1912 election.[33] At the same time, independent developers Frederick Sweet and Moroni Heiner, who were moving their local political fight against the Rio Grande to the national level, had brought other charges against the railroad in the Interstate Commerce Commission. Hastily, the Rio Grande also agreed to their demands, ending the ICC cases.[34]

But the Progressives struggled locally, as the Braffet machine swung into action against them. At Sunnyside, during the 1912 campaign, Utah Fuel officials, with Braffet on hand to observe, drove Progressive candidates from the rented (but company-owned) public hall into the street and then into the cramped Post Office where they could give their speeches on federal—not company—property.[35] Ultimately, such tactics won Utah Fuel few friends. After the votes were counted, two pro-independent Progressives had won seats on the Carbon County Commission, where they joined the lone Democrat serving out his term.[36] Thus, the Carbon County Commission became the battle-ground for further political strife.

A host of other changes came with the 1912 election. The Progressives could not deliver Utah to Roosevelt, who only got 24,000 votes to Taft's 42,000 throughout the state. America, as a whole, went for Wilson. Consequently, the first Democrat since Cleveland and only the second since the Civil War now sat in the White House.[37] Other 1912 electoral outcomes put Castle Valley squarely on the Utah political map. Voters uncharacteristically often crossed party lines, voting for nominees based on their integrity, rather than their party affiliation, or, as W. F. Olson put it, "the donkey and the elephant climbed in bed together" to elect the best candidates.[38] Republicans won most races, such as Orangeville's Jesse D. Jewkes, who became state treasurer. He had won his first statewide office four years earlier, running against Huntington's James W. Nixon, Democrat, for state auditor. Another Castle Valley stalwart, William J. Seely of Castle Dale, retained his seat in the state House of Representatives, where he was elected Speaker in 1913. The post of Carbon County Recorder went to Miss Josie Fitzgerald, Republican, the top vote-getter overall. (After her success, all subsequent twentieth-century recorders except one were women, culminating with Ann B. O'Brien, who served for thirty years.)[39] Elected on the same ballot, progressive-minded Carl R. Marcusen (technically a Republican) began his long tenure as school superintendent from which he later rose to many high state offices.[40]

In short order, political changes swept all levels of government. President Wilson, backed by a Democratic Congress, pushed numerous national reforms. Recognizing the growing power of workers, Wilson named the former secretary of the United Mine Workers as the first Secretary of Labor in a new Cabinet post. Congress, in 1913, passed both the Sixteenth Amendment, allowing a graduated income tax, and the Seventeenth Amendment, mandating direct election of Senators, taking those officials out of the pockets of the trusts. The much lower Underwood Tariff, strongly championed by Wilson, removed much of the protection American business had previously enjoyed. The loss of governmental revenue it presaged was compensated by the newly-authorized tax structure, allowed by the Sixteenth Amendment and carried as a rider on the Underwood bill. (The highest tax bracket, on annual incomes over $500,000, paid a whopping six percent.) At the very end of 1913, Congress passed highly controversial legislation that created the Federal Reserve Board and its affiliated federal banks to regulate the national currency. Further evening the balance between capital and labor, in 1914, Congress passed the Clayton Anti-Trust Act, which specifically exempted strikes from prosecution under the Sherman Anti-Trust Act, previously used to break unions such as the 1894 Pullman strikers.[41]

In Castle Valley, politics see-sawed. The Utah Fuel machine seemed to stage a come-back, making significant electoral gains in 1913. Then, the independents mobilized their women. In February 1914, about twenty-five female relations of leading Progressives and independent coal operators organized a Women's Betterment League. They elected officers and formed committees on Finance, Publicity, Morals and Research, Children and Working Girls, and Pool Halls and Boys (an interesting and indicative combination).[42] A month later these activists presented the Price City Council with a petition signed by 215 women demanding the suppression of "flagrant gambling and prostitution," vices long ignored in the town's outlaw section. No men had been allowed to sign, since the women were determined to clean up Price by themselves. Red-faced, the city councilmen tabled the petition "pending an investigation."[43]

In fact, prostitutes had long plied their trade locally and had occasionally been arrested, fined, and/or driven out of town, particularly since the passage of the federal Mann Act (or White Slave Act) in 1910.[44] Reflecting the carnival atmosphere surrounding these arrests, one 1912 article noted in its entirety, "In the neighborhood of a dozen of the dissolute women who have been making Price their hangout for the past year left on No. 3 Sunday. There were quite a number of male friends at the depot to bid them farewell."[45]

Many upstanding citizens had tired of open vice, and the *News* tried alternating anti-machine news articles with poetry throughout the spring and summer of 1914. Penned by Castle Valley's own anonymous Muckraker, a fictitious "Mrs. Grundy" (contemporary slang for an old-fashioned complainer), rhymes such as this issued regularly: "Little bits of grafting,/ With audacity,/ Bring to mind a certain/ Fuel company. . . . Little decent people,/ Trying to kill vice,/ Find it mighty hard work/ In this town of Price."[46] In this reforming atmosphere, Progressive Carbon County officials reassessed coal company town lots, increasing the valuations of taxable property in Carbon County three-quarters of a million dollars and spurring Mark Braffet to seek a court injunction forestalling foreclosure when Utah Fuel refused to pay.[47] Under fire, Utah Fuel's general superintendent felt compelled to justify publicly his company's involvement in local politics, which he dated to the Castle Gate payroll heist "a few years ago" (actually 21 years earlier, when Butch Cassidy did the job). He complained in the *Advocate* of the unsavory crowd drawn to saloons outside company towns (but presumably, not to company-run enterprises) and threatened to raise the rent on company houses if the November election went against company desires—a poorly-veiled threat to his captive employees.[48] Despite this blustering, in 1914, Carbon County's Progressive candidates defeated a fused, pro-railroad Republican-Democrat ticket, with the exception of Republican Ernest Horsley who retained his seat as county clerk (and whose wife served in the Betterment League).[49] Locally, although the pro-liquor Utah Fuel machine won back Price City in 1915, it lost everywhere else. The company promptly replaced its political king, Mark Braffet, with a new elections manager, although Braffet retained his formal employment.[50]

At the state level, the 1914 election marked a political watershed whose ramifications spun out over the next few years, centering on machine politics and the liquor issue. Thanks to the Seventeenth Amendment, Republican Senator Reed Smoot, head of the Federal Bunch machine, had to face the general electorate in a contest with Democrat James H. Moyle. Smoot won in a very close race, although both Carbon and Emery went for Moyle. Concurrently, Utah's temperance advocates, who had succeeded in getting a local option law passed in 1911, failed to gain statewide support for full prohibition in 1914 and again in 1915, but kept trying. In 1916, the liquor issue came to a head as Smoot and his Federal Bunch openly backed Prohibition for the first time, no longer fearing a revival of the old gentile-Mormon split. Their Democratic opponents, headed by gubernatorial candidate Simon Bamberger, also backed Prohibition. Bamberger won, becoming Utah's only Jewish governor. The Federal Bunch collapsed, and

Utah went dry. Bamberger, backed by a Democrat-dominated legislature, also sponsored the successful enactment of a host of other Progressive programs. Most important for Castle Valley miners, Utah adopted stringent workmen's compensation laws supervised by a new Industrial Commission, becoming one of thirty states in the Union with these important provisions. Locally, despite the demise of the Progressives (including the Women's Betterment League), Carbon County, in 1916, elected a slate of officers outside railroad control. Two months later, Utah Fuel fired Mark Braffet.[51] Thus, with two political machines gone, prohibition well-established (at least on paper), and compensation available for industrial accidents, the state and the valley seemed more in tune with national trends, and, for once, with each other.

Nationally, however, the old Progressive impulse was losing steam. In 1915, Wilson's administration had set up the Federal Trade Commission to regulate business. However, the president ignored or sabotaged other reform measures. He vetoed a bill that would have helped farmers with a rural credits system and failed to support drives to abolish child labor and to give women the vote. In 1915, he had also vetoed a bill requiring a literacy test for immigrants; a new Congress passed it over his veto two years later. This measure, strongly favored by labor, limited the number of immigrants allowed entry into the United States, thus aiding labor organizers who were regularly undercut by newly-imported foreign scabs whenever they struck. Wilson also increased black-white segregation in federal agencies, eliciting a storm of protest in the North and Midwest but support in the South.[52] His attitudes on race would shortly come to gain a national foothold, even within Castle Valley.

Meanwhile, Castle Valley's physical environment had begun to show visible distress. More and more animals grazed along the Wasatch Plateau, leading to heated confrontations between Sanpete sheepmen and Emery cattlemen. In 1911, Manti District Forester Sherman had taken voluminous testimony in hearings held in Sanpete County, Huntington, Cleveland, Lawrence, and Ferron. A year later, the government reduced sheep allotments on the Forest by 27,000 head with additional limits on cattle.[53] The Forest Service charged twelve cents per head, per season, sometimes giving permanent and sometimes temporary allotments.[54] Rangers also began monitoring the size of local herds on driveways. By the late twenties, Ranger John Brockbank allegedly counted thirteen hundred head of cattle belonging to the Staker family of Lawrence coming up Huntington Canyon bound for summer range, but only let six hundred head go through.[55]

Reduced cattle meant increased forage, and so the Forest Service introduced elk to benefit future hunters. In January 1916, twenty-four of them staggered down from the train in Price after a long trip from Jackson Hole, Wyoming. They were penned on the Del Peacock ranch near Orangeville until the grass greened in the mountains. That summer, as a group of men

In 1914, miners posed for this photo before the mantrip descended deep into the Hiawatha mine, taking them to their work stations. One of the men in the foreground (sixth from left), Charlie Pettiti, a nineteen-year-old Italian immigrant, later opened Wattis, then farmed, living into his ninth decade in Castle Valley. Courtesy of Western Mining and Railroad Museum.

and boys on horseback tried to drive the elk up Cottonwood Canyon, they scattered. A few hung around the Peacock and Miles ranches, becoming a nuisance to the farmers' crops until they were driven away.[56]

While the government tried to regulate rangelands, coal extraction flourished unmolested. In 1912, a new major corporation moved into Castle Valley coal when the United States Smelting, Refining, and Mining Company (USSR&M) bought Hiawatha in a deal brokered by Frederick Sweet, the head of Consolidated Fuel since the death of his brother, Arthur, in 1910. Hiawatha's sale allegedly enriched individual Salt Lake stockholders to the tune of $5,000 to $10,000 or more, a potent lure to others. USSR&M also bought out Mohrland and Black Hawk.[57] The entry of this smelting giant into Castle Valley coal also helped bring to conclusion another struggling railroad: the high line building north from the Black Hawk vein. It shortly connected with the D&RGW north of Helper and became known as the Utah Railway. Then, the D&RGW came to terms, allowing the Utah

Railway—which owned a right-of-way all the way to Provo—to share its tracks, eliminating the need for double tracks further north.[58]

Some local enterprises took longer to materialize. Former railroad grader and prison warden George A. Storrs, in a new career as an official of the Knight Investment Company, paved the way for the entry of Mormon capitalist "Uncle" Jesse Knight into eastern Utah coal. As an agent for the Knight Power Company, Storrs purchased coal lands in Cottonwood Canyon in 1911, and in Rock Canyon, also in Emery County, two years later.[59] He later recalled that in "1912 I was riding . . . on the train with Uncle Jesse Knight and he told me he had about three quarters of a million dollars in the bank and he was wondering how he could use it to do the people the most good." With this backing, Storrs visited another Knight property in Spring Canyon, west of Helper, where he and an old Pennsylvania coal miner located and opened a seven foot vein. Knight decided to open a mine, and Storrs directed the project: building a tipple, a tramway, sixty-three rock houses (with hot and cold water), a hotel, store, and hospital, and the beginning of a railroad. The town also sprouted a saloon, although probably not instigated by the high-minded Storrs. When the new mine began shipping in 1913, Knight insisted it be called Storrs for the man who built it.[60] Following Knight into Spring Canyon, the Sweets, after selling Hiawatha to USSR&M in 1912, founded the new Standard Coal Company and a town called Standardville—intended to represent the "highest standard" in coal mine development. It initially lacked culinary water, so residents had to haul a couple of five-gallon cans to Helper each time they went and fill up at Merrill Bryner's service station, where he kept one small room open with an available tap and attracted a healthy business.[61] The Sweets also cooperated with Knight to build a railroad down the canyon to connect with the D&RGW above Helper. In 1914, the Liberty Fuel Company opened another Spring Canyon mine called Latuda, which began humbly with small, horse-drawn, wooden mine cars and a wooden tipple. Former opera singer Leon F. Rains, who worked for the Standard Coal Company, quietly acquired water rights in Spring Canyon using Standard's water surveys and won a nasty lawsuit after he opened his own camp at Rains in 1915. He formed the Carbon Fuel Company with investors L. R. Wattis of the Utah Construction Company, A. A. Armstrong, and others.[62]

By 1914, Utah had become the most industrialized inter-mountain state thanks to ore processing, an industry based on coal shipped on an ever-expanding web of railroads. Castle Valley became increasingly commercial, attracting new developers to old coal seams. For example, Frank N. Cameron opened the Panther Mine of his Cameron Coal Company at the base of Price Canyon near Castle Gate in 1912, selling out a year later to rifle manufacturers M. S. and Mariner Browning. Beginning in 1913, the Ketchum Coal Company, under Truman Ketchum, also tapped the Castle Gate seam and tried to acquire more of the old Pleasant Valley operation through creative litigation. Mergers increased by 1915 as USSR&M acquired Panther. In 1916, the smelting company created a new subsidiary, the United States Fuel Company. Moroni Heiner, the prime mover behind this last consolidation, became the president of U.S. Fuel, serving for the next seventeen years.[63]

Transportation also diversified, even in Castle Valley. By 1911, the whole nation had become enthralled with car-worthy roads. An eastern promoter envisioned one stretching coast-to-coast, hard-surfaced all the way, a project adopted by the privately-funded Lincoln Highway Association after 1913. The resultant Lincoln Highway cut through Salt Lake City, and the federal government took over road-building with the Federal Aid Road Act in 1916.[64] At the state level, Castle Dale's Ira W. Browning, elected to the state legislature from 1914 to 1916, authored Utah's first automobile licensing act and later became the chief engineer on the State Road Commission, serving until his death in 1926.[65] Elsewhere, private endeavors continued, as the Indiana Auto Club, in 1913, drew up plans for another transcontinental route, the Midland Trail, which wove down Price Canyon and along the Castle Valley corridor. Castle Valley residents quivered with excitement. In Green River, "Midland became a magic word. . . . The Midland Hotel was built to the specifications of Belle Waddel who ran it for years."[66] The Utah State Road Commission authorized Midland Trail construction, but cautioned that the state's portion would cost an alarming $100,000, the bulk of it for the Price Canyon road. Accordingly, Price residents spearheaded a fund drive, raising $50,000 in work pledges under the auspices of its own Midland Trail Association with Arthur W. Horsley, president; James M. Whitmore, vice president; George Nelms, secretary and treasurer; and Clarence H. Stevenson, its strongest promoter. Construction of this difficult passageway began in early summer 1913 and was barely finished when the first representatives of the Indiana Auto Club arrived on July 16. Two weeks later, a couple motoring from New York to San Francisco diplomatically pronounced the connected roads comprising the Midland Trail "not what may be called good, but they are far better than those of the northern route." After all that work, the published *Midland Trail Tour Guide* of 1916 disappointingly (but realistically) warned motorists to avoid Price Canyon when it was wet, to use the horn frequently on its twisting road when it was dry, and to reduce their speed at the end of the steep canyon grade to ten miles per hour.[67] Also in 1916, California boosters began quietly studying what became the Arrowhead Trails Highway, a Los Angeles-to-Salt Lake route that, by 1918, took drivers on less dangerous roads well west of Castle Valley.[68] As a result of all this road-building, most transcontinental motorists easily avoided the difficult Midland Trail in favor of other routes. Castle Valley remained, as ever, largely isolated from the mainstream.

Consequently, the earliest automobiles along this rural corridor mostly chugged back and forth between valley towns. Two locals earned the title

Cars, drivers, and passengers, in appropriate protective clothing, line up in 1914 to showcase the Price Auto Club trip to Emery, then an arduous and exciting venture. Courtesy of Emery County Archives.

of First-to-have-a-car. In 1908, Frank Cook of Green River bought an automobile, as did Helper's Dr. Frank Fisk who used it to make his rounds.[69] In his open-air Stanley Steamer, hauled in on the railroad, Fisk wore "one of those linen dusters and cotton gloves, and a cap with a drop-screen over his face to keep the dust out," an absolutely essential outfit on the unpaved roads of Castle Valley.[70] Merchant Sam Singleton had one of the first cars in Ferron. He gave ten-year-old Richard Behling a ride "as far as the bottom of the dugway. It was like a trip around the world!"[71] Along the base of the Wasatch Plateau, where Castle Valley flattened out, the one good road seemed an invitation to excursions. In 1913, the *Carbon County News* reported that Max Alexander had taken an auto trip from Price into Emery County and particularly enjoyed the stretch from Ferron to Emery, proclaiming it "the best in eastern Utah."[72] Ferron residents took their roads seriously. As a local historian observed, "Every rain washed roads out, every hard wind storm made sand dunes across them," in the early years of settlement.[73] In 1914, when the Price Auto Club made the same trans-valley trip with a parade of forty cars (holding 150 people), Emery County townspeople met them all along the way with bands and flowers. On the celebrated Ferron-Emery stretch, some cars cruised at an astonishing fifty-two miles per hour.[74]

While some Castle Valley residents became increasingly mobile, men in company towns often felt trapped by the will of the bosses, with sometimes tragic results. For example, in 1911, several newly dismissed Kenilworth miners congregated in the hills and opened fire on the camp. Company watchman Thomas Elias Jackson died. His brother, Robert, returned fire and killed Greek immigrant Steve Kolozakis. Four other Greek men were arrested for riot and murder; two were dismissed. The body of Jackson, then a Helper resident, was taken back to Huntington for burial. Rumors of strikes

at other camps swept the community.[75] Later, people told two different stories about what caused the violence. The state coal mine inspector wrote,
"A number of Greek, Austrian, and Italian miners . . . requested the mine
superintendent to allow them to select a check-weighman, as they claimed
they were not getting correct weights over the mine scales." Although the
boss agreed, the men became "very boisterous and insulting," so were "discharged and escorted out of camp." They later returned to involve others
in shooting up the town from the hills.[76] One of the surviving miners told a
different story. According to Italian immigrant Peter Aiello, when a new superintendent came from another mine, suddenly miners got short weights.
"[I]f a car used to weigh about 3 or 4 ton . . . they only give you about 2 ½,
3 ton . . . at the most." When the miners asked that one of their own be chosen to work alongside the company checkweighman, the superintendent
agreed. Then, "about two days after, we see a car or two of gunmen come
. . . You see, the superintendent wanted to make a big name for himself.
They had to put the gunmen [to work so] . . . they laid us off. . . . But," he
added, "if I could talk [English] then like I do now, we would have had him
[the superintendent ] fired. Because the men didn't want no strike. . . . But
that superintendent forced the strike [on] to the miners."[77] The local paper
claimed that the foreigners implicated in the strike had gone to other local
camps or to Colorado. Aiello himself went to work at Hiawatha, still employed by the Sweets, along with two others from Kenilworth.[78]

This deadly encounter was but a muted version of increasingly harsh
confrontations between capital and labor all over the West. In Los Angeles,
the dynamiting of the virulently anti-labor *Times* building, in October 1910,
killed twenty men. Accused bombers James and John McNamara and Ortie
McManigal were brought through Price on "separate trains" with "locked
Pullman compartments," headed back to Los Angeles to trial.[79] Most workers believed them innocent due to the 1905 frame-up of union leaders
from the IWW/WFM in the murder of Idaho's ex-Governor.[80] Even highly
conservative Samuel Gompers of the American Federation of Labor (AFL)
hailed the accused *Times* bombers as "innocent victims of capitalist greed."
Labor thus felt hideously betrayed when, just prior to trial, famous defense
lawyer Clarence Darrow filed a guilty plea. Ortie McManigal had turned
state's evidence, revealing that the Los Angeles bombing, orchestrated by
the McNamaras, represented the last of eighty-seven other attacks nationwide instigated by the AFL-affiliated International Association of Bridge
and Structural Iron Workers. (With the exception of the *Times,* none of
them was fatal). This revelation horrified the public, eviscerated unions,
and strengthened corporate capitalists all over America.[81]

Despite this major setback, labor organizers kept on plugging away
throughout the West and in Utah. In 1912, the WFM called an unsuccessful strike at the Utah Copper camp of Bingham, west of Salt Lake City.
There they championed hundreds of newly imported Greek miners, who

were chafing under the yoke of the *padrone*, Leonidis Skliris, also one of the labor recruiters for Castle Valley mines. Skliris made his raw recruits sign a paper in English, which none of them could read, promising to pay him one dollar per month to be deducted from their paychecks. They were also forced to patronize the businesses he preferred. Utah Copper officials studiously denied that the padrone system even existed (although Utah Fuel had, in 1908, posted warning signs in Greek and English that employees should not pay money to interpreters for securing employment). The 1912 Bingham strike failed to bring in the union; it did, however, finally break Skliris's power.[82]

Meanwhile, the IWW (Wobblies) independently moved in on other Utah locations including Tucker, where, in June 1913, they led a strike of approximately 3,000 Utah Construction Company workers who were grading a new line for the D&RGW into Castle Valley from the north. The company, owned by Wattis and Eccles family members, brought in deputized guards, as usual, to confront the IWW picket line whose vocal members tried to dissuade strike-breakers from going to work. Utah Construction had another 4,000 men simultaneously building the Utah Railway from Mohrland to Castle Gate. General Manager Wattis discounted the possibility of an additional strike and Carbon County Sheriff Thomas Kelter guaranteed that "agitators will be shown out of the country at the first intimation of any act of violence."[83] In fact, no violence occurred, and the Wobblies succeeded in winning a wage increase at Tucker. They then converged on Salt Lake City, singing rousing songs composed by Swedish immigrant Joe Hillstrom (known as Joe Hill) to motivate the crowds.[84] Joe Hill himself came to Salt Lake City, and was arrested on circumstantial evidence for the January 10, 1914, murder of a former policeman and one of his sons. After Hill's trial and an appeal, the Utah State Supreme Court upheld a guilty verdict in 1915. An international "Save Joe Hill" campaign even prompted President Woodrow Wilson to request a pardon for Hill from Utah's Governor Spry, all to no avail. On November 19, 1915, at Salt Lake's Sugarhouse Prison, Hill was seated in a chair with a paper target pinned over his heart and officially shot to death. His execution created a lasting labor martyr. Spry became a marked man, and Ed Johnstone, who had killed Gunplay Maxwell in Price, became one of the governor's bodyguards.[85]

This growing strife mirrored even more deadly international conflicts, marking the end of optimistic progressive reform. From 1910–1920, the U.S. meddled in Mexican revolutionary struggles. In Europe, World War I had begun in the summer of 1914, when a Serbian nationalist assassinated the heir-apparent to the throne of Austria-Hungary. Shortly, secret alliances pitted the Central Powers led by Germany and Austria-Hungary against Great Britain, France, Russia, and their allies. As war devastated many nations, markets crashed world-wide, even affecting Castle Valley. By November 1914, the Utah mine inspector noted that U.S. smelter shutdowns and tariff readjustments in the disrupted global copper market had reduced the demand for Utah coal. Utah Fuel and the independents showed their commercial desperation by banding together in the midst of their political struggle to solicit Navy contacts on the Pacific, a plan ultimately doomed by lack of reliable railroad connections. Eastern coal now had an advantage, as, almost without fanfare, America's seas had just been connected by the Panama Canal. German U-boat (submarine) activity in the Atlantic forestalled the canal's full use during wartime, however. In fact, the war's outburst had quashed a grand celebration planned for the canal's inauguration in 1915: instead of sea-going pageantry, the first ocean-going boat to use the canal hauled cement. The glittering San Francisco Panama-Pacific International Exposition went forward all the same, not just to celebrate the canal but to show that the city had risen from the ashes of the earthquake and fire of 1906. At the Mines Palace, one of several exhibition buildings, A. C. Watts of the Utah Fuel Company supervised the installation of a thirty-foot high obelisk of solid Castle Valley coal, costing $6,000 and modeled on the famous Cleopatra's Needle. Displays proliferated and medals abounded in every category: for inventions; for products; for the best display of books. Emery's long-term LDS Bishop, sometime state senator, and renowned stockman, Alonzo Brinkerhoff, brought home the gold medal for honey.[86]

This self-congratulatory fervor died as the shadow of war loomed closer. On July 22, 1916, San Francisco businessmen staged a Preparedness Day parade disrupted as a black satchel left on the route exploded, killing ten and injuring dozens. Immediately, police rounded up five labor leaders and charged them with the explosion. Despite unreliable witnesses and proven perjury, the most visible labor organizer, Tom Mooney, was convicted and sentenced to hang. Just as President Wilson had done with the Joe Hill case in Utah, he pressured California's governor to pardon Mooney. Postponing Mooney's execution date until after the 1918 election, California's re-elected governor then commuted Mooney's sentence to life in prison—for a crime he clearly did not commit.[87]

By then, Wilson had been reelected in 1916 on the slogan, "He kept us out of war." Once back in the White House, however, he had had to face the realities of intensified diplomatic pressures and the renewal of German submarine warfare. Only a month after Wilson resumed the presidency, U-boats sank the *Lusitania.* Wilson promptly asked Congress for a declaration of war, and on April 6, 1917, the United States officially joined World War I. Seventeen men from Carbon County and several from Emery County immediately volunteered. The United States instituted its first draft of males between ages twenty-one and thirty in July 1917. Some 801 men eventually served from Carbon County plus thirteen from Emery, whose farmers earned exemption because of the importance of food production to the war effort. Some local foreigners faced difficult choices. Paul Dupin, a Hiawatha coal miner, while totally committed to American victory, realized he had a brother in the Austro-Hungarian army. Rather than chance meeting him on the battlefield, Dupin got a job herding sheep in the mountains throughout the war. A German from Scofield attracted Justice Department investigation when he claimed to have been born in Switzerland of Swedish descent. Another German from Mohrland was arrested for his pro-Germany statements, shipped to Salt Lake's Fort Douglas, and held there with the other enemy alien prisoners of war. Nonetheless, Mohrland's heavy patriotic contributions helped Emery County to lead Utah in exceeding its quota in the first Liberty Bond drive, and eventually Emery doubled its allotment. Carbon County, too, exceeded its quota, and in the fourth Liberty Bond drive compiled the best record in the entire Twelfth Federal Reserve District. Consequently, its residents got to choose the name for a U.S. ship launched at the Alameda yards near San Francisco on July 31, 1919. With great ceremony, the 11,000 ton oil tanker, *Utacarbon* (a name suggested by Mrs. C. H. Stevenson of Price) slipped into the ocean, christened by Utah Governor Bamberger with a bottle of Colton Springs water and by Miss Margaret Horsley, the head of women's work on the Price City council, with a bottle of champagne.[88]

Despite all this patriotic fervor, significant counter-currents favored peace. The Socialists heartily criticized the war as a ploy of the rich. William Henry Price, who spent most of his life in Ferron, remained a lifelong Socialist. He urged others to "wield the sceptre of freedom mightily at the ballot box" to "vote on war and peace," imagining a "nation wide referendum in which those voting for peace would stay at home . . . [and those] voting for war being drafted to the front and given the priveledge [sic] of breathing poison gas and catching the shells cannon balls and cartridges as they come red hot out of the guns." But, he added realistically, "those for war have never fought in them. . . . [It] has always been a rich mans war and a poor mans fight."[89] This same view aired nationwide thanks to the efforts of Eugene V. Debs, the nation's leading Socialist. Debs gave his most famous anti-war speech in June 1918 in Canton, Ohio, in which he proclaimed that working people should control their "own jobs . . . own labor and be free men instead of industrial slaves," forced to manufacture war materiel solely to kill other working people. Debs closed with a call for "emancipation of the working class and the brotherhood of all mankind."[90] Arrested and convicted under the federal Espionage Act of 1917 for allegedly dissuading recruits, Debs ran his last presidential campaign in 1920 from a federal penitentiary, polling almost a million votes—his best showing—as Prisoner 9653. Meanwhile, Congress had also passed the Sedition Act in 1918, the backbone of a crusade against dissidents and labor under the guise of wartime necessity.[91] These new, restrictive laws would soon be used against Castle Valley labor.

Despite his eventual militarism, even President Wilson had expressed his concern with the coming war when he wrote: "Every reform we have won will be lost . . . for we shall be dependent upon the steel, ore and financial magnates."[92] Ironically, shortly thereafter he headed the most so-cialistic administration ever to govern the United States. Federal agencies, staffed by corporate giants working for a dollar a year, ran virtually every aspect of the economy. To coordinate the war effort, the National Council of Defense met in Denver in May 1917, where Charles N. Strevell, long associated with the IC&C, represented Utah. To counteract a nationwide coal shortage in 1916–1917, Congress created a Food and Fuel Admin-istration, soon split in two. Herbert Hoover headed the Food Adminis-tration; Harry A. Garfield took over the Fuel Administration.[93] To solve the continuing coal shortage, the agency set up regional divisions that regulated production, prices, labor, and wages and, in 1918, set up a zone system for hauling coal.[94] The following June, Moroni Heiner of Emery County's U.S. Fuel Company became the coal distributor for Utah and southern Wyoming.[95]

During wartime, foreigners, particularly the Greeks, had become conve-nient targets. Although over sixty Castle Valley Greeks had returned home to fight Turks in 1912, they were reluctant to volunteer for World War I. Helper's Tom Avgikos explained why: Greece had already been partitioned between the Turks, English, and Italians, and, even though Greeks hated the kaiser, defeating him would not make the other Europeans give them back their country. Castle Valley's Greeks had done well in America, too, and gave thanks for their prosperity through the construction of Price's Church of the Assumption, the second Greek Orthodox church in Utah and the thirty-third in the United States. Consecrated on August 15, 1916, it also welcomed Serbs, who share a belief in Orthodox Christianity. This Byzantine-style, domed, brick building, constructed by Lars Gunderson (who had also built Price's Carnegie Library in 1913), soon saw a parade of marriages, funerals, and the celebration of holy days.[96]

In 1918, surging anti-Greek nativism led to a scam against Greek sheep-herders, the most well-to-do of their countrymen. Speculators, with the col-lusion of the State Land Board, obtained land leases at five cents per acre, but failed to mark the corners of the land leased. Instead, they lay in wait for "trespassers" (Greek sheepherders) and sued them for thousands of dollars. This mistreatment had two major results. First, local men formed the Carbon County Greek Association. Second, some Greeks bought lands to run their sheep, and this land would bring some families substantial for-tunes in the late twentieth century—surely an unintended consequence of those who sought to fleece the Greeks in World War I.[97] As the war contin-ued, in April 1918 the *News-Advocate* (successor to the *Carbon County News*) claimed that "American boys . . . are fighting to make America safe for them [the Greeks] to accumulate wealth." By contrast, the *Sun* (previously the *Eastern Utah Advocate*) complimented Greek patriotism on the recent oc-casion of the celebration of Greek independence day, singling out stirring addresses by the Greek priest and by Stylian Staes (Stylianos Stagapoulos), a local leader. It added that "the [Price Greek Orthodox] church subscribed for a thousand dollar liberty bond. This is the first church in Carbon County" to do so. It also noted that fourteen Greeks had already left for the war; ten more were to follow in two weeks' time.[98]

But before the war ended, a Greek nearly lost his life at the hands of a lynch mob—not for any lack of patriotism, but for taking a non-Greek girl for a ride in his yellow Buick. "Tony Michelog's brother [John Michelogiannis —the name had been shortened] . . . was going with a little Anglo-Saxon girl from Huntington or Cleveland," John Sampinos later remembered. "They were going to get married, but her parents didn't want her 'running around with a Greek.' So they said he molested her and threw him in jail." As a lynch mob massed, so did thousands of Greeks, pouring in from all the mining camps. "P. O. Silvagni gathered the Italian miners. . . . They actually had Price under siege! . . . They said if they hung Michelog, there wouldn't be any (white) person breathing the air the next day in Price. They would annihilate them. So Michelog was released, and the situation went back to normal."[99] In Europe, the Greeks and Italians had been historic enemies, but in Castle Valley, as Silvagni said when he rallied his countrymen, "If it's a Greek this time, it'll be an Italian next."[100]

As the war dragged on, men from throughout the Castle Valley corridor and from the Uinta Basin shipped out together from the Price depot. The *Advocate* listed them by name—a litany of Greeks, Italians, French, British, Americans, and others. As late as May 1918, dozens of recruits, of all nationalities, got a grand send-off from the Sunnyside Italian Band—directed by Prof. Giovanni D. Colistro—which had been passing through on the way back from Salt Lake City. There, the seventy-five-piece brass band had played in the Italian Day celebration and won the state-wide band competition. At the depot, Price officials delivered moving speeches and the recruits went through a military drill in a show of fervent patriotism that matched that of the nation at large.[101]

Many Castle Valley men served in France; at least one went as far as Vladivostok, on Russia's Pacific coast. Rolla West, a skilled carpenter, spent most of the war in France constructing airplanes for the new, more impersonal style of warfare. No longer would a soldier necessarily see his enemy face-to-face. Instead, bombs dropped from miles up, or mustard gas slid stealthily into the trenches and killed thousands. Some men died as exploding shells sliced their bodies with shrapnel. Shell shock among some survivors became the inevitable result. Price's Guy Thomas was wounded on the battlefield and put on "the finest, fastest American train you ever saw," recalled West, who saw him on the way to the hospital. Thomas, however, could not be saved. West also remembered the constant mud and the lack of food. German submarines torpedoed American supply ships crossing the Atlantic, and "the French didn't have any [food]"—though he did take advantage of their bourbon and cognac to kill the hunger pains.[102] George Rowley of Spring Glen also went to France to the thick of the fighting. He pushed through the Hindenberg Line and captured eighteen German military single-handedly. Later, after surviving a gas attack, he won the Purple Heart. Rowley returned home to become a school principal and juvenile judge and later served as a hospital ship chaplain in World War II.[103]

Fred Voll, later one of Helper's leading citizens, fought World War I on the other side of the world. Voll joined the Navy on June 7, 1917, and was sent to Russian Siberia where his outfit joined British, Japanese, Chinese, French, and Italian military in an attempt to control the Bolsheviks. Now called the Communists, these political dissidents had begun a three-way civil war in Russia with their capture of the government in St. Petersburg in October 1917. Opposed by royalists and republicans, the Bolsheviks in March 1918 signed a separate treaty with Germany, effectively taking Russia out of World War I. Over 40,000 Czechs and Slovaks, caught behind the lines when the war ended, could only get back to Europe by going the long way—through Russian Siberia. They commandeered the Trans-Siberian Railway and headed east. Their plight helped galvanize a cautious President Wilson to send American troops, Fred Voll among them. Voll saw no Bolsheviks, but he did meet the Czechs and Slovaks and learned of their toughness and resolve. He and his shipmates helped them to cross the Pacific to San Francisco, and they eventually got back to Europe by going virtually all the way around the world. The international presence in Siberia had done nothing to stop the Bolsheviks. Russia soon became solidly Communist, despite the fact that America still had 8,477 troops in Siberia in September 1919— including Voll, who was finally mustered out on October 12, 1919.[104] By then, the Great War had been officially over for nearly a year.

At home during World War I, most people simply did their patriotic best. Mines expanded to meet factories' fuel demands. In early April 1917, just before the declaration of war, a new camp, named for leading developer William H. Wattis, opened just north of Hiawatha. Developed with backing of Ogden businessmen M. S. Browning, Edmund O. Wattis, and Royal Eccles, it began shipping in March 1918 over a spur connected to the Utah Railway. With men gone overseas, women worked on the coal tipples, the huge, warehouse-sized shaking machines that sorted coal by size before it was dropped into railroad cars. Many also helped with the Red Cross, working as nurses or rolling bandages at home. They collected clothing for the troops, where Green River excelled by providing 4,442 separate articles.[105] Local medical care improved when Dr. C. T. Rose built his own hospital at Price, offering Red Cross classes to "a limited number of ladies . . . between the ages of 19 and 25." In 1918, the Rose Hospital changed hands a couple of times, becoming Carbon Hospital. By 1921, it belonged to Dr. W. P.

A photographer recorded the devastation at Castle Gate when the Gooseberry dam above Scofield broke in 1917. Note the warped and washed out railroad tracks at left and the splintered bridge in the background. The Castle Gate store, which remained standing, is at the far left. Courtesy of Albert Fossatt.

Winters, previously of Castle Dale and Mount Pleasant.[106] During the war, Red Cross women from all the Castle Valley chapters also flocked to the railroad station in Price, supplying the estimated 18,250 men who passed through with "coffee, sandwiches, fruit, chocolate bars, cigarets [sic], cookies, doughnuts, cantaloupes, watermelons, chewing gum, etc."[107] Women and children raised Victory Gardens to augment food supplies, so that excess produce could go to feed the troops. By January 1918, school children were tagging coal shovels to remind householders to conserve one shovel a day to save an estimated 50,000,000 tons a year nationally.[108]

Natural disasters also took their toll on Castle Valley. In June 1917, just after U.S. entry into World War I, the Gooseberry Dam above Scofield broke. Floodwaters roared down Price Canyon, through Castle Gate (where they smashed the railroad depot to splinters), past Helper and Spring Glen and out through Price. The new steel bridge south of town withstood the flood, although the older Southern Utah and Castle Valley Railroad bridge crumpled. The Gooseberry Dam had been completed in 1910 by the Price River Irrigation Company, successor to the older Utah Irrigation and Power Company which began actual construction in 1907. For seven years, it had helped foster local agriculture, especially apple trees and oats. When crops suffered in the dry winter of 1915–1916, developers had raised the dam by five feet and let the subsequent winter's snowmelt rise to within ten inches of the top of the dam. That was just too much water, so the dam failed. In May 1919, six months after the war ended, Helper's main street caught fire, and residents rushed from their homes, believing the whole crowded town would go. Firefighters from Helper and Price managed to douse the blaze, but not before it created property damage estimated at between $80,000–$100,000. It destroyed Peter Bozone's bakery and four of his houses; Antone Labori's rooming house; three commercial buildings belonging to Baptiste Flaim, and the four-story hotel and store building owned by M. P. Bergera, housing some $20,000 in merchandise belonging to C. A. Bertolina.[109]

However, the worst affliction—not only locally, but throughout the world—was the flu. A rapidly-spreading influenza epidemic had begun late in the summer of 1918, springing up almost simultaneously around the globe. In the European trenches before it started, the calculated death rate of soldiers from disease equaled a modest five-per-thousand–per-year. By October, men died at the rate of four a week. The Armistice on November 11, 1918, put an end to the shooting, but death by disease continued to spread. As the feverish, cold-like symptoms clambered through Castle Valley towns, schools closed, events were canceled, and businesses suffered. Children and adults alike wore little, foul-smelling asafetida bags on strings around their necks in the hope that the nasty odor would ward off the disease. Some local residents tried garlic instead, with equally unsuccessful results. The flu started with a headache, body aches, and continuous chills with a high fever. In a few days, or hours, faces turned purple, people began to cough up blood as their feet turned black. They began gasping frantically for breath as they slowly drowned in the reddish fluid that filled their lungs—unstoppable, incurable. Children under five, elderly over seventy, and, oddly, those between twenty and forty were the most susceptible. Over 25 percent of America's population fell ill; 2.5 percent of those died. Consequently, the average life span in the U.S. fell by twelve years in 1918, from age 51 to age 39.[110]

Communities pulled together to tend the sick and bury the dead. For example, in Huntington, practiced healer Mary Susannah Fowler, with her two youngest boys in unknown condition overseas, aided her town's one overworked doctor in successfully nursing countless influenza victims.[111] In Hiawatha, Wilhelmina "Stecky" Holdaway remembered when the flu hit. The brand new company amusement hall became a pest house, where bachelors and those at the far end of camp were quarantined until they either died or recovered. Huntington native Dr. Ernest Nixon, the new company doctor, tended the victims with one registered nurse and two aides: Bill Berenson, who helped with the men; and Frone Myers, the superintendent's mother-in-law, who aided the women. Those still healthy took over jobs left by the sick as the disease whipped through the isolated camp. Nine-year-old Stecky found herself replacing her mother as the company telephone operator, using knowledge she had absorbed while hanging around the mine office after school. She ran the switchboard all by herself every night from 10 to midnight when her father, the town marshal, came to take her home. In the room behind her, the dead were stored in wicker baskets until the area's only mortician, Mr. Flynn, had time to retrieve them. "The superintendent said he'd kill anybody that told me that there were bodies in there," recalled Holdaway, but I heard this basket one night, squeaking, and I started to open the door." She recognized Flynn and could identify the baskets from scenes she had seen in movies, "So I hurried up and shut the door because I didn't want him to pick me up." Then, one night when Flynn and an assistant came to get the bodies, the door to the office swung open, and a heavily-loaded basket "came in right by my seat where I was sitting talking to the Price operator," Holdaway remembered. She screamed, and a drunken Flynn spoke into her mouthpiece, "She's all right; I just scared her." But the Price operator called back shortly thereafter just to make sure. Holdaway concluded, "He [Flynn] was getting worn out; it's no wonder he came up there drunk." Hiawatha's quarantine, established in November, was finally lifted in March.[112] By the time the epidemic ended, over 50,000 American troops would be dead, and perhaps ten times that many U.S. civilians.[113]

Holdaway remembered, too, when the soldiers came home. Hiawatha then christened its new amusement hall with "a big dedication dance. . . . All the women got formals, real elegant. . . . The men wore tux."[114] By 1922, Hiawatha's Henry Holdsworth Post of the American Legion (named for one of the five town residents killed in action) had raised $4,000 to buy a bronze Doughboy statue, erected between the amusement hall and the U.S. Fuel office building. One of probably hundreds dedicated nationwide, it showed an American soldier charging the Germans with his right hand extended holding a hand grenade and his field equipment on his back. By 1990, this statue was one of only two or three still left in the United States. The American Legion sponsored its retention in Castle Valley, and the Price mayor originally suggested moving it to sites rejected as too obscure. "'Where do you want it, next to city hall?'" the mayor asked. "'That would be nice,'" answered American Legion post commander Mario DiCaro. Former doughboys, J. Bracken Lee and Ted Thomas (whose brother, Guy, had died in the Great War), attended the 1990 dedication on Price Main Street. The statue now stands next to City Hall, refurbished by local metal artist Gary Prazen with a new plaque funded by the Price Kiwanis listing casualties in subsequent foreign wars.[115]

After World War I, veterans returned to a changing America. Thomas, for example, got a job driving his Tin Lizzy behind the privately-contracted Murdock Stage Line carrying mail from Price to Vernal. He picked up mail sacks that fell off its truck. In the spring of 1919, the Post Office took over this 121–mile route. Thomas became one of the original twenty-six Post Office drivers, handling rural deliveries that increased 200 percent in the first eight months. "We hauled anything they'd put stamps on," Thomas recalled. "The Uintah Bank in Vernal was built completely from bricks we hauled . . . [at] 74 cents for 70 pounds of bricks." The only bank ever built by mail in the United States, its bricks came parcel post, since rates were based on circles drawn with Salt Lake City as the center regardless of the route packages actually traveled. Driving over 9,100–foot Indian Canyon, the mail trucks sometimes got stuck in such deep snow that the drivers walked the distance between them, dragging up the mail sacks to exchange at the top. "Once a round trip to Vernal and back took me and my partner seven days because of the snow and deep mud," Thomas recalled. When the state improved roads west of Salt Lake City, in 1934, America's longest Star Route (so named for special, rural conditions) finally shut down.[116]

Less positive changes came, too. As Wellington's Don Carlos Grundvig rode the train home to Utah from California where he had been demobilized, he faced another, more unpleasant American reality. As he argued for the pardon of labor organizer Tom Mooney, framed for the 1916 Preparedness Day parade bombing, Grundvig said, "Why not? They never did find him guilty." A big sergeant across the aisle jumped to his feet and thundered, "I think I will take you in and file charges." Seeing the man in uniform carrying his sidearm, Grundvig "apologize[d] very meekly." The sergeant got off at the next stop, and the car's other occupants then wondered out loud if the soldier was with the Army Intelligence Division and if he had been in the parade itself. They warned the nervous Grundvig that he might find federal investigators on his doorstep back home.[117]

This was no idle threat. While the nation adjusted to peacetime, the triumphs of Russia's Communists–Reds—and their political strength in western Europe increasingly disturbed American conservatives and stimulated American leftists, guaranteeing a clash. Although Grundvig did not get a visit from government agents, 1919 brought a widespread spate of hysteria. It began with the Seattle general strike in January. In May, thirty bombs (most unexploded) went out in the mail to national political figures, including Utah politicians Frank Nebeker, William H. King, and Reed Smoot. A month later, another bomb detonated at the home of U.S. Attorney General A. Mitchell Palmer. The alarmed Palmer promptly spearheaded a national "Red Scare," rounding up dissidents and deporting aliens. The fever peaked in January 1920, then quickly faded as Americans lost interest in the exaggerated Communist menace. Palmer's raids, however, left the Socialist Party shrunken, the IWW permanently crippled, and heavy-handed criminal syndicalism laws on the books of many states, including Utah. In one year of labor unrest, 3,600 strikes had flared nationwide; fourteen of them in Utah. The only one in the Castle Valley coal mines, on November 1, 1919, came spontaneously. The UMWA, trying to align members' wages with capitalists' new, post-war profits, had called for a nationwide strike but had declined to include partially-organized Utah. Nonetheless, UMWA members walked out at Scofield, Castle Gate, Kenilworth, Hiawatha, Storrs, and Rains. The strike failed. Subsequent internal friction in the union led to Utah's reassignment from Colorado's District 15 to Wyoming's District 22 in 1921. That realignment and Utah's strict criminal syndicalism law were the strike's only major legacies, but both would have major local repercussions.[118]

Labor's struggle to keep wartime gains mirrored the post-war strains of the nation. During World War I, the federal government had created a marvelous business machine, but it had no brakes. Skeletal emergency government agencies ran for years after the war ended; the Railroad Administration until 1920, for example. Unneeded coal, hastily mined, remained stockpiled; farm prices began to drop. Preoccupied with foreign affairs, President Wilson stumped the country seeking support for the Treaty of Versailles which he had helped to negotiate. It included his prized Fourteenth Point, calling for a League of Nations to offer a diplomatic alternative to war. A hostile Senate killed the Treaty; a stroke nearly killed Wilson. He spent the rest of his term as a semi-invalid; the U.S. never joined the League of Nations and had to sign a separate peace to officially end the war.[119] Post-war America had changed from the optimistic, progressive nation it had been just a few years before. Not knowing quite what went wrong, people longed for normalcy, and turned to a variety of explanations and diversions in the ensuing years.

# 8

# Roller Coaster, 1920–1929

*There was much drinking in those days. . . . It was smart to out-wit prohibition offi-
cers, smart to be wild and woolly, to attend "Speak-Easies" where one could purchase
drinks, dance, and have a "ball". . . . I had thought [this behavior] would never get
started in Emery County. I was wrong. These practices seep outward from the centers
of the populated areas into the most remote corners.[1]*
— Eva Westover Conover, farm wife and state legislator

For many, the 1920s was a roller coaster ride, some of which felt distinctly
uncomfortable. Historian Robert Wiebe claimed that World War I made
America "tough and plural . . . [facing the] unfamiliarity of new relationships and the ambiguity of new principles."[2] Everywhere, people felt drawn
to new ideas and modern lifestyles. Expectations rose for the "good life,"
and many plunged headlong into a round of fun sparked by movies, spread
by automobiles, and spiked with bathtub gin. At the same time, a gathering
depression in both mining and farming drove Castle Valley residents first
to private organizations, then to the federal government for desperately
needed aid.

Initially, Castle Valley rode the tail end of wartime prosperity. For example, in 1921, the Utah Oil Refining Company accidentally struck carbon
dioxide gas in the Farnham anticline a few miles east of Wellington and
helium in the Woodside anticline. Fresh from the military use of "lighter-
than-air" balloons, the U.S. government created a local Helium Reserve to
conserve the non-explosive gas. Never used for warfare, the carbon dioxide
eventually was loaded into cartridges to shoot down coal. It also supplied
Wellington's long-lived dry ice plant (useful for all sorts of applications,
even making home-made root beer or fog for stage productions), in lieu of
the tremendous power normally required, such as the Dry Ice Corporation
of America used to take from Niagara Falls.[3]

Farming did even better, including "patches of onions that netted the owners $1,000 an acre," crowed the 1920 *New West Magazine*. Harvests boomed in sugar beets, cherries, alfalfa, sweet clover, potatoes, and other lucrative crops.[4] This prosperity nonetheless had a tenuous natural basis. As a county agricultural agent noted, ten-inch precipitation, "low humidity and strong wind movement" meant that the "practice of farming during the summer and working in the mines in the winter has [of necessity] existed since the beginning."[5] Farmer-miners joined recent immigrants in a total of "eighteen mining camps running full time, with an output annually of 5,000,000 tons of bituminous coal" and became some of the "more than 5,000 miners."[6]

Job opportunities grew as more mines opened and old ones expanded. For example, Lion Coal Company merged with Wattis Coal in 1919 to further develop mining along the Carbon-Emery County border. Kinney Coal Company at Scofield was poised to open as the *New West* article went to press.[7] Another new mine, called variously Little Standard or the McLean Mine, also opened in 1919 in Spring Canyon. Older developments also thrived: U.S. Fuel, now encompassing Hiawatha, Mohrland, and Black Hawk, had just produced over one million tons of coal, the only company besides Utah Fuel ever to do so.[8] Latuda, in Spring Canyon, in 1920 drove a new 2,200–foot rock tunnel from the tipple into the coal seam, which lessened the grade, increased production, but still allowed an innovative method for generating electricity. The coal-filled cars of the mine trip, as they dropped down the canyon, generated enough power to run a new large, powerful electric substation, added in 1921. At the same time, in another rocky canyon over forty miles east along the Book Cliffs, the Columbia Steel Corporation developed a new mine in 1919. In 1921, it began shipping coal over a spur of the Sunnyside railway, and a year later opened an accompanying town, named—of course—Columbia.[9]

As production increased, the price of coal began to drop: from $3.35 per ton in 1921; to $3.14 in 1922; to $2.89 in 1923; to $2.69 in 1924; to $2.53 by 1928; and to $2.47 as the Stock Market buckled a year later.[10] In 1919–1921, domestic copper production dropped by 54 percent, slashing demand for coke.[11] Utah's grand jury later uncovered coal operators' resultant price-fixing when, in coordination, they raised coal prices from $9.50 to $10.00 a ton. It indicted Frank N. Cameron of Utah Fuel; Frederick N. Sweet of Standard, Sweets, and others; Moroni Heiner of United States Fuel; Jesse W. Knight of Knight Fuel Company (which owned Storrs); and J. H. Tonkin, general manager of Kenilworth's Independent Coal and Coke.[12]

Nationwide, the economy faltered late in 1920. A lot of Americans ignored the sectional downturn that affected largely textiles, farming, and mining, (consequently devastating Castle Valley). Elsewhere, people were having too much fun. Part of the impetus came from Prohibition, adopted nationwide thanks to the Eighteenth Amendment and the accompanying

Volstead Act. Everywhere, bootleggers proliferated. In Castle Valley, they brewed or distilled the "good stuff" in sheep camps, basements, orchards, and old pioneer dugouts. The popular Wilberg Resort, halfway between Huntington and Castle Dale, attracted Saturday night dance crowds who "only had to walk along the road between the long rows of parked cars, and someone would come up to you and ask if you were looking for a drink."[13] Out on the San Rafael Swell, Moonshine Tanks Canyon earned its name from local whiskey makers who would use the water from the sandstone holes to make their product, posting a guard at the top of the nearest ledge where the country could be viewed for miles. They sold their hundred proof to bootleggers, who would color it with boiled coffee, "dilute it 50 to 100 percent, and sell it for $1 a flat pint (12 ounces) or $4 a gallon. A pint was strong enough to get your mind off your troubles," wrote Castle Dale's Owen McClenahan.[14] Some Castle Valley residents who had never before tried beer or liquor tried it then; for others, particularly immigrants, alcohol had always been part of their lives.[15] Although American temperance reformers had high expectations, in 1924 Castle Gate's T. L. Burridge summed up the common attitude in his diary: "Jack had some very good moonshine and I think it did our cold a world of good. Still we are breaking the law when we drink even though it is given to us, but [it] is mighty hard to live up strictly to a law that you are not in sympathy with."[16] This noble experiment finally died an ignoble death in 1933, after stimulating organized crime and new roles for women, for whom clandestine speak-easies had become daring new retreats.

In part, the enactment of the Twentieth Amendment—Woman Suffrage—in 1919, had also altered women's roles. Nineteen-twenties women moved in larger circles than their forbears and had new experiences. For example, Eva Conover spent her senior year of high school in Provo in 1926–1927, leaving a quiet farming town where girls did not drink and returning to find that many did. While she refused to drink alcohol, she did love "the Jazz music that kept one's feet tapping, those fads in dances, the flee-hop, the Charleston, the fox-trot, the two-step, and always the waltz. . . . I remember watching, before I was old enough to dance, the 'Shimmie', and 'The Rag'. They were something else!"[17] Others expressed their modernity by moving away from home, such as Alda Vee Lambson Alger, who left her home in Circleville, Paiute County, to teach at Consumers coal camp in 1926. "I think that everyone was horrified that I wanted to come to Carbon County, but I did," she recalled, "because it was metropolitan."[18]

Perhaps the greatest influence of all was the movies. Women copied the stars, bobbing their hair, raising hemlines all the way to the knee, becoming the ultimate "flapper," a cartoon creation of Salt Lake native John Held, Jr.[19] While the technical, mechanical ability to make moving pictures had surfaced in the 1880s and 1890s, the idea of a theatrical narrative matured (in the U.S.) with *The Great Train Robbery* in 1903, and the first feature-length

176 NEW PEOPLE, NEW WAYS

film aired in 1912.[20] World War I had severely hampered European competition since celluloid (the basic material for film) and high explosives required the same ingredients, giving America the global lead in film.[21] Locally, by 1908, beloved "Uncle" Bert Martin and his wife, Mae, started bringing silent films to the valley every two weeks. They charged twenty-five cents for adults and ten cents for children. Martin originally arrived with a hand-cranked projector and showed one twelve-minute reel at a time. As an elderly man, he was still making the rounds in the 1930s, showing films for two nights at the Finn Hall in Clear Creek, then traveling down to Castle Gate for another two-night stand.[22] Everyone went; one former Helper child billed movie night as "a big event."[23] Building on Martin's success, Price businessmen opened the first newly constructed motion picture theater in 1911. By 1913, Price had two theaters, the Isis and the Eko. The latter had contracted with the Orpheum Theater circuit, which promised "talking pictures [with the aid of accompanying phonographs], acquired at a cost of $75,000 for ninety days."[24] A year or two later, Abraham Greenhalgh bought the old Killpack store building in Ferron where his family's orchestra played for dances. When few people came, the Greenhalghs turned the large hall into a movie theater. People crowded in once a week on "show night," getting "a glimpse of the outside world, breaking down the barrier that had isolated the community," later reported a local historian.[25] When a second theater failed, the Greenhalghs took it over, too, but the over-expanded business faltered. After that, the LDS Church committee sponsored motion pictures at the chapel to maintain that link to the world outside, as it later did in the ward meetinghouses at Castle Dale, Emery, Huntington, and Cleveland. By the 1920s, Ferron could boast the presence of the Star Theater, which, in 1930, showed the first "talkies" in Emery County. Other Castle Valley towns had their own movie palaces: the Bonita Theater in Huntington; the Rex Theater in Castle Dale; and the Gem Theater in Green River. In Helper, movies aired in the Liberty Theater, then patrons folded up their chairs, rolled up the protective floor canvas, and the dancing began (at least until the Strand Theater opened in 1922). In the basement of the Strand, storekeeper Harry Eda showed silent Japanese movies, and provided a stage for occasional traveling Kabuki theater groups, pool, and gambling.[26] At Kenilworth, the company offered free silent movies every Thursday night and another ten-cent show on Sunday afternoon.[27] Castle Gate, too, offered "Dances on Saturday night. The picture shows weren't talking . . . you'd read underneath what they were saying," remembered Walter Borla, the child of Italian immigrants.[28] At Standardville, Nedra Monroe Richardson and Kay Leavitt also remembered the silents, with piano accompaniment first provided by Mrs. Harmond from Price, and later by town resident Mrs. Beebe.[29]

This lighthearted, multi-ethnic entertainment contrasted with a growing post-war national perception that dangerous immigrant hordes were taking American jobs.[30] As the door swung shut, foreigners still kept coming to Castle Valley: South Slavs, driven out of their homeland as Italy got their villages by treaty after the war; Japanese, who had originally followed the fad of seeking work in the modern land of America.[31] For example, seventeen-year-old Masaki Okura had left his native village in 1904, and sent money back to Japan ever since, creating favorable press with his illusion of easy prosperity. His cousin, Kosuye Tsugawa Okura, had been married to him by proxy although she was only four when he left and did not remember him. Masaki returned to claim his bride when she was nineteen. "The day I went to the station to go after him I said to my family, 'I will be back in a little while.' Everybody was laughing at me because . . . officially I was [already] an Okura." She never lived with her natal family again. Masaki had told Kosuye he was a railroad section foreman (which he had been in Wyoming) but, months later, upon arrival in the U.S., he brought her straight to the better-paying Kenilworth coal mines. "I felt so degraded to be lowered that low from being raised in such a high [samurai] class," recalled Kosuye. "I cried every day . . . [for] a year." To help meet expenses, she started cooking for the bachelors in the "Jap" boarding house. That November, the company doctor delivered her first daughter whom she named Utah, the only English word she knew.[32]

American nativists, caught up in pseudo-scientific racism, wanted no such "inferior races" breeding on their shores. Consequently, in 1921, Congress established a quota system, limiting new arrivals to three percent of the total number emigrating from each European nation based on the 1910 census. Already-established Asian restrictions remained untouched; the Western Hemisphere was excluded. According to historian John Higham, "the law of 1921 proved in the long run the most important turning-point in American immigration policy." Its hallmarks—the quota system favoring northern Europe and its sharp limitations generally – allegedly insured that "in a generation the foreign-born would cease to be a major factor in American history."[33] He may have overestimated the new law's impact; nonetheless, its stringency very nearly had tragic results for the Bikakis family who arrived from Crete in 1921. Nick Bikakis recalled that his father, already working in America, had sent for him, his sister, and their mother to come join him. When they got to Ellis Island, they had to wait almost a month while their papers were processed. By then, "the immigration quota had closed and they were going to send us back to Greece." Luckily, another Utah-bound traveler had gotten through and informed their father of their imminent deportation. Through Stylian Staes, he got in touch with a U.S. senator who interceded with immigration officials. A week later, the family was reunited in Castle Valley.[34] As far as Congress was concerned, however, the 1921 law still admitted too many "undesirables," so it passed a revision in 1924. The new act set a two percent limit based on the 1890 census until a survey of "national origins" of all previous immigrants could serve as the basis for parceling out a total quota of 150,000 by 1927 (actually implemented in 1929). The Japanese, like the Chinese in 1884, were completely excluded.[35]

Unions welcomed immigration restriction because it signaled the end of imported foreign strike-breakers. The new immigration laws, coupled with the prolonged economic downturn, created an explosive labor situation. When in 1922 Castle Valley mine owners cut workers' pay by thirty percent (also lowering the cost of coal camp housing and mining supplies by fifteen percent), the imbalance in favor of the company was all too obvious.[36] When the UMWA walked out nationwide, still partially organized Utah went, too.[37] The Strike of 1922 had begun.

Different camps had different experiences. At Winter Quarters, company man Stanley Harvey remembered how the "head guard," Sam Dorrity, rode horseback down to Scofield, attracting gunfire from striking miners. "They [the strikers] were shooting low [to avoid a fatality] it looked like," Harvey later recalled. Dorrity survived, but his horse died.[38] Two strikers were also wounded, one shot thorough the lungs with a bullet in the back, and the other through the right shoulder. Often, Scofield teachers kept children in after school and made them lie on the floor to protect them from the shooting.[39] The companies continued bringing in strikebreakers from other states and counties, including Huntington and Castle Dale. "Sometimes they would bring them in over the hill on saddle horses from . . . Sanpete," Harvey remembered. "It was an awful job trying to break them into mining coal because they didn't know a thing about it."[40]

When companies needed still more miners, they turned to a previously almost untapped population: African Americans. As Howard Browne, Sr. recalled, "In 1922 or 1923 . . . they started bringing people from down South to come in here to break strikes. And that's the main reason why most of the blacks (including my stepfather) got in Carbon County."[41] By the 1920s, the South seemed a good place to leave. As blacks there became better educated and more articulate, many whites tried to keep them from advancing with highly discriminatory Jim Crow laws, often backed by violence. Thus, they made ideal recruits for Castle Valley coal operators, who had run out of other pliant populations to import. During the strike, Browne's family went to Rains. "There were about twenty blacks living there, working in the mine. There were ten or fifteen black people living in Helper . . . Latuda . . . Castle Gate . . . Kenilworth; and another twenty or thirty living and working in . . . Hiawatha. "[42] Unknowingly, the African Americans had moved into camp quarters recently emptied by threats and violence.

In camp after camp, company men had evicted the striking miners and their families from corporate property. Sometimes men in the boarding houses lacked even the time to pack their clothing.[43] At Sunnyside, while company guards prepared to throw a woman in labor out into the street, the company doctor, Andrew Dowd, stood on her porch with a shotgun and threatened to shoot any guard who entered.[44] All up and down the Castle Valley corridor, evicted families settled where they could. Some farmer-miners went home to Emery County. The UMWA provided displaced members with tents shipped in from Wyoming, fostering colonies of strike towns, often just outside the coal camps. At remote Hiawatha, every day the town marshal, William Steckleman, rode his horse down to the strike camp to escort one or two people into town so they could buy necessities and pick up the mail for all of those on strike. When one of the women in the tent camp became seriously ill, Steckleman approached the company doctor for help. He refused to come to the strike camp, but the superintendent agreed to send his car to fetch her if his chauffeur would drive. The chauffeur assented. Consequently, with the armed Steckleman in the front seat, they brought the patient to the company hospital, where she recovered.[45]

At Sunnyside, those evicted included Albert Vogrenic and Anna Marolt Tolich, then striking miners' children. Vogrenic, born in Sunnyside in 1916, particularly recalled the "great big wire fence across the bottom end of town there, and us kids used to get up on the fence and throw rocks at the scabs." One night when they climbed the fence, the company's searchlight swung across and lit them up and guards shot at them.[46] Tolich remembered their tent with a hard-packed dirt floor. She also described the machine gun stationed on a hill above the mine entrance, and the National Guard with their guns: "It was quite a harassment . . . [although] they didn't hurt anybody." Most warmly, she remembered the United Mine Workers' organizer, Frank Bonacci, who "helped to put the union in."[47]

Bonacci's family suffered severely when the strike began at Kenilworth. Frank Bonacci was run out of town, and mine guards moved his family to a run-down, old house at its outskirts without water or electricity. Guards kept them prisoner, denying them food. "Several days later Ann Dolinski defied the guard and walked to the house," wrote Helen Papanikolas. "The younger children could not keep down the omelet she brought after their long hunger. The oldest child, Marion Lupo, said, 'My mother was never the same after this experience. She was silent and withdrawn.'"[48] Bonacci and his brother moved down to their married sister's farm in Spring Glen. The company set up a searchlight that raked the little community all night long. "I'd go to bed every night with fear and worry," recalled their niece, Filomena Fazzio Bonacci. "The searchlight put fear in us. [We thought] they knew everything that was going on down here. They could tell who was here and who wasn't here."[49]

Plenty of others came to Spring Glen, the only heavily ethnic farming village in Castle Valley. The family of John Kosec, driven from Mohrland when the strike started, moved to a 12 x 15–foot tent there, one of dozens stretching clear to the railroad tracks.[50] "Wherever they could find a place, there was a tent," said Francis Dupin Vouk, remembering the sight in front of her father's store, where plenty of strikers lived on credit (some

of which they never repaid). A few others made money working for Martin
Millarich across the street, putting up a brick building called Millarich Hall
that replaced the old wooden building standing since 1907. Millarich had
run a tavern there until Prohibition. After that, he turned to bottling soda
water and, some said, selling bootleg out the back. Fellow Austrian Leonard Mahorich did the carpentry work on the new building to earn his living.[51] Other families helped out on local farms, such as the one shared
by Dominic Conca, Virginio Marzo, and John and Camillo Manina. "The
men, the kids, they'd come up and give you a hand and take vegetables,"
remembered Jack Marzo, Virginio's son. A lot of strikers also worked on the
highway from Helper to Castle Gate, using teams with scrapers, and digging
the road by hand.[52]

Invariably, with typical American xenophobia, officials blamed a particular ethnic group for the strike. In 1903–1904, Italians had been targeted. In Kenilworth, the blame shifted to Greeks in 1910 and stayed there
through 1922. This pattern of always finding a new scapegoat replicated the
American dislike of the newest foreign arrivals, and the Greeks had come in
great numbers only since 1900. (For that matter, so had the Japanese, but
they remained too few in number—and too disinclined to strike—to con-
stitute as much of a "menace.") As historian Helen Papanikolas explained,
the Greeks' "asking for army exemption during the war [World War I],
their refusal to attend Americanization classes, their sending large amounts
of money to Greece, and their bootleg and assault charges" made them
special targets of the newspapers and the American Legion.[53] In response,
they banded more closely together to confront growing prejudice. In the
early 1900s, the Greeks had formed Pan Hellenic Unions, admitting all
their countrymen. During the 1922 strike, the old organizations foundered
as men separated into new groups based on their Greek provinces of origin.
Almost all also joined one of the national lodges: the American Hellenic
Educational Progress Association (AHEPA), founded in 1922 to foster as-
similation, and the more conservative Greek American Progressive Association (GAPA), established a year later, which emphasized the preservation
of Greek culture.[54] The first death in the 1922 strike was also a Greek. On
May 14, 1922, striker John Tenas (Htenakis) died from a bullet fired by
deputy sheriff Lorenzo H. Young from Huntington. The unarmed Tenas,
strikers claimed, had been shot in the back, but Young said he had shot in
self-defense. At Tenas's funeral, the Price band marched in procession with
seven hundred Greeks following his casket, many waving small blue-and-
white Greek flags.[55]

Friction increased. Strikers consistently picketed the entrances to coal
camps and along the Utah Railway, the artery bringing strikebreakers to the
more remote mines. Sporadic shooting erupted: twice at Kenilworth and
once at Standardville, with no injuries. Dynamite was often the weapon of
choice in America's labor wars, and Castle Valley had plenty of it, for shooting

Spring Canyon members of the United Mine Workers of America man the picket line, display-
ing both their "STRIKE" placard and the American flag to show their right to strike. Courtesy of
Western Mining and Railroad Museum.

down coal in the mines, or for heralding the beginning of a celebration
like Dewey Day, Independence Day, or July 24th. But no one ever used it
in a strike. Instead, men loaded their rifles, seeking specific, not general,
targets. On June 14 some strikers prepared for a confrontation when word
came of a group of about twenty Colorado men riding to Standardville in
a single car on the Utah Railway. When the unionized train crew learned
the passengers' identities, they refused to budge, stranding the "scab train"
at Castle Gate. So, R. J. Vaughan, former Union Pacific engineer and new
Utah Railway superintendent, decided to drive the train.[56] Standardville's
Arthur P. Webb, county deputy and company guard, agreed to be the fire-
man, shoveling coal into the engine box to keep up a head of steam. H. E.
Lewis, general manager of the Standard Coal Company, and a number of
other armed guards rode with them. "My dad rode the train in the cab,"
later recalled Wilhelmina Steckleman Holdaway (or Stecky). "But when
they went through the tunnel at Martin, and came out. . . . these men
[striking miners] were up on the hill. My dad looked up there and said he
didn't see anyone . . . [but] of course, they were behind bushes. And then
he looked to see if there was any on the other side of the track and just then
the shots were fired and Mr. Webb was killed."[57] The strikers told it differ-
ently. As always, they said, they were picketing along the track to let the

men on the train know they were taking jobs of striking miners. According to their attorney, Sam King, "[W]hen the train left the tunnel . . . a number [tried] approaching the train on the track and in the open. . . . [F]iring at once started from the train . . . [and] judging by the number of shots fired from the train, the strikebreakers must have been armed."[58] One Greek striker was shot in the arm and later arrested. He escaped from custody, although fourteen other Greeks and one Italian were later identified by H. E. Lewis as the perpetrators—in fact, some had been present and some had not. Prejudicial news articles followed. After quick local trials, initial defendants received long sentences. Subsequent trials were later moved to Castle Dale, and dragged on into 1924.[59] Union miner Vito Bonacci put the whole incident more bluntly: "when this train . . . came through the tunnel, somebody shot him [Webb] . . . .. That's when the soldiers came down."[60] Governor Mabey had ordered in the Utah National Guard to patrol the coal fields.

Guards fanned out to the coal camps, Scofield, and Helper. About three hundred local miners were rounded up and those found with weapons disarmed; three-man patrols prevented street meetings; sentries guarded all the roads to and from Helper, and machine guns threatened strikers' tent camps from the heights. When Margaret Marzo Ariotti and her siblings left their Spring Glen farm to attend St. Anthony's Catholic Church in Helper, oncoming soldiers frightened them so they hid in the sagebrush by the canal. They watched wide-eyed as the soldiers stabbed the wet ground with their bayonets, probing for buried guns.[61] Eight-year-old Elizabeth Jackson Ciochette, living in Kenilworth, remembered the "guard at the entrance of town, and people had to have a pass coming and going. . . . The curfew was ten o'clock at night and every light had to be put out, except the search lights. If the lights were not out at curfew, guards would rap on the door with their gun butts. . . . if arms were found, they were confiscated."[62] Charlie Saccomanno, also eight, took his dog with him when he went with his father and uncle to peddle produce from their Spring Glen farm. "As you would enter Kenilworth," he remembered, "a guard would pull the ropes to open the gate. Once we got in, they would check our wagon for any guns or artillery we might be trying to smuggle in. . . . One day I was sitting along side of the road when one officer was riding up on his horse. My dog started to bark at him; the officer took out his gun and shot my dog. I went home, got a shovel, and buried the dog."[63]

In August, the UMWA called off the strike as, back East, John L. Lewis forged a settlement. Utah mine owners restored the wage scale prevalent before the thirty percent reduction. Companies refused to recognize the union. As Charlie Saccommano summarized, "Soon after the strike ended, the men went back to Kenilworth. Some to their homes and to their jobs, some to find out that someone else was living in their homes and working at their jobs."[64] Some of those who replaced blacklisted strikers had left their farms only in desperation as nature seemingly turned against them. For example, alfalfa and clover, the staple crops since before World War I, repeatedly suffered from the perennial local problem of insufficient water plus a severe infestation of the alfalfa weevil. In Ferron, Cliff Snow managed to combat the insect pests with a machine he made from old binder parts that beat the insects off the high alfalfa onto a canvas. Then the bugs were dumped out in a pile and burned. But in the 1920s, alfalfa prices went into a slide, and by the mid-1930s, farmers no longer grew it as a cash crop. Likewise, the 1920s saw a decrease in apple trees, home-made butter, and honey production.[65] Consequently, some families chose the coal camp life, and the company assigned them houses vacated during the strike. Those arriving in Kenilworth in 1922 included Calvin Jewkes from Orangeville, who began as a teen-aged miner and went on to a long career in the company store. This talented musician and singer became leader of the Cal Jewkes Orchestra, the "Music Venders," arguably the best dance band in Castle Valley. He also played trombone in other orchestras, joined a quartet which sang at the Price Theater's intermissions, and by the end of his life had sung for over 2,500 funerals and in a lot of other places.[66] Another new Kenilworth resident, Wilford Coleman Burton, came with his wife, Coila Otten Burton, and their baby, Jeannette, following his brothers into the camp. As another daughter put it, they had to move because "their farm was unable to provide enough due to depressed times."[67]

As Castle Valley's economy tottered, some people tried to made a living in business. For example, John Skerl, Sr., a Slovenian immigrant who had first mined coal at Sunnyside then gone into cattle with the Millarich brothers during World War I, found his herd destroyed by a freak freeze. Then, prices dropped. Cattle he had bought at $75 a head he sold for $25 a head. He lost the farm, moved to Spring Glen, and went to work for Frank Dolinsky at a pool hall there until the Strike of 1922 undercut that business, too. In 1924, Skerl partnered with Italian James Rolando in what became Helper's Mutual Furniture and Hardware, but not without a long struggle. (Nonetheless, their enterprise lasted for over seventy years.)[68] In short, as the economy rose and fell (and fell some more), hard times shuffled the population up and down the Castle Valley corridor.

More affluent businessmen also took a gamble. Frederick Sweet pioneered the development of a new mining district on Gordon Creek, just south of Spring Canyon. His timely purchase of a block of land just pre-dated the new federal Mineral Leasing Act of 1920, which mandated that coal deposits could never again be sold to private owners. After 1920, only the surface lands above them could be bought. Coal mining rights had to be leased from the federal government, putting money into the national coffers rather than into private, corporate pockets.[69] On his recent coal land acquisition, Sweet founded two new developments: the town and mine of Sweets in 1921, and the nearby National mine and town. At about the same time, Arthur E. Gibson opened his own mine in Gordon Creek Canyon, soon to be known as Consumers for the parent Consumers Mutual Coal Company. George A. Storrs secured a lease on land that became the Gordon Creek Mine and planned a town he called Coal City. In 1924, the new National Railroad, under President F. A. Sweet and Vice President George A. Storrs, began serving all these developments.[70] Storrs also put his own assets into a would-be utopian project just four miles from Spring Canyon. On the advice of John Pettit, the new state coal mine inspector, he had approached brothers Shekry [Shekra] and Jim [Nedje] Sheya, Syro-Lebanese immigrants, about the purchase of their grazing land which covered a potentially lucrative coal vein. The Sheyas had followed 'Brahim (Abraham) Howa, Utah's earliest Syro-Lebanese settler, into Castle Valley. Howa had come to Carbon County around 1896, originally peddling carpets and jewelry. He had settled down and tried both mining and farming, a pattern emulated by the Sheyas who had become substantial landowners by the time Storrs contacted them. Eventually, Jim bought out his brother and he and George Storrs incorporated Cedar Mesa Farms and stocked it with cattle and sheep. The farm company also legally owned eighty acres of coal land, and Storrs began a long, frustrating attempt to get financing for a railroad to tap the area and to develop a new mine.[71]

Storrs planned a grand future for his holdings. Through his newly-established Great Western Coal Company, Storrs sought to build a railroad spur, the National Coal Railway, to connect his development with that of Fred Sweet. As expenses mounted, Storrs borrowed money where he could. "I have even taken the shoes off my feet and given them to teamsters on the [railroad] grade in order to keep the teams going," wrote Storrs later. Storrs himself drove scraper teams, "plow teams, and put on a blacksmith[']s apron and shod horses," doing "any and everything I could think of to keep this company going."[72] Saddled with incompetent bookkeepers, rising expenses, and a mine unready for production, Storrs continued sinking a great deal of his own and borrowed money into the venture, holding fast to his utopian vision of employee profit-sharing: a town where each miner would own his own land, "a little spot of ground on which to raise his vegetables during the slack period in the mine industry," where "every miner . . . [would] become a stockholder with us." He wanted to "build a town that would be a credit to other American coal camps . . . for the betterment of humanity in connection with the coal industry inasmuch as we thought it would prevent at all times coal strikes or coal mine troubles such as have been the menace to the coal mining industry in the United States."[73] To this end, he established Coal City next to the proposed mine. After a great many other deals fell through, Storrs went to Hollywood, where his daughter, Beulah Storrs Lewis, had joined Hollywood's Universal Film Company in 1916, and made several appearances in the serialized episodes of Graft.[74] "I . . . went to see Charlie Chaplin, whom I knew personally," wrote Storrs, but his bad luck held. "Charlie's interest was for the proposition but his manager was not."[75]

Storrs's choice of Charlie Chaplin as a potential investor was no idle whim, but based on the sound realization of the star's incredible wealth. As America's star system matured, actors' incomes grew phenomenally. Charlie Chaplin, who had begun at $150 per week in 1913, went to a second studio in 1915 for $1,250 per week. The following year, he signed with a new studio for $10,000 a week with a $150,000 signing bonus. By the time Storrs contacted him, Chaplin was worth millions. The film industry was becoming Big Business: by 1920 studios routinely owned their own theaters to showcase the films of their stars. At least one Castle Valley native achieved modest success: Castle Dale's Artimus Ward (Art) Acord. He had begun show business in Buffalo Bill's Wild West Show in 1898 and reigned as World's Champion Cowboy from 1912–1914. After service in World War I, Acord went to Hollywood, making movies there and in Mexico, South America, and England before his death in 1931. He saw movies make the transition to talkies, in 1927, and the addition of newsreels—beginning with Fox Movietone News—as millions paid their quarter every weekend to see the latest show.[76]

George Storrs's dogged quest for funding ultimately brought a touch of all-American "ballyhoo" to Castle Valley. According to 1920s journalist Frederick Lewis Allen, "ballyhoo" erupted when "millions of men and women turned their attention, their talk, and their emotional interest upon a series of tremendous trifles—a heavyweight boxing-match, a murder trial, a new automobile model, a transatlantic flight."[77] Castle Valley shared in this tendency, never more so than when heavyweight boxing champion Jack Dempsey came to Storrs's Coal City. Here is how that happened. Discouraged and headed home from Hollywood after his failure to interest Chaplin, Storrs encountered Jack Dempsey and his manager, Jack Kearns, traveling on the same train. Dempsey knew something about mining, having worked in the mines at Cripple Creek in his youth. Storrs's project piqued his interest, and he sent his brother, Bernard, to view Storrs's property. After a good look around, Bernard advised his brother to invest.[78] A contract was duly signed, making Jack Dempsey the president of the Great Western Coal Company and Kearns the secretary-treasurer. Planning to raise more development money from his wealthy friends, in 1923 Dempsey moved his training camp to Coal City (sometimes referred to as Dempsey City) where he trained in the fields and in the basement of the Andreini store, one of three cinder block buildings amidst the tiny cluster of frame houses that constituted the town. While locals touted the little coal camp as "Coal City with a punch behind it," miners preferred to live near their work at National, Consumers, or Sweets, and Dempsey's rich friends failed to donate. Then came the Gibbons-Dempsey fight in Montana. Jack left to train. "After that," recalled Storrs, "notwithstanding the fact that they had absolute control, they paid no attention to this proposition. Again we were left to hold the sack."[79] Storrs managed to buy back his stock, and wound up selling his nascent railroad to the Utah Railway Company in 1926 for over half a million dollars.[80] Dempsey, of course, went on to his momentous loss to Gene Tunney that same year in front of over 130,000 spectators who had paid a total of almost two million dollars to see the fight. A year later, 145,000 people (roughly six times the population of all of Castle Valley) brought in gate receipts of $2,600,000 in a Chicago amphitheater so huge that many in the outermost seats did not know who had won when the fight ended. Tunney did, aided by the infamous thirteen-second "long count" in the seventh round, which allowed him to regain his feet and go on to vanquish Dempsey.[81]

As Allen claimed, Castle Valley, like the rest of the country, also had a love affair with cars. The 1920s was the car's heyday, as numbers grew nationwide: from eight thousand in 1900 to over eight million in 1920 to almost twenty-three million—one for every five Americans—in 1930. In 1914, for the first time, the country manufactured more cars than wagons and carriages.[82] Consequently, Price's John Redd, among many others, switched from running a livery stable to managing Redd Motors. Just after World War I, Redd bought a Franklin and chauffeured those who paid for the ride, including Rolla West and his fiancee to Helper and back for $5.00. "A man couldn't treat his girl to anything nicer than that!" West said.[83] Henry Ford's innovative assembly line pushed down the $850 price of a 1908 Ford Model T to $585 for a Ford roadster in 1926. Eighteen-year-old coal miner Clifford Smith had already put down $265 toward the roadster when a mine accident blew out his right eye and, before he recuperated, his father died. When he requested a refund, the Ford Garage owner told him, "'No, I can't do that, for we have already ordered the car, and you have already payed [sic] more than the [official] down payment.'" Then, Smith explained that he did not want the county to have to bury his dad. "So he gave me all the money back," Smith recalled.[84]

Local residents started getting their own cars in larger numbers around 1923 or 1924, although for many, like Smith, cars remained a luxury. Automotive infrastructure had to keep pace. For example, Arthur W. Horsley, Price Mayor in 1916–1917, established the town's first street and traffic ordinances and backed a "camping ground for automobile tourists" at the old freighting grounds. Tourist traffic increased, particularly after 1921, when the Pikes Peak Ocean-to-Ocean Highway was routed through Castle Valley, running west from Green River to Price, then south down the face of the Wasatch Plateau and again west over Salina Pass.[85] Out-of-the-way roads remained terrible, however. In 1924, Mrs. Elsie Huntsman, schoolteacher at Kiz, tried to drive to Price and the car in which she was riding overturned in the bottom of a flooded wash. She drowned.[86]

To serve the public, garages, service stations, and transportation lines sprung up all over. Would-be coal developer George Miller opened Hun-

Every day, Wellington's Bill Norton drove his town's older children to Price to attend high school. Children from more distant coal camps had to take weekly buses and board in Price at their own expense. Courtesy of Western Mining and Railroad Museum.

tington's first garage in 1917. Competing auto lines tried serving remote camps. Guthiel-Broecker originally served Emery County, beginning in 1915, but by the 1940s, Parley P. Johnson had that contract. Star routes to the coal camps remained contracted out: later the Arrow Stage Line (or Arrow Auto Line), served Hiawatha, Wattis, the Sunnyside district, Wellington, and National, at least until 1918, when the state public utilities commission granted exclusive rights to Huey and Bell of Price, the pioneers of the route, ousting the competing Star Line.[87] In 1926, Mohrland bought a school bus to transport students to North Emery High School in Huntington, and children from all the other coal camps rode the bus to Price, where they boarded during the week at their own expense. The Millerton Dairy also became motorized. For years, it supplied milk to the U.S. Fuel camps on the Black Hawk vein. The dairy, some four miles outside Hiawatha, had begun under the Miller brothers and eventually came under the administration of Reuben G. Miller, Emery Stake president and active polygamist.[88] As former Mohrland resident Max Finley remembered, "Milk from the company dairy located at Miller Creek was delivered in glass bottles. It would arrive on the doorstep before dawn and with luck, in the wintertime, would be brought in before it froze solid and pushed the paper lid off the top and made the cream available to the family cat."[89]

Others turned to trucks to make a living. Maude Marsing, who with her husband, Orson, and family ranched 3,000 acres on Miller Creek, remembered buying a 1927 Chevrolet truck that allowed them to make two or three trips to Price daily rather than one with the wagon. "We never enjoyed any other truck as much," she later recalled—and certainly not for its accessories, because it had none.[90] In the mid-1920s, Luke Cormani also turned to his truck when his hours got cut on the D&RGW. "I had this brand new Rio truck that my dad bought and I bid for the mail." He got the contract to drive the stage from Helper to Latuda at the top of Spring Canyon, stopping at each mine on the way. "I went every day when the train came here [to Helper] and would bring the meat and everything for the stores in Spring Canyon." Loading up the truck and driving the route took about two or three hours a day, "Made about $250 a month. . . . That was big money."[91]

Cormani's reliance on his truck as the railroad reduced his hours mirrored the reality of American transportation. Cars and trucks made tough competition for the railroads. Trains became longer and heavier, going from an average freight train of thirty-seven cars weighing 1,443 tons in 1920, to an average of forty-five cars weighing 1,750 tons six years later. Railroads consolidated, and, by 1928, the United States had about eight hundred lines, down from over six thousand a few years earlier.[92] Upgrading technologically, locomotives switched to diesel, cutting down the demand for coal, a decision that reverberated through the Castle Valley mines. Furthermore, the car had immediate environmental consequences. By about 1930, so many motorized residents had turned their horses loose that Carbon County hired John Prince to round up all the wild bands foraging in farmers' fields and gardens—up to two hundred at Sunnyside alone.[93] Although Joe Swasey, still erect and barrel chested, mourned the destruction of the desert horses that had primed his long livestock career, the day of horse-drawn transportation was over.[94]

As more and more people got cars, they found new uses for their vehicles. For example, Castle Valley baseball fans would drive up to one of the many diamonds sprinkled throughout the area to watch the game from their cars, since most had no grandstand. At sunset, they turned on their headlights to light the field. Everyone played baseball—boys and girls (usually on separate teams), miners and farmers, immigrants and native-born. Ferron's Irma Petersen Snow remembered her after-school baseball games: "That was one of the most important things in my life. I hardly even ate. Whoever was early got to pitch. We played in the street."[95] Nationally, baseball's roots went back to the eastern U.S. in the 1850s and 1860s, where the Cincinnati Red Stockings emerged as the first professional team in 1869.[96] The game had arrived in Castle Valley by 1895, when the pious Teancum Pratt complained, "Helper is a baseball center [as it still remains;] the towns above & below come here to play match games on Sundays, & my children are in some danger of breaking the sabbath."[97] A year later, the Orangeville baseball team posed for a formal photograph sporting new uniforms.[98] Ernest Horsley described Price's celebrations for July 4 and 24, 1899, with "baseball, [a] new game, included."[99] After the turn-of-the century proliferation of commercial mines and company towns, a "coal camp league" developed. Each of the companies hired men, ostensibly as miners, who could swing a bat, pitch a strike, or heave a ball in from mid-field. "The miners . . . started it," remembered Joe Myers, the son of Austrian immigrants. "They wanted a ball club. And it originally started from importing ball players . . . We had [Hall-of-Famers] Heinie Manush, played with the Washington Senators . . . We had China Brown and we had Mike Kreevish . . . and Carl Mays."[100] Legendary local player Frank Zaccaria, a Helper native, later signed with Ty Cobb to play for the minor league San Francisco Seals. He spent five years on this farm team for the New York Yankees before accepting a job (really to play ball) for Utah Copper Company in the state's Industrial League. In the 1930s, too, a woman's league flourished. Millie Vogrenic Babcock and Frances Day Vogrenic played on the King Koal women's team. At the same time, Carbon County organized junior and senior softball leagues, all of which created a foundation for a passion that would last well into the twenty-first century.[101] Helper's Luke Cormani moved abruptly from waterboy to substitute catcher in 1915, "because the catcher got hurt," he recalled. "We played all over. . . . Kenilworth had a ball club, Hiawatha, Mohrland, Castle Gate, Price, even down at Castle Dale we used to go down and play occasionally" although they were not in the league.[102] Harry Conover pitched for the Ferron team, and became its manager for years after he stopped playing.[103] Mohrland, despite being located in Emery County, won the Carbon County league championship in 1915 and therefore got to play the Chicago White Sox in an exhibition game in Price. The contest attracted an estimated 10,000 spectators—from a valley with fewer than 20,000 total residents. The White Sox won 17–1.[104]

Nationally, the whole baseball world was rocked four years later when the much-favored Chicago White Sox lost to the Cincinnati Reds in the 1919 World Series. The Sox, originally favored 3–to-1, saw the odds shift to favor the Reds 8–to-5 before the eight-game series ended. Cruelly underpaid by tight-fisted Charles Comiskey, eight White Sox players had allegedly agreed to throw the series for $10,000 apiece. Reduced payoffs, an attempted double-cross, and crucial miscommunications enriched only the gamblers in the end. In a 1921 trial, all the players were acquitted when key records disappeared. Regardless of this outcome, the tough new commissioner, Judge Kenisaw Mountain Landis, banned all eight men from baseball for life. Forever after, they were known as the Chicago Black Sox.[105] "The only thing they could do was organize a team and barnstorm throughout the country," Myers remembered. He had the opportunity to see them play the Sunnyside team. The Black Sox won, 2–0. "We had [other] teams coming through," Myers remembered. "We had the colored Jefferson Giants from Chicago; Kansas City Monarchs; . . . the House of David came through here. And then the Hollywood Bloomer Girls . . . [and the ] Tokyo Giants, from Tokyo, came and played."[106]

All over Castle Valley, children, too, played baseball. Heated rivalries developed between coal camps, such as that between Hiawatha and Mohrland. "I was mascot for these [Mohrland] guys in 1927 and 26," remembered Remo Spigarelli, who chased balls during games, took care of balls and bats and gloves for the players, and helped collect the used baseballs (bought by the company) when they became too scarred for league use. Somehow, he remembered, "we had a lot of friction tapes come out of the mine" which were used to wrap and rewrap the used balls to keep them playable for sandlot games.[107] At Sunnyside, Joe Myers also caught baseball fever, especially after he went into a game as a pinch hitter and hit a double, giving Sunnyside the win. The ecstatic crowd, as always, showered the field with money. "I took my ball cap and went out picking up those dollars all over here and there. Fifty cent pieces and dollars—there was no paper money then, it was silver dollars. I got 75 bucks!" He was fourteen-years-old. He went home and dumped it on the kitchen table and told his mother he wanted to be a professional ball player. She told him to go into the mine like his father; she would not take his money. But it was 1926, and the mines were only working one day a week, so he went to California, enrolled in high school, and played ball. He made all-city in Los Angeles and was scouted by Rogers Hornsby of the Chicago Cubs. He also played winter league throughout his high school years, rubbing shoulders with Hornsby, Babe Ruth, Charlie Gehringer (called the "Mechanical Man," because of his consistency at second base), and other major leaguers. Each of the movie studios had a team and so did several companies. "One time, in LA, I had 17 uniforms in my locker," recalled Myers. "Played a different team every night." Among them, he played for Metro-Goldwyn-Mayer, "for Joe E. Brown. . . . [He] was part owner of the Pittsburgh Pirates. . . . And then he'd get us in pictures. Joe E. Brown made *The Big Leaguer, Diamond Dust* . . . we went out there in uniform and we'd just play catch . . . and they'd give us $10 an hour." The great Negro League pitcher, Satchel Paige, came down and played "winter league, for Metro-Goldwyn-Mayer. I played with him about two months," remembered Myers. "Satchel would have been in the big leagues years before [Jackie] Robinson ever was" had the major leagues not been segregated. All the big names came to California. "They'd stay maybe two months. I know when Babe Ruth was down there, he stayed three . . . and he got in shape. Played for the White King soap company."[108]

Much as all this 1920s hoopla helped unite Castle Valley's diverse people, shared tragedy did sometimes even more. For example, when in 1923 Castle Gate's Japanese miners learned that a great earthquake had just leveled much of their homeland, the whole town gathered for a benefit concert and dance with all profits earmarked for Japanese earthquake relief.[109] A year later, all the Castle Gate miners suffered when the local economy slowed and the company cut forces, concentrating its workforce in the No. 2 mine. Ann Slavensky Spensko remembered March 8, when "We heard

the big shots . . . go off and we thought it was the boys, just shooting dynamite." Then she saw a man running down the hill from No. 2. "He was all
black and torn 'cause he was outside in the fan house and he said, 'The
mine blew up.'"[110] Residents rushed to the portal. In Price, Greek immigrant Tony Kontgas heard about the explosion and ran to get the Greek
priest. "I told him what I learned, and he got hold of a Greek who owned
a Cadillac. He was a politico; nobody else could afford such a car. And
we drove up to Castle Gate." There, they saw a huge mass of debris piled
hundreds of feet across the wash, blasted there by the explosion. "Wom-
en were standing by the entrance screaming, yelling, hollering, crying,"
recalled Kontgas. "I watched the fire departments from both Price and
Helper come and pull out their fire hoses and try to pump water into the
mine. But that was just an absolute waste of time; it didn't do any good at
all."[111] Meanwhile, up at Winter Quarters, safety crew chief Stanley Harvey
gathered his men, joining others from Clear Creek and the Kinney Mine.
They piled their heavy rescue gear into a boxcar and climbed in for the
hurtling ride down ice-filled Price Canyon as the D&RGW passenger train
waited at Colton to give them the track. Wearing their helmets and carrying their forty-pound breathing apparatuses on their backs, they struggled
over the debris into the black, smoky mine, looking for survivors.[112] As they
tired, the Standardville team spelled them. George Wilson, Standardville's
captain, had his nose clip knocked off by a struggling teammate whose
safety helmet leaked. Wilson, stranded in the gassy mine for five long minutes, became the first corpse laid out in a makeshift morgue.[113] People
outside hoped for survivors, like at the well-remembered Winter Quarters
disaster. But as rescuers spoke in hushed voices of that sight in the tunnels
of the two steel motors (coal cutting machines) torn and twisted by the
blast, everyone realized that all 171 miners had died. Twelve of them came
from Emery County; others from other parts of Castle Valley, Utah, the
nation, and the world. The final total listed 74 American-born miners, 49
Greeks, 22 Italians, 8 Japanese, 7 English, 6 Austrians, 2 Scots, 2 African
Americans, and one Belgian.[114] Women without family in the mine worked
on the outside boiling water, sterilizing doctors' instruments, collecting
blankets, cooking over open fires, heating milk for babies, and manually
operating respirators for hours in unsuccessful attempts to revive gassed
miners.[115] Salt Lake members of the Utah Salvation Army and Red Cross
rushed down on the train to help to feed and console the living. They advised mothers, wives, and sisters of the deceased not to view the bodies that
were already identified, since "it would be better for them to remember
their loved ones as they had last seen them," noted the night watchman,
T. L. Burridge.[116] Some insisted, including the mother of Ann Slavensky
Spensko. Mother and daughter went to identify the dead boy. His "gray
coffin was opened and he had blood running through his nose, and he
must have fell in water, 'cause he was white around his face, and the rest

Two of the casualties of the 1924 Castle Gate mine explosion are laid to rest in the Castle Gate ceremony. This photo would be sent back to an immigrant's homeland, to reassure relatives there that he had received a proper, sanctified burial. Note the grieving widow with four small children to the right of the black coffin, and, behind them, an African American man wearing his lodge badge. Such racial solidarity would soon break down in Castle Valley. Courtesy of Western Mining and Railroad Museum.

was . . . you know," Ann remembered. He was eighteen.[117] One man was "all in pieces but his wife was able to identify him by one of his toes." Another, who had lost his father in the Scofield explosion in 1900, had to be buried without his head. When it was located a day later, the grave was reopened so he could be interred intact.[118] As rescue teams worked toward the back of the gas-laden mine, they often had to make three or four rest stops on the way out, each time checking their heavy, cumbersome breathing apparatus and oxygen gauges. Once a hissing, whistling noise frightened Harvey, and he stopped to check for leaks in his crew's apparatus. He found nothing. Shortly thereafter, "we found a body that had been blown into an empty mine car . . . [It] was badly swollen, and was giving off gas around the mouth, making a hissing sound." In the flickering light of their safety lamps, the rescue work "was spooky to say the least," he added.[119] By Wednesday, March 12, Castle Gate's Doctor McDermid forbade any further viewing of the bodies except for identification purposes. "The order was necessary," Burridge wrote, "for the sanitary protection of those of us who were still left alive."[120]

The emotional fallout continued. Anton Dupin, a Croatian immigrant who spoke English with a slight southern accent, having learned it from African-American coworkers back East, had worked in the coal before opening a Spring Glen store. He wanted to help out with his delivery truck, so "he went up to the mine and picked up all the bodies there and took them to the amusement hall," remembered his daughter, Frances Dupin Vouk. "[H]e knew a lot of the men and a lot of them were hurt just real bad. After that he was sick. It was the first time my dad had ever been ill."[121] From Sunnyside, Slovenian immigrants and brothers-in-law Joe Bon and John Tolich also went to help with the rescue work. John's wife, Anna Marolt Tolich, remembered, "When they came home neither one said a word. . . . they were so moved emotionally."[122] Tony Kontgas returned with the Greek priest to assist in the burials. "We opened up this one casket a little, but we couldn't tell what it was. We knew it was a human being. . . . That's how badly many of the bodies were burned. We just hoped we were burying the right individuals—I mean, Greek."[123]

Opening the mine again also cost quite a struggle. As Burridge explained, the "fires had to be fought and put out before the work of getting out the men" could continue. Fighting fire "in a coal mine is slow and dangerous. Fresh air cannot be drawn into the places where these fires are for fresh air feeds the fire with oxygen and makes them impossible to handle. The fire itself is all the time giveing [sic] off the deadly gas known as after damp but [which] is mainly Carbon-dioxide and Carbon-monoxide."[124] The best timbermen were called from other camps to shore up tunnel roofs so rescue teams and later, miners, could enter safely. Dave Parmley, Sunnyside foreman, again asked Bon and Tolich to help out in retimbering Castle Gate. They agreed to go, so moved their families to the devastated camp. It was hard, recalled Anna Tolich, for "the men working in the mine. Many times the odor of the human remains" lingered. "It took quite a while to ventilate the air . . . [but] gradually the men started working again."[125]

In the close-knit communities along the Castle Valley corridor, everybody suffered. For weeks thereafter in Castle Gate, no church meetings were held; fraternal lodges remained closed; no one frequented the amusement hall even when all the bodies had been buried in distant hometowns or in the newly-expanded graveyard in Willow Canyon, to the east.[126] The tremendous loss of life also led to new mine safety measures, replicating the Winter Quarters explosion of 1900. While Winter Quarters had started with an explosion of giant powder (dynamite) which suspended coal dust in the air, resulting in a series of explosions, the "Castle Gate mine explosion appeared to have been caused by methane gas being ignited by an open flame and then propagated through the mine by coal dust being raise in suspension," wrote Harvey. Now, instead of sprinkling the mine with water to settle the coal dust, begun after the 1900 disaster, mines started rock-dusting, and Utah passed a law mandating "the use of electric cap lamps to prevent ignition by open flames of gas or coal dust in suspension." At the cost of over 170 lives, Castle Valley coal mining had become a little bit safer.[127] Utah's Governor Mabey authorized a relief fund collection and established a committee to administer it. Under the direction of one of Utah's earliest social workers, relief payments lasted for the next twelve years.[128]

Concurrently, some divisive ideas also oozed down the Castle Valley corridor. Some six months after the Castle Gate mine explosion, some strangers drove into Helper in three or four cars, lit a 10 x 15–foot cross on a hill east of town, and drove away as it flamed.[129] Joe Barboglio's daughter, not quite six-years-old, knew it meant "that there were people who hated us, and all the other foreign born families."[130] The Ku Klux Klan had arrived. Founded to suppress African Americans in the post-Civil War South, it had been resuscitated to terrorize foreigners as well in America's post-World War I xenophobia. In Utah since 1921, the Klan now descended on the state's most ethnic enclave.[131] It swayed the 1924 elections, influencing the defeat of incumbent Carbon County Attorney Henry Ruggeri, of Italian descent, by reputed Klansman, Oliver K. Clay.[132] One of Helper's Greek residents, Stan John Diamanti, was not impressed: "[I]f you had any problems in those days there were always neighbors and the town behind you. . . . [T]he Italians, Slavs, Czechs, and everybody else banded together."[133] Within a year, an elaborate spy system linking Greeks, Italians, Slavs, and Irish Catholics revealed the identities of Klansmen. Lawyer LeRoy McGee's ethnic clients rapidly found another attorney after Price residents recognized him in an open-air Salt Lake Konklave (Klan meeting). The Klan, moribund, went underground and officially disbanded in 1930.[134]

But in 1925, the Klan still burned crosses on Castle Valley hills—at the Blue Cut between Price and Helper, up in Pleasant Valley where Elvie Hurskainen Stevens, the daughter of Finnish immigrants, remembered a cross "way up on the corner of the Scofield Cemetery, clear to the top . . . burning like everything."[135] Its opposition answered with enigmatic, flaming circles. In this tense atmosphere, on June 15, 1925, African-American miner Robert Marshall allegedly shot and killed Castle Gate's popular night watchman and Klan member, J. Milton ("Milt") Burns. Marshall seized Burns's gun and fled, pursued unsuccessfully by a posse of forty men.[136] Three days later, Marshall returned to the shack that he had shared with another black miner, who reported Marshall's presence to camp officials, maybe hoping for the $250 reward for Marshall's arrest and conviction. But Marshall never went to trial. Camp officials captured Marshall and set off toward the Price City jail in a three-car caravan. They passed the sheriff, headed out of town, as a crowd gathered at the courthouse in front of the jail. Two fourteen-year-old boys, Francis Prince and his friend, Tom Shield, headed out on horseback to check Prince family cattle, saw other cars near the underpass west of Price. Their occupants were yelling, "They got the nigger! They got the nigger!" The boys knew exactly what that meant, so they followed the cars to town. Meanwhile, a deputy had left Marshall alone in the car surrounded by an angry mob when he stepped into the courthouse. By the time he exited the building, Marshall was gone.[137] As a procession now estimated at 100 vehicles started down the road east toward Wellington, the boys tied up their horses and got a ride "to the hanging tree east of Price," as Prince's daughter later wrote. "They were walking across the railroad tracks toward the trees when they were greeted with cries of 'There he goes!' Forty feet from them, Marshall's body rose in the air. . . . Francis watched the rope tighten around the man's neck until the neck was only inches around."[138] Almost ten minutes later deputies arrived at the hanging tree and cut Marshall down. When he was found to be still living, the mob wrested Marshall from the deputies, slung the noose over his head, and jerked him up again several times until he died of a broken neck.[139] An unknown photographer took pictures of the hanging body and several shots of the crowd which were soon reprinted as a packet of postcards (a common practice for "exciting events" of that day).[140]

The Price *Sun* reported the lynching, noting that members of the lynch mob hardly fit the usual image of a disorderly crowd of violent strangers. Instead, many locally prominent people attended and "participation in the affair seemed to be a matter of boasting."[141] District Attorney Fred Keller and County Attorney Oliver Clay swore out arrest warrants for eleven men.[142] Under pressure from Utah Governor George Dern and State Attorney General Harvey Cluff, Keller and Clay reluctantly withdrew the eleven arrest warrants as the county impaneled a grand jury on June 30. The eleven men were released on bail. When none of the 125 grand jury witnesses could remember any of the lynchers, the accused were permanently freed on August 11.[143]

The event left an ugly mark on Castle Valley. After watching Marshall swing, Tom Shield decided he had had enough and went home. Francis Prince had to go on to check on his family's cattle, but spent a fearful night in the mountain cabin at Mud Water. As he tried to sleep, the "Negroes hung from the walls, the rafters, and all over the cabin. They swung up, cried out, and strangled. They writhed in torment in the cabin darkness. The boy turned from one side to another as Robert Marshall was repeatedly lynched throughout the night."[144] Castle Valley, too, felt the nightmare for a long, long time. A 1998 Day of Reconciliation, spearheaded by former Kenilworth resident Matt Gilmour, a high school student at the time of the lynching, prompted a spectrum of reactions. People of diverse races and backgrounds variously viewed the event as a healing gesture, an attack on racism, rewriting history, or pandering to political correctness.[145] In 1925, Carbon County's 100–150 African Americans had taken up a collection to bury Marshall but they had lacked the money for a marker. The 1998 event culminated in the addition of a headstone to his grave, donated by Caucasian Bernie Morris of Price's Morris Monuments and unveiled by him and African-American Pastor France Davis of Salt Lake City's Calvary Baptist Church. It reads, "Robert Marshall: Lynched June 18, 1925, A Victim of Intolerance. May God Forgive."[146]

Community spirit had foundered on the rock of race. Marshall was lynched because he was black. In its only lynching, Castle Valley regrettably fit the American mainstream. Booker T. Washington's Tuskegee Institute, a training school for African-Americans, kept national lynching records beginning in 1882, a year after the school opened. For over eighty years it published yearly tallies. After 1886, when seventy-four blacks and sixty-four whites were lynched, black lynchings consistently outnumbered every other group. Tensions heightened after World War I when black veterans, having fought in the trenches side-by-side with their white compatriots, refused to accept an inferior status back home. Thousands joined the Great Migration, one of the largest voluntary population movements in American history, that took blacks out of the South and into northern cities. There they joined New York's Universal Negro Improvement Association (founded in 1917); wrote prose and poetry in the Harlem Renaissance, and created the era's signature music: jazz.[147] Their visible creativity spawned a violent backlash, and in 1924 and 1925 only blacks were lynched, Robert Marshall among them. Not until 1952 did the United States have a year without a lynching; they occurred sporadically for over a decade after that.[148]

Furthermore, African Americans had always been few in number along the Castle Valley corridor. For example, when the state coal mine inspector first reported nationalities of miners in 1905, he listed 14 Negroes among over 1,700 men. By 1910, they numbered 10 among 3,422; by 1916, 34 of over 3,700 miners.[149] The census reported only 1,400 blacks in all of Utah in 1920, dropping to 1,100 in 1930 in a total state population of about half a million.[150] Not only did African Americans represent the smallest local ethnic or racial group, they had almost all arrived as strikebreakers in 1922–1923. Even then, coal company managers had assigned them the worst accommodations. In Mohrland, for example, the Italians lived closest to the center of town, near the railroad yard and mine tipple. "Above this came the Greek boardinghouse, then Jap town with its lovely flower and vegetable gardens built along the stream bed, and finally colored town just below the mine portal," remembered superintendent's son, Nevin Wetzel. With this arrangement, only black and Japanese children could not go home during school lunch break; the walk up the canyon to their homes was over a mile—too far, too steep, and too slippery to manage. "In 1927," Wetzel continued, "some of the black coal miners there had families and children, with a reputation as good miners, uncomplaining about poor working conditions or bad treatment by the company. However, bitter strife would frequently occur within this group, and by 1930 all blacks had left Mohrland."[151]

Other immigrants were far too plentiful to make effective targets, although numerous negative stereotypes pocked Castle Valley—every camp had its "Jap Town," "Wop Town," and people commonly referred to "black Dagoes," "square-headed Bohunks," and "greasy Greeks." Nonetheless, living in tiny coal camps, sharing holidays and activities, and risking death or maiming in a mine explosion, created a strong sense of community, particularly among the young. Iris Mangum Potts, a mechanic's daughter, remembered her childhood in Spring Canyon and her Italian neighbors: "on New Year's we would always go down to the Anselmos. . . . We had our food . . . and then we [little kids] would go to bed [on the floor]. . . . [W]hether they was Italian, Greek, Mexican, Japs, it didn't make any difference, we all slept there." She summed up the general coal camp outlook, "We never realized there was anything different until we came to Price and outside people started to tell us we had foreign elements."[152]

Castle Gate, the incubator for events that led to the lynching, had its own expression of solidarity in a 1926 commemoration of the March 1924 explosion. The local paper reported, "Largest Crowd Mining Town Has Ever Seen Attends Services." Castle Gate's amusement hall, the former morgue, could hold 900 persons but attendees still had to be turned away. Representatives of churches, welfare associations, lodges, and civic and military associations all participated, including Heber J. Grant, president of the LDS Church. The Knights of Pythias had raised $25,000 throughout the U.S. for care of widows and children and for the children's education, three of whom had already benefited from the fund. Afterwards, participants formed a procession to the cemetery and decorated each and every grave.[153]

Other camps had their activities, thanks to the welfare fund to which each working miner contributed an obligatory dollar a month (taken out of his pay by the company). The fund paid for company picnics, for dances, for a town band (or two), and an orchestra. Coal camps also had their football teams, if not level playing fields. For example, for one July 24th match, Clear Creek won the toss and made its opponent, Winter Quarters, "face the incline." Clear Creek won, five goals to two.[154] Within a few years, however, Winter Quarters faded. This grandfather of all the Castle Valley coal mines closed in 1928.[155]

Winter Quarters's demise showed the silent, icy spread of the 1920s mining depression. Like the downturn in agriculture, it seemed somehow hidden from a public caught up in wild music, rising stock prices, bootleg whiskey, movies, and fast cars. For a while, active residents made their own energetic fun, such as the "Balanced Rock Gang"—a group of young men who made it a challenge to climb Helper's trademark rock formation. They made the dangerous climb first in May 1929, later installing a flagpole with a flag that blew off, and was replaced, and blew off, and was superseded by a fifty-five-gallon victory drum that lasted into the twenty-first century (with a few mishaps) that may soon be replaced once more.[156] Then, suddenly, the fun stopped. On October 24, 1929, the bottom dropped out of the stock market. Wall Street rocked as stockholders dumped over twelve million shares that day. Leading bankers pooled their assets to keep the crash from becoming absolute, but even they could offer only a brief bump on the way to the bottom. Five days later, on October 29, a sixteen-million share day, marked the beginning of the end. So-called securities provided nothing of the kind as stock prices tumbled for three-and-a-half years.[157] Republican President Hoover did what he thought best to manage a supposedly temporary downturn, asking business for voluntary adjustments. Utah's Republican Senator Reed Smoot, head of the Senate Finance Committee and also pro-business, saddled the country with the highest protective tariff in American history, oblivious of America's involvement in the global economy. His masterpiece, the Smoot-Hawley Tariff, created such international backlash that it deepened the Depression world-wide. In the spring of 1931, the European banking system collapsed. At home, more than 2,000 banks failed that year.[158] Economically, the rest of America started to look like Castle Valley.

# PART III
# CRISIS AND COMMUNITY

# 9

## Depression, 1930–1941

*The story that has made the rounds more than any other about those days was about Omar shoplifting a small can of chili powder. We couldn't get home for Thanksgiving one year, and, of course, had no money for holiday food. We did have beans and tomatoes and fifteen cents for a pound of hamburger. I hope we will be forgiven for that little infraction that made a Thanksgiving chili dinner a little more palatable.*[1]
—HELEN E. BUNNELL, WIFE OF FUTURE UTAH STATE SENATOR

Studs Terkel, famous for his books of collected oral histories, had his own unfocused memories of the 1930s, of his youth. "That there are some who were untouched or, indeed, did rather well isn't exactly news," he wrote. "This has been true of all disasters. The great many were wounded, in one manner or another. It left upon them an 'invisible scar,' as Caroline Bird put it."[2] Castle Valley, scarred already by the mining and farming depression of the 1920s, suffered further from spreading poverty and cyclical drought. Depression conditions became so severe, money so scarce, and human suffering so acute, that local residents actively sought federal aid, inviting in authorities whom they had previously avoided. From the 1930s onward, Castle Valley became more and more connected to the big, outside world, seeming smaller and less significant by comparison. Like its people, its future became more uncertain.

In Castle Valley, folks initially carried on much as they had for a decade, their long-standing poverty seemingly untouched by the Wall Street Crash. In 1930, the Thompson brothers opened a new coal mine in the walls of Price Canyon above Castle Gate, driving two inclines and constructing a modern tipple to handle it. Their New Peerless absorbed all their capital in its construction. Faced with a continuing depression, they had to close the mine in 1931.[3]

Green River soldiered on: farmers had expanded their melon crops and introduced sugar beets during the 1920s, bringing back Green River Melon Days in 1925 after several years without a celebration. By 1928, special trains had brought in visitors who enjoyed over forty tons of free melons. Egg production also increased due to commercialization of poultry operations. This expansion made them all the more vulnerable when agricultural prices dropped an average of forty percent between 1929–1933. Finally, beef prices fell and valley land turned more alkaline, so many livestock owners switched from cattle to sheep. But Castle Valley farmland values kept dropping.[4]

Even the Ku Klux Klan sold its property in one of the strangest land deals in American history. The Klan had acquired the hilltop at the south end of Gordon Creek Canyon which it had used for cross burnings. In February 1930, Carl Nyman, former KKK member, surveyed, subdivided, and platted this plot. Then, Glen Jackson, who had originally come from Tampa, Florida, probably as a Klan organizer, sold forty acres of it for $150 to a group of Slavic lodges filled with exactly the kind of foreigners that the Klan had loved to hate. Slovenian Martin Millarich and Croatian Anton Dupin, respectively president and secretary of the Austrian Central Cemetery Association, received the land transfer in time for the first burial: Dupin's twenty-one-year-old daughter, Annie, a tuberculosis victim. Meanwhile, Jackson had become good friends with John and Louis Kosec, sons of Slovenian immigrants, as they worked side-by-side in the mines. So in 1930, he gave John Kosec his old electric Klan cross, which folded up and fit nicely into a box for easy transportation to the next rally, frequently held in the field below the cemetery hill. Kosec's oldest boy later took some of the red lights out of the cross and substituted green; for decades the cross hung on the front of their house in Spring Glen, lit up every year as a Christmas decoration.[5]

After the Great Crash, President Herbert Hoover had led a conservative approach to recovery. A self-made man, he hesitated to provide massive federal aid since he believed it would weaken the country's moral fiber. Businessmen and workers, scared by the continuing slump, failed to cooperate. As voluntarism fizzled and the economy sank to its lowest depths in 1932, Hoover sponsored the Reconstruction Finance Corporation to give banks easy credit in order to jump-start the economy. This program briefly bolstered what was left of America's banking system, but did nothing to ease the Depression. In the elections that fall, the Democrats swept into office nationwide, including Franklin Delano Roosevelt (FDR) as president. Utah's Republican stalwart, Reed Smoot, lost. His Senate career was over.[6]

By then, the Great Depression had come to Castle Valley. It reached its nadir during the winter of 1932–1933, before Franklin D. Roosevelt's inauguration the following March. "There was no work!" remembered Helper's Ann Slavensky Spensko. "If people are getting laid off and they say, well, where are we going to get work? There was no work to go to."[7]

Price's Helen Bunnell felt particularly badly for her parents, who finally had to abandon their farm in 1934. "Four children, a couple of month's supply of canned food and farm produce, and $1,000 were all they had to show for five year's hard work on the farm and twenty-three years of married life."[8] Not everyone had to leave. Eva Westover Conover survived the Depression on a "small, run-down farm, three miles up the canyon from the town of Ferron," bought by her husband, Harry Conover, whom she married in 1933. He had found a job at Mohrland but lost his right eye in an industrial accident the first day on the job. His settlement money paid for the farm, and Eva counted herself lucky that the house lacked electricity, a telephone, and running water, so they had no utility bills to pay. She remembered seeing "entire families riding freight cars. . . . People lost whatever was not paid for, their cars, their homes, their farms, lost all they'd struggled a lifetime for."[9] Some of those who rode the rails stopped at the Bee Cafe in Helper, begun by Japanese immigrant Masaki Okura and partners who had left Mohrland as workdays dwindled. "While the train loaded up," remembered his daughter, "we would all rush around like mad and get them fed and then they would leave without paying. Other times we would have nothing to do but sit around." After a year they sold out and opened a restaurant in Price, catering mostly to the local trade.[10]

When FDR came into office, he faced similar financial distress all across the country. He immediately declared a "bank holiday," closing all banks nationwide until, after investigation, only the sound ones could reopen. Green River's Commonwealth Bank, the town's third, had begun with great hopes in the mini-oil boom of 1921. It closed on March 5, 1933, during the bank holiday. After paying depositors in full, it stayed closed.[11] Two other local banks had already reorganized. The Emery County Bank, founded by Manti sheepman and Orangeville winter resident James Crawford, Jr., had opened in 1906 and had operated successfully ever since. Farther north, in the early 1920s Wallace Lowry had helped found the Carbon County Bank to provide more sympathetic treatment to fellow sheepmen than the old First National Bank. In February 1932, directors of the Emery and Carbon institutions agreed on a merger, becoming the Carbon-Emery Bank with $633,000 in assets and preserving all their depositors' savings.[12]

To restore public confidence, Roosevelt began broadcasting his famous radio Fireside Chats. His first Hundred Days ended with the creation of the New Deal and its original plethora of federal agencies: the Agricultural Adjustment Administration (AAA); the Federal Emergency Relief Administration (FERA); the Civil Works Administration (CWA); the Civilian Conservation Corps (CCC); the Tennessee Valley Authority (TVA); and the New Deal's centerpiece, the National Industrial Recovery Act (NIRA).[13]

Labor delighted in the passage of the NIRA in June 1933. Its famous Section 7(a) contained three major provisions working people had long been fighting for: employees could organize in groups of their own choosing and elect representatives with whom business must bargain collectively, no one seeking work could be forced into a company union nor be prohibited from joining a labor union (the end of the "yellow dog" contract), and employers had to comply with maximum hours, minimum wages, and other conditions of employment stipulated by the president. Other sections of the act protected business in an attempt to insure reasonable profits, prevent unfair competition, and avoid overproduction, while compelling companies to pay a living wage.[14] Unionization and collective bargaining had just become legal. Nationwide, miners' expectations for a better life soared.

Even before the passage of the NIRA, the coal industry began changing. The Anaconda Copper Company switched from coke to natural gas for smelting, closing out one major buyer for the Castle Valley product.[15] Back East, disaffected members of the United Mine Workers of America (UMWA) felt that they had been sold out by John L. Lewis in the 1927–1928 strike in Pennsylvania and Ohio. They formed the militant National Miners Union (NMU) to lead "the miners' struggles against the capitalist owners of the mining industry, and their agents, for better working and living conditions . . . to participate in the struggle for abolishing the capitalist system and replace it by socialism."[16] In May 1933, NMU organizers arrived in the Castle Valley coal fields. Their union tried to spread its appeal among entire families. Organizers rented the Millarich Hall for their rallies, created a women's auxiliary and a youth section, and sponsored Saturday night dances and Sunday meetings. They also relied on the silver tongue of leaders like Charles Guynn, Charles Weatherbee, and Paul Crouch. "Charles Guynn had what they call charisma now. He could really put it across," remembered Frances Dupin Vouk. "Once we went to a dance up at what used to be the roller rink . . . out of Spring Glen on the highway, and they had this big symbol, this Communist symbol, with this sheaf of wheat. . . . They didn't do that until they got everyone really interested."[17] At that point, some people left the NMU. Some stayed, not caring if the union was communistic or not. While Helper mayor Frank Porter refused to take sides, Price mayor Rolla West branded every NMU supporter a Communist and forbade the organization to march in the July Fourth parade, which alternated between the two towns. Incensed, NMU parents pulled their children out of the Carbon High School marching band, which had just won first place honors at the national competition and marched in the 1933 Chicago World's Fair Parade. If the parents couldn't march in Price, neither could their newly-returned children.[18]

Breaking up the band underscored how divisive the Strike of 1933 had become. Band participation and competition had long helped unify not only the diverse communities of Castle Valley, but had helped connect this isolated corridor with the rest of Utah and the region. Children joined the Price band from every coal town in the region (except Mohrland, whose children went to school in Emery County), riding buses from Columbia,

This 1933 Carbon High School band, the pride of the county, won the right to appear at the 1933 Chicago World's Fair and was the smallest band there. Upon its triumphant return, tensions of the 1933 strike prevented it from marching in Price's Labor Day parade. Courtesy of Western Mining and Railroad Museum.

Standardville, Latuda, and elsewhere to board in Price and study at Carbon High. Edgar M. "Toot" Williams, an Emery County native and the Carbon High School music director since 1923, had brought his students to a nationally recognized pinnacle with considerable local support. With the backing of the Price Chamber of Commerce and the cooperation of the entire area, throughout which people opened their homes to visiting musicians, Price had begun hosting the Intermountain Music Meet in 1931, welcoming bands from other Utah towns and from western Colorado. By 1932, Price hosted thirty-two bands with 1,450 students. In the state contest at Logan that year, the Carbon High School band won the right to represent Utah and Region Ten at the national competition at Evanston, Illinois. There, in 1933, although the smallest band there, they were "acclaimed by the judge as the greatest marching unit ever to enter a national contest," according to the Price *Sun Advocate.* Dorr Williams Hanson, who played clarinet in his Uncle Edgar's band, rated the Chicago trip a highlight of his early life. Thelma Mathis Jewkes, who chaperoned the students, credited Williams with their success not only for his insistence on music and drilling, but because he never let the students run around in their uniforms and made sure they were well fed and well rested. While Castle Valley missed seeing these champions that July Fourth, the Intermountain Meet returned to Price in April 1934, drawing a number of bands second only to the national competition. Williams worked on the state patriotic music committee

in World War II, and music meets continued on and off until 1953, drawing
together a community periodically split by mine disputes, different backgrounds, religions, and social classes. But well into the twentieth century,
everybody loved bands.[19]

In 1933, bitterness continued escalating after the July Fourth parade
fiasco. Some NMU members felt unfairly accused of violence. Stressing that
they worked peacefully, John Spensko remembered, "We [even] went down
here to Emery County mines . . . to Huntington and down in Salina." The
men parked their trucks on the county road (public property) "and when a
truck comes we'd stop them and we'd talk to them and tell them, . . .'Don't
go up there and get that coal, if you want to join with us!. . . . But they
wouldn't listen."[20] When local coal companies cut miners' wages in defiance
of the Reconstruction Finance Corporation's rules, miners, in general, became more pro-union. One local mine boss even took young Remo Spigarelli aside and said, "'I'll tell you, you'll be better off belonging to a union
than without it. . . . Of course, I can't say what I feel [publicly] . . . but' he
says, 'We're not stupid enough not to know that organization is the best
thing.'"[21] The UMWA's John L. Lewis, hearing of NMU inroads in the Castle
Valley coal fields, started his own, belated recruiting drive. But the NMU
was gaining steam. With a prelude of two quick strikes at Mutual in August
1933, on Labor Day many miners walked out for good, with standoffs centering on Gordon Creek, Spring Canyon, Castle Gate, and Kenilworth.[22]

In subsequent months, the competition between the NMU and the
UMWA, and between strikers and strike-breakers, drove deep wedges be-
tween Castle Valley's people. In general, the Helper area and the South
Slavs (Croatians, Slovenes, and Serbs) supported the NMU. Price, the
American Legion, and Carbon County government sided with the UMWA.
Italians, Greeks, native-born Americans, and other ethnic groups were split.
The divisions became so bitter that, in August, UMWA members, armed
with pick handles, rifles, and shotguns, tried to break the NMU picket line
in Spring Canyon and Gordon Creek. The UMWA also joined the local
power structure in successfully requesting Utah's Governor Blood to send
in the National Guard and cooperated in aiding the coal companies: the
only known instance of such an "unholy alliance" in American labor history.[23] UMWA flyers secretly distributed at the coal camps read, in part:

> Please do not mistake the United Mine Workers of America for the Na-
> tional Miners' Union which is now in your midst blowing their trumpets of
> discord. . . . The United Mine Workers of America is really an American in-
> stitution, working under American ideals and ideals. . . . The National Min-
> ers' Union, on the contrary . . . [follows] policies dictated from Moscow,
> Soviet Russia . . . [and] is a menace to the coal miners, to the coal industry,
> and to our nation.[24]

The ghost of the old Red Scare walked again.

Soon, newly-deputized UMWA members moved in against NMU strikers at the Gordon Creek camps, joined by the National Guard. At Consumers, strikers had barricaded the road with railroad ties, mattresses, and a truck. Women joined men guarding the entrance to the camp, and when the women caught superintendent David Parmley (also chair of the Carbon County Commissioners) trying to leave, six big Slavic women seized and disarmed him, then held him down and peed on him in a typical old-country insult. Parmley soon reached the shelter of the approaching deputies. When a dozen NMU hotheads followed him down the canyon, the first three of them were felled by punches from Bill Stapley, the Mormon bishop of Castle Gate who had replaced Bishop Thomas, killed in the 1924 explosion. The bested NMU sympathizers escaped back up the canyon, and Stapley was known as "Bill the fighting Bishop" ever after. At nightfall, the posse took down the barriers and proceeded to Consumers, where a group of deputies stayed to patrol the camp. The next day, they made military preparations to take Spring Canyon.[25]

As the strike began, Joe Myers had come back from California after suffering an injury that ended his professional baseball career. He went to visit the Spring Canyon picket line where his mother and other Austrian women helped picket and feed the strikers. Meanwhile, lawmen began massing from all over the state. Walt Borla recalled seeing a "plane . . . flying around." He added, "I always remember sitting in the front yard, 'cause we lived off the highway, and watching those old Model-A patrol cars. . . . I bet I counted about sixty . . . as they went by." He worried about his father up on the Spring Canyon picket line. "Pretty soon over the hill he came, over that tunnel. And he came down through those fields and came home and I was so relieved." The clash had started. At Spring Canyon, the National Guard began lobbing tear gas canisters at the strikers, whom, they claimed, were on company property. Myers, with his great baseball arm, picked up one of the canisters and threw it right back at the soldiers. After a scuffle, he was arrested and locked up in the bullpen with over two hundred other men, "and I wasn't even working here!" he remembered.[26] For a full day, the men in the bullpen were denied food, water, and blankets as the Carbon County deputies concentrated on cleaning up Helper. After twenty-four hours, the prisoners got food and coffee. After forty-eight hours, Price mayor Rolla West led seven truckloads of deputies into Helper, made searches of NMU-affiliated houses without warrants, and arrested Charles Guynn and Charles Weatherbee, talking his posse out of a plan to lynch the NMU organizers.[27] Most of the previously arrested men stayed in the Price bullpen; some, together with Guynn and Weatherbee, were booked into the Price city jail.

Two weeks after the raid on Spring Canyon, the state championship baseball game was scheduled to be played in Helper, the best ballpark in all of Castle Valley. Due to the strike and resultant ordinances forbidding public meetings, the game was transferred to Provo. Joe Myers, still in jail, was on the Helper championship team. Popular Carbon County Sheriff

Marion Bliss, the only Republican elected in the county in 1932 (and the last for quite a while) offered deputies his car to take Myers to Provo. Myers rejected the whole idea: "bring me up in the sheriff's car with bayonets and [they think] I'm going to play ball? I said, 'You either let me go on my own, or I'm not going.'" So the Helper mayor put up $5,000 bail so Myers could get out of jail. Sheriff Bliss lent Myers his car. Myers drove to Provo, played in the ball game, "drove back, parked the car and knocked on his [Bliss's] door, and he put me back in the cell." (The Bliss family lived adjacent to the courthouse and jail.) "Bliss says, 'I sure hate . . . to do this to you, Joe . . . but you know the law's the law.' . . . Mrs. Bliss kind of liked me," Myers continued, so "Marion used to come over and say, 'Joe, somebody outside wants to talk to you. It's important.' He'd take me back into the kitchen. . . . And she used to let me eat with the family. . . . But they booked me for criminal syndicalism. That's a felony!"[28] Myers, however, was released without trial and only learned of the charges years later when his sister, working at the county courthouse, found the old records. By then, Myers was a World War II veteran and Helper's police chief. Meanwhile, humane Sheriff Bliss was killed in a disorganized shoot-out in 1945.[29]

After the NMU organizers went to jail, a peaceful march down Price Main Street to protest their incarceration ended in a fire hose and tear gas attack by armed county deputies. J. Bracken Lee, later Price City mayor and subsequently Utah's governor, filmed the melee from a nearby rooftop. Some liberal Salt Lake City Mormons compared the terrorizing of the NMU members to the actions of U.S. marshals ferreting out cohabs over a generation earlier. In subsequent trials of NMU organizers for criminal syndicalism, one of the former deputies served as jury foreman but no mistrial resulted. Instead, the defendant was found guilty, although the conviction was set aside and the case remanded on appeal. Investigative articles in Salt Lake's *Deseret News* never appeared. In the words of historian Helen Papanikolas, "The organizers' trials. . . . crushed the NMU. . . . From the day the UMWA and management signed their agreement [bringing in the union], Carbon County ascended in union affairs." Price became the headquarters of District 22 covering Utah, Wyoming, and Colorado; it remains so today.[30] The Strike of 1933 made other changes in Castle Valley. It thoroughly discredited the NMU, while the United Mine Workers and its members became more popular. Frank Bonacci, long-time UMWA organizer whose family had suffered so at Kenilworth in 1922, was elected to the Utah State Senate in 1936 and for five terms thereafter.[31] Nationally, the unionization process took longer. In 1935, the Supreme Court overturned the NIRA, forcing Congress to repass it in modified form. On its second try, the Wagner Act passed the judicial test.[32] Utah responded quickly to solidify labor's gains: it became one of five states nationally to approve a statewide labor relations law modeled on the Wagner Act.[33] Nonetheless, the 1933 strike left an uncomfortable bitterness in Castle Valley. Almost half a century later,

Joe Myers asked, "How would you feel if you worked in a mine with me and I was on the picket line and you packed a gun for the company? How would you feel?"[34] Speaking of a recently deceased neighbor and former strike deputy, he added, "For years and years nobody would have nothing to do with him. . . .Up to this day . . . [certain people] don't even talk to each other. . . . and that don't happen in Carbon County. But it did."[35]

The strike's bitterness soon became drowned in the desperation of the Great Depression. As livelihoods dried up and mine workdays dwindled, municipalities and counties, as well as individuals, faced ruin. People without work could pay fewer and fewer taxes. In the midst of the strike, the state had attempted to boost county coffers with new legislation that transferred to them a share of the coal royalty (lease) payments that the federal government returned to the states. In November, 1933, for example, Carbon County had almost $17,300 extra income, which its commissioners ear-marked for roads, bridges, and schools.[36] But the mining sector was becoming increasingly unstable as a 1936 study of the Utah coal industry showed. Mines had long overcapitalized and, by 1934, produced over eighty percent more coal than the existing market could absorb. Demand disappeared as railroads turned to diesel; homes to electricity. Although twenty-nine percent of the nation's electricity was generated by coal, even electrical demands had dropped from 1927 to 1934. Freight rates for coal remained high, and a national fuel economy movement, stabilized population growth rate, and environmental concerns about smelter smoke all hurt the coal market.[37]

As the Depression worsened, U.S. Fuel, like the other companies, struggled to keep its highly seasonal workforce intact. It began the innovative practice of working Mohrland and Hiawatha on alternate months so everyone earned half a paycheck.[38] People did what they could to survive. For example, the family of Albert Vogrenic spent Mohrland's off months on Joe Penovich's farm near Consumers. They swapped labor for cabbages and potatoes, getting a few wiener pigs as well, so they did not starve. After doing other odd jobs, Vogrenic started mining coal for forty-three cents a ton, but when summer came his workdays almost ended. The company finally gave up working the mines on alternating months. Mohrland closed in 1938, when U.S. Fuel decided to take the coal out through tunnels connected to Hiawatha. Emery County lost its only large, commercial coal mine to date and individuals scrambled for whatever work they could find. Newly married, Vogrenic went down to the farm of his wife's folks, the Oviatts, in Elmo. Her father and brothers taught him how to farm.[39]

Mohrland's demise hit the county's coffers particularly hard. During 1931–1934, Emery County could collect only about three-fourths of its taxes, and hard-pressed residents banded together to form local Tax Reform Leagues. Green River, seeking better access to government, made particularly strong demands. Its residents had to drive through Price (the Carbon

County seat) to get to Castle Dale (the Emery County seat), while Moab (the Grand County seat) was half the distance of that to Castle Dale. Consequently, Green River wanted to be annexed to Grand County. Restructuring counties, in Utah, remains a virtual impossibility, but Green River's dilemma was finally ameliorated in 1938 when the Civilian Conservation Corps (CCC) built a cutoff road roughly following the Old Spanish Trail that reduced the distance from Green River to Castle Dale by almost half. The road is still in use. Other Depression-era road projects done with state and federal funding greatly improved Castle Valley's internal communications and did a small bit to help alleviate crushing poverty. In 1932, workers paved Highway 10 all the way from Price to Huntington and realigned and rebuilt the road from Woodside some fifteen miles northwest to Icelander Wash. Two years later, pavement of Highway 10 extended to Castle Dale and of Highways 50 and 6 from Green River to Woodside. Castle Valley's main north-south artery gradually received a complete upgrade: Highway 10 pavement reached Ferron in 1938 and Emery in 1941, while the spur to Orangeville was paved in 1940.[40]

Even if one could find work, wages remained dismal, even in the newly-unionized mines. Before Mohrland closed, Remo Spigarelli earned just over three dollars there for an eight-hour shift loading coal. Consequently, he (like others) sometimes doubled back for a second continuous shift despite the physical toll of working sixteen straight hours shoveling coal. Brandishing his pay statements for March and April 1934, he later explained, "We didn't work March. So you see, the Medical Department was a dollar and a half [per month], but they took off three dollars [for March and April], and the rent of course was ten bucks!. . . . And there is ten more dollars [rent deducted]. And the Welfare Association was a dollar a month, so two dollars, now that's the store, $27.03 and our union dues was $3.00, a dollar and a half a month. I made a total of $55.03, and my take-home pay was 54 cents, for two months!"[41]

Life was no better on the farms. As Castle Valley's jobs dwindled, the Great Depression drove almost forty percent of Emery County families to federal relief. Ironically, some natives had worse problems elsewhere and came home. For example, Huntington's Willard Sandberg, a son of miller Olaf Sandberg, had left Castle Valley for college and an LDS mission. For eight years, he had been at a New York bank with "7,500 employees," he remembered, "and they let 2,500 go at one crack." He came back to Huntington, started in the mill, and remained until 1970, replacing his father as miller.[42] Clawson actually grew during the Depression. People took over all available housing—sometimes even two families to a dwelling—because there they could grow a garden to survive. Many folks stayed put and made do. Karl Seely of Castle Dale creatively juggled his assets when the price of wool went from forty-seven cents per pound to nothing. Under rigorous bank loan restrictions, he bartered old ewes for coal, lumber, oats, lettuce, his daughter's dance lessons, and other commodities to keep himself and his herders going. And he paid off the loan. Mohrland's closure also allowed people to buy the surplus, wood-frame, four-room, camp houses and have them hauled away by teams, so they could use the lumber or place the houses on new foundations where they competed with other Depression-era homes built with sweat, barter, and ingenuity, yielding a frugal comfort.[43]

Everyone practiced daily economies, regardless of background or social standing. As Helen Bunnell of Price explained, she "cooked and canned and sewed and made over, turned collars and put hems up and down, relined coats, and patched sheets. Instructions to my sister to 'double the recipe and use one egg' became a family joke. Using up the annual supply of venison was also a family tradition, but no joke."[44] For all that, she also joined Price's selective New Century Club, formed in 1933 (before the Bunnells came home). Founding members created this women's literary, entertainment, and community service organization, admitting only a portion of those who applied until its demise in 1985. It and its predecessor, the Literary League, both had roots in the old Woman's Club of the 1920s. Bunnell surmised that "the club probably provided an outlet for the energies of some young women who were being prevented by the Depression from going away to college," the closest one got to being "elite" in Castle Valley.[45] At home, Bunnell's economizing efforts were paralleled by those of her husband, future state Senator Omar Bunnell. Usually, he worked "patching up used cars and performing other odd jobs for his dad's foundering automobile business, selling Fuller brushes, and raising sugar beets for a couple of summers. . . . Actually, the most profitable work he had during that time was *not* raising sugar beets—a New Deal program that really helped us."[46]

She referred to the Agricultural Adjustment Administration (AAA), which attempted to eliminate farm surpluses by paying farmers to reduce production until "parity prices" (those earned during World War I) were attained. In Utah overall, the AAA paid out over half a million dollars during fiscal 1933–1934 alone, or approximately one dollar per person. The Soil Conservation Service also had a major Castle Valley impact. Conditions got so bad that in 1936, local farmers invited the federal government to help, and in 1948, the Huntington Soil Conservation District became the second in the state of Utah.[47]

Castle Valley's rangelands also demanded stricter conservation, although they had already been regulated for decades. By 1934, however, the local livestock industry teetered on the brink of extinction due to one of Castle Valley's periodic freeze-drought cycles. First, in the winters of 1931–1932 and 1932–1933, severe cold and snowfall had killed thousands of sheep on Castle Valley's rangelands. Then, the blessedly mild winter of 1933–1934 became a scorching summer drought. Instead of the usual thirteen inches, Utah's annual precipitation for 1934 equaled just over nine inches for the state as a whole; only two inches fell at Hanksville, just

southeast of Castle Valley. All over the range, springs dried up and forage withered. Stock died.[48] Moore received limited help through Utah's
drought relief fund, which paid to raise the dam that fed the irrigation canal and financed construction of a large storage cistern on a plateau above
the town, allowing piped-in culinary water.[49] To save their stock, desperate
ranchers began agreeing to further federal regulation. James Allred, speaking for many of his neighbors, opined that lands near Cleveland suffered
from considerable overgrazing "due to grazing in the summer as well as
winter making it necessary to feed stock in the winter much heavier" than
previously.[50] Consequently, Castle Valley ranchers generally accepted the
federal 1934 Taylor Grazing Act, sponsored by Utah Representative Don B.
Colton (although he had left Congress by the time it passed). Designed to
regularize use of federal grasslands, it impressed Preston Nutter, who with
control over 180,000 acres (281 square miles) owned Castle Valley's—and
Utah's—largest privately-held cattle ranch. He appreciated "its intent 'to
stabilize the livestock industry,'" according to his daughter, Virginia Price.[51]
Historian Carl Abbott noted, "Within two years, the Taylor Act removed
142 million acres of western lands from potential sale and reserved them
for grazing under federal control. . . . The new Grazing Service of the
Department of the Interior was to lease grazing rights at reasonable rates
while controlling use of the fragile rangelands."[52] The Taylor Act also superseded a clutch of federal homestead laws, ending "forever the fantasy of
free public land, and the hope of someday 'proving up' on a picturesque
homestead," in the words of historian Stanford J. Layton.[53] By 1935, that
long-lived fantasy had been largely swallowed by Depression realities. Hard-
pressed Castle Valley stockmen consequently also embraced the livestock
program of the Federal Surplus Relief Corporation, which purchased unwanted animals (usually culls), paid for their slaughter, and allowed the unemployed to pick up the meat, free of charge. Over five thousand head of
Castle Valley cattle and several thousand head of sheep came off the range
under this plan. Unnecessary animals, particularly wild horses, had to be
eliminated. Harry Mahleres noted that some Greek sheepmen, rather than
buy permits for iffy federal rangelands, had purchased their own acreage
to run their stock. "In this way," he added, "the sheepmen have entrenched
themselves here, especially in Carbon County."[54]

The 1930s freeze-drought cycle not only killed animals, it destroyed
farms inhabited by thousands of desperate people driven home or to a
neighbor's place to try to weather the Great Depression. Weather conditions dropped irrigation water to less than a quarter of the normal supply.
In southern Castle Valley, around Emery and Moore (formerly Rochester),
eighty-five percent of the crops died, leading to an almost total unemployment rate by the end of 1934. Crops also failed at Cleveland. Ferron's water
system sporadically went dry. Castle Dale's flowed so sluggishly that residents received emergency typhoid immunizations to protect them from a

disease known to be spread in bad water. Federal records revealed that during 1934–1935, in Carbon County, where the mines barely scraped along, over 3,900 families lived on 408 farms which received eighty federal loans totaling over $52,000. In Emery County, almost 1,500 families on 924 farms received 140 loans for $25,000 in the federal drought relief program.[55] This local dependence on federal relief funds exemplified Utah's acceptance of "the economics of ambivalence," a phrase coined by historian Wayne K. Hinton to describe the attitudinal reversal in a state previously highly suspicious of federal "meddling."[56]

In addition to those that helped livestock and farming, other New Deal agencies made a lasting impact on Castle Valley, particularly the Works Progress Administration (WPA), the Civilian Conservation Corps (CCC), and the Farm Security Administration (FSA). The WPA, part of the Second New Deal inaugurated in 1935, made practical improvements at Clawson where it hired virtually every man in town to gravel streets and sidewalks. Overall, however, it had its greatest influence in art. Nationally, it hired artists and provided them with materials; it also arranged locations for muralists in an attempt to promote art education and provide community service. Utah received approval to hire 15,000 heads of families; by November 1935, the state's monthly WPA payroll exceeded $1,000,000. Helper first took advantage of this largesse, applying for a WPA grant to create an art center. Its leaders agreed to spend $250 to remodel the civic auditorium and to pay $25 per month for an exhibitor fee. As a result, Helper acquired a traveling art exhibit that, in the first three weeks, attracted 3,057 people to a town of only 2,700. Price, not to be outdone, also sent in a grant proposal and thus Castle Valley became home to two of the four art centers in Utah (the other two being Salt Lake City and Provo).[57] Helper also utilized New Deal funds to construct an underpass connecting Main Street to Janet Street under the railroad, opening up the east side of town for further development and greatly improving access to the city park. The new Helper Junior High School, another Depression-era project, greatly relieved crowding at the old Central School (which burned down in 1965, to be replaced by Sally Mauro Elementary School).[58] Finally, in 1937, the WPA funded construction of the Helper Post Office from construction plans identical to others used nationwide (to save time and money), but financed a distinctive mural of a "typical western town" by Jene Magafan on the interior.[59] In Price, Carbon County artist Lynn Faucett earned $1,600 to paint another mural on the top half of the new WPA-funded Price Municipal Building. Laboring from 1938–1941, Faucett created a pictorial history of early Price. He included such figures as Caleb Rhoades, Abraham Powell, Chinese railroad workers, business people, religious leaders, educators, coal miners, and his own blind grandfather being led by the artist as a boy. Simultaneously, Fausett achieved a "dramatic turning point" in his artistic career, painting three more WPA murals which led to commissions in Salt Lake City, New

CCC enrollees hauling large chunks of rock pose for the camera. They helped support their parents and left lasting traces in Castle Valley. Hurst Thygerson Collection. Used by permission of the Utah State Historical Society, all rights reserved.

York, and elsewhere.[60] Other WPA workers in Utah also worked on roads, other public buildings, sidewalks, flood control, insect eradication, and recreational facilities, to name a few.

In the mid-1930s, the federal government not only added new programs but expanded projects around since the First New Deal. One example of this continuity was the long-lived CCC, signed into law in April 1933. It had come to Castle Valley the following month with the arrival of the first thirty men of Company 959 at Joe's Valley. Eventually numbering two hundred, of which about fifty came from Emery County, they united to fight the biggest fire ever on the Manti Forest in the droughty summer of 1934. "I'll never forget the night a week after the fire started," remembered a former CCC man. "We was lying in bed during a light drizzle hoping it would bail out a good rain, and it did. No one cared if his bed and person got wet, if we could only get the fire under control." They did, earning an unprecedented eight-day leave thereafter.[61] Company 959 left in the winter of 1934, worked on various Utah projects (such as building the Skyline Drive and the Huntington-Fairview Road over the Wasatch Plateau), and returned to the area three years later. Meanwhile, the CCC established other camps near the coal mine in Dog Valley, south of Emery; at Castle Dale; at Green River, and at Price, mostly to build roads. Ferron received a year-round camp built in the town park under local supervision with locally-milled lumber, a real boon to the economy. Since all CCC participants had to be unmarried, unemployed men from the ages of seventeen to twenty-five whose parents were on relief, romances flourished. Bill Anderton, who wed Ferron's Genevieve Funk, later remarked, "We could [have] control[led] the elections in Ferron by telling our wives how to vote because so many of us

The San Rafael bridge, now one of only two known suspension bridges remaining in Utah, is obscured at the back of this photograph of its glorious dedication ceremony. Dozens of cars arrived in the San Rafael Swell to celebrate the 1937 opening of this Civilian Conservation Corps project, which allowed safe passage for local herds over the San Rafael River. Courtesy of Emery County Archives.

married Ferron girls"—assuming the wives would have obliged them.[62] Other benefits came to the Price Steam Laundry of Angelo Georgedes, who had learned to make soap in his native Greece. To survive the Depression, Georgedes bid successfully against state-wide competitors for the CCC laundry contract, then had to collect blankets and sheets over a 1,300–mile route in Utah and parts of Nevada, Wyoming, Colorado, and Arizona.[63] Locally, in addition to fire-fighting and road-building, the CCC terraced hillsides to prevent erosion, marked several mountain trails, built the swinging bridge over the San Rafael River, prepared picnic grounds, built fences and ranger dwellings, and otherwise promoted conservation, sending (by law) $25 of the $30 earned monthly home to their parents.[64]

These federally-funded local improvements, valuable though they were, did nothing to help Castle Valley's always-marginal farmlands. Northern Castle Valley farmers had been struggling with recurrent water problems ever since the Gooseberry Dam went out in 1917. In 1921, A. W. Horsley, Henry Mathis, and others had organized the Price River Water Conservation District to purchase a new reservoir site in Pleasant Valley, relocate the old railroad, and build a new dam. The Horsley Dam at Pleasant Valley was finished in 1926, its construction funded by $750,000 worth of bonds bought (mostly at a discount) by area farmers, miners, and town residents.[65] Castle Valley, then caught in one of its periodic droughts, could not fill the reservoir until the spring of 1928, by which time the dam's earth fill had dried out. As the reservoir filled, the earth cracked and settled. Water poured through holes in the dam's face. The watchman sent out a flood alarm; men rushed to the dam, opening outlet gates to their fullest as the water slowly lowered. The dam held, but the local irrigation district could not handle the extensive repairs needed.[66]

Although a state committee made basic improvements that kept the Scofield dam functional for over a decade, only federal money could finance a new dam. This seemed an ideal New Deal project since big dams became major federal pets during the Great Depression. Nationwide, they provided multiple benefits: mainly flood control, irrigation, and electrification. In the East, the government originated the Tennessee Valley Authority (TVA); in the West, it sponsored Boulder (Hoover) Dam. Both of these grew on politicized foundations. Private utilities fumed impotently as the federal government built the "socialistic" TVA, still a model for developing nations. Hoover Dam had been affected by the Teapot Dome scandal of 1924, which had led the Interior Department to abandon the use of federal employees in preference for outside contractors. The low bid on Hoover Dam—by almost ten million dollars—came from the Six Companies, a consortium which included brothers Edmund O. and William H. Wattis, who owned (together with the Eccles family) the Utah Construction Company, target of the 1913 IWW strike. They also owned the Wattis coal mine in southwest Carbon County, but had long invested their Castle Valley earnings elsewhere. For example, in California, they built Yosemite's highly controversial Hetch Hetchy dam, the only such structure ever erected in a national park.[67] Among the others connected with the Six Companies, entrepreneur Henry Kaiser would soon have a major impact on Castle Valley, drawing rural Utah ever closer into the national economic net. One of Teancum Pratt's grandsons joined the rush to build Hoover Dam, attracted by wages of about fifty cents an hour for unskilled labor and about seventy-five cents for skilled carpenters.[68] He found "a forbidding hole . . . [to become] the mighty daddy of all dams," but did not stay long in this world of shanties, dynamite explosions, and heat prostration.[69] After four years of struggle, effort, and human misery, officials dedicated Hoover Dam in September 1935.[70]

Despite its desperate water needs, no such grand plan touched Castle Valley, where, by the mid-1930s, most farms along the Price River had become so unproductive that an estimated three-quarters were subject to foreclosure. The federal Resettlement Administration of the FSA took note of this dismal situation and seriously considered buying out 17,000 farmable acres, reorganizing the nineteen local canal companies (the major stumbling block), and resettling 250 families on the only 70 arable acres left by 1936. To assess the situation first-hand, both the Western Regional Director, Jonathan Garst, and the Regional Labor Advisor, Paul Schuster Taylor, visited northern Castle Valley, accompanied by photographer Dorothea Lange. Her unflattering photographs of snowy Consumers coal camp each bear the phrase, "controlled by absentee capital," to underscore the Resettlement Administration's view that the miners' only chance for improvement came from federally funded homes and subsistence farms.[71] (Two years later, its back to the economic wall, Consumers closed abruptly in the spring of 1938, after hiring new miners that very morning. The buildings were sold and carted off; the iron tracks torn up and sold to Japan.[72]) In 1936, based on the FSA study, the Price River Reclamation Project manager concluded that water was the main problem and made "some very startling discoveries" (to a government employee) that the farmers with the poorest lands owed the most back taxes.[73] Officials also noted the unsettling economic affect of the coal industry's volatility and pinpointed problems associated with handling a highly diverse population "from the standpoint of nationality." Director Garst also observed that "some of this land is rapidly being spotted by the infiltration of alkali caused by irrigation and poor drainage," officially recording what Castle Valley residents had known for generations. Finally, remarking that "the income of the Price River area comes largely from the range livestock, mines and railways; so the community is not entirely dependent upon the irrigated area," the Resettlement Administration put the project on hold.[74] A local 1937 attempt to revive it received little better than a form letter, stating, "It is regretted that the project . . .could not have been included in our present program."[75]

While the federal government shelved the Castle Valley resettlement effort, the state stepped in to foster local education. In 1937, after considerable lobbying, the Utah Legislature passed an act to create a junior college at Price. Carbon College, built for just under $200,000, began operating in the fall of 1938 on the site of the old baseball field used as a bullpen in the strikes of 1922 and 1933. The first year, it enrolled 731 students who could take technical, mine-related instruction as well as the usual range of academic courses. Thereafter, the federal government boosted the college technical program through the National Youth Administration (NYA), which hired 100 local youth (and students) to make additions on the vocational building.[76] As the college readied for opening, an official contacted Leonard Shield, then working at Rolapp as a night welder and mechanic. Shield, born in Sunnyside of English parents in 1907, welcomed the proffered instructional job although he had spent the 1930s trying to develop a mine of his own. After being laid off at Kenilworth, he had accompanied his father, William, a former assistant state coal mine inspector, in walking across the face of the Book Cliffs eastward from Deadman Canyon, tracing a known coal vein. At Soldier Canyon, the potentially workable vein disappeared, hidden by dirt slides. The men laboriously dug a trench along the mountainside, uncovering seven veins of coal, from six inches to twelve feet thick. Initially working with his father, brother, and Charlie Baker, Shield hauled coal to Price in a truck during the winter of 1931–1932 until he got hired back at Standard. Then he went to Los Angeles for training in welding and diesel mechanics, and later in Cleveland, Ohio—certification later crucial to his college job. In 1940, Shield became a full-time college welding instructor, selling his coal lease to Andrew Marinoni who eventually sold it to California Portland Cement.[77]

By the time Shield began teaching, all eyes had turned to world events. Fascism had spread through Europe and North Africa. The Italians conquered Ethiopia in 1936; Spain's Fascist leader Francisco Franco, with Italian and German backing, defeated the Loyalists in 1937; and in 1938, the German Nazis annexed Austria and invaded Czechoslovakia. As the world waited, hoping Hitler's conquests had sated his imperialistic demands, America began quiet preparations for war. On March 28, 1939, President Roosevelt issued an Executive Order which revoked all private-stock driveways in the state of Utah—the only state so restricted. He wanted to get animals off the Salt Flats, freeing up land originally regulated under the Taylor Grazing Act for the creation of Wendover Field. Activated in July 1941, it was the largest military reserve in the world.[78]

By then, Europe had exploded into World War II. The German invasion of Poland, in September 1939, triggered a declaration of war from France and Great Britain. Italy sided with Germany to form the Axis powers. In the spring of 1940, Hitler launched his blitzkrieg, conquering Denmark, Norway, Belgium, the Netherlands, and France by summer. The war separated some Castle Valley families such as the Ariottis, who had traveled back and forth between the American West and northern Italy several times. They had to endure the war with their father, Rocco Ariotti, in Italy, and their mother, Albina Giacoma-Rosa Ariotti, and her five children in Castle Valley.[79]

As the rest of the world slipped into war, FDR won an unprecedented third term in 1940. His administration continued to support the British and their allies, billing the U.S. as "the arsenal of democracy." In this spirit, he signed the Lend-Lease Act in March 1941, sending war materiel to nations the U.S. considered vital for its own security—in essence, an economic war on Germany. Thanks to this pact, federal money filtered into America's agrarian hinterlands. Castle Valley enjoyed "increased employment, and war markets through our exportation of foodstuffs and materials to Britain," noted C. C. Anderson early in 1941, emphasizing "quality [stock] production at a peak of the carrying capacity of the range." Anderson also remarked on increased consumer buying power and the possibility of "boom days" ahead as war, not the New Deal, finally pulled America out of the Great Depression. His prediction was realized when the Nazis invaded the Soviet Union in June 1941, and Roosevelt extended Lend-Lease to it.[80]

While all eyes remained on the European Theater, the Japanese continued their conquests on the other side of the Pacific. Few Americans paid much attention, but Fred Wataru Taniguchi, an American citizen born in 1914 in Dinuba, California, understood the seriousness of Japanese military aggression. Shortly after his birth, his father fell ill and went back to Japan to die. His mother had to take the infant Fred back, too. Raised near Hiroshima, Taniguchi grew up hearing all about Japanese military exploits in China and Korea from returning veterans. Although neighbors greeted the soldiers as heroes, lavishing them with food and drink, their boasts of killing dozens of men, women, and children repelled Taniguchi. Therefore, as the world-wide Great Depression deepened and his guardian (an uncle) offered Taniguchi the choice of joining the Japanese navy to fight in Asia or a return to the land of his birth, Taniguchi chose America. The sixteen-year-old disembarked in Seattle in 1930, speaking no English. After years of hard manual labor, he finally established himself in southern California. In June 1941, Taniguchi contracted an arranged marriage with Ferry Hiroko (formerly Utah) Okura, born in Kenilworth's "Jap" boarding house, who joined him in California, feeling she had finally left the coal dust of Castle Valley behind.[81] Then, on December 7, 1941, the Japanese attacked Pearl Harbor. America could no longer stay out of the war, which sucked men and minerals even out of such remote corners of the nation as Castle Valley.

# 10

# America's Arsenal, 1941–1960

*They asked me if I would go down and find it [the uranium deposit] with my geiger
counter, and find it I did. It made them so happy they put my name on the claims. . . .
We mined five tons of ore, slid 200 pounds at a time down a rocky slope in a tin
bath tub to the place where we loaded it into a truck. Now, that doesn't sound like
much, but by the time we got through we didn't ever want to try it again.*[1]
—OWEN MCCLENAHAN, BUSINESSMAN AND AUTHOR

World War II ushered in another chapter in Castle Valley's saga of extractive industry. The American military machine needed more and
more minerals to fight Nazism, Fascism, and later the Communist threat.
Castle Valley had plenty—some known, some forgotten. The transition
from a diversified economy—stock-raising, farming, and mining—to almost
complete mining domination marked the mid-twentieth century, spurred
by the Great Depression, intensified by World War II, and solidified during
the Cold War. Particularly World War II firmly entrenched new, govern-
ment-sponsored corporations that gradually acquired local wagon mines
(now truck mines) and bent Castle Valley industry to national requirements
and distant market demands, ignoring local ramifications. After the war, as
America sought to build bigger and bigger bombs, people explored Castle
Valley in the heat of uranium fever, a siren for many, a chimera for most.

Once America entered World War II, virtually everyone worked, and
they worked a lot longer. To fuel outside factories working around the
clock, coal production doubled: from 3,576,000 short tons in 1940, to
7,119,000 short tons four years later. Coal miners got deferments because
industry needed fuel and mines put on extra shifts. The fourteen small
mines in Huntington Canyon formed a cooperative (in a traditional pattern) to handle large orders. To get their output to market as gas rationing
took hold, men constructed a new route, known as the Burma Road for

its sharp curves and steep grades, to connect with the nearest railhead at Mohrland. As Vernon Leamaster wrote, "The building of this road again brought out the cooperation of the mine operators as they had to arrange for the maintenance of the road after it was completed." The Leamaster and Co-op mines in Huntington Canyon even received federal and state permission to run diesel-powered equipment underground—an apparent first for Castle Valley, and an application so uncommon that it remained without federal safety standards until the late 1990s.[2]

Individuals were also affected. After working a lifetime in the mines, Slovenian immigrant Frank Kraync, Sr., had retired at age sixty, considered too old to mine. Then World War II started. "At age sixty-five," joked his daughter, Hilda Kraync Yoklovich, "he was no longer too old to work—he was young again. The Standard Coal Company hired him, and he worked there until his retirement at the age of seventy."[3] Clifford Smith, a long-time miner raised on a farm near Wattis who had been blackballed after the Strike of 1933, was welcomed back in the coal and learned to run the hoist that pulled the cars in and out of the mine. "The war was going full blast," he remembered, so "I had to run enough coal to have empty cars for the night shift to load. . . . I worked 16 to 19 hours a day until 1947."[4] This grueling schedule "caused a considerable increase in accidents," remembered Dr. J. Eldon Dorman, who had arrived as company doctor for Consumers in 1937 and gone on to specialize in ophthalmology. "I saw many severe eye, head, and facial injuries as a result of this mad effort to mine more coal at all costs."[5] Underweight and therefore unable to get into the military in World War II, "Doc" had joined the Civil Air Patrol and become part of the Price Flight, training at the Price Municipal Airport, moved twice since its 1919 founding. By 1940, with approval of the Civilian Aeronautic Authority, the airport had become part of the national defense system. Members of the Price Flight learned to fly, learned to march in formation under the direction of Pacific war veteran "young Bill" Lines, and eventually won the statewide marching contest.[6]

Those who trained the local workforce also worked incredibly long hours. At Carbon College, Leonard Shield spent a full year teaching double shifts: welding from 8 a.m. to 2 p.m. and war production classes from midnight to 8 a.m.[7] Likewise, Shefton Gordon, a long-time Hiawatha miner and later foreman, worked as a Carbon College instructor in the daytime and a mining instructor and foreman at night. At the mine, he trained "all those fellows from Oklahoma and Arkansas . . . taking care of those."[8] Gordon's workforce represented one of the major mass migrations in American history: the westward exodus of Midwesterners in the late 1930s and early 1940s. Driven out by technological unemployment and the depression-era Dust Bowl, hundreds of thousands of men, women, and children traveled west. Many went to California, becoming the despised Okies of John Steinbeck's novel, *The Grapes of Wrath*, a stereotype created largely by Californians for their own purposes.[9] Those who came to Castle Valley included non-stereo-typical Jeanette McAlpine, who left Oklahoma in 1935, coming to Rains in Spring Canyon with her mining engineer husband and their two children. A highly educated woman, she later became a mainstay in Carbon County's cultural events. In 1945, future teacher Nadine Marx came to Hiawatha with her parents at the railroad's expense (later deducted from her father's wages), part of a group of "defense Okies" who filled wartime jobs.[10] They augmented the "jump in the number of miners from 2,600 to 3,800," not-ed by Dorman, who treated a good many of them in his career.[11]

Not only miners, but women and children voluntarily supported the war effort. Denied sugar, candy, new furniture, nylon hose, fabrics, and a host of other items, women used little ration books with their many-colored stamps to purchase available goods. These ration stamps had expiration dates, and storekeeper Ross Boyack remembered the pandemonium at his men's shop "when shoe stamps neared the expiration date. Customers not wanting to lose the use of the shoe stamps, rushed in, bought shoes regard-less of size, color, or style. They would return in a day or two to exchange the shoes for a better choice and size."[12] To help in the face of limited food availability, Mrs. Viola Ross of Castle Gate bought one of the state-accred-ited victory cooking schools to Price to help women maintain proper nutri-tion during rationing.[13] Throughout Castle Valley, female Red Cross units got busy. For example, Molen women, under Ella Beach, "salvaged all clean newspapers and boxes. Every tin can was opened on both ends with the covers folded inside and then crushed flat. These were hauled to the rail-road shop in Price," recalled Lucy Hansen Nielsen. The women also knitted socks of all sizes from wool provided by the Red Cross; washed, dried, and packed white cotton cloth for bandages; and organized nursing classes to learn how to treat common ailments.[14] With men overseas, households ad-justed. Stecky Holdaway moved back in with her mother at Hiawatha; her husband had shipped out to the front, and her father worked over at Mohr-land. She made the move, she said, since "I knew that Hiawatha was a better place [than Price] to raise my kids when I didn't have a husband to help me. And it turned out to be just that."[15] The Boy Scouts also supported the war effort. The Hiawatha troop collected scrap metal from long-abandoned Mohrland. Helper's Troop 271 not only collected waste paper, but devel-oped their own mobilization plan to direct residents to shelters if necessary as part of the burgeoning national emphasis on civil defense.[16]

According to historian Karen Anderson, the long duration of World War II created another more profound effect: it altered societal views and behavior of American women. Women entered jobs previously considered only for men, and when the reserve of single women dried up in 1943, employers actively recruited married women. Whether for patriotic reasons or because of psychological and financial gains, women responded. "At the wartime peak in July 1944, 19 million women were employed, an increase of 47 percent over the March 1940 level," wrote Anderson.[17] Castle Valley, with its huge demand for labor, reflected this national pattern. Beginning in May, 1943, an all-female road striping crew consisting of supervisor Alma Anderson, Ruth Minere, Sylvia Branch, Tillie Anderson, Jessie Williams, and Edith Richmond, all of Price, got busy in Price Canyon. The work lagged in October because military requirements delayed the delivery of basic paint materials including white lead and uranium.[18] Women also started work on coal tipples in 1943, after the Utah Industrial Commission relaxed its gender restrictions. That November the first twenty-nine women began picking boney (rock) out of the coal as it slid by on the tipple's conveyor belts.[19]

Castle Valley's people, no matter what their age, gender, or backgrounds, felt united by a common patriotism. Many local men served in the military: 2,375 from Carbon County; 803 from Emery County.[20] A few women served, too, including Velma Frances Juvan Cole, the daughter of Slovenian immigrant John Juvan of Spring Glen. She had joined the Navy, serving at the bureau of personnel in Washington, D.C. Betty Avery of Kenilworth joined the Marines.[21] Ann Bishop of Sunnyside joined the SPARS, the women's branch of the Coast Guard, but received a medical discharge after a belated diagnosis of rheumatic fever. (She later married Ted Self, and became the founder of the first local school for handicapped children, now the Ann Self School.)[22] Twenty descendants of Anna Draper Tidwell of Wellington served in various branches of the military—grandsons, great-grandsons, grandsons-in-law, and a single great-granddaughter who was an army nurse.[23] At home, the miners at Royal staged a wildcat strike because they wanted the American flag to fly over the mine portal where they worked, rather than over the company office, seat of the bosses.[24] People lined up to buy war bonds from Jack Dempsey, who briefly returned to his old haunts near Coal City and made appearances elsewhere throughout the valley.[25] Residents also supported the unknown soldiers in transit who came through on the Rio Grande, just as they had since the Spanish-American War. When troop trains stopped in Wellington, the children ran over to talk to the soldiers and offered to mail letters for them. Helper townspeople fed undersupplied, recent graduates from the Hoffman Island Radio Officer School who pulled into the depot in 1943. "I don't know how the [troop] train got word [out]," emotionally recalled a veteran decades later, "but when we pulled into the station, there were people all around with all kinds of food."[26] Folks at home thought often about the soldiers at the front. "Most of the boys that I had taught in my first four years . . . were old enough to go to war," remembered Eva Westover Conover. "They were everywhere—the Suez, Rome, Germany, England, on about every Pacific island and I would listen every evening to the radio news about the war where my boys were. And I would cry and worry about them."[27] Greek immigrants Angelo and Effie Georgedes worried, too, when they heard that their son, John, had been captured in battle as the Allied troops fought south from Normandy into France. Fearing that John had died, Angelo nonetheless kept selling war bonds just as enthusiastically as before, and was later greatly relieved to hear that John, taken prisoner, had been released in time to help liberate Paris.[28] Bill Hall, son of Mohrland's postmistress, came back with the Congressional Medal of Honor. A Naval Reserve pilot from the carrier *Lexington*, he had dropped a bomb down the smokestack of a Japanese battleship in May 1942 and returned a day later to fight twelve Japanese planes, bringing three of them down despite his own severe wounds. Consequently, he became one of five Utahns to receive this highest military decoration, and "one of the few who ever received that decoration and lived to wear it," according to his childhood friend, Nevin Wetzel.[29]

Not all the men made it home, and losses struck very deeply. For example, Huntington's Marie Cowley, a former high school cheerleader, had married Pete Grange, the basketball captain, in June 1941. Pete was working in the Hiawatha coal mine and could have had a deferment for essential war work, but he insisted on going if called. He was drafted in August 1944, leaving behind his pregnant wife and a year-and-a half old son. The family got news in June that he was wounded; then, nothing. Early in September her sister-in-law came in sobbing with a package of Marie's letters sent to Pete. They were labeled "Deceased." "This is how we found out he was dead," remembered Marie. "They didn't let us know . . . [that] there had been a telegram there [in Price] for quite a while and they never called or sent anyone over." All of Huntington mourned. "It seemed like we were such a close town and to have a war hero right here. . . . it shook up everybody, not only me but the whole community."[30] Many others also died, and other communities suffered. Dr. Dorman noted a "plaque listing 39 names of former students of Carbon College who were killed in World War II. There are 13 names with an ethnic lineage such as Amador, Angotti, Nogulich, Bikakis, Protopappas and Kochevar. Carbon County had a total of 87 men who did not return from World War II; one third of these had ethnic names."[31]

While ethnicity made little difference in most of Castle Valley, national lawmakers became preoccupied with race. China had joined the U.S. in fighting against Germany, Italy, and Japan. Consequently, the 1882 Chinese Exclusion Act became an international embarrassment, so Congress repealed it in 1943. In other ways, old racist attitudes had changed very little. Congress still provided a quota of only 105 for persons of Chinese descent regardless of country of origin (the only admission law based solely on race). "A Chinese born in Canada, for example, would be chargeable to the tiny Chinese quota; while a native of Canada could enter as a nonquota immigrant," noted historian Roger Daniels. For the first time, however, Chinese could become U.S. citizens on the same basis as other immigrants.[32] Congress also dissuaded the Japanese American Citizens League (JACL), which stressed patriotic support of government policies during the war despite their unconstitutionality, from expressing public support for this bill. The JACL's silence, Daniels noted, meant that "Japanese unpopularity might not adversely affect that bill and so that the inevitable question of quotas and citizenship for all Asians might be forestalled."[33]

American Japanese suffered terribly during the war. Many people myopically lumped together Japanese-American citizens, resident Japanese aliens (ineligible for U.S. citizenship by American law), and the enemy overseas. At Sunnyside, for example, the day after Pearl Harbor, Nisei children (American-born citizens) did not come to school. When they arrived on December 9, "the class bully was extremely verbally abusive to them, especially to my good friends Henry, Harry, and Harold Nitsuma," remembered Paul Turner. "He made it sound like they were personally responsible for the bombing."[34] The same attitude went all the way to the top. On February 19, 1942, President Franklin Roosevelt issued Executive Order 9066, allowing the military to remove all suspected enemies from designated areas. Commanding officers used this power sweepingly. After the Federal Bureau of Investigation made an initial roundup of suspected disloyals of all nationalities, the military incarcerated all people of Japanese ancestry from the coasts of Washington and Oregon, all of California, and the southern part of Arizona. Those imprisoned totaled about 120,000 individuals, two-thirds of them U.S. citizens, ignoring their birthright: the protection of the U.S. Constitution. In 1943, the Supreme Court upheld the internment. Thirty-eight years later, historian Peter Irons discovered military intelligence reports showing that federal officials had lied to the Court to justify the imprisonment.[35] A 1981 federal Commission on Wartime Relocation and Internment of Civilians concluded: "Executive Order 9066 was not justified by military necessity, and the decisions that followed from it—exclusion, detention, the ending of detention, and the ending of exclusion—were not founded upon military considerations. The broad historical causes that shaped these decisions were race prejudice, war hysteria, and a failure of political leadership."[36] Well before that, American Japanese military units—the 442nd Regimental Combat Team, the 100th Infantry Battalion, and the Military Intelligence Service—had more than proved their patriotism overseas.[37]

That belated realization did no good during World War II. As the government geared up for mass internment in early 1942, some American Japanese became voluntary evacuees. Among them was Fred Wataru Taniguchi and his new bride, Ferry (formerly Utah) Okura Taniguchi, both American citizens married in California the previous June. They sold their newly-acquired possessions for what they could get and boarded a train back to Ferry's parents in Castle Valley. Ferry's mother and sister had obtained a letter addressed to the U.S. military from their landlady, local businesswoman Clara Miller, guaranteeing that they would not become a public charge. (A letter from Ferry's parents, "aliens ineligible for citizenship," who had

The Okura family, father and chef Masaki, with daughters (right to left) Toshiko, Chieko (Cherry), and Hiroko (Ferry), stand outside their restaurant in Price about 1940. All three girls waited tables in the restaurant while their mother and father cooked. After more than a decade as a coal miner, Japanese immigrant Masaki Okura had finally found a road to prosperity in Castle Valley. Courtesy of author.

to rent, because they legally could not buy, would have done no good.) As soon as she returned to Castle Valley, Ferry went back to working in the family cafe.[38]

Fred Taniguchi found employment as a motorman at Sweets, up Gordon Creek Canyon, where numerous American Japanese worked throughout the war. While he drove coal cars in and out of the mine, Columbia laid off all its American Japanese workers as military risks. They were also forced out of Kenilworth, and the company turned the old "Jap" boardinghouse into apartments.[39] Sego Takita Matsumiya remembered that officials confiscated her father's "old five-tube radio . . . his camera, and . . . a .22 that he used to shoot rabbits. . . . down in Carbon County before he was forced to move." He became a share-cropper on a Bear River farm in northern Utah.[40] Only two or three Japanese were still mining at Hiawatha when the war broke out. One remained throughout the war and lived in the camp's hotel for the duration. Another, Mr. Sugihara, moved his family into Price, where unknown persons set his house on fire, trying to burn him out.[41] One group of American Japanese voluntary evacuees, driven off the coast, leased 1,500 acres from W. F. Asimus, George Thurman, and the Wilson Produce Company at Green River, settling some forty families there and growing sugar beets. While 200 Green River citizens initially protested this voluntary relocation, the rest of Emery County absolutely rejected any resettlement of "the Japs." The government forcibly located others there, however, at the old CCC barracks near the Dog Valley coal mine south of Emery where they had to dig coal for Utah's only concentration camp at Topaz, near Delta, at the edge of Utah's Salt Flats. Topaz housed most of San Francisco's Japanese for the duration, including its sizable art colony and the head of the Buddhist Churches of America, which was administered from Utah until 1945.[42] The Castle Valley wartime experience with American Japanese mirrored that of the rest of the nation: not one single act of domestic sabotage occurred.

War also brought new corporations to Castle Valley. U.S. Steel expanded its mines at Columbia, located three miles southeast of Sunnyside. This area, originally patented by a Midwestern consortium in 1911 for investment purposes, as of 1912 was billed as "the only large veins of coking coal left in eastern Utah."[43] Columbia Steel Company had acquired these prospects and established a mine and camp in 1922, processing the coal to make coke and shipping it by rail to its steel-making plant in Utah County. Production had reached a million tons by the time the U.S. Steel acquired the plant in 1930.[44] Under U.S. Steel, in the 1940s, the steel plant at Geneva became "Utah's most significant war-related industry" according to historians Roger D. Launius and Jessie L. Embry.[45] The company supplied its mines at Columbia with the latest coal mining equipment as wartime demand grew. It also opened another mine called Horse Canyon (just over the Emery County line) in 1942, one of the most modern in the country at that time. Five hundred new coke ovens rose at Columbia, although they saw only brief service before the war ended.[46] Castle Valley coke exclusively supplied the $200–million Geneva plant, which turned out three-quarters of a million tons of plates and shapes for Henry Kaiser's prolific Pacific coast shipbuilding plants, earning him the nickname "Sir Launchalot."[47] Kaiser himself, seeking vertical integration for his shipbuilding companies, leased the old Sunnyside No. 2 mine (closed after a disastrous fire in 1921) as well as Nos. 3 and 5, to supply his Fontana Steel plant in southern California. His seven-day-a-week schedule, remembered Frank Peczuh, guaranteed that "we could feel the blasting in the mine in our home."[48] Kaiser's Fontana Steel and the Geneva plant were the "only major steel manufacturing . . . [factories] west of the Mississippi River" according to historian Gerald Nash. Both of them ran on Castle Valley coal.[49] Without a doubt, Castle Valley, once ignored as worthless, had become the epitome of America's role in World War II: the arsenal of democracy.

This front-line importance brought other major changes. Increased demands for manpower immediately resulted in coal camp housing shortages. The old Utah Fuel town of Sunnyside could not manage the manpower crunch; builders threw up 250 homes for 1,500 people in only six weeks at nearby Dragerton and Sunnydale. In 1942, the Defense Plant Corporation built a new, six-mile railroad spur from the Carbon County Railway at Columbia to Horse Canyon. The Sunnyside company store closed down, replaced by the new store in the new town, run by the privately-owned Price

Wartime labor demands generated a building boom in Castle Valley as a new, planned community, called Sunnydale, sprouted up beside the venerable Sunnyside Mine. This 1942 photo shows construction well underway. The old machine-gun nest from the 1922 strike is at the base of the rocky cliff on the left canyon wall. Courtesy of Western Mining and Railroad Museum.

Trading Company. This firm had long since started operating other coal camp stores, including Mohrland and Hiawatha in 1936, and Latuda in 1942. The willingness of giants such as U.S. Fuel, U.S. Steel, and Henry Kaiser to move toward privatization meant that coal camp populations were no longer "captive" in company towns. It also meant that companies no longer needed to build housing and infrastructure for what was correctly adjudged to be a brief, wartime boom.[50] Federal money poured in to improve the area, however. The long-delayed Scofield Dam project took shape in the mid-1940s after surviving a judicial challenge and receiving a federal grant of almost $400,000, augmented by $31,000 from the Utah Fish and Game Commission. Even so, some Castle Valley homes still lacked culinary water for decades. Those in Miller Creek finally received it thanks to the formation of the Miller Creek Special Services District in 1983–1984.[51]

In the meantime, as men flocked to fill round-the-clock shifts at all of Castle Valley's mines, local population shifted dramatically. Between 1940–1950, Carbon County's population increased by over one-third as 6,000 new people arrived, a quarter of those drawn to the Sunnyside district.[52] Paradoxically, Emery County lost almost 700 people, or ten percent, as students left to join the armed services; industrial jobs beckoned elsewhere, and Castle Valley's difficult farmland faced unbeatable competition from more fertile American valleys. These shifts made immediate impacts as the towns of Victor and Desert Lake closed down. Emery County also suffered "the most bitterly fought consolidation battle in the county's history," according to historian Edward Geary. In early 1943, the county school board voted to close Central High School, which served Orangeville and Castle Dale. Students in grades nine through twelve were to be reassigned to North Emery High (for Orangeville students) and South Emery High (for Castle Dale's). Some Central High School parents brought suit, but the court allowed the procedure for the duration of the wartime emergency. In the fall, Central High students refused to board the buses sent to remove them, and only abandoned their boycott when students from both communities could remain together at South Emery. In 1947, Central High burned to the ground.[53]

These local tensions fairly evaporated when Castle Valley heard that the war had ended. As Eva Conover remembered, "When news came that it was finally—for sure—over, we climbed into the pick-up, children standing in the back next to the cab, and headed for town. On the way every neighbor joined us, on tractors, walking (we picked them up), in their cars, on horse back. . . . A crowd had gathered by the post office, waving flags, crying for joy, laughing, cheering. Then, we decided to go to Emery to join them in celebrating. We hadn't gone past the first old blue hill until we met them coming to Ferron."[54] Kenilworth had a huge victory bonfire, and the whole town gathered around, celebrating. The Price newspaper reported crowds pouring into the streets when the news first came over the radio. "Residents from the many camps surrounding Price and Helper began to arrive in these centers late in the afternoon, which increased the snarled traffic and already thick crowds." Patrons stripped the state liquor stores completely bare. Price officials closed off the center of town to cars, "and E. M. Williams' Carbon high band furnished music for a public dance on the pavement that lasted until after midnight." The following day, a public victory and thanksgiving program drew hundreds. Meanwhile, all the local mines shut down for lack of miners, and rationing on gasoline and canned goods ceased. The celebrations were all joyous and orderly; the sheriff made no arrests.[55]

With the war over, people had time for increased recreation. In the winter, many turned to skiing. The sport had been gaining in popularity along the Wasatch Front since the 1930s, when the CCC cut roads into old mining towns such as Alta. In Castle Valley, Clear Creek had its ski lift and groomed course, as did Sunnyside. Both had rope tows powered by old car engines; at Sunnyside the power supply actually "included an old Model A Ford with an extra rim on the outside back wheel, with the back wheels in the air. The rope went around the spare rim a couple of times and was anchored on top with another rim hooked to a solid pole," remembered Paul Turner. The mine superintendent, Bob Heers, had helped clear the hill by sending a Caterpillar crew. When Grant Turner, Paul's brother, got his heavy clothes twisted in the winch rope and was left dangling in mid-air just short of the top pulley, Heers and his electricians installed an automatic

shutoff switch to prevent similar accidents. Turner also remembered rent-
ing several railroad cars to take students from Carbon High School and
Carbon College up to the Clear Creek ski run.[56] "When Clear Creek started
dropping down [in population], the Josi boys and our boys, all the school
teachers in town . . . built a ski lift up above Finn Canyon," remembered
Elvie Herskainen Stevens. Those Finn children could ski. "The houses . . .
were built so close to one another that when the town went down, they
took all the doors out . . . and those silly boys would ski from the mountain
slope and go through all these doors through this house." They could also
jump—one "never even left his skis after they hit the bottom, he stayed
on them." The school principal though he could do as well, went over the
jump, and broke his hips. Weino Josi was the best skier. "He could come
down those hills . . . take those beautiful bends, . . . and just circle down
and stop like that." All wore hand-made skis buckled on with leather straps,
the ski tips heated in the coal stove boiler until they were warm and soft so
they could be bent up with the weight of a rock.[57] In the 1950s, 1960s, and
1970s, Utah's ski industry, based on its famous powder, became more com-
mercialized and sophisticated. Meanwhile, Castle Valley's ski runs folded
together with the coal camps they had served.[58]

In the immediate post-war years, as Castle Valley relaxed and celebrated, international tensions mounted. Based on a series of international conferences culminating at Yalta, Russia, in 1945, the Big Three—the U.S.,
Soviet Union, and Great Britain—agreed to support for a United Nations,
to a Soviet offensive against the Japanese after V-E (Victory in Europe) Day,
and to mediate future hot spots, including Egypt, the Middle East (especially a future Jewish state), China, and Viet Nam. Three weeks later, FDR
died. Foreign policy novice Harry S. Truman became president and faced a
rising tide of U.S.-Soviet misunderstanding that matured in an Iron Curtain
descending across Europe, in the words of British Prime Minister Winston
Churchill. The U.S. unilaterally ended the Pacific War on August 6 and 9,
1945 with two atomic bombs, partly fueled by Utah uranium.[59]

President Truman faced difficult challenges at home and abroad. Trying to improve domestic relations, he sent Congress a new reform program
which was whittled away after the Republicans won a congressional majority
in 1946. Congress revised the old Wagner Act with the passage of the Taft-
Hartley Act of 1947 which mandated a "cooling-off" period before a union
could strike. Truman vetoed it, but Congress overrode his veto. Meanwhile,
coal miners struck nationwide (including in Utah), creating a coal scarcity
that spurred consumers to convert to natural gas or oil for home heating.[60]
Truman also attempted major civil rights reforms. He appointed African
Americans to major federal offices, integrated the U.S. military, urged federal prosecution in civil rights cases, attempted to eliminate lynching, and
tried to overturn the poll tax, used to keep blacks from voting. These actions
angered southern Democrats (or Dixiecrats) who ran Strom Thurmond for

president in 1948, giving Republican candidate Thomas Dewey hope for victory with a split Democratic vote. Truman battled on the Democratic ticket to win the presidency in his own right. In the heat of the campaign, ten-year-old Edward Geary of Huntington went with his father, the Emery County Republican chairman, to hear Dewey speak at the LDS Tabernacle in Salt Lake City, and got to shake his hand. Campaigning just as hard, Truman made a 30,000–mile whistle stop tour of the country, including Castle Valley. Geary joined other students dismissed from school to go see him, "despite my dislike for the man because . . . he was The President in spite of everything, and also because I liked trains." Geary laughed with the rest of the crowd when Truman remarked that he had been looking out of the window and saw "one of the lovely garden spots of America." (Geary's father charitably opined that maybe the President had fallen asleep somewhere in Kansas.) On election night, Geary, like many, went to bed content, after early returns showed Dewey well in the lead. But California went for Truman, and Dewey lost. In later years, Geary marveled at the immediacy and reach of national politics in those days, "when a ten-year-old boy living in an obscure southern Utah village could see both major presidential candidates in person and shake hands with one of them."[61] Even Castle Valley had found a spot on the national political map.

Utah had already made national news in the 1950 Congressional elections as the only state where two women vied for a single seat. Republican Ivy Baker Priest ran against Democrat Reva Beck Bosone, who had begun her law practice in Helper in 1931. In 1932, Bosone had run for the state legislature and won in the Democratic landslide: the first female state legislator from Castle Valley. In 1935, she had returned to the state legislature, representing Salt Lake County, her new home, and, in 1936, she was elected a Salt Lake City judge. Bosone went from there to the U.S. House of Representatives in 1948, becoming the first woman to represent Utah in the U.S. Congress and one of only nine women in the House. (There was one woman in the Senate.) Two years later, she beat Priest. In 1952, Priest became U.S. Treasurer under newly-elected President Dwight D. Eisenhower (the first Republican since Hoover), a position she held for eight years. Bosone became a casualty of a new Red Scare. Congress, spurred by the House Un-American Activities Committee (HUAC, authorized in 1945) and the Senate's McCarthy hearings—televised from 1947–1954—ferreted out alleged American Communists in Hollywood and elsewhere, irreparably damaging some reputations while boosting more favored politicians. Bosone suffered accusations that she was a Communist sympathizer (quite possibly because some of her Castle Valley clients had been members of the NMU). She nonetheless remained politically active and encouraged other women to do likewise.[62]

This new anti-Red hysteria grew, in part, from serious international problems, particularly during Truman's second term. The U.S., following

As this photo from the early twentieth century attests, very little changed in uranium prospecting over the decades. When the rush arrived in the fifties, men still traveled out on the Swell, carrying canteens of precious water, found likely outcrops (foreground), and often shoveled the valuable rock into burlap bags for transportation (right, rear). Courtesy of Emery County Archives.

the foreign policy of containing the Communist threat, had rebuilt Europe under the Marshall Plan and got more and more deeply involved in Asia, beginning with the Korean War (officially a United Nations police action) from 1950–1953. In 1954, two years after Truman left office, the Geneva Conference failed to bring a lasting peace to Korea, initiating events that would bring America into the war in Viet Nam. The conditions for a protracted Asian involvement began under Truman, as policy-makers simplified foreign relations into the U.S. versus the Communists. In 1947, President Truman had spurred Congress to pass the National Security Act, establishing a consolidated Department of Defense, the Joint Chiefs of Staff, a National Security Council, and the Central Intelligence Agency to fight the new Cold War.[63] Concurrently, the government had created the Atomic Energy Commission (AEC) and a Joint Committee on Atomic Energy to explore both military and peaceful applications. The federal government turned to South Africa and Canada for their uranium, although locals— and Europeans—had tapped deposits on the San Rafael Swell for a very long time.[64]

The first strange rocks had been discovered in the late 1800s, but only in 1898 did the Smithsonian Institute identify them as uranium. French scientists immediately built a concentrating plant in southwestern Colorado to process local ores, including some brought out mule-back from Joe Swasey's Temple Mountain Mine. The Polish Nobel Prize winner, Madame Marie Curie, who had first isolated and named radium, arrived a year later and got samples.[65] By 1904, the *Emery County Progress* invited its readers to visit the newspaper office to see "a radiograph, a recent scientific invention ... [and] Emery County production" painstakingly devised by Ira Browning. He had created a picture of "a common-size trunk key ... made after eighteen hours exposure" on a "photographic plate by Rotengen [sic] (or X-) rays" using minerals from his Orinoco claim, sixty miles southeast of Emery on the San Rafael Swell, which he shared with Oscar Beebe and Seymour Olsen.[66] Only two tons of Castle Valley uranium concentrate were shipped to Europe before World War I. Although Madame Curie revisited the West after the war, receiving a gram of radium (then worth $80,000 wholesale; $120,000 retail), interest in these deposits dwindled. In the 1930s, the Vitro Manufacturing Company of Pittsburgh, Pennsylvania, sought uranium ore mixed with vanadium, so Moab's Howard Balsley established one of his storage facilities at Green River to supply it. World War II created limited federal interest in these uranium deposits: in 1942, as a steel-hardening agent, and, after 1944, for its World War II atomic bomb project which culminated in the bombing of Japan. The government then became the sole buyer for the mineral, taking over the Vitro operations and its feeder storage facilities while belittling the size of Castle Valley deposits.[67]

When the Soviets detonated their first nuclear weapon in 1949, and their Communist allies concurrently conquered China, the U.S. sought more bang for the buck. The AEC suddenly instituted an extensive national uranium survey, provided monthly maps, and offered $10,000 for a paying mine. The rush was on.[68] The frenzy really began when a determined Texan, geologist Charlie Steen, discovered a multi-million-dollar mine in an unexpected geological formation southeast of the San Rafael Swell.[69] Former coal camp doctor and respected ophthalmologist Dr. J. Eldon Dorman, joined the thousands who "went crazy. . . . I hocked my life. On Friday, I'd work maybe a couple of hours . . . and then, I'd take off." Together with two other men he formed the Southern Cross Uranium Company, filing 106 claims near Hite, across the river from the uranium mill at White Canyon.[70] People went out on the Swell in trucks and on horseback; some even flew over dangling scillenometers out of open-cockpit planes. The Emery County Recorder's Office struggled to keep up with the paperwork: 910 claims filed in 1949, and another 410 in the first three months of 1950 alone. Among them, Ferron's Frank Blackburn, Ervin Olsen, Elden Bryan and Thomas Worthen, all over 60 years old, staked their claims, did all their own mining, and soon "were riding around in Buicks and Lincolns," according to Owen McClenahan.[71] Other mines in the area included the Conrad, the mines at Tomsich Butte, and one in Hondoo Canyon found by McClenahan and Albert Hunter. Albert's brother, dentist L. T. Hunter of

"Here It Is" says the sign, which points to a mushroom cloud over Fremont Street, Las Vegas, on April 18, 1953. These above-ground nuclear tests created the deadly fallout sensed by Geiger counters on Utah's San Rafael Swell. Courtesy of Las Vegas News Bureau Collection, University of Nevada, Las Vegas Library.

Castle Dale, had owned one of the earliest Geiger counters in the area and helped set off the boom.[72]

A clicking Geiger counter did not always mean pay dirt. McClenahan reported one particularly exciting trip when "the amplified click came through too fast to count." He and Fame and Owen Price "started to check everything in sight," finding the hottest deposits in "low spots like gullies in the flat" as they searched their entire camping area. "Finally it dawned on us," he wrote, "that it was fallout from an atomic bomb test at the Nevada testing ground." They quit and returned to Castle Dale, where "it was announced that they had tested a bomb a day or two before."[73] Like the rest of uninformed America, Castle Valley simply took these deadly tests in stride.

Those lucky enough to find a genuine claim then had to find investors to pay for development such as machinery to dig tunnels and to haul out the ore on roads not yet built. Dr. Dorman recalled, "We built a road . . . and in came some big shot from Pasadena. He was supposed to be an authority. Everybody was an authority. . . . We bought a caterpillar tractor . . . and a big truck. We hauled out, I think 50 tons" of uranium, but it was high in lime content, which incurred a penalty. "We got maybe a couple hundred dollars."[74] Spring Glen's George Rowley fared better. After showing sixty uranium cores as proof of his finds, he sold his claims for $85,000 to the Warren Oil Mining Company of Fort Worth, Texas, leaving development work to others.[75] Price's Lawrence Migliaccio also prospered as principal owner of the historic Vanadium King Mines in the Temple Mountain district, among the mines he passed to his lovely, talented daughter, Brenda M. Kalatzes, still a successful mine manager.[76] Outsider Vernon Pick did magnificently, selling his Delta No. 4 (renamed the "Hidden Splendor"—and later, the "Hidden Blunder") for $9 million to the Atlas Corporation, but he left Castle Valley with a reputation tarnished by bad debts in Green River and "bullshitting" about his so-called death-defying prospecting trip along the trickle called the Muddy River.[77] Emery County's Hyrum Knight and Jesse Fox, on the other hand, never got to develop their Temple Mountain claims, losing them to the Consolidated Uranium Corporation of Temple Mountain after a year of litigation. Consolidated then brought in small loading machines, disassembled them, and lowered the pieces into holes drilled in the rock. The machines were reassembled at the face of a sizable, buried ore body—enough to support forty Anglo families at Temple Mountain and five Mexican families at North Temple, although all their water had to be trucked in forty miles from Green River by a man who also brought the mail.[78] The cumulative output was staggering. According to USGS reports, "From 1948 through 1956 the [Temple Mountain] district produced about 261,000 tons of uranium ore."[79] In 1960 alone, Emery County produced more than 94,000 tons of ore, valued at almost two million dollars.[80]

While some painstakingly dug ore, others tried selling stock. Many prospectors sold their claims to penny stock companies for part cash and part stock. Then stock company geologists came down, glanced around, and wrote glowing descriptions guaranteed to attract investors. Most buyers didn't care about details as penny uranium stock became the rage, sometimes even handed out free with a bag-load of groceries. According to newspaper clippings from the boom, in 1954, uranium stock sales in Salt Lake hit five million shares, then seven million.[81] Carbon County residents Francis Scartezina and Floyd Adams "formed a company called Mountain Valley Uranium" to sell stock, but made more just selling the name of their company, remembered Dr. Dorman. Commonly, "stock started at a penny a share . . . then, they'd go up to ten cents."[82] As stock companies proliferated, the federal Securities and Exchange Commission (SEC) dispatched an investigator who infuriated the state government by trying to impose stricter requirements than those of Utah's own Securities Commission. The SEC filed several indictments, and the stock boom ended after a little over eighteen months. But it had stimulated domestic uranium exploration, replacing a national shortage with a bonanza.[83]

Before everything ended, some Castle Valley residents got crushed in the uranium vortex. Huntington residents Bud Nielson and Shorty Larsen and their wives had helped out Charlie Steen when he needed money, so he had pointed them to a potential uranium deposit. They sold an out-of-town entrepreneur a sixty-day option for $40,000, only to receive a later offer of $200,000 (which they legally could not accept) for the same claims. In another case of unintended consequences, Price's Henry Ruggeri became Steen's lawyer and negotiated the purchase of the land for the Atlas uranium mill alongside the Colorado River. It later became one of America's unsavory radioactive clean-up sites under the 1978 bill signed by President Jimmy Carter. The act provided federal funds for removing hazardous waste, not only at the Moab Atlas mill but at the old Green River Vitro holdings.[84]

During the uranium boom, the deadliest threat came from radon gasses released by radioactive decay, often highly concentrated in poorly-ventilated mines. Dr. Geno Saccomanno, whose family had been the first immigrants to pay off their Spring Glen farm, became one of the first physicians to provide reliable data about radioactivity-induced lung cancer. During the Great Depression, the young Saccomanno had sold peaches from the family orchard for twenty-five cents a bushel to make money for school. He had to pay his own way through high school at Price (where out-of-town students had to pay their own room and board), then funded a biology degree in 1940 and a medical degree in 1946. By the 1950s, he was the visiting pathologist at the Price City Hospital, providing laboratory services there and in many small hospitals throughout the Colorado Plateau. During the uranium frenzy, a handful of medical professionals became concerned as uranium miners contracted lung cancer at an unusually rapid rate. In 1954, the National Cancer Institute (NCI) agreed to run a controlled study. In 1955, the Seven-State Uranium Mining Conference on Health Hazards met in Salt Lake City, with representatives from the federal government, Utah, Arizona, Colorado, New Mexico, Idaho, South Dakota, and Wyoming. Poor-quality medical slides hampered the NCI's attempt to gather data substantiating miners' lung damage. Dr. Saccomanno invented a vastly improved method and machinery for making the necessary slides. He also became the director of the annual sputum cytology (cell study) program in Salt Lake City, taking yearly samples from miners and attempting to autopsy all of those who died. The first settlement awarded to a uranium widow came only in 1961, in Colorado. Although Saccomanno provided compelling statistics in the leading Utah case, the state supreme court refused to recognize the danger of lung cancer in uranium miners as an occupational hazard. Next, Utahn Esther Peterson, then assistant secretary for Labor Standards under the Secretary of Labor in Washington, D.C., tried hard to involve the federal government in adequate workman's compensation for uranium miners during the next decade. Peterson would go on to become a prime mover behind President Kennedy's Presidential Committee on the Status of Women, chaired by Eleanor Roosevelt, but, in the meantime, she and her boss battled fruitlessly for dying uranium miners. They did succeed, however, in establishing a legal maximum amount of allowable radiation by federal law. By then, others had contracted cancer, including Orangeville's

William Hannert who mined extensively around Temple Mountain until he died of the disease. His sons inherited his mines, but by then the uranium boom was over. In the 1960s, the United States government had become the only buyer, and it eventually authorized purchase only from ore reserves developed prior to November 28, 1958.[85] There was no point in further prospecting.

The boom left a number of legacies. One recent journalist ascribed Utah's status as the "fraud capital of America" to the old uranium penny stocks: "Salt Lake City had a U.S. Securities and Exchange Commission office that fights investor fraud . . . by far the smallest city with such a presence."[86] More ominously, some holes remain near Buckhorn Wash, ten miles east of Castle Dale, where, in 1948, the War Department tried to determine "the action of an atomic blast on underground habitations," according to local mining man Arthur E. Gibson. "The public is aware of the fact that tests are being made," he wrote in 1948, "but results of any tests will remain a secret for the present."[87] Only through persistent efforts by Price mortician and former Emery County resident Greg Fausett did concrete facts emerge a half-century later. In identifying a site for NORAD, the federal front line of defense against nuclear attack, the government had built a series of gigantic tunnels (some 20 feet high and 150 feet long). Fausett discovered they had then detonated huge dynamite charges above them to gauge the effects. Local men, including Arthur Cox and Max Jensen, were hired to cart away the dislodged rock and brush in wheelbarrows but sworn to secrecy. At least one man was killed when rainwater rose in a higher tunnel and broke through a debris dam to flood a lower tunnel where men were working. Morrison Knudsen Company, a major World War II contractor, assumed control of the project, today known as the MK Tunnels and used for teenage parties.[88]

The uranium boom had other repercussions. Aside from its tests, the national government developed a greater appreciation of the strategic importance of the Colorado Plateau. Historian Arthur Gomez noted that federal monies soon financed many more access roads for strategic purposes that were later utilized by tourists and other outdoor recreationists.[89] However, lone prospectors, not federal officials, ultimately had the biggest effect on much of the remote San Rafael Swell. The old prospector's adage, "Beaten trails are only for beaten men" spurred would-be uranium developers to sculpt dozens of jeep tracks into this geologic dome, now usable by those attracted to its scenic wonders. Building a road in the Swell often meant creative use of a bulldozer in steep canyons on brittle sandstone. Owen Price was one of the best road-builders, though it sometimes appeared that his "bulldozer was going to roll down the mountainside," remembered McClenahan. "At the last, second, he could stop and back up for another load."[90] In another spin-off, Dr. Geno Saccomanno, remembering his own hard struggle to fund an education, took some of the proceeds from his uranium-related medical innovations and established a $2.5 million endowment fund in 1991 for residents of Carbon County, Utah, and Mesa County, Colorado, which still benefits numbers of students at the College of Eastern Utah.[91]

Despite certain improvements, the post-war economic boom left Castle Valley out in the cold. The national commercial boom did not penetrate this far, neither did the regional pattern sketched by historian Gerald Nash, who claimed that World War II had liberated the "colonial economy" of the American West from sole dependence on the exploitation of raw materials.[92] While Utah as a whole reaped diversification through the establishment of ten major military establishments and subsequent support industries, Castle Valley merely changed masters.[93]

Those masters owned the coal mines. In 1950, Emery had sixteen truck mines (down from twenty in 1947) and one rail mine; Carbon had thirteen truck mines (down from sixteen in 1947) and twenty-three large, rail mines. By 1966, each county had but ten producing mines, total, with Carbon County's Mutual Mine slated to close by the end of the year.[94] Production dropped in response to national markets which had less and less use for coal. In 1958, the two counties together produced 5,222,000 short tons, a performance approached only once, in 1961, as total coal tonnage hovered in the mid-four millions into the 1970s.[95] As one business analyst explained, "with the release of resources at the war's end, railroads throughout the nation began a modernization drive," turning out 21,000 new diesel locomotives between 1945–1955. By 1958, steam locomotives equaled "less than 2 percent of total railroad freight haulage." He also pointed to another problem for coal producers: "Coal had lost markets to oil and natural gas not only because the fuels were cleaner and more convenient, but because of lower prices and seeming abundance." As a result, coal's competing fuels increasingly generated most of the electricity in the United States.[96]

Towns died. "It got to where there was no kids," remembered Margaret Marzo Ariotti. "And if there's no kids, you just don't have this [togetherness]"—no picnics, no holiday celebrations, no big community events.[97] Based on census data, the 1950s saw the demise of Clear Creek, Columbia, Consumers, Kenilworth, Latuda, Peerless, Rains, Rolapp (formerly Cameron, or Royal), Spring Canyon, Standardville, Sweets, and Wattis.[98] As the 1950s gave way to the 1960s and 1970s, mines struggled and died. Miners listened daily to radio KOAL (originally KEUB, established 1937) for the mine report, broadcast daily at precisely 6:30 a.m. and 5:30 p.m.:

> With the co-operation of the following coal mines and through the courtesy of Price City, we bring you the mine report. Mines working tomorrow are Castle Gate, Columbia, the Geneva Mine at Horse Canyon, Hiawatha, Kenilworth, Latuda, Peerless, Rains, Royal, Spring Canyon, Standard, Utah Fuel at Sunnyside, and Wattis.[99]

Sometimes, fathers were working underground during the mine report. Children then had the responsibility to listen in and tell their returning fathers if there were work tomorrow. If the mine worked and an able-bodied miner failed to appear, he was usually fired. Half a century later, many of those children, grown to late adulthood, can still rattle off the names of then-working mines in perfect order.

Agriculture also faltered after reaching its maximum potential by 1940. In the late 1950s, the federal government proposed to reduce the number of grazing allotments. Although this reduction affected the nation as a whole, Utah became the lightning rod for tension for two reasons. First, a unidentified highly-placed official in the LDS Church accused the federal government of "tyrannical" practices, equating proposed range management limitations with days when mobs "burned, raped and murdered" the fleeing Saints. Second, Ezra Taft Benson, Mormon Apostle (later LDS Church President), was the Secretary of Agriculture, accepting President Eisenhower's cabinet appointment only after receiving permission from LDS President David O. Mackay. In the heat of the grazing controversy, Secretary Benson made a conciliatory trip to Utah in February 1958, calming the public with assurances of local autonomy. Federal range studies done from 1962–1967 indicated severe overgrazing, however, and the government subsequently reduced allotments by fifty percent. By then, the agrarian towns of Lawrence, Molen, Rochester (or Moore), and Woodside had all disappeared from the census as well, since the tiny handful of residents in each location got counted with larger neighboring towns. Highly agricultural Emery County lost almost twenty percent of its population (from 6,304 to 5,137) as over one thousand people moved away between 1950–1970. Between the economic assaults on mines and farms, Carbon County lost even more. Population plummeted from a total of 24,901 in 1950 to 15,647 two decades later. Better than one-in-three people left.[100]

In this dismal economic climate, the attempt by one of their own to close Carbon College came as an unprecedented shock. Republican J. Bracken ("Brack") Lee, a Price native, had served six terms as mayor of his home town before beating incumbent Democrat Herbert Maw for Utah governor in 1948, when Truman won the presidency in his own right. Lee had campaigned on the promise that he would run the state "just like my own business, on a sound basis, for the benefit of the people," which for Lee meant less spending, reduced taxes, and a balanced budget.[101] This strategy soon earned him national recognition in such magazines as *Time, Life,* and the *Saturday Evening Post* and he won a second term in 1952.[102] Lee began to take issue with newly elected and wildly popular Republican president Dwight D. Eisenhower, who was reelected in 1956. According to historians Louis Galambos and Joseph Pratt, "Eisenhower set the tone for what would become an era of good feelings toward business" while Lee carped about federal spending and the national debt. Lee continued cutting Utah state services, beginning with the salaries of public school teachers, then proposed the closure of Carbon College and the return of the other three state-run junior colleges to the LDS Church.[103]

Castle Valley residents fought back with a "Save the College Committee" spearheaded by Emery County native Gomer P. Peacock. College supporters had only sixty days to gather 33,000 signatures—more than the entire population of Castle Valley—to get a referendum on the next ballot. The committee formed an alliance with Weber College which objected to losing its secular status. CEU student body president Dominic Albo, Jr., mobilized as many local people as he could. Price businessman Angelo Georgedes hired two petition-carriers and paid their expenses to go to three counties to collect signatures. Many Castle Valley residents returned to former hometowns carrying petitions. When the deadline came, over 56,000 names had been collected. In the November 1954 election, voters rejected closing Carbon College by almost four to one and refused to return the other colleges to the LDS Church by a three-to-one margin. As the newspaper noted, "Despite the fact that the schools are located in comparatively small and widely separated communities, the trend even in heavily populated areas was strongly against the bills." For many of the campaign's participants, this success marked their lifetime achievement. Lee's popularity dwindled, and in 1956 he lost in the Republican primary.[104]

Even while Lee's short-sighted, anti-education campaign flourished, Castle Valley's school population began shifting due to business decisions. As company towns closed down, people left the area or drifted to established centers like Price, Helper, Castle Dale, and Huntington. This was a gradual process, and, for a while, children of families who had not yet relocated were bussed from the fading camps to schools in town. Classrooms there became overcrowded, and a new, ambitious building program resulted. In the Sunnyside district, Kaiser Steel, while reducing its workforce at the nearby mine, donated land it no longer needed for East Carbon High School. U.S. Steel had sold off many of its houses constructed in 1946, but it, too, joined Kaiser in donating money to build the school and a swimming pool in 1959. The same year, a new high school was constructed in Price to house approximately 900 students in three grades (later expanded to four), a move which separated it physically from its former housing at Carbon College.[105] In a final gambit of the education shuffle, also in 1959, Carbon College became a branch of the University of Utah, permanently ending the drive to close it.[106]

One more change awaited the local college. In 1965, thanks to a bill co-sponsored by all the state legislators from Carbon and Emery counties, it officially became the College of Eastern Utah. Among its co-sponsors, Emery County representative Eva Westover Conover mirrored another change in Castle Valley and the United States. She represented a new wave of feminine leadership, identified by President Kennedy's Council on the

Status of Women, chaired by Utahn Esther Peterson. "No year since the passage of the Nineteenth Amendment in 1920 can be compared to the period October 1963 to October 1964, in terms of new opportunities offered to women," said the first Council report.[107] Originally encouraged to run by Reva Beck Bosone, in 1963, Conover became the first woman to represent Emery County in the State Legislature (and the second to represent Castle Valley, after Bosone) serving until 1967. Conover's determination emerged in her campaign, as a local man extolled her opponent as "the best man for the job." "That may be true," she replied, "but I am the best *person* for the job." Once in the legislature, Conover surprised some of her colleagues with the breadth of her knowledge—speaking intelligently on bills regarding education, agriculture, coal mining, wilderness, BLM land, forest reserves, soil conservation, water rights, and so on. She explained, "I'm a former school teacher. My sister and brother are teachers. Many of my friends' husbands work in the coal mines. I taught school one winter in a coal camp, and became good friends with the mine foreman who used to tell me what was needed in the mine and what the miners needed. Men collect at our home for the ride to and from the canyon and talk cow talk." How could she not know?[108] Trying for a third term in 1966, after redistricting included Grand County with Conover's district, she lost by some 500 votes.[109]

In part, the redistricting that led to Conover's defeat resulted from the dwindling population in Emery County. By 1970, it had one of the lowest per capita incomes in Utah.[110] Job-hungry people moved away; only the elderly remained. Or, as more vividly put by Edward Geary, describing his native Huntington between 1955–1965: "the median age was over fifty. The high school was closed, the old meetinghouse demolished, and the Prickly Pear Flat was littered with empty houses, sagging barns, junked cars, and dead trees."[111] What would become of Castle Valley?

# 11

# The Preservation Instinct, 1960–1980

> *We were the owners and operators of the geyser property . . . which included an excellent rock crystal museum, mineral fluorescence display along with some antique items. Everyone enjoyed the burros and the animals on exhibit and especially the peacocks. . . . If Woodside was a "tourist trap," all we can say is that Utah should have had more of them to promote tourism and increase the time out-of-state visitors stayed in the area. It meant money for the state and all the other businesses in the area.[1]*
>
> —MRS. ROY COOK, SERVICE STATION AND ATTRACTION OPERATOR

In 1938, Roy Cook and his wife had built a store and service station at Woodside, roughly twenty miles northwest of Green River and twenty-five miles southeast of Price. Their backyard geyser gushed forth about every thirty minutes (in those days), and the Cooks charged fifty cents (twenty-five cents for children under twelve) to enter a rock crystal and fluorescent mineral museum, a desert zoo, and to watch the geyser erupt. The attached gift shop sold Indian jewelry, pottery, Navajo rugs, and other items. They allowed people to camp for free in the trees south of the service station. Until the early 1970s, when the Cooks gave the Woodside geyser (renamed the Crystal Geyser) to the state as a potential, unique rest stop, they and their employees catered not only to locals but to traveling motorists from all over the nation.[2] The state never developed the Woodside attraction, and as Castle Valley's water table dropped, the geyser erupted less and less frequently.

By the end of the twentieth century, Castle Valley was tired of being ignored by everyone except volatile extractive industries. As mining once again faltered, the area turned to its past—not only local history, but archaeology, paleontology, and geology, too. Residents scraped up development dollars where they could as the economy rapidly rose and fell. Before

Drilling at the edge of the San Rafael Swell created the Woodside geyser, a tourist attraction that exploded to the surface about every half hour until Castle Valley's growing population severely lowered the water table in the late twentieth century. It still erupts occasionally, but not predictably. Courtesy of Emery County Archives.

they could celebrate their distinctiveness, however, they had to weather one of the most divisive times in American history. Outside pressures created cultural and social divisions, challenging residents to find their own ways of keeping this historic community together. As always, the landscape, the mines, and people's shared activities insistently reminded everyone that, despite their differences, they were unalterably joined at the roots.

Nationally, the 1960s was an era of transitions. Many remember the tragedies of the assassinations of President John F. Kennedy, Rev. Dr. Martin Luther King, Jr., and the president's brother, Robert Kennedy. For others, it was the era of flower children, drug-inspired music, and rallies featuring banners (and behavior) saying "Make Love, Not War." Remembering his own youth, bituminous coal extractor Kirk Olsen remarked, "The sixties didn't happen here."[3] In the sense of hippie-youth culture, Summer of Love, and psychedelic drugs, the decade largely missed Castle Valley. In other ways, though, the era generated plenty of excitement, particularly in Emery County, where the two high schools, long heated rivals, merged in 1962. The old North and South schools became junior highs. According to Allan Kent Powell, then a high school junior, attending the new school was "like entering a whole new world." Not only was the school bigger and more populous, but the students got to choose their own mascot and school colors, field their first football team, and enjoy a host of stimulating new teachers. One of the faculty members actively promoted the Allosaurus as the school emblem, but the student body overwhelmingly voted for the Spartans, attracted by its powerful sound and not at all concerned (or aware) that it might reflect the heritage of some of those Greeks in Carbon County, where the Dinosuars (too much like the Allosaurus!) represented Carbon High School. When the formerly rival North and South students asked their principal, "Who is our rival now?" he answered, "Everyone is!"[4] Competitively, Emery County had reached a whole new level.

Less benign national tensions also haunted the area. Americans in the 1960s typically defined themselves by membership in certain groups and emphasized the boundaries between them, something like probing the edges of a wound. In some ways, this was necessary for national healing, a process begun in the courts. Cases from California and Texas prohibiting the segregation of Mexican children in 1946 and 1947 became precedents to the famous 1954 Supreme Court decision in *Brown v. Board of Education of Topeka, Kansas*. In a unanimous decision overturning *Plessey v. Ferguson* (1896), the justices ruled, "in the field of public education the doctrine of 'separate but equal' has no place."[5] By extension (and later court decisions), the separation of people by race became illegal all over America.

While Castle Valley, with a minimal African-American population, escaped the violent black-white confrontations making news all over the nation, racial discrimination still survived. Blacks had largely left the area, except for a handful of coal miners, a few teachers, and the sizable Ellington family. Japanese Americans stayed and worked hard, pushing their children to succeed in education, which frequently meant leaving the valley. Mexican Americans, however, remained in sizable numbers. First attracted by railroad and mining jobs during and just after the Mexican Revolution of 1910–1920, a huge influx had arrived during World War II to mine the coal that kept America's war machine humming. Coal camps, always segregated ethnically, put them in the poorest housing. For example, Paul Turner, in describing the far southern end of Sunnyside, recalled the "sorry little two room houses where a couple of Mexican and Black families lived."[6] Whether by choice or not, Mexicans also formed their own five-trailer camp during the uranium boom, coming into much larger Temple Mountain, with its cook house, boarding house, bath house, laundry building, and machine repair shop, to buy food.[7] In Price, Mexicans formed a *colonia*, or ethnic neighborhood, in Little Hollywood, a section which allegedly got its name from the silhouetted dramas played out nightly against pulled-down window shades. In the face of discrimination, like other ethnic groups before them, Chicanos founded their own lodges. In 1949, Helper residents created the *Sociedad Mexicana de Cuauhtemoc*, which largely promoted Mexican social and cultural activities and remained in contact with the Mexican consul in Salt Lake City. Lorenzo Jaramillo, raised in Helper, helped organize two chapters of the GI Forum, one in Salt Lake City and one in Price. This group, a predecessor to the nationally known SOCIO (Spanish Speaking Organization for Community, Integrity, and Opportunity), had been founded in Texas when a whites-only funeral home refused to bury a World War II Mexican veteran killed in action in the Philippines. The Forum initially aided disabled and needy Spanish-speaking veterans but got involved in court cases and strongly stressed education as a way to combat anti-Mexican discrimination. After the Utah chapter of SOCIO formed in Salt Lake City in December 1967, focus shifted to aiding Mexican Americans with all phases of adjustment in Anglo society. This goal helped to override internal divisions in the Spanish-speaking community, since those born in Mexico tended to look down on those born on the north side of the border, calling them "manitos" because of their relative loss of culture and language skills. Particularly after 1965, when the new federal immigration act did away with the old quotas based on country of origin and instead favored admission of U.S. citizens' immediate family (parents, minor children, and spouses), Hispanic immigration rose.[8]

As numbers of "brown" people grew, people's attitudes shifted. In the East Carbon area, where many Hispanics had been living since World War II, Hispanic Catholic women organized the Guadalupana Society in 1958 to celebrate the feast day of Our Lady of Guadalupe, inviting neighbors of all backgrounds. East Carbon's Good Shepherd Parish, dating back to the 1920s when Italians were the mainstay, also attracted a Spanish-speaking priest in the 1970s.[9] At the same time, Lorenzo Jaramillo's daughter,

Dahlia Jaramillo Cordova, born in 1956, remembered difficult school days in Carbon County when she felt "excluded socially and academically from all the activities. People of color were put down, taunted, and told—even without words—that we would never amount to anything."[10] When Dragerton's Rosa Sandoval complained of discriminatory firing, the local SOCIO chapter, under Sunnyside resident and president John Medina, tried to mediate, leaving bitterness on both sides.[11] To complicate matters, not all Spanish speakers agreed that those of Mexican heritage faced discrimination in Castle Valley. For example, Colorado-born Valentine Arambula, who had worked as a miner for Kaiser and as a section foreman, stated in a 1972 interview that "there's no discrimination if you don't want to be discriminated against. . . . It's how hard you push yourself is how high you will go." Long-time Castle Valley resident Floyd O'Neil, who, with Vincent Mayer, was conducting the Arambula interview, remarked "how very wide the opinions among the Spanish-speaking [are] about the amount of discrimination there is."[12] Other responses bore out his observations. Richard Cordova of Dragerton remembered a bar owner who would not serve Mexican Americans, driving them out with a billy club. Yet he insisted there was no discrimination in a coal mine, and his wife added, "Ever seen a miner when he comes out of a coal mine?" she asked. "They're all black, every last one of them. You can't tell a white man from a black man."[13]

Locally as well as nationally, other racial barriers began to fall. The issue of racial intermarriage came before the Supreme Court in the aptly named *Loving v. Virginia*. Although the case arose from a black-white marriage, the Japanese American Citizens League was allowed to file a friend-of-the-court brief, indicating that its members had a vested interest in the outcome, because often (as in Utah) intermarriage between any two people of different races was prohibited. In 1967, the justices issued a unanimous opinion on the case, written by Chief Justice Earl Warren, overturning all anti-miscegenation laws nationwide.[14] This decision came too late for Castle Valley's first American Japanese girl to marry outside her race. In 1964, Joanne Taniguchi and Terry Black had been wed in Idaho, where interracial marriages were legal. They returned to Castle Valley and then moved on to stay with Black's sister at Richfield. In all those years, Taniguchi remembered nothing but kindness from her new, Mormon relations. Yet her younger sister, Jeanne Taniguchi, recalled, "When I was in high school I asked a boy to the preference ball. His father would not let him go with me because I was Japanese—that was in 1969." A year later, she married Caucasian Darel Gagon. She later remarked, "I don't think the people in Carbon County cared about it [the inter-racial marriage] as much as the Japanese community did. . . . I never did give 'race' much thought living in Carbon County."[15]

Another insidious division flourished not far below the surface, however. As Charles S. Peterson, former CEU history professor and then head of the Utah State Historical Society (USHS), wrote in 1976, although "Utah society forms groups along such conventional lines as political persuasion, profession, education, place of origin, age group, ethnic background, and level of income. . . . the Mormon/non-Mormon division cuts through and influences all other grouping arrangements."[16] This historic split gained new emphasis beginning in the 1950s, as the LDS Church members arrived in the aftermath of World War II, the church sponsored building programs, and increased its missionary activity throughout Europe and the Pacific. In the 1960s, church programs extended to South America and Southeast Asia. As a result, converts flocked to Utah, outnumbering child baptisms, a trend that continues to the present. As Utah became more and more multiethnic, the LDS Church stressed conformity to Mormon traditions to replace old ethnic practices, making greater Utah resolutely mono-cultural.[17] Most importantly, Saints everywhere increasingly followed the Word of Wisdom (abstinence from alcoholic or stimulating beverages, tobacco, and other vices) in what historian Jan Shipps called "boundary maintenance." She defined this as "a clearly articulated behavioral code . . . so that Latter-day Saints are constantly reminded of their chosen status by what they eat and do not eat" and by wearing special undergarments, to keep them "ever mindful that they are God's people,"[18] or that they were "in" while all others were "out." In 1957, the LDS Church also organized ward education committees, "to encourage and enroll young people in a seminary," meaning classes in religious instruction.[19] Utah allowed LDS children "released time" from regular public school classes to attend seminary, a system extended to students of other denominations only in the 1980s. While creative class scheduling helped juggle the various resultant educational experiences, school age children became increasingly aware of religious differences. These attitudes started to wear away at the traditional tolerance of Castle Valley people towards each other, although not everyone felt the tension with the same keenness.

But LDS cohesion had its positive side. The very arrival of television in Emery County illustrated the benefits of traditional Mormon communalism combined with modern technology. In 1953, before he died of uranium-induced cancer, William Hannert joined with William R. Justesen and Lavar Sitterud to locate the television signal broadcast from Salt Lake City in an attempt to erect a translator station for Emery County. Justesen subsequently headed a committee staffed with men from Orangeville, Castle Dale, Ferron, Huntington, and Cleveland. They erected a tower on Horn Mountain, and hooked it to a power line that failed to meet the electrical standards of Utah Power and Light Company (UP&L), which was supplying electricity. When UP&L offered to build a suitable power line for an unaffordable $30,000, the men found an old-fashioned, LDS communitarian solution. Each potential user donated $60 cash and $60 in labor, and they built the line for $10,000. Political pressures finally garnered a permit from the Federal Communications Commission, and, in 1956, Emery County got

television. Only then did the committee approach the county commissioners and offer to turn it over to them for maintenance. The commissioners
accepted, and added a one-half mill levy tax on recreation to support the
system.[20]

By then, Carbon County also had television, so throughout the 1950s
and 1960s, increased advertising and popular culture bombarded the area
with images of the white, middle class wallowing in consumer goods. Grainy
black and white screens showed such popular TV programs as *The Donna
Reed Show, Our Miss Brooks, Ozzie and Harriet,* and others. Children of miners,
farmers, or ethnics found little to relate to on these shows, which nonetheless shaped their aspirations. Most powerful of all were the cowboy serials,
as kids watched Roy Rogers or Gene Autry or Hopalong Cassidy ride out
of the movie serials and onto their home TV screens, whipping the bad
guys as they upheld the Code of the West. As Wellington's Tom McCourt
noted, "They fought to a set of unwritten rules, a code of conduct that
seemed to be universal. . . . Even in the heat of battle there was a measure of self-control. Justice was sure and swift, and God and your neighbors
were watching."[21] As many urbanites on the Wasatch Front looked down on
Castle Valley residents, either for their multi-culturalism or their economic
backwardness, the area largely kept the peace among its own and fought for
outside recognition through sports.

Fortunately for valley unity, local residents had always loved athletics,
going back at least as far as the nineteenth-century baseball teams. More
than anything else, sports helped bridge the ready-made gap created by
sharpening national and Utah attitudes. It was hard to dislike people of
other backgrounds when teamwork brought so much success against respected, talented opponents. "Basketball was the great game in rural Utah,"
noted Huntington native, Edward Geary, of his boyhood in the 1940s and
1950s. "There was scarcely a granary that did not have a hoop nailed to its
side and a beaten patch of ground where the boys played after school, drib-
bling cautiously to avoid chicken droppings."[22] Helper residents mirrored
this enthusiasm, and organized a city league beginning in the mid-1930s,
when the new civic auditorium provided a city court. In 1949, the Helper
Basketball Association began sponsoring the Helper Invitational Basketball
Tournament, the oldest continuous non-school meet in the state.[23] This
local devotion to the sport met with frequent success, such as in 1954 and
1955, when South Emery High School boys won the Region 5 basketball
championship and broke the region record by winning twenty straight
games. As soon as the all-county Emery High School opened in Castle Dale,
it became a basketball powerhouse. In its first year, the Emery Spartans took
second place in the league, and in 1964, sixth place in the state for schools
of its size. A year later, it rose to the pinnacle of third in state.[24] Meanwhile,
in 1960, the Carbon High School Dinosaurs from Price won their first
Region 8 boys basketball championship and went on to place third in the

state.[25] Following this winning tradition, 1965 became a big year for Castle Valley boys basketball. East Carbon's multi-racial, multi-ethnic team earned a berth in the state class B high school tournament after Leroy Martinez scored 18 points in the deciding game. At the same time, the College of Eastern Utah (CEU) team triumphed under Curtis Jenson, former University of Utah standout in his first year as coach. Castle Valley boys, including African-American John Ellington and Caucasian teammates Jerry Hutchens and Randy Moors, joined with blacks and whites from other parts of the state and nation on the CEU Eagles. First, they enjoyed a satisfying win over all their Utah rivals in the Intermountain Collegiate Athletic Conference, where out-of-state African Americans Ron Cunningham and Wilson Watkins earned spots on the all-conference team. Then, the Eagles defeated all challengers from the western region in the National Junior College Athletic Association contest hosted in Price, earning a berth in the national tourney. At Hutchinson, Kansas, they joined America's sixteen best junior college basketball teams. They took third place as Cunningham scored a record-breaking forty-seven points in the final game and earned a slot as one of the tournament's top ten players. When the team returned to Price by chartered plane, a line of cars over two miles long stretched bumper-to-bumper along the road to the airport. Local residents had spontaneously turned out to welcome their boys back home. The newspaper reported an even larger gathering "earlier in the day when the Eagles were originally scheduled to arrive," their plane having been delayed by bad weather.[26] Following this great basketball tradition, in the 1990s, before he finished college, Emery County native Shawn Bradley was drafted into the NBA, where he now plays for the Dallas Mavericks.

Other Castle Valley athletes reached personal pinnacles in other sports. Football had long been a tradition in Carbon County, where the high school tied for state champion in 1924 and won the state championship outright in 1938 and again in 1950–1951. Helper native Rex Berry, the "Carbon Comet," went from all-round athletic stardom at Carbon High School, to Brigham Young University, to the San Francisco 49ers football team, where he played for six years, earning a spot in the Utah Hall of Fame in 1973. Meanwhile, in 1967, Emery County's Michael Tedd Johnson, pole vaulting at the B team level, bested all state A team contestants by 13 inches, setting a Utah record and helping his team to the state championship. A year later, Johnson again triumphed with a new record of 13 feet 5 inches, and the Emery County track team again took state. Girls sports came to Green River High School only in 1975–1976, but the girls went to state in volleyball that year. They topped all other Utah schools in 1977–1978 and 1978–1979, also fielding strong teams in basketball and track.[27]

Baseball ruled the summer. As far back as the 1920s, Castle Valley teams had played in the Coal League, the Eastern Utah League, Central Utah League, and Utah Industrial League. In 1936, Helper's Central Utah

When the Price National league WBBA team beat the perennial local powerhouse, Helper, in August 1957, this photograph made front page news. The undefeated team members, twelve-year-old boys, also exemplified Castle Valley's multiethnicity. Shown (front row, left to right) are Joe Ori, Max Thomas, Dane Larsen, and Ray Littlejohn. Second row, left to right, Norris Wiseman, Donnie Henderson, Joe Morgan, and Paul Scartizina. Back row, Gary Bliss (manager), Mickey Maglioccio, Bobby Taniguchi, Allen Winters, Donnie Salzetti, and Kent Jensen. Bob Henderson, the assistant manager, was not shown. Photo from the author's collection.

League team took the state amateur championship in Salt Lake City. In 1940, while Helper hosted the state's American Legion tournament, local pitcher Angelo Venturelli pitched a successful 12 innings before collapsing, exhausted, on the mound as his team beat Brigham City, 8–7. Following World War II, Helper installed lights on its ball field, the first to do so in Castle Valley, and marked its status as the best field in the area (which it still retains). Boys' Little League started out strong as Helper's first all-star team took second place in the 1952 state tournament. Scores of boys played in the PONY league or, after 1956, on Western Boys' Baseball Association (WBBA) teams, sponsored by towns, local businesses, and fraternal organizations. In 1957, the Price National league team (made up of the best players from half of the Price teams) stunned Helper by winning the county championship. It made front-page news. Men also played softball, as did women. The all-female Mitchell's Mummies dominated the entire region: in 1951, they defeated all-comers, taking the Provo Gold Cup; and in 1954, after a grueling traveling schedule of over 1,700 miles, they took third in the Utah State Women's Softball Tournament and won the sportsmanship trophy.[28]

Locals also played a host of other sports. Indoors, bowling leagues proliferated for women as well as men, many of whom honed their skills at the lanes in coal camps such as Sunnyside or at Hiawatha (where hand-setting pins remained the rule until the amusement hall was closed and the town sold to private interests in the 1990s). Outdoors, people enjoyed fishing, hunting, golf, and most of all, rodeo. Nationally, rodeo dated back to a cowboy tournament held in conjunction with the 1887 Denver Exposition, held while pioneers, railroad workers, coal miners, cohabs, and federal marshals scattered down the Castle Valley corridor. By the 1930s, the sport had become professionalized, as rodeo sponsors and then cowboys organized and tried to come to working agreements on purses, participants, and judging. By 1940, cowboys could choose from an estimated 105 officially sanctioned rodeos, including Castle Valley's Robbers Roost Roundup, established in 1937 and later renamed the Black Diamond Stampede. Throughout Castle Valley, almost every little town had its rodeo, often connected with a local riding club. For example, in the 1940s, Emery's Riding Club sponsored its annual rodeo, went dormant for a couple of decades, and came back in the late 1970s, first as a Junior Riding Club, then reorganized in 1979 as the South Emery Riders for enthusiasts of all ages. In 1953, riders largely from Cleveland and Elmo formed the nucleus of the Blue Ridge Riding Club, formalized in 1954. Elmo's Veda Merlene Jones earned fame as the only girl bull rider in the first Junior Rodeo at Elmo's old rodeo grounds.[29] Wellington's Tom McCourt described the rodeo atmosphere when he competed in the early 1960s as a "proving ground" where "riding rough stock in the hometown rodeo . . . was like having a Bar Mitzvah." Generations of families clustered around the dusty arena—babies in wicker baskets, lovers fumbling under the blankets thrown over their shoulders, kids dropping snowcone and bubble gum bombs from the tops of the bleachers, grandparents relaxing on cushions or folded blankets, and drunks in parked cars by the arena fence. The P.A. system blared the names of the contestants, their scores, and polkas or cowboy music between the events. Pretty girls on horses circled the grounds, trolling for boys; mothers worried about their sons; and fathers watched proudly. For McCourt and others, "The whole thing was an act of communal bonding."[30] "I had daydreams for years," wrote McCourt, "about all of the young girls' hearts I could have broken if only I could have carried the flag in the grand entry of the Black Diamond Stampede."[31]

The fall brought new, valley-wide activities. Most men, and a few women, joined the deer hunt. Hunters still hope to return with "their deer," labeled this way in conversation as if it were pre-tagged. Families developed hunt traditions, often returning to the same areas year after year. Communities staged pre-hunt, full-dress (including sometimes hunting weapons) Deer Hunt dances. So many children skipped school the day before the hunt to make camp on the mountain before daybreak (when shooting could legally begin), that Castle Valley public schools declared Deer Hunt a holiday to prevent losing considerable funding due to the extraordinary number of absentees. In the 1950s and 1960s, two Deer Hunt days were allotted; now, with improved transportation, school children get only one. This annual event still unites families throughout the valley, regardless of hometown, ethnicity, or religion.

Increasingly, too, Castle Valley's love of its unique history started binding people together. The schools had made an early attempt to record the passing scene, starting in 1913 when Wellington's school principal had sponsored interviews with local LDS pioneers. Eight years later, Helper students wrote a short history of their town. Superintendent C. H. Madsen compiled these efforts and others and mimeographed the history of Carbon County towns aided by the "Teachers, Pupils and Patrons of the Carbon [School] District" in the early 1930s.[32] Indefatigable Ernest Horsley wrote his own history of Price in 1937, excerpted in the newspaper, and passed the manuscript along before he died.[33] Up and down Castle Valley, devout Latter-day Saints had written reminiscences or kept a diary or journal, as urged by their ecclesiastical leaders. Therefore, when the Daughters of Utah Pioneers (DUP) decided to commemorate the 1947 centennial of the LDS Church's arrival in Utah with a series of local histories, Castle Valley's DUPs wrote their own. The results—*Centennial Echoes from Carbon County* published in 1948, followed a year later by *Castle Valley: A History of Emery County*—captured history in danger of disappearing. Of course, LDS sponsorship limited the focus of these works somewhat, neglecting some of the ethnic, gentile, and industrial stories that also characterized this distinctive valley. The lack of an adequate history of the non-Mormon, non-Indian Utah past soon prompted the editor of the *Utah Historical Quarterly*, published by the USHS, to seek new research. He asked Cameron-born, Helper-bred Helen Zeese Papanikolas, the daughter of Greek immigrants, to write the first history of the Greeks in Carbon County. Published in 1954, her article began her tenacious pursuit of non-Mormon, ethnic and labor topics and later launched a generation of historians inspired by her work.[34]

While her influence was just beginning, a fictional account of Castle Valley (unfortunately, not pinpointed as such) received national acclaim. In 1955, Price native John D. Fitzgerald published a thinly-disguised history of his Castle Valley upbringing. Born in 1907 to a Danish LDS mother and an Irish Catholic father, Fitzgerald wrote about his parents, his saloon-owning uncle, Basque sheepmen, a Jewish merchant, and LDS-gentile conflicts and resolution in *Papa Married A Mormon*, published by Prentice-Hall.[35]

Although set in fictitious East and West Adenville in the late nineteenth century, the events he described in this book and in his subsequent, popular "Great Brain" series for young readers, based on his entrepreneurial brother, Tom, mirrored much of Price's history in the early twentieth century.[36] Because of Fitzgerald's novelistic approach, however, most readers who have delighted in his family's exploits think they represent greater Utah, not unique Castle Valley.

Filling this factual gap, the Utah State Historical Society began other efforts to preserve Castle Valley's history, along with that of the rest of the state. The federal government stimulated these efforts, beginning in 1969, when Congress passed the Historic Preservation Act. It mandated a Historic Preservation program in each state, and the USHS hired Dr. Melvin T. Smith as State Historic Preservation Officer. He soon added a coterie of eager graduate students from the University of Utah, including Huntington native Allan Kent Powell and Philip F. Notarianni, whose grandfathers had mined at Sunnyside. Powell began part-time in 1970, moving to a permanent position in 1973, when the agency expanded, then to editor of the *Utah Historical Quarterly* in 2002. Notarianni began on contract in 1976, became full-time in 1977, and the head of the Utah State Historical Society in 2003. Also in 1973, USHS hired David Madsen to launch the Antiquities Program, rescuing archeological sites and materials. Helen Z. Papanikolas (who had been appointed to the first Board of Editors of the *Utah Historical Quarterly* in 1969), joined Price's Dr. J. Eldon Dorman on the Board of State History, which had to approve all additions to the state and national registers of historic places.[37] In short order, Papanikolas nominated Price's Greek Orthodox Church, and Dorman nominated Castle Gate's Wasatch Store Building, robbed by Butch Cassidy. Other sites followed. In Castle Dale, the old Justus Wellington Seely house, still in excellent condition and then inhabited by Wink's youngest daughter, Dora Seely Otterstrom, and the old Castle Dale School also achieved listing.[38]

Sometimes preservation nominations built on local efforts. For example, in 1963, South Slavs, long active in their respective lodges, had acquired Spring Glen's Millarich Hall and converted it to a Slovenian Home—one of only five west of the Mississippi. "It really isn't a lodge in itself," explained Frances Dupin Vouk, one of those involved in the purchase. "They take other people in; you don't have to be Slovenian. This is a private club; it doesn't belong to any national organization." She also remembered lively dances there, featuring polkas danced to the inspired music of the accordionist Matinka.[39] Its inclusion on the State Register of Historic Places in 1976, and on the National Register four years later, gave concrete recognition to Castle Valley's history of South Slav coal miners, to the 1922 strikers who built it, to the NMU meetings held there in 1933, as well as ongoing community associations.[40] This drive to preserve local historical buildings matured when the USHS decided to use federal preservation grants to hire a group of interns and put them in communities throughout the state. One was assigned to Castle Valley (as well as Grand and San Juan Counties). In cooperation with long-time community residents, a host of local listings followed, including Helper Main Street, the Huntington Flour Mill, Price's Sampinos-Mahleres commercial building, and the brick Peter Johansen house in Castle Dale.[41]

As part of its internship program, the USHS helped promote the formation of local historical societies statewide. Castle Valley residents leapt at the chance, and the Castle Valley Historical Society drew up by-laws and formally organized in July 1978. Its stated purpose included to:

> discover and collect material which will help establish or illustrate the history of our counties . . . [to] cooperate with officials in insuring the preservation and accessibility of records and archives . . . [and of] historic buildings, monuments, and markers . . . [to] disseminate historical information . . . by publishing historical material; holding meetings, pageants, addresses, lectures, papers, and discussions; marking historical sights . . . [and] using media . . . to awaken public interest.[42]

As ambitious as this sounded, it eventually all came to pass. Initially, under president Eva Conover, the society met alternately in Carbon and Emery counties, where two chapters coalesced under presidents Pruda Trujillo and John L. Jorgensen, respectively. In 1980, the initial society formally dissolved and in its place a separate, forty-member Emery County Historical Society and a twenty-four-member Carbon County organization were established. Numerous local people collected important records and took oral histories, including energetic Sylvia Howard Nelson of Huntington.[43]

At precisely the same time, members of the Castle Dale Second Ward inaugurated an historical pageant based on local family histories. After an uncertain beginning, Montell Seely took over the script-writing job, prompted, in part, by stories of his own grandfather, Wink, and family difficulties in coming to Castle Valley. Stumped after writing a number of scenes, Seely turned to prayer and "the little dark blue Emery County history book," published by the local Daughters of Utah Pioneers in 1949. He completed the script and the pageant was first performed in 1978 in a natural outdoor amphitheater with local actors and live animals. It was an immediate success. Over the years, expanded formal seating and a host of other activities have been added, including opportunities to view a Pioneer Village with a living museum inhabited by mountain men, a blacksmith, spinners and weavers, and various other pioneer crafts; a traditional Emery County sheepherder's lamb fry added in 1983; and a flag ceremony initiated in 1991, originally to honor the veterans just returned from the Gulf War. As Seely proudly wrote, "The Castle Valley Pageant has grown from a one-ward production, up through the Stake- and Region-sponsored levels, to become one of eight pageants sponsored annually by the general body of The Church of

The Castle Valley Pageant has reenacted the LDS saga of local settlement for the last two decades, drawing hundreds of thousands of people to witness this church-sponsored extravaganza. It is the only known Utah pageant that uses live animals, a tribute to Castle Valley's continuing links with its agrarian, pioneer past. Courtesy of Ben and Dottie Hawkins Grimes.

Jesus Christ of Latter-day Saints."[44] Following this tradition minded trend, Huntington native Edward Geary wrote a literary salute to his hometown, *Goodbye to Poplarhaven: Recollections of a Utah Boyhood*, published in 1985.[45] Meanwhile, in Carbon County, an historical writing contest catalyzed the *Carbon County Journal*, (still published) initially edited by Frances Blackham Cunningham, descendant of some of Spring Glen's LDS settlers. In the first issue, published in 1982, she wrote, "Our heritage is unique, different from most of the state of Utah. It is one of early Mormons, of the immigrants, of railroading and of mining."[46] She also worked with the Carbon County Commission, securing a $2,000 grant to amass and duplicate historical materials, and obtaining an office in the basement of the courthouse.[47]

While local residents avidly collected and disseminated Castle Valley history in various guises, the USHS actively supported and aided their efforts. Particularly through the efforts of co-workers and close friends Dr. Kent Powell and Dr. Phil Notarianni, a series of lectures for Emery and Carbon counties took place in 1979 and 1980, respectively. These lectures yielded two books, edited by Powell (for Emery County) and Notarianni (for Carbon). The books were published with the aid of both county commissions as projects of the respective county historical societies. Emery County also published a huge local history book, *Emery County, 1880–1980*, in time for its centennial.[48] The state of Utah further promoted Castle Valley history when it held Statehood Day in Price in 1987. A decade later, the massive, state-sponsored Utah Centennial County History Series issued a volume each for Emery and Carbon counties (in 1996 and 1997, respectively), and in 2003 Montell Seely and Kathryn Seely published their 440–page *Castle Valley Pageant History*.[49]

While all these efforts attracted attention, local dinosaurs drew even more wide ranging interest. Desert-savvy ranchers such as Neilus Ekker of Green River and Ferron's Joe Swasey had known about some fossil beds for years, but only in 1928 did a group of University of Utah paleontologists investigate one such site east of Cleveland where they soon excavated 800 bones. William Lee Stokes, born at Black Hawk but raised in Cleveland, knew about this deposit and about the dig that ended in 1931. He tried to sell some of the fossils to finance his bachelor's and master's degrees at Brigham Young University. When no one would buy, he worked for the WPA's National Youth Administration instead. Then Stokes went to Princeton University to earn a doctorate, where he learned that the university lacked a dinosaur skeleton because they were so rare and expensive. "I know where you can get dinosaur bones. Lots of them," Stokes exclaimed. Philadelphia lawyer Malcolm Lloyd, Jr. donated $10,000 to Princeton University for the collection and mounting of a dinosaur. Stokes received $1,000 of this sum for fieldwork, uncovering (with the help of his brother, Grant) some 1,200 fossils in three summers. Another part of the funding paid Jim Jensen and Arnie Lewis to create the so-called Princeton mount of an Allosaurus. In 1941, Stokes received his Ph.D. degree in geology, and, because of his knowledge of the uranium- (and dinosaur-) bearing Morrison formation, he got a seven-year job with the USGS. "Fortunately," Stokes later remarked, "the bones at Cleveland-Lloyd contain very little uranium. Otherwise they would have been claimed as an ore deposit and hauled to the mills long ago." He also knew about the Red Seeps finds in 1932, the Smithsonian's excavation at North Horn Mountain in 1937, and the fossil beds east of Molen studied by the California Institute of Technology in 1941. Therefore, after Stokes began teaching geology at the University of Utah in 1947, rising to chair the department thirteen years later, he began Utah's Cooperative Dinosaur Project to supply international museums with affordable dinosaur skeletons from the Cleveland-Lloyd Dinosaur Quarry, established in 1960. In 1966, it became a National Natural Landmark, and by the end of the twentieth century had yielded over 12,000 individual bones, over thirty complete skeletons, and several dinosaur eggs.[50]

Despite Stokes's interest in supplying fossils to museums world-wide, or perhaps because of it, he initially took little interest in establishing a museum in Castle Valley. Instead, Donald L. Burge lit the fuse. He arrived in 1959 to teach math, geology, and physics at Carbon College (later CEU) and offered a night class in geology in the spring of 1960. Local businessmen and professionals, many of them members of the Castle Valley Gem and Mineralogical Society (the Gem Society, for short), took his class. Afterwards, they began adjourning to a local cafe for doughnuts and coffee and began a sort of "show and tell," bringing specimens garnered from a lifetime of prospecting the ledges and "Eastering" down on the Swell. Burge, who had explored part of the area during the uranium boom, finally announced, "You know, you people are crazy!" Why keep these treasures hidden away when they could open a museum?[51] According to Dr. J. Eldon Dorman, one of the class members, "He hounded us so damn much he convinced us we should do it. Every time we saw him he would bring it up, even when we'd meet him on the street."[52]

Burge was rightfully enraptured with over 200 million years of geologic time that lay exposed in a fifty-mile stretch from Soldier Summit to the San Rafael Swell, looming above the newly opened Cleveland-Lloyd Dinosaur Quarry.[53] The men who formed the core of what became the College of Eastern Utah Prehistoric Museum (after the college changed its name) had already been associated not only in the Gem Society but in the Jeep Patrol, admitting Dorman because he could fly an airplane, thanks to his participation in the wartime Price Flight. He sometimes acted as spotter for them or flew them to remote areas for prospecting.[54] Exploring on the ground and in the air, the men soon exhausted their own knowledge of the area, so they contacted Dr. Stokes. They first took him to the fossilized mammal beds near Joe's Valley, where he initially claimed that he had been brought to the wrong area. When he saw the photographs in a scientific journal they had brought along describing the mammal beds, he realized they were parked on top of the site and immediately got out of the car and started collecting fossils. Subsequently, Stokes arranged to sell the new museum an Allosaurus skull for its earliest display and later assisted in the curation of many exhibits.[55]

As collection plans developed, the dilemma became where to house what was then called the Carbon College Museum. Price City eventually volunteered a large room in City Hall. The Independent Coal and Coke Company had recently closed down the towns of Castle Gate and Kenilworth, so donated cases from old company stores, probably including the one where Butch Cassidy grabbed the payroll. As the rockhounds refurbished these much-painted cases, sanding, sweating, and digging splinters out of their fingers, they also discussed the many well-known local collections of Indian artifacts tucked into homes, barns, and basements. The idea dawned that their new museum should not only house minerals, but archeological specimens, too. But people held back their carefully amassed artifacts until Fred Keller, the famous "Cowboy Judge" and composer of the beautiful cowboy ballad, *Blue Mountain,* offered his fine collection of Anasazi pottery. Then others stepped up, including Dave Nordell of Nine Mile Canyon and Keith Hansen of Sunnyside.[56] Thus, the local weekend diversion (and federal offense, if conducted on federal lands) of "pot-hunting" started to benefit the public. Museum organizers rushed to increase their archaeological knowledge to create exhibit labels, prompting chairman Dr. Quinn A. Whiting to put Dorman in charge of "finding out all there is to know about this stuff." Dorman started studying, and years later earned statewide recognition for his expertise on local rock art.[57]

Initially, Dorman and Burge had sought help from the college's institutional superior, the University of Utah, a relationship established by the state legislature in 1959. But, despite this formal bond, no one at the university wanted to take the Price group seriously. After communications stalled, Dorman heard of Dr. Jesse Jennings, head of the University's Anthropology Department, and sent him a carbon copy of the last letter he ever intended to write to the uncooperative University. Jennings called Dorman the very next day and was in Price a day later. The museum had found its anthropology liaison, and thirty years later Jennings stated, "They treated me as a friend and eventually borrowed almost half of the exhibits at the university (U of U) museum."[58]

Although the University of Utah lent its resident experts, artifacts, and bestowed its official blessings on the college's museum, it could provide no money. Instead, Price's Chamber of Commerce and Lions Club contributed $1,000 and $800, respectively. Together with lesser amounts from other sources, they funded the museum's official opening on June 3, 1961. Local businessman George Patterick, owner of Kilfoyle Krafts, convinced the Carbon Art Guild and Fine Arts League to paint a lush 4 x 24–foot dinosaur mural for one wall of the room. Twenty women and two men lavished hours on the scene, some of which had to be redone to reflect actual prehistoric conditions. When Dr. Stokes arrived, he started pointing out additional errors, and sketched in charcoal the necessary changes. A third rendition resulted in complete scientific accuracy.[59] In the first year, 1961–1962, the museum attracted over 14,000 visitors from the region, the state, and several foreign countries. The museum subsequently expanded its collections and exhibits, outgrowing a second home in the old basketball courts in Price City Hall. In 1991, relocated in a newly-constructed $2 million facility next door, the museum became one of only four in the state of Utah (and the only one outside Salt Lake City) to receive accreditation from the American Association of Museums, the guarantee of professionalization. In 1997, a 32–cent U.S. postage stamp commemorated the discovery of a new dinosaur, the *Gastonia Burgi*, named after long-time curator Don Burge, who with his associates had uncovered seven new dinosaur species, six of them still awaiting a scientific name as this book went to press.[60] In 2003, Burge officially retired and the museum welcomed a new curator of paleontology, Dr. Reese Burdick, who seized the chance to "live and work where there are dinosaurs out your back door."[61]

Not to be outdone by Price, Helper had also started its own museum showcasing railroad and coal mining history. Around 1963, Helper

Don Burge, founding curator of the College of Eastern Utah Prehistoric Museum, displays *Gastonia Burgi,* one of his many finds and the dinosaur named for him. Remains of this nodasaur include fossilized skin. This dinosaur is featured both on a postage stamp and at the small exhibit of a dig in progress at Disney World. Photo by the author.

businessmen Chris Jouflas, Al Veltri, John Skerl and others formed the North Carbon Industries to attract tourists to their historic railroad town. They spent $1,800 for the twenty-foot statue of Big John, the famed coal miner, to display in front of the Helper City Auditorium. Jouflas kept inviting newly retired railroad machinist Fred Voll to their meetings. Voll finally came. When he told them they needed some pictures of the coal industry on the wall, they "scraped up enough money to buy the boards and gave me a few dollars for paint, brushes, and stuff," Voll recalled, and he began painting. First working at the old telephone company building, Voll soon moved to the Helper Auditorium where he could set up three panels at once, "to get the continuity of the background," he remembered. "I started the first day in November [when] I took my pension . . . and painted three years on it." Through the years, he kept adding little touches. In 1980, when one of the museum workers asked him when he was planning to finish the "ghost mule" originally blocked out with quick brush strokes, "I went over there one afternoon with a few tubes of paint and finished him up." After sixteen years, the murals were finally complete.[62] Meanwhile, attorney Stanley V. Littizetti had sparked the Helper City Council to provide a permanent room in the auditorium for the museum. William Branson, the first curator, had assembled a collection of his own rock samples in a case and accessioned the growing number of donations that came in from all over the area. James Diamanti, a strong museum supporter, donated a fossilized tree stump from the coal land he later sold to Price River Coal. Voll became the second curator, and tried to organize the expanding collection. He consulted with photographer Bill Fossatt, who had served with the Signal Corps in Germany during World War II, then studied at the Brooks Institute of Photography in Santa Barbara on the G.I. Bill. Declining the offer of a position at Brooks, Fossatt came home to Castle Valley and opened a photo studio on Helper's Main Street from 1955 to 1990. He was later joined by his brother, Albert, after the latter's retirement, and they became known as distinguished landscape photographers. To help the Helper Museum, they mounted and hung over 500 photos. Voll built a coal mine replica. Periodic open houses stimulated community interest, although, said Voll, "one woman said we ought to remodel all the photographs and have all the different camps in . . . one place." People "don't stop to realize that there was a period of seventeen years" over which exhibits arrived; "you didn't get that all at once, you know!" he added, with a grin.[63]

As with other museums, success meant continued expansion. Spearheaded by city councilman Bryon Matsuda, the Helper museum got a grant to help with the refurbishing of the old Helper Hotel, previously home to numberless railroad crews and other guests (including, reputedly, ladies of the night). This new space accommodated more varied exhibits, and the next curator, Frances Blackham Cunningham of Spring Glen, former president of the Carbon County Historical Society, made sure that local women had a place. She immediately collected an early electric stove, four washing machines, a butter churn, and a bottle capper (for homemade root beer— or bootleg) to add to the mining and railroad items on display. A long-time independent researcher, Cunningham also oversaw the initiation of a professional archives, funded in part by a federal grant handled through the Utah State Historical Society. "We have acid free boxes and folders in which to store historical records . . . [including] both oral and written histories" as well as bound copies of local newspapers and many other documents and photos, she told a local reporter.[64] Much of this material came through the cooperation of the county clerk, Norman Pritchard; Dr. Nelson Wadsworth, who, as visiting editor of the *Sun Advocate* spent countless hours in a darkroom making archival copies of donated photographs, and Samuel Quigley, executive at Tower Resources (later Andalex), who worked hard to get records of the uranium boom for the archives and mining machinery for outdoor display. Many of these plans matured under subsequent leaders like Madge Tomsic and Edna Romano at what was now named the Western Mining and Railroad Museum. It became a major draw on Helper's Main Street, listed on the National Register of Historic Places and protected by a city ordinance passed in 1994.[65] In 1998, after ten years of effort, the museum acquired the first longwall (giant coal-cutting machine) in the western United States, brought to Helper from Sunnyside with widespread community cooperation. According to city councilman Frank Scavo, when the Carbon County Commission lacked the money to pay for moving the machine, they offered the services of the county's road, maintenance, and weed abatement departments to assist in its transportation and installation. Helper city crews pitched in, and the Coal Operators Association, Genwal Resources, Energy West, and Morgantown Machine donated to the project. Speaking for much of Castle Valley, Scavo explained, "This artifact is precious to our heritage as a mining community. This display historically marks when Carbon County entered into longwall technology, which now dominates production in the Utah coal fields."[66] After long neglect, Castle Valley's history had become attractive.

The same impulse sparked activities in Emery County. Enrollees at the Castle Valley Job Corps, located south of Price, traveled down to the edge of the San Rafael Swell to construct a visitors center at the Cleveland-Lloyd Dinosaur Quarry, opened in 1968, the first such center ever administered by the Bureau of Land Management (BLM). That same year, a Fremont burial site yielded the mummified remains of a woman and small child, which went on display at the College of Eastern Utah Museum until Emery County had a facility to house them. The Emery County Jaycees spearheaded converting the old Castle Dale elementary school, listed on the National Register of Historic Places, into a museum. It opened on May 1, 1970, combining exhibits on prehistory with pioneer artifacts, later adding historic farm and mining displays and a model of a co-op store.[67]

Growing excitement over ancient local artifacts and deposits brought a number of results. In the late 1980s, Utah authorized a pilot amateur archeology training program to be held at CEU, conducted by archeologists Blaine and Pam Miller. Their timing proved prescient, for in August 1988 construction workers at Huntington Reservoir unearthed the truly remarkable Huntington Mammoth. As the *Emery County Progress* later reported, this almost-complete skeleton was the most "well-preserved Columbian Mammoth species known to science, attracting worldwide attention" for a variety of reasons: its extremely high location (9,000 feet); association with human-manufactured artifacts; evidence of damage due to disease and old age; and "association with a rich assemblage of other fossils such as the giant bear, insects, and plants." Controversy ensued over where it would be displayed, helping to delay the unveiling until 1992 at the Utah Museum of Natural History on the University of Utah campus.[68] From there, the skeleton eventually came to stay at the CEU Museum in Price, thanks to its national accreditation.[69]

Emery County, now galvanized, acquired funding for its own new, spacious building, the Museum of the San Rafael, which debuted in 1993 in Castle Dale, just a block from the Emery County Museum. Opening in time for the county fair and the Castle Valley Pageant, this new museum sported impressive mountain and desert landscapes painted by Clifford Oviatt as

settings for natural history exhibits. Gene Talbot and Dixon Peacock spearheaded initial collection efforts and arranged displays in "a 3–week project
which included work seven days a week and up to 12 hours each day." Acquisitions included numerous Indian artifacts such as the rare willow figurines,
pipes, ornamental bowls, a bead collection, woven blankets, arrowheads,
knives, and "the extensively studied Sitterud Bundle which is believed to
be the only arrowhead kit of its kind." (This prehistoric tool kit contained
all the implements necessary for making arrowheads, and some impressive
examples of the owner's craft.) The museum added dinosaurs, including
the impressive Allosaurus, Chasmosaurus, and Albertosaurus, all found in
the nearby Cleveland-Lloyd Quarry, as well as dinosaur teeth, claws, and
footprints. As a result of this new facility, the older Emery County Museum
confined itself solely to historical displays, while the Museum of the San
Rafael concentrated on natural history, archeology, and paleontology.[70]

While Castle Valley residents began serious preservation efforts of their
own surroundings, their socio-economic life heaved like a bucking horse,
up one year, down the next, sometimes sideways. For example, a new federal
interstate highway, an extension of the Defense Highway System, had to pass
somewhere near the area. When local officials heard of the Congressional
authorization secured by Utah's Senator Wallace Bennett in 1957, they
made elaborate plans to welcome the federal delegation, hoping the chosen route would follow the Old Spanish Trail through Emery County. They
included a two-day tour of the San Rafael Swell on the fact-finders' itiner-
ary, figuring its beauty would sway the road their way. This plan backfired
when the government built Interstate 70 (I-70) right through the Swell,
avoiding all the Emery County towns except Green River. The finished
highway from there to Salina—all 110 miles of it—remains the longest
stretch without services in the entire nation. During its construction—from
1963–1967—local people often made excursions across the desert to the
work sites, familiarizing themselves with lonely pockets once known only
to ranchers, sheepmen, and prospectors. Conversely, some construction
workers also moved into Emery, Castle Valley's southernmost town, often
traveling the road through Moore. According to Jean Christiansen and
Arminta Hewitt, they added "greatly to the sheltered education of many of
the citizens. A gradual change began to take place, a shift from being a lot
the same as the neighbors, in thought, financial means, and occupations,
to an awareness that different lifestyles, religions, and occupations existed
in the world out beyond."[71] Green River also benefited, particularly during
1964–1979, when it also housed the Utah Launch Complex, home to Athena
and Pershing missiles fired off to White Sands, New Mexico. New residents
moved in, Green River's school population boomed, and churches sprung
up to serve Protestants, Catholics, and LDS.[72] Eventually, religious hetero-
geneity also gained a concrete permanence throughout the rest of Emery
County. Catholics built the Mission San Rafael south of Huntington under

the direction of Price's Notre Dame Catholic Church, breaking ground in November 1976, and celebrating the first Mass there at Easter 1977.[73] A year later, Pastor Milton Carr inaugurated the First Baptist Church in Castle Dale, which moved to Ferron in 1981, and raised an impressive building on the town's main street.[74] An Evangelical Free Church rose on the south end of Huntington, adding to the area's religious choices.

These congregations prospered as workers of all backgrounds flooded into Castle Valley, many of them drawn by energy-related jobs at two new coal-fired electricity-generating plants built by Utah Power and Light (UP&L). The introduction of major coal-fired plants to Castle Valley mirrored a nationwide trend of large-scale energy production, spurred by America's growing environmental awareness and unpleasant international political realities. Environmentalism, catalyzed by the 1962 publication of Rachel Carson's *Silent Spring*, led Congress, in 1970, to pass the National Environmental Policy Act, establishing the Environmental Protection Agency as a few dedicated environmentalists celebrated the first Earth Day.[75] The Clean Air Act, passed a year later, brought a sudden demand for reduced pollution, including the use of Castle Valley's low-sulfur coal. At the same time, the federal land leasing program expanded, ignoring a 1967 warning to "put a brake" on the process because "the stakes are too high, and the public interest too transcendent, the pressures too great and the questions too many."[76] Under pro-business Republican president Richard Nixon, a prototype program for leasing oil shale stalled in Utah due to legal obstacles before Nixon's abrupt departure following the 1974 Watergate scandal. Meanwhile, America's pro-Israel foreign policy angered certain Arab nations, resulting in an oil embargo by the Organization of Petroleum Exporting Countries (OPEC) in 1973–1974. Suddenly, oil no longer arrived at the docks to fuel the nation's electricity-generating plants. Worried about energy vulnerability, in 1978 Congress passed the Power Plant and Industrial Fuel Act. It mandated utility and industrial conversion to coal. Eager energy corporations first targeted the Kaiparowits Plateau in southern Utah, but a host of difficulties led to the suspension of their plans, a decision later seemingly made permanent by creation of the Escalante-Grand Staircase National Monument. During the Kaiparowits fight, the government approved construction of the Intermountain Power Project (IPP—also known as Son of Kaiparowits) in the desert north of Delta. UP&L, previously involved in the Kaiparowits development, forged an agreement with the Bureau of Reclamation to trade its now useless leases for federal coal leases in Emery County, creating a huge new market for local coal. In short order, UP&L contracted to supply twenty-five percent of the coal needed for the massive IPP from its own mines.[77] An era of domination by international energy giants was about to dawn in Castle Valley.

# 12

# Energy Crisis, 1980–2004

*We are as close to the frontier as you can get in the United States. We have the San Rafael and not too many people know about it but more are finding out. The secret is out. But we'll do what we can to save as much as we can for those of us who still live here. It will be interesting to see what the next hundred years bring.*[1]
—KENT R. PETERSEN, FORMER EMERY COUNTY COMMISSIONER

In 1994, Kent Petersen, Ferron native, Army veteran, and former Utah Power and Light (UP&L) environmental engineer noted, "When I was traveling the world I always knew Emery County was one place the air was still clean. But that was because nobody lived there."[2] He was right. As Castle Valley got sucked into the vortex of international price wars and market fluctuations, the energy industry on which it traditionally depended entered a new period of volatility. By the twenty-first century, farming the valley's alkaline soil no longer offered an adequate living, and ranching suffered from increasing environmental pressures. The federal government no longer concerned itself with aiding farmers and relocating displaced miners (as it had during the Great Depression), and the flood of cash brought in by the uranium boom was long gone. Without a new economic base, what would happen to Castle Valley?

Like riding a mechanical bull, remaining residents tried to stay astride as the economy bucked and heaved. Increasingly mechanized coal companies needed fewer and fewer miners, and repeated energy company mergers guaranteed that distant corporate officers knew far more about the contents of local coal veins than about the people and traditions of Castle Valley. As always, the first priority for community health remained jobs. Trying to forestall employment cutbacks, when the UMWA labor contract ran out in 1977, the union staged its longest strike in recent memory: 111 days. Men stayed out of work, previously stay-at-home wives sought jobs to support the family, and tensions between union and non-union members' children flared on school playgrounds. Louis Pestotnik, then the local UMWA secretary-treasurer, remembered, "If it's handled right, that's [the strike is] the only weapon that the miner has." Recognizing a growing split between union leadership and the rank and file, he added, "Now you take this last [1977] strike. . . . The miners was the ones that got the contract. If they would've ratified that [original] contract, like the leadership wanted them to, they've lost more than what they did lose."[3] The miners held out, but the growing weakness of the UMWA added to local uncertainty.

Much of that uncertainty also stemmed from confusion over who, exactly, owned the mines. Even front office employees sometimes lost track as the dizzying pace of far away corporate mergers surged during the late twentieth century. International energy companies, in particular, started diversifying in Castle Valley coal lands. For example, Plateau Mining (a subsidiary of Getty Oil Company and later of United Nuclear) bought Wattis in 1967. In 1971, the Diamantis sold Plateau their mine in Hardscrabble Canyon, west of Helper, which brothers George and John G. had first leased in 1916 and incorporated (with John's sons) as the Hardscrabble Coal Company in the 1930s and renamed the Carbon Fuel Company when Rains sold out in the 1950s. In 1968, North American Coal Company (part of McCullough Oil Company) bought Kenilworth, also acquiring Castle Gate in 1974. North American then began working both mines through the Castle Gate entrance.[4]

The old LDS mines also went through a series of owners. In 1938, the LDS Church had acquired well-known coal land surrounding the old ghost town of Connellsville, at the head of Huntington Canyon, and had added acreage originally prospected by "Uncle" Jesse Knight during the Progressive Era. Worked as a Welfare Project, this church-owned Deseret Mine closed from 1941–1946 due to plentiful jobs elsewhere in the wartime boom. After the war, it reopened under direction of Shirl McArthur, who supervised the building of a reservoir, acquisition of two other nearby mines, and the purchase of up-to-date machinery. Also stimulated by the immediate post-war boom, in 1945 Cyrus Wilberg bought an old wagon mine that had been idle for most of the 1930s and operated it with his son until 1966, when they offered it to Peabody Coal Company. Peabody had first come to the area in 1961, when McArthur put together Castle Valley Mining Company and contracted with Peabody to mine local coal for sale to the Nevada Power Company. There, the coal was used to generate electricity, an obvious need in a state where the Las Vegas lights glowed ever brighter, but water power, the usual energy source, was in conspicuously short supply. By 1967–1968, Wilberg coal also flowed to Nevada under contract with Peabody.[5]

The suitability of local coal for generating electricity inspired a brand new construction effort that brought a host of jobs to Castle Valley. UP&L

decided to build electricity-generating plants at the source of the coal, and move the power, rather than the mineral, over the miles to distant markets. Therefore, in 1969 and 1970 UP&L started buying coal from Peabody's Wilberg mine. By this time, the LDS Church, faced with increasing safety restrictions, was ready to sell the Deseret Mine. UP&L bought it. This deal freed McArthur to organize the American Coal Company in 1971 to mine coal for UP&L, and American established its offices in the renovated North Emery High School building on Huntington's main street. UP&L was thus well supplied with coal when the Huntington Plant came on-line in 1974, with an additional unit added in 1977. In 1979, however, a policy disagreement led UP&L to force the sale of American Coal's contract mining rights to Savage Brothers of American Fork. Savage then organized the Emery Mining Corporation, which consolidated the coal contracts of all five coal mines supplying UP&L's Castle Valley plants: Deseret, Beehive, Little Dove (known as Des-Bee-Dove), Deer Creek, and Wilberg. By 1980, Emery Mining Corporation, employing approximately 1,600 people, supplied both plants (including the Hunter Plant, completed in 1983).[6] For a time, the energy industry seemed the salvation of Castle Valley.

But this new industry proved a mixed blessing, providing needed jobs but insistently demanding much of Castle Valley's precious water. The electricity-generating process utilized steam for power and a water cooling system.[7] Knowing this, in 1969, even before publicly announcing its intent to build the generating plants, UP&L had purchased a total of six thousand water shares in the consolidated irrigation companies serving Orangeville, Castle Dale, Huntington, and Cleveland, adding another six thousand acre-feet from Joe's Valley Reservoir. This water had been stored thanks to the 1956 federal Colorado River Storage Act, which included authorization for the large reservoir in Joe's Valley on the Wasatch Plateau as part of the Upper Colorado Reclamation Project. As drought had gripped Emery County, farmers long divided into separate water districts had finally agreed to form the Emery County Water Conservancy District in 1961, headed by O. Eugene Johansen of Castle Dale. Looking on the positive side, at the 1963 groundbreaking of the Joe's Valley Reservoir, a dignitary had noted the dam's benefits not only included irrigation water, but potential earnings for Emery County residents, one-third of whom then made less than $3,000 per year. These construction jobs successfully reduced outmigration, which had reached almost thirty percent between 1950–1960.[8]

As the plants came on line, they required still more water, but brought unprecedented prosperity. The entire Emery County Project, completed in the 1970s, included not only the Joe's Valley Reservoir and recreation area, but canals, a road alignment, and Huntington Lake. The projects indeed provided seasonal construction work and training for numbers of Emery County men, who thus spent at least part of every year at home in Castle Valley. They worked on the Millsite Reservoir, begun six years after the Joe's

Valley groundbreaking. This new project was sponsored by federal, state, and local entities: the Soil Conservation Service, the Forest Service, the Utah Power and Water Board, the Utah Department of Fish and Game, Ferron City, and the Ferron Reservoir and Canal Company. The Huntington Plant, a new employer nine miles northwest of the town of Huntington at the mouth of the canyon, got its additional water from Ferron Canal and Reservoir Company and from Electric Lake, created by a dam on Huntington Creek. Its sister Hunter Plant, three miles south of Castle Dale, used additional water from a thirteen-mile pipeline to Millsite Reservoir west of Ferron.[9]

For a few years after all this development, once-poor Emery County boasted the highest per capita income in Utah. Increased wealth permitted long-desired improvements, such as a new piped-in culinary water system demanded by some serious housewives of Lawrence, Bernice S. Culloms and Utanah Wilson. Such grass-roots activism prompted the formation of the North Emery Water Users Association, which, in turn, negotiated with the Farm Home Administration for a ninety-two-mile-long pipeline running east from Huntington, the longest single culinary water system in Utah. It connected to Lawrence, Cleveland, and Elmo, and ended the practice of hauling water and dumping it in family cisterns, which had continued for ninety years.[10] At Huntington, the old airport, opened in 1945, acquired improvements including a resurfaced runway, taxi-way, fuel tank, and administration building. For the Hunter Plant dedication, over a dozen private aircraft sat tightly packed on the freshly-finished parking ramp.[11] At Emery, in 1975, Consolidated Coal Company (Consol) bought the old Ira Browning Mine, the town's main employer. Browning had sold it in about 1920 to E. H. Duzett, who had leased it to his sons-in-law before selling it to Kemmerer Coal Company, Consol's predecessor. The new population attracted to Castle Valley's far southern settlement also demanded new recreation, so Scott Christiansen built a motocross track and organized two major annual events, which draw participants from as far away as Helper.[12]

The overall impact of this energy development was tremendous. According to local historian Montell Seely, this major shift in water use "began the change of Emery County from agricultural to industrial, but water continued to be its lifeblood."[13]

In one of Castle Valley's many trade-offs, this water reallocation led to the slow death of bedrock rural traditions. In 1980, long-time stockraiser LaVora Kofford noted the realities of local change when she wrote, "Many families still own horses for pleasure and recreation, and there may be a few families who are still making profit on the livestock industry, but as they old saying goes, 'All good things must end.'"[14] As the economics changed, Orangeville native Roger D. Curtis reminisced about the great "summer ride": "The sense of community was never more strongly felt than on that great, looked-forward-to event. . . . Here was the opportunity to get away from hot farm work and spend four or five days driving the cattle from the lower ranges to the upper ranges and brand the calves which had been born since the cows left the valley for the mountain pastures. And to sit around the camp fire at night and listen to the tales of the older men of life in a more distant past than ours."[15] With the land wearing out, water going to the generating plants, and the range industry withering, few people moved their cattle anymore.

On the other hand, perhaps this shift to an industrial economic base also helped mute the impact of the Sagebrush Rebellion in Castle Valley. In the 1970s, this widespread western movement sought to transfer public lands from federal to state control, where elected officials would be more responsive to local constituencies. The rebellion began when Congress passed the Federal Land Policy and Management Act of 1976, the organic act for the Bureau of Land Management (BLM). The law gave the federal government more control of land management, while, as a compromise, allowing ranchers a moratorium on grazing fees and granting them mandatory ten-year grazing permits. As ranchers across the West howled, the Assistant Secretary of the Interior declared, if the Sagebrush Rebels succeeded, "You could kiss goodbye millions of acres of our best hunting, fishing, and hiking territory, because it would soon be fenced and posted with 'no trespassing,' 'private property—keep out.'" The fight continued in Congress with the Public Range Lands Improvement Act of 1978, which did little to raise the cheap fees western stockraisers paid for federal grazing permits, and worked against those who did not have access to public lands.[16] As federal reform efforts slowed to a glacial creep and long-standing relationships remained largely intact, the Sagebrush Rebellion died.

But this tighter link with international corporations brought ever more violent shifts to Castle Valley's economy. By the late 1970s Castle Valley was locked into what oil historian Daniel Yergin called "the hydrocarbon civilization" of America and the world.[17] Painful changes in the national and international economy ever more rapidly impacted small towns everywhere as the global information age matured, and Castle Valley proved no exception. For example, as the nation entered the deepest recession since the Great Depression late in 1980, the Price newspaper warned of nationwide coal mine takeovers by major oil, steel, and utility companies, particularly since, due to extensive federal environmental regulations, independent mining companies could no longer compete economically. Citing the *Wall Street Journal*, the article mentioned widespread concerns that the oil companies would try to manipulate the coal market, quoting a 1979 Tennessee Valley Authority report "that said the oil companies 'exercise sufficient power in the (fuel) markets to be able to hamper interfuel competition.'"[18] Nonetheless, local coal production kept expanding as it had since 1972, and in 1981, a development district spokesman claimed the area had finally learned to manage the energy boom.[19] A year later, the layoffs began. In April, Huntington's Emery Mining Corporation laid off 200 workers.

In June, Price River Coal and U.S. Steel at Sunnyside announced a two-week "idle time" period in addition to their two-week summer vacation. By December, layoffs at Consolidated Coal Company near Emery reached over 180 as the mine closed for "an indefinite period."[20] In 1982, Horse Canyon mine closed.[21] Addressing the deteriorating economic situation, the Carbon County planner tied layoffs to problems in the steel industry, to low oil prices that discouraged conversion to coal, and to the Clean Air Act which required scrubbers on all coal-fired electricity plants rather than limiting the amount of sulfur a plant could emit. "There is no competitive advantage to [Castle Valley's] low sulfur coal as a result," he concluded. To combat the downturn, Carbon and Emery Counties had developed cooperative agreements for mutual support, in essence codifying a century-old tradition.[22] Meanwhile, in 1981, the U.S. completely deregulated the oil industry, and, in 1982, the national economy headed for its most severe depths since the Great Depression.[23] By July 1983, the newspaper shrieked, "Jobless flee coal country." Part of the distress began in the previous April, when far north of Castle Valley, a winter-soaked hillside slipped, blocking a creek that drowned the old town of Thistle and cut off rail and highway connections from the valley over Soldier Summit to the Wasatch Front for several months. Losses were placed at between $200 and $337 million, and Thistle was never rebuilt. Subsequently, Castle Valley unemployment rose to over twenty percent, and coal operators and the UMWA bickered over the root cause. Don Ross, president of the Utah Coal Operators Association, blamed reduced demand for coal on slowing conversions from oil-fired to coal-fired electric plants, and the end of sales to the Japanese, who had briefly purchased U.S. coal when faced with an Australian miners' strike. UMWA District 22 president Mike Delpiaz countered, "'It was the oil companies buying up all the coal mines. . . . All of a sudden it was the end of the road, and roads just don't stop that quick.'"[24]

In many respects, both were right. Oil, not coal, had become the foundation of world energy production. As producing nations in and out of OPEC jockeyed for position and oil companies entered an era of hostile takeovers, the industry became a free-for-all of buyers and sellers competing in a glutted market. Oil production also fell more and more under the control of nation-states as colonialism evaporated in the late twentieth century and newly established indigenous regimes nationalized private, corporate holdings. Thus losing direct access to many international supplies, long-lived oil giants often had to reinvent themselves as integrated energy companies, suffer buy-outs, or give way to simple energy brokers who had no involvement with actually pumping or refining oil.[25] In addition, the United States increasingly entered wars to protect actual or potential oil supplies, including the Gulf War, the invasion of Afghanistan, and the war in Iraq under father and son Presidents Bush, schooled in the oil industry.

Meanwhile, the great, international energy scramble brought another potential extractive industry in Castle Valley. In 1980–1981, the Carter and Nixon administrations had not only urged conversion from oil to coal, they had promoted a synfuels (synthetic fuels) program to convert kerogen, found in oil shale, into low grade petroleum. According to a national study, "The world's richest known shale deposits are located in the Green River formation, a 17,000–square-mile area where Colorado, Utah, and Wyoming intersect; the Green River, one of the principal tributaries of the Colorado, flows through this area."[26] Their extraction promised an antidote to an industry poised at a precipice on the "oil mountain," where supplies might decline abruptly, gutting oil companies and idling the thousands of machines and factories built to run on oil. A Texas company began prospecting in Whitmore Canyon, dangling promises that a local synfuels refinery would eventually produce up to 125,000 barrels a day, employ 2,000 residents during construction and some 1,000–1,200 thereafter.[27] Castle Valley entrepreneurs had long exploited the asphaltum beds in Whitmore Canyon, filing on locations in 1907, that had, by 1912, promised "extensive development."[28] Some of this gooey substance was used to pave streets and highways, and developers built an aerial tramway to haul it from the face two miles down to what was then a "good wagon road."[29] Ownership changed hands in the 1930s, and by the 1940s teenage boys, such as Paul Turner, supplemented the handful of men employed there during the summer, when the canyon (and rockpile) wasn't too frozen to work. Turner described jackhammering rock at the face so it fit into a crusher, then watching it move by conveyor belt to one of several large metal bins, hung every three hundred feet along the gravity tram. These loaded buckets, weighing over half a ton each, traveled some eight miles down to the discharge using solely the power of gravity, the weight of the loaded buckets lifting empty buckets back up to the rock face in one continuous loop. At the discharge site, dump trucks large enough to hold one bucketful waited to haul the coarsely crushed rocks to the mill. There, the rock was further smashed until reduced to the size of paving material. The whole process ended in 1948, and, by the twenty-first century, only a line of sagging buckets hung forlornly over the canyon. When the recession hit, all plans for synfuels development ceased. Hope flickered briefly for its renewal again in 1984 and 1985 before it fizzled.[30]

The continuing sense of Castle Valley community endured, however, and, despite unsettling shifts, belied at least one national trend remarked by historian Thomas Michael Power. Viewing the period from 1980–1990, he aptly described new industrial techniques, which, "adopted worldwide, have increased supply potential, driving commodity prices down… [and raising coal] productivity… 7.3 percent per year over a decade [which] would reduce the direct labor content of coal by half."[31] As a consequence, he concluded, "miners are wary of setting down roots in a mining dependent town."[32] But not in Castle Valley, where a lot of people, like Kent Petersen, were born with local roots and never quite severed them. Residents also continued to treasure reminders of the distinctive local past, even as economic changes cut into the local landscape. For example, when North American Coal closed down the venerable town of Castle Gate to make way for increased preparation plants, storage plants, loading facilities, and unit trains, most residents chose to buy their old coal camp houses and move them to a free lot in the newly established Castle Gate subdivision of nearby Spring Canyon, keeping the community together. A minority took a monetary payment. At the time, North American also promised to maintain the town cemetery with its many mine victims and planned to salvage the historic Wasatch Store where Butch Cassidy stole the payroll. The store was later torn down but, thanks to the considerable pull of Dr. J. Eldon Dorman, the staircase and front step—the immediate scene of the heist—were saved for display at Helper's Western Mining and Railroad Museum.[33] Likewise, another salvage effort targeted the Standardville bandstand. It had remained in place when the mines there closed in the 1950s, but it was slated for destruction when remaining town structures were razed two decades later. So, Ernie and Stella O'Green bought it and moved it to their Spring Glen orchard. In 1999, Rob Metzger of the Helper chapter of E Clampus Vitas accepted the O'Greens' offer to move it to downtown Helper. Principal Tom Montoya of Helper Junior High offered his students for restorative work. Orlando Ochoa supervised construction of the cement foundation by Helper City workers. The old building thus got repositioned and restored in time for the Canyon Days Reunion in August 1999, an event when many former Spring Canyon residents get together to reminisce.[34]

In the midst of modern economic uncertainties, some permanent social changes also bloomed. Women got more job opportunities in a floundering economy that needed their productivity. Utah had long recognized women's contributions, although 1970 marked the first time that three women from the same area earned recognition as "Young Woman of the Year": Sherril Burge, Janis Siggard, and Mary Helen Powell, all from Castle Valley.[35] Even more atypically, Castle Valley women started mining coal. Although women had worked outside the mines during World War II, only in 1973 did the first women go underground, in West Virginia. A year later, five women entered Castle Valley's mines. Many male miners objected to their presence, and the UMWA remained thoroughly unenthusiastic about female miners until 1983. Then, at the fifth national conference of Women Miners, UMWA president Richard Trumka finally denounced the old British belief that bad luck follows a woman down a mine: "You have brought us good luck, not bad luck. Courageously, you have destroyed myth after myth." He also pledged to help stop sexual harassment and discrimination in what remained a highly male industry.[36] By this time, fistsfuls of women worked in the Castle Valley mines: Shirley Haycock, the initial pioneer; followed by others including Ann Byerley, Fay Hall, Joy Huitt, Elnora Clark,

Carolyn Booker, and Judy Franco. In 1981, these last six women formed an organizing committee for female coal miners and affiliated with the nationally active Coal Employment Project, founded in 1977 in eastern Tennessee. By the 1980s, the percentage of women coal miners had increased nationally from .001 percent in 1973, to 11.4 percent in 1979, retreating to 8.7 percent in 1980 (still amounting to 3,600 women) due to layoffs of the least senior miners as the economy constricted. In 1985, the National Conference of Women Miners met in Price. Former state senator Frances Farley, whose three uncles were injured in the Missouri coal mines (two fatally), delivered one of the keynote speeches and chatted with the lady miners. Price's Ann Byerley told Farley she chose mining after a divorce, leaving her with two children and a pile of unpaid bills. When she started in the mines in 1980, she reported, "there was more flippancy, rudeness, and downright harassment on the part of men toward women miners." In 1983, as the downturn began, however, the younger men got laid off under mine seniority rights, and the miner's average age rose from twenty-two to thirty. "Byerley finds men over 30 to be more respectful of women," added Farley.[37] To learn how to confront harassers, conference attendees heard from Sunnyside's John Medina, formerly head of the Castle Valley chapter of SOCIO and now anti-discrimination director for the Utah State Industrial Commission. Other speakers addressed women's achievements and their ongoing campaign for parental leave for family emergencies such as care of a seriously ill child. Inevitably, speakers such as the UMWA secretary-treasurer referred to the recent Wilberg Mine disaster, where miner Nanette Wheeler was among the twenty-seven killed, the only woman to die in the mine fire and the sixth killed underground in the nation.[38]

The Wilberg Mine tragedy, still so much on people's minds, had flared just six months earlier, on December 19, 1984. Then, fire had broken out 5,000 feet from the entrance and 1,800 feet below the surface. As the smoke thickened, trapped miners had struggled blindly through the darkening tunnels, shouldering breathing apparatus—when they could find them—and affixing the attached nose-clips. Kenneth Blake, wearing his safety equipment which provided one good hour of oxygen, headed for the mine opening. In the smoky darkness, he soon ran into three or four other miners, halted by the growing fire. Then Leroy (Tom) Hersh appeared out of the inky blackness. At sixty, the oldest of the trapped miners, Hersh "maybe knew something I didn't" remembered Blake, who followed him into a dog-leg tunnel. Groping their way, the men got separated. Blake finally came through a mandoor (an exit provided for miners) into a current of fresh air and eventually emerged through the snow-covered portal. He was astonished to find that no one else had come out of the burning mine.[39]

Twenty-seven people remained underground, trapped inside the Fifth Right section where the fire raged. Atypically, company men counted among them, because the crew was attempting to set a world's record for tonnage

The Wilberg mine disaster of December 1984 brought widespread sorrow to Castle Valley as twenty-seven people died in the mine fire. Here, smoke billows out of the portal (as it did for days), visible for miles around Orangeville. Courtesy of the Emery County Archives.

produced in twenty-four hours on longwall operation (a large, sophisticated cutting machine). As all of Castle Valley prayed for the miners' welfare, Emery Mining officials alleged that those missing could have barricaded themselves in a safe haven underground. Hope slowly strangled as repeated rescue attempts failed to quell the fire and rescuers found only bodies, not survivors. The safe haven idea collapsed as fireballs shot from the mine portals, hampering rescue efforts. By December 23, all but two bodies had been located (which could only be removed a year later when the mine had cooled). The entire valley spent a grim Christmas. Many churches—Catholic, Greek Orthodox, and others—took up special collections for the families of the deceased. A huge community memorial ceremony on December

26 made front-page news as far away as Washington, D.C. Emery Mining sealed off all entryways to stifle the fire, and Castle Valley faced the numbing reality that its economy—already weakened in the 1981 recession—would soon hit bottom. Emery County's workforce had already dropped from over 8,400 to 3,300; Wilberg employed fifty percent of those left, and the connected Deer Creek and Des-Bee-Dove mines employed thirty percent more. Official investigations of possible arson followed, conducted by the federal Mines Safety and Health Administration (MSHA), the Emery County Sheriff's Office, and the FBI. In 1987, MSHA investigators finally pinpointed the source of the fire as an underground air compressor. Emery Mining officials revealed that no updated emergency training had been provided in years; no safety training included longwalls, and that the most recent evacuation and firefighting plan had been submitted in 1974 by its corporate predecessor, the Peabody Coal Company. While no criminal charges resulted, in 1990 a jury declared UP&L and Emery Mining negligent, and therefore responsible for the loss of twenty-seven lives. They became liable for millions of dollars in fines. By then, as with all former Castle Valley mine disasters, new federal regulations for fireproofing helped improve the safety of surviving miners.[40] Meanwhile, in the weeks immediately following the tragedy, counselors aided residents dealing with grief. One remarked on an almost "visible cloud of gloom" over Castle Valley. "But," he added, "people in the Carbon-Emery area have an ability to draw together in time of trouble and to support one another."[41]

The Wilberg Mine disaster also resulted in new MSHA regulations for a so-called two-entry system of mining, demanding a review of those mines which had only two entries into their workings. This new directive adversely affected the double-entry Kaiser mines at Sunnyside, which already had number of difficulties. In 1987, Kaiser declared Chapter 11 reorganizational bankruptcy, eventually laying off over 200 employees while it sought a new buyer for various properties. These included the Sunnyside mines, untapped coal leases, a longwall machine, its coal-washing plant at Wellington, and the Carbon County Railway, which it had acquired in 1984 and 1985 when it bought the Columbia (Horse Canyon) mines from U.S. Steel. After a year of complicated negotiations with other corporations and the bankruptcy court, in 1989, the Colorado-based Sunnyside Reclamation and Salvage Company beat out BP American (British Petroleum American) to acquire the bulk of this property. Only half the previous workforce was called back, but when the first eighty-car, 8,000–ton coal train left Sunnyside that March, the UMWA women's auxiliary held a grand celebration and attached a festive banner to the train's engine. As the *Sun Advocate* reported, the event "was a sign not only of rebirth to the mine, but to the entire East Carbon community."[42]

Even with the mines' reopening, poverty still haunted the Sunnyside area, formally incorporated as East Carbon City in 1973. A San Diego newspaper described streets containing boarded-up homes with weeds and desert plants in the yards, sometimes separated by broken-down autos and rusting mobile homes. But by 1993, it held one main attraction for that southern California city: it took some of San Diego's trash. Since September 1992, rails that had previously carried coal trains allowed everything but hazardous and radioactive waste to be hauled hundreds of miles to a 2,400–acre waste dump with a projected 30–40 year lifespan opened just west of East Carbon City. The town's mayor, Paul Clark, avidly cooperated with the East Carbon Development Corporation (ECDC), originally founded by a group of Utah businessmen, to woo trash from places as far away as Boston Harbor. Opposition coalesced into a group called CAN (Citizens Awareness Now), but, although they were able to force a referendum on the landfill, they could not stop it. While environmentalists complained that this waste hauling once again allowed richer communities to control more poverty-stricken areas, East Carbon received fifty cents a ton for garbage collected, accepted a minimum of 400 tons daily (especially from ten northern Utah towns), kept East Carbon High School open, and provided scholarships for the seventeen of its twenty-nine graduates in 1992 who went on for further education. By 1993, sixty percent of ECDC belonged to USPCI, Inc., a subsidiary of the Union Pacific Railroad. This acquisition was hardly surprising; by then, trains all over America hauled waste from New York to Illinois and Georgia, from Seattle to rural Oregon, from New Jersey to Virginia, and, of course, from San Diego to Sunnyside. By August 30, 1995, the ECDC landfill had accepted two million tons of trash.[43]

Castle Valley concerns for its ecological future fit right in with America's twenty-first century environmental debate. According to historian Daniel Yergin, the first global environmental awareness wave, born in America, concentrated on clean air and water. The second focused on stopping nuclear power, especially after the explosion of the Chernobyl reactor in the Soviet Ukraine in 1986. The third, he wrote, "concerns every environmental hazard from the depletion of the tropical rain forests to the disposal of waste products. . . . [A]t the top of the concerns are the consequences of hydrocarbon combustion—smog and air pollution, acid rain, global warming, ozone depletion."[44] Concern did not necessarily translate into improvement. When nations met in 1997 to forge the Kyoto protocol regarding global warming, not only did the United States not sign, the UMWA—concerned about members' employment—came out publicly against it, claiming it would cost two million jobs.[45]

By that time, lack of coal mining jobs preoccupied all of Castle Valley. In many ways, this uncertainty tightened when a host of major extractors converged on the area, in the frantic spate of mergers that accompanied oil deregulation and wildly fluctuating international events of the 1980s and 1990s. In 1980, for example, Tower Resources incorporated and began acquiring mines along the Book Cliffs north of Price and in Crandall Canyon.

A subsidiary of foreign-owned Andalex, by 1996 Tower had become "one of Utah's top coal exporters," according to Price's *Sun-Advocate*, finding markets world-wide. Likewise, from 1980–1982 Coastal States Energy Corporation, a subsidiary of Getty Oil Company, developed the Skyline Mine above Scofield in a joint venture with Utah Fuel Company, covering a lease area of some 6,400 acres in Carbon and Emery Counties. The 1982 recession slowed construction, and when Texaco bought out Getty in 1984, Coastal States purchased Getty's fifty percent. In 1993, Coastal States, now with its western headquarters in Salt Lake City, also acquired the old Soldier Creek Mine northeast of Wellington, originally located by William and Leonard Shield. By the mid-1980s a host of other major corporations had shifted back and forth through Castle Valley, including American Electric Power, Quaker State Oil Company, Atlantic Richfield Coal Company (ARCO), Continental Oil Company, and several more. Despite the arrival of all these giants, by 1998 Carbon County employment had declined.[46] In short, Castle Valley's mines increasingly belonged to fewer and fewer, and bigger and bigger, international energy or mining corporations. These companies cannibalized each other, mined more coal with machines, employed fewer miners, and gutted the coal veins as quickly as possible to shore up share prices and prevent hostile takeovers. By 1996, Utah coal production had reached an all-time high of almost twenty-eight million tons (as compared to the seemingly phenomenal output of over seven million tons just two decades earlier).[47] Experts informed coal industry officials that a thirty-year supply remained underground throughout the state, one-third of which remained in Castle Valley. Optimists argued that up to sixty years of coal remained, but that estimate allegedly depended on the ability to "mine down to [a vein] four feet high and under cover 3,000 feet thick. That just won't happen," stated Coastal States executive Vernal Mortenson. Even considering Utah's estimated 10.6 billion tons under the Wasatch Plateau, and the 3.93 billion tons in the Book Cliffs, given environmental, economic, and other factors, only 1.6 billion tons could be actually mined. Some major state reserves remained off-limits due to environmental laws, particularly the huge Kaiparowits deposit located inside the newly-created Grand Staircase-Escalante National Monument.[48] Within a single remaining lifetime, Castle Valley coal mines might close down for good.

With so much global uncertainty in oil and coal, the United States took a harder look at natural gas. By 1996, officials at UP&L (now acquired by PacifiCorp) worried that utility deregulation and a cheaper process using natural gas to burn coal would cripple them economically before their power plants reached their 2020 projected closing date.[49] In the meantime, coal's great competitor, natural gas—specifically coal bed methane—had been discovered in Castle Valley. As early as 1980, a Texas-based geophysical crew had surveyed the area around Kenilworth, using a ground vibrating technique previously employed in the known oil and gas fields in

Wyoming, Kansas, and California, among other places. Other companies had already partially mapped the huge Overthrust Belt, a geological feature formed by the long-ago collision of two giant land masses, driving one thousands of feet above the other. Described as "a 40 to 50–mile wide strip that snakes its way from Alaska to Mexico, through Canada, Idaho, Montana, Wyoming, Utah, Nevada, and Arizona," its creation frequently left ancient surface rocks 5,000 to 10,000 feet below the present surface. As of 1980, parts of it were known to contain oil and gas deposits, but no one knew for sure about Castle Valley.[50] Development of these deposits took on some of the air of a free-for-all, although, in 1982, Congress passed the Federal Oil and Gas Royalty Management Act requiring stringent record-keeping and cooperation with the states, and set sanctions for violations of royalty payment provisions, all under supervision of the Department of the Interior. Subsequent events, including problems with bidding procedures, lack of federal inspectors, and Interior Department non-cooperation suggest that these requirements have not adequately been met.[51]

Development certainly boomed. In the 1960s, companies sank eighteen wells in Castle Valley, followed by a handful of others in the 1980s. At the time, in order to release the gas, water had to be removed from the coal, although water production decreased as gas production increased. A new process called reverse osmosis eventually allowed for salt removal, creating usable water out of Castle Valley's notoriously alkaline subsoil.[52] Further energy developments surged in the 1990s, as engineers refined coalbed methane gas extraction technology. Late in 1995, the U.S. Forest Service began considering new gas drilling applications from two outside corporations on the Manti National Forest. Down in the valley, residents debated the spacing of wells, their noise, and environmental impacts. In September 1995, one of Texaco's exploratory gas wells four miles west of Orangeville caught fire, its flames leaping fifty feet into the air as the ground vibrated for several hundred feet around the well. An Orangeville resident went out the following night and saw "the flame [on] Horn Mountain . . . the whole mountainside flickering in a bright orange light." The fire was doused the following day, and a company spokesman explained that flares sometimes occur when compressed-air drillers hit a natural gas pocket.[53] Two weeks later, an editorial questioned the comfort of "living near a full-blown gas field. . . . Residents close to the wells tell horror stories of drilling taking place after dark and air releases coming from the wells in the middle of the night."[54]

Company officials tried to quiet their concerns. With their persuasion, by the end of 1996, Castle Valley housed "the single largest petroleum project ever in the history of Utah," according to the Utah state geologist. Prospects and wells dotted the so-called Ferron (Sandstone) Fairway, eighty miles long and some ten to fifteen miles wide, stretching all along the Castle Valley corridor from Price to Ferron. The methane gas, embedded in coal seams ten to forty feet thick, could potentially support 3,200 gas wells. Each well promised an economic life of twenty years, with an estimated thirty-year lifespan for the entire field. In 1996, River Gas and Texaco sunk wells; Anadarko Petroleum Corporation joined them by 1997, leasing extractive rights from the federal government and a host of private owners. Leases on state-held school trust land generated hundreds of thousands of dollars for Utah, beginning to rival the old coal lease funds. This increased valuation even led to unusual state litigation over coal land ownership by 2004.[55] Echoing this renewed interest, in 2003 President George W. Bush's administration began targeting much of the Intermountain West as a new sort of "American arsenal," and instructed his agencies to expedite oil and natural gas drilling in such archaeologically sensitive areas as Nine Mile Canyon. Even before this recent incentive for energy companies, dozens of grasshopper wells rhythmically rocked all along the Huntington-Price road, and visitors to once-quiet landscapes like Pinnacle Peak could no longer escape the insidious whine and metallic thumps of continuously operating pumps.[56]

While the old, extractive, boom-and-bust cycle began again, Castle Valley officials sought economic alternatives. The area had become "Castle Country" on the state's tourist maps, and, given its unique geology, paleontology, and history, residents more actively sought tourists. In 1997, the *Advocate* announced as front-page news: "Tourism rapidly becoming key driving economic force." A recent meeting of the Colorado Plateau Forum (covering Utah, New Mexico, Arizona, and Colorado) had attracted participants like Emery County Commissioner Kent Petersen, who stated, "Whether we want it or not, we have tourism in the San Rafael Swell." Carbon County Travel Bureau director Kathy Hanna added, "Tourism . . . gives us something besides energy production to rely on."[57] Thanks to impressive natural beauty and agressive marketing, throughout Utah, tourism was booming. Between 1975–1985, income from tourism rose twenty-seven percent, then doubled between 1981–1986. In 1986 alone Utah earned almost two billion tourist dollars—over half the income generated by all the coal, oil, and uranium production that same year.[58]

Consequently, Castle Valley energetically pursued the tourist dollar. By the twenty-first century, a partial list of local events included the St. Patrick's Day Parade, San Rafael Bike Festival, Nine Mile Canyon tours, Green River Friendship Cruise, Scofield Pleasant Valley Days, Wellington Pioneer Days and Rodeo, Greek Festival Days, Castle Valley Pageant, Price International Days, Ferron Peach Days, Green River Melon Days, Labor Day Parade (one of the few left in the nation), and the Electric Light Parade in Helper, now Utah's "Christmas Town."[59] Virtually the whole valley got involved in one way or another. The Helper City Council and numerous citizen volunteers developed a River Parkway, eventually intended to connect with a non-motorized trail up Spring Canyon, formally dedicated in 1996. Unfortunately, due to restoration by the state's Division of Oil, Gas, and Mining, the

This watermelon on wheels has helped has helped publicize Green River's Melon Days since the 1950s, a tribute not only to Castle Valley's agrarian heritage, but to its continuing appeal. Courtesy of Emery County Archives.

canyon lost its old coal camp structures despite community protests and the publishing of a tour guide to these abandoned towns. At least Cyprus Plateau and its new partners, American Electric Power and Blackhawk Coal, donated to Carbon County twenty acres of Spring Canyon cliff face, called the Indian Rock Climbing Ledges, now the area's only developed rock climbing site. Further west, to lure backpackers, mountain bikers, and equestrians, Manti Forest personnel created the Castle Valley Ridge Trail System stretching from Clear Creek to Huntington Canyon. They also prepared an Energy Loop Tour into Emery County, where the Hunter Plant gives tours. Golf lured people to the valley to play at the Millsite course just west of Ferron, or, for a while, on the five-hole course at East Carbon. In 1996, the Carbon County Club, just north of Price, expanded its golf course to eighteen holes, although the former owner retained trail rights, resulting in hundreds of sheep delaying golf carts on occasion. The Cleveland Lloyd Dinosaur Quarry Visitors' Center continued upgrading, particularly after 1996, when an unprecedented burglary of real dinosaur bone (not casts) led to tightened security and other improvements. In 1997, after six years of planning, BLM officials, local landowners, the Carbon County Travel Bureau, and a host of local residents cooperated in building a Nine Mile Canyon recreation site with tourist facilities and road-side guides for those interested in historic buildings and prehistoric rock art. At the far southern reaches of Emery County, Goblin Valley State Park advertised sandstone goblins that everyone could climb, as well as a state-of-the-art photovoltaic system to provide electricity in the rangers' cabins and heat water for the park restrooms. In 1996, Emery became the first Utah county with its own web page, brainchild of internet-savvy Wesley Curtis, local rural development specialist.[60]

But there was more to Castle Valley's self-promotion than some slick, facile soft-sell. Its history held too much tragedy for that, and plenty of local people remembered the bad times, including stone mason Harry Liapis. For years, he dreamt of erecting grand monuments to commemorate local mine disasters. Liapis spoke with metal artist Gary Prazen, who had started as a skilled welder and moved on to create magnificent bronze statues. For example, Prazen's first bronze, a statue of John Wayne as Rooster Cogburn, was the last artwork approved by Wayne before he died. By 1980, Prazen had established his own foundry and gallery in Spring Glen, where he eventually saw life-size bronzes through every step of the lost wax process. Liapis, who had built numerous local rock walls and a several-ton picnic table and benches by the Price underpass, had learned stone cutting from his Greek immigrant father. At one time, Castle Valley had numerous stonemasons, particularly among the Italian immigrants—men like John Biscardi, the Seppi brothers, and one-armed Ross Gigliotti, who, with his father Felice (or Franklin), had hauled rock down from the ledges on stoneboats. The Gigliottis used their stone at Martin (just north of Helper) to build a combined service station and general store, allegedly the first convenience store in the nation. But, by 1985, all the traditional ashlar masons were gone except for Liapis and another Greek immigrant's son who had moved to Salt Lake City. Creating a work that still draws curious tourists, Liapis and Prazen collaborated on a monument erected in October 1987 near the mouth of Price Canyon along Highway 50 and 6, honoring those who died in the 1924 Castle Gate mine explosion. Attendees at the formal installation included an honor guard, friends and families of those killed in the explosion, and two members of the original rescue teams, Stanley Harvey and Thomas Hilton. Three weeks later, Liapis ceremoniously helped unveil another massive red sandstone and bronze plaque in Scofield recognizing those killed in the Winter Quarters mine disaster. On Price's Main Street, Prazen unveiled their third and last collaboration honoring Castle Valley immigrants in 1989, a year after Liapis's untimely death.[61]

Others who remembered past tragedies included Scofield's Ann Helsten Carter, a descendant of one of the rescue workers at the Winter Quarters mine disaster. In February 1999, she remarked to her husband, Durwood (Woody) Carter that the following year would mark the disaster's centennial. She suggested replacing the old wooden markers tottering over the victims' graves, their painted-on names fading fast in the snows and sun of Scofield. They contacted Dr. Craig Fuller of the USHS, and, from there, a simply cemetery spruce-up mushroomed into a major international commemoration. Scofield neighbors Bill and Marilyn Nielsen put hundreds of miles on their new pickup, checking Colorado burial sites of victims; Paul and Linda Helsten arranged for the reprint of J. W. Dilley's 1900 *History of the Scofield Mine Disaster*, originally written to raise money for families of the victims and long out of print. The two Castle Valley newspapers cooperated in creating a thirty-two-page commemorative booklet which included a list of the ten worst mining accidents to date in Castle Valley: the first and worst at Winter Quarters, 1900; the second at Castle Gate in March 1924; five men killed at Rains in September 1924; twenty-five dead, including three rescue workers, at Standardville in February 1930; two months later, five men killed in a New Peerless explosion; eight dead at Kenilworth in March 1945; the following May, twenty-three killed at Utah Fuel's Sunnyside mine; four men dead at Spring Canyon in January 1958; nine at Hardscrabble Mine, Spring Canyon, in December 1963, and the Wilberg Disaster of December 19, 1984, that killed twenty-seven miners. This continuing loss of life meant that many, many people locally and elsewhere could relate to the Winter Quarters story. Consequently, countless groups and individuals lent a hand in preparation and on May 1, 2000, an estimated 1,800 people flocked to the tiny town of Scofield. They heard descendants of the victims, historians, religious leaders, and the Consul General of Finland (flown in from Los Angeles) speak about the tragedy and its effects. Flags of all the nations of the dead fluttered in the wind. Visitors could view a photo exhibit and professional video, take tours of the mine area, and record their own oral histories and family stories. Major Utah newspapers reported the commemoration and the unprecedented turnout.[62]

Castle Valley's coal industry again made state news in 2003 and 2004, when workers at the Co-op Mine near Huntington struck over their right to unionize. *Salt Lake Tribune* reporters Mike Gorrell and Rhina Guidos broke the story on October 12, 2003, with the tale of Bill Estrada, who for a year had dug coal for less than $6 an hour. When he tried to organize a union, he claimed, the Co-op Mine fired him, allegedly for falsifying a safety inspection record. Around seventy other miners, mostly recently immigrated Hispanics, joined him on the picket line at the base of Huntington Canyon. They protested exploitative conditions, defective and dangerous machinery, lack of health-care benefits and training, and low wages. Backed by the faith-based Utah Jobs With Justice and the Disabled Rights Action Committee, in 2004 the protests spread to several others of the 160 businesses (worth an estimated $150 million) owned by the 1,200–member polygamous Kingston clan, Co-op's owners. The polygamists themselves, an inbred group firmly repudiated by the LDS Church, were originally exposed by a 1998 indictment and subsequent conviction for incest of one of the patriarchs who forced a sixteen-year-old niece to become his fifteenth wife. In January 2004, another male family member was convicted of felony incest for similar behavior. As this book goes to press, the strike remains unresolved, but, once again, Castle Valley events highlight historic issues, this time of polygamy, of immigrants seeking better lives in the mines, and of union organizing.[63]

Other issues also spurred Castle Valley controversy in the twenty-first century. An increasing influx of visitors catalyzed public debate about

competing land use and potential wilderness designation, a national pre-
occupation ever since the passage of the 1964 Wilderness Act. This legislation honored preexisting federal leasing and mining until 1983, but
then restrictions tightened in an attempt to preserve, untouched, approximately four percent of the American land mass.[64] Of course, what other
people called wilderness has always been Castle Valley's back yard. Many
people still go Eastering, and most hunt, fish, hike, or camp in the nearby desert and mountains. In fact, by the late twentieth century, students
got college credit for wilderness experiences. About 1980, the College
of Eastern Utah developed a Wilderness Program as part of the regular
curriculum, meshing classes in the sciences and humanities with faculty-
supervised backpacking expeditions and river runs. Under drama professor Lee Johnson, the college eventually operated its own river running
company, possibly the only arrangement of its kind in the nation.[65] While
students studied wilderness first-hand, the first Utah-sponsored Wilderness Bill failed in Congress in 1995. A flurry of others followed and failed.
In response, in 1997, Emery County officials devised the idea of a Western
Heritage Park to include a national conservation area on the San Rafael
Swell and a national heritage area for towns along the Wasatch Plateau.
Officials invited Carbon County to join them, to highlight local events and
vistas, including:

> ...natural history and wildlife such as the big horn sheep management
> area being proposed on Sids Mountain; dinosaur sites such as the Cleve-
> land Lloyd Dinosaur Quarry, the CEU Prehistoric Museum and the Mu-
> seum of the San Rafael Swell; the Ancient Ones, Fremont Indian ruins and
> rock art sites; trails, such as the Walker Trail and Spanish Trail; cowboys,
> Sid's Leap, Swasey Cabin and other outlaw and pioneer locations; and the
> nuclear age, which would include mining (uranium and coal) and power
> generation locations. Those sites could include Temple Mountain, local
> coal mines, and the three power plants.[66]

Much of the impetus for Emery County's continuing effort (with or without
the rest of Castle Valley) grew from increasingly raucous debate over the future of the San Rafael Swell, one of a number of Utah areas under study for
potential federal Wilderness designation. In early 2003, the Sierra Club's
widely-circulated magazine featured the Swell in its full-color cover story,
stressing the damage done to nature by off-road vehicles.[67] In response, a
letter dated February 2003 appeared on the Emery County website, solicit-
ing the public's comments and ideas for continuing to pursue Heritage
Area status after "three [unsuccessful] attempts to have Congress designate
the County as a National Heritage area."[68]

Castle Valley's current goal—to attract "heritage tourists," identified by
state officials as the number one spenders—mirrors a nationwide trend of

visiting historic places. According to historian John A. Jackle, the uses of a "romanticized past" included "bind[ing] the tourist closer to the national body politic," teaching lessons to children, evoking heroism, and enshrining forebears and their lifeways. "Landmarks rooted in the past," he wrote, "enabled tourists not only to locate themselves in space, but . . . in time, as well."[69] On the other hand, most recent studies of tourism point to its unintended consequences, described by historian Hal Rothman as a "devil's bargain." He cautioned that "places devolved into caricatures of their original identities, passing from . . . unique heritage . . . to colorful backdrop for . . . visitors [who] understood themselves to be" at the center of the tourist experience.[70] Finally, business professor Patrick Long recently warned, "No one can or should presume to know the exact outcomes of tourism development; however, a community must continually focus on the degree to which it is willing to alter its character—its soul—to attract and satisfy visitor needs."[71] In 2003, eighty-nine-year-old rancher Owen Price, a veteran of the uranium boom, talked to journalists publicizing the Swell. He recalled his youth, when he rounded up wild horses where I-70 now bisects the Swell, and his mother's admonition when he left the house: "You better be back home for Thanksgiving." Lee Jeffs, a fourth-generation rancher on the Swell's north end, lamented "the destruction of fences and grazing habitat by illegal use of all-terrain vehicles. . . . 'I don't think there's much future for ranching out there,' Jeffs said."[72]

A different confrontation, this time between historic preservation and federal energy policy, spilled into national news in mid-2004. On May 24, the National Trust for Historic Preservation named Utah's Nine Mile Canyon one of the eleven most endangered historic places in the entire nation. Identifying Nine Mile Canyon as "a world and national treasure," Trust president Richard Moe called the canyon, "the world's longest art gallery" for its astonishing expanse of native rock art. The National Trust noted that the canyon contained "more than 10,000 images . . . [as well as] many historic sites—including stagecoach stations, settlers' cabins, ranches, and iron telegraph poles installed by the famed 19th-century Buffalo Soldiers—that stand as reminders of the area's pioneer history." Already impacted by tourism and recreation, the canyon now faces destruction from ongoing energy development. The race for increased oil and gas supplies "could transform the historic landscape into an industrial zone with heavy industrial trucks rumbling through the narrow canyons in close proximity to fragile Native American rock art. Currently proposed projects for energy development and exploration would result in tens of thousands of trips by these trucks, in addition to numerous wells being drilled." The dust alone would radically erode fragile cultural remains. Consequently, the National Trust for Historic Preservation championed "raising public awareness, planning and increased program funding," thereby bringing this fascinating rim of Castle Valley to new national attention.[73]

While new pressures for change loom over Castle Valley, those who call it home continue to carry its unique identity with them as a turtle carries its shell. In addition to being a concrete, physical place, by the turn of the twenty-first century, Castle Valley had become the psychological home of those who left. For example, the youngest judge ever named to the Utah bench, Sharon Peacock McCully, admitted in 1986, "When people ask me where I'm from, and it has been sixteen years since I've lived in Orangeville, I tell them I'm from Emery County. It seems like more of a place to be from than Salt Lake, you know." She also reflected on the Wilberg Disaster, when, home for Christmas, she had seen the black smoke pouring out of the mine from her sister's back window. "The whole town could have been holding hands, as far as the feeling that was there . . . [and] Carbon County was surely just as affected."[74] Edward Geary, long a resident of Provo, came back for a special lecture in his native Huntington and spoke of "we" and "us" as though he had never left. He observed that "nothing is long ago in Castle Valley. . . . We have homesteaders' cabins in the shadow of giant power plants, empty chicken coops at the back of trailer courts, idle hay derricks standing on their long legs like gaunt giants beside highways busy with commuter traffic." Surveying the economic scene, he added, "the Carbon County coal mines have always contributed largely to the economic well-being of Emery County. At first, [Emery County] people would spend part of the year in the coal camps and part at home on the farm. Later, they lived entirely in our communities and commuted to work, mostly to Hiawatha but some as far as Sunnyside . . . [still following] the seasonal rhythms of an agrarian way of life."[75] More recently, the traffic has reversed, as plenty of Carbon County residents work in the Emery County power plants. Paul Turner, a child of Sunnyside now resident in Richfield, wrote about a recent visit: "The houses are gone, as is the barn, the school house, the tipple, the bath house, the amusement hall, the tennis court, the depot, the store, and the post office. But the memories those of us who lived there have are as vivid and enduring as though Sunnyside was still alive."[76] Steven D. Bunnell, for decades resident in Spokane and Salt Lake City, even scripted audiocassettes of stories based, in part, on his Price childhood. Such tales included "The Birth of My Values" and "My One Real Adventure," which described youthful shenanigans around the Bunnell garage and "borrowed" cars that would have caused a lot of trouble, had he ever been caught. He even offered fellow Castle Valley aficionados a newsletter.[77] Finally, former Latuda teacher and school principal Mary Rynio thought about her childhood and youth in Castle Gate, Helper, and later life up Spring Canyon, where by the 1990s, nothing but ghosts remained. She closed her eyes, imagining "the tipple loading coal cars, dogs barking, people playing softball, children playing, lawns being mowed, mothers hanging laundry out." Proud to have been part of "the good old days," she added, "Thanks for the memories."[78] Now very much connected to the larger world, Castle Valley people feel its changes, but remember who they are and what makes them a unique island in the mainstream. In the face of Castle Valley's consistently uncertain future, its past sustains us all.

# Notes

## Preface

1.　David A. Hollinger, "The Historian's Use of the United States and Vice Versa," in *Rethinking American History in a Global Age*, ed. Thomas Bender (Berkeley: University of California Press, 2002), 383; Joseph A. Amato, *Rethinking Home* (Berkeley: University of California Press, 2002), 191.

## Introduction

1.　John Donne, "For Whom The Bell Tolls," *Poems That Live Forever*, comp. Hazel Felleman, (Garden City, NY: Doubleday & Company, Inc., 1965), 300.

2.　Dr. Philip Frank Notarianni referred to Carbon County, the northern part of Castle Valley, as Utah's "industrialized island." His concept has been extended here to encompass the entire valley. See Philip F. Notarianni, ed., *Carbon County: Eastern Utah's Industrialized Island* (Salt Lake City: Utah State Historical Society, 1981).

3.　See, for example, Thomas Bender, ed., *Rethinking American History in a Global Age* (Berkeley: University of California Press, 2002) and Patricia Nelson Limerick, *Something in the Soil* (New York: W. W. Norton & Co., 2000).

## Chapter One

1.　Oliver Huntington, quoted in Andrew Jenson, "The Elk Mountain Mission," *Utah Geological and Historical Magazine* 4 (1913): 191. This is a partial typescript of the journal of Oliver B. Huntington, secretary for the Elk Mountain Mission of the LDS Church. The source of the name "Castle Valley" has been lost to history, but it was obviously in common use in 1855 when Huntington made this journal entry.

2.　Francis J. Blumberg, "History of Helper," [Price] *News-Advocate*, 24 February 1921. This seventh-grader thanked "Messrs. Stovoll [sic: Stowell], Fitch and others" for their information.

3.　James Albert Jones, "A Story of the Settling of Huntington, Utah," privately printed, 1975, copy in possession of the author, 2.

4.　Alfred W. Crosby, "Virgin Soil Epidemics as a Factor in the Aboriginal Depopulation in America," *William and Mary Quarterly* 3 ser. 33 (April 1976): 289–99.

5.　Stella McElprang, comp., *Castle Valley: A History of Emery County* (Emery County Daughters of Utah Pioneers, 1949), 172.

6.　Wayne L. Wahlquist, ed., *Atlas of Utah* (Provo: Brigham Young University Press, 1981), 18.

7.    Price's Dr. J. Eldon Dorman popularized the term, "the backside of the
       Wasatch Front," indicating the less-than-important position of Castle Valley
       in Utah perceptions of the 1980s.
8.    Discoveries dating from 20–110 million years ago include new finds of the
       1990s: a new and unnamed brachiosaur, iguanodon, nodosaur, ankylosaur,
       *Utahraptor ostromaysi* (similar to the raptors in the movie *Jurassic Park*) and
       *Gastonia burgei,* named for the College of Eastern Utah's long-time curator,
       Don Burge. See pamphlets, CEU Prehistoric Museum.
9.    J. Eldon Dorman, ed., *The Archeology of Eastern Utah with Special Reference to
       the Fremont Culture* (Price: College of Eastern Utah Prehistoric Museum,
       1980), 15–21. This is a collection of all the previously-published articles on
       the subject, including David B. Madsen to J. Eldon Dorman, 18 April 1979,
       71–72; Polly Schaafsma, *Indian Rock Art of the Southwest* (Santa Fe: School
       of American Research, 1980), 179–81; Jesse D. Jennings, *Prehistory of Utah
       and the Eastern Great Basin* (Salt Lake City: University of Utah Press, 1973),
       184–206.
10.   Mae Grames Brown, "Biography of Albert James Grames," 3, unpublished
       typescript, copy in possession of the author.
11.   Owen McClenahan, *Utah's Scenic San Rafael* (Castle Dale, Utah: privately
       printed, 1986), 22.
12.   Charles L. Camp, "The Chronicles of George C. Yount—California Pioneer
       of 1826," *California Historical Quarterly* II (April 1923): 28. Although
       Orange Clark, the chronicler, refers to the area as "St. Joseph's Valley," his
       description of the route taken indicates that it is really Castle Valley. Those
       who agree with this interpretation include J. Cecil Alter, *Utah: The Storied
       Domain* (Chicago: American Historical Society, 1932), i, 23; Leland H.
       Creer, *The Founding of an Empire* (Salt Lake City: Bookcraft, 1947), 32; LeRoy
       R. Hafen and Ann W. Hafen, *The Old Spanish Trail* (Glendale, CA: Arthur H.
       Clark Co., 1954), 152.
13.   Herbert F. Bolton, *Pageant in the Wilderness* (Salt Lake City: Utah State
       Historical Society, 1950), gives the most complete account of their journey.
14.   Clifford Duncan, "The Northern Utes," in *A History of Utah's American
       Indians,* ed. Forrest S. Cuch (Salt Lake City: Utah Division of Indian Affairs
       and the Utah State Historical Society, 2000), 173–77. Ute spellings vary
       widely, even within the same piece. For example, on pages 176 and 177 of
       this work, the San Pitch are also listed as the Sanpits, the Tumpanawach
       additionally as the Timanogots, and so on. I have chosen the most common
       spellings based on the works consulted.
15.   Ibid., 182.
16.   Sondra Jones, "'Redeeming' the Indian: The Enslavement of Indian
       Children in New Mexico and Utah," *Utah Historical Quarterly* [hereafter
       *UHQ*] 67 (Summer 1999): 220–25; Creer, 28; Hafen and Hafen, 260, 83.
17.   Joseph J. Hill, "Spanish and Mexican Exploration and Trade Northwest from
       New Mexico into the Great Basin," *UHQ* 3 (January 1930): 16–17. See also
       the account in Joseph P. Sanchez, *Explorers Traders, and Slavers* (Salt Lake
       City: University of Utah Press, 1997), 99–100.
18.   Hafen and Hafen, 263–66; Sanchez, 101–2.
19.   Floyd A. O'Neil, "A History of the Ute Indians of Utah Until 1890" (Ph.D.
       diss., University of Utah, 1973), 16, 96–100; David J. Weber, *The Taos
       Trappers* (Norman: University of Oklahoma Press, 1971), 74–80.
20.   George R. Brooks, ed., *The Southwest Expedition of Jedediah S. Smith* (Glendale,
       CA: Arthur H. Clark, 1977), 47. Spelling and capitalization (or lack of it)
       reflects the original.

21. Hafen and Hafen, *Trail*, 94–97, 102, 170–71, 229, 198; McElprang, 182; James H. Knipmeyer, "The Denis Julien Inscriptions," *UHQ* 64 (Winter 1996): 52–69.

22. Kathryn L. MacKay, "Indian Culture c. 1840," in Wahlquist, 77; O'Neil, 21; Duncan, 184; Stephen P. Van Hoak, "Waccara's Utes: Native American Equestrian Adaptations in the Eastern Great Basin, 1776–1876," *UHQ* 67 (Fall 1999): 319–21.

23. Solomon Nunes Carvalho, *Incidents of Travel and Adventure in the Far West*, ed. and with an introduction by Bertram Wallace Korn (New York: Derby & Jackson, 1857; reprint, Philadelphia: The Jewish Publication Society of America, 1954), 266.

24. George William Beattie and Helen Pruitt Beattie, *Heritage of the Valley* (Pasadena: San Pasqual Press, 1939), 65–66.

25. Harlan Hague and David Langum, in *Thomas O. Larkin* (Norman: University of Oklahoma Press, 1990), effectively establish Larkin's role as President Polk's confidential agent (see especially pp. 3–5 and 126–30), but the nature of Pratt's commission is unknown.

26. Hafen and Hafen, 341–42, 358; Hubert Howe Bancroft, *History of California*, vol. 7 (San Francisco: The History Company, 1890), 223–24. The journal is published in full in Hafen and Hafen, 344–58, quote on 350.

27. Hafen and Hafen, 357.

28. Ibid., 358.

29. David L. Bigler, ed., *The Gold Discovery Journal of Azariah Smith* (Salt Lake City: University of Utah Press, 1990), 108.

30. Whitney R. Cross, *The Burned-Over District* (Ithaca, NY: Cornell University Press, 1950; reprint, New York: Harper Torchbooks, 1965).

31. The standard account is in "Joseph Smith, Jr.," *History of the Church of Jesus Christ of Latter-day Saints*, B. H. Roberts, ed., 7 vols., 2nd ed. rev. (Salt Lake City: Deseret Book Co., 1964), 1: Chs. 1–8. Much of this history, intermixed with theological revelations, is also found in *The Doctrine and Covenants* (1833, 35, 76; reprint, Salt Lake City: Church of Jesus Christ of Latter-day Saints, 1968), iii–47 [hereafter *D&C*].

32. *D&C*, 10:55–56, summer 1828. "Gentiles" by LDS definition encompasses all non-Mormons, including members of the Jewish faith.

33. Klaus J. Hansen, *Mormonism and the American Experience* (Chicago: University of Chicago Press, 1981), 139.

34. There are many versions of these events. A considered view by LDS authors is found in James B. Allen and Glen M. Leonard, *The Story of the Latter-day Saints* (Salt Lake City: Deseret Book Company, 1976), 53–215. The most balanced description describing violence on both sides is found in D. Michael Quinn, *The Mormon Hierarchy: Origins of Power* (Salt Lake City: Signature Books, 1994), especially 646–60.

35. A useful list of dates can be found in the annual LDS *Church Almanac*. I have used the Church of Jesus Christ of Latter-day Saints, 1991–1992 *Church Almanac* (Salt Lake City: Deseret News, 1990 [sic]), 282.

36. Robert Bruce Flanders, *Nauvoo: Kingdom on the Mississippi* (Urbana: University of Illinois Press, 1965), 330–32.

37. Quinn, 653.

38. Samuel Brannan, "Fragmentary remarks re: his expedition to California with the Mormons," c. 1878, California file, Henry E. Huntington Library, San Marino, California. See also Will Bagley, *Scoundrel's Tale* (Logan: Utah State University Press, 1999), 75–168.

39.  "Account of the Mormon colony landed in San Francisco 1846," California file, Huntington Library. It appears to be in the same handwriting as the "fragmentary remarks" attributed to Brannan. California in those days was a much larger area than the present state, as can also be seen from the account of Orville Pratt, previously cited. In the minds of many, it encompassed areas of Nevada, Utah, and possibly part of Arizona.

40.  Allen and Leonard, 233–34.

41.  Frank Esshom, *Pioneers and Prominent Men of Utah*, (Salt Lake City: Utah Pioneers Book Publishing Co., 1913; reprint, 1960), 126.

42.  Norma Baldwin Ricketts, *Historic Consumnes and the Slough House Pioneer Cemetery* (Salt Lake City: Daughters of Utah Pioneers, 1978), 7.

43.  Norma Baldwin Ricketts, *The Mormon Battalion: U. S. Army of the West 1846–1848* (Logan: University of Utah Press, 1996), 334–35 n. 8; idem, *Consumnes*, 7; Daniel Rhoads to Jesse Esrey [California, Spring of 1847], in Rhoads Family Papers, Bancroft Library, University of California, Berkeley, 5. The family name is spelled variously; I have adopted the spelling used by Caleb.

44.  David L. Bigler and Will Bagley, eds., *Army of Israel* (Spokane, WA: Arthur H. Clark Company, 2000).

45.  Bagley, 255–57; Ernest S. Horsley, "Historical Sketch of Price," MS 112, Jean M. Westwood Collection, Box 31, Fd. 1, Special Collections, Marriott Library, University of Utah, Salt Lake City, Utah, 15.

46.  Wimmer Family Group Records, LDS Church; Mary P. Winslow, "Mrs. Wimmer's Narrative of the First Piece of Gold Discovered In California, December, 1847," San Francisco *Daily Evening Bulletin*, 19 December 1874, reprinted in Rodman W. Paul, *The California Gold Discovery* (Georgetown, CA: The Talisman Press), 174–76. Sam Brannan also stated that the first piece of gold was given to Mrs. Wimmer (Weimer). It is now on display at the Bancroft Library, University of California, Berkeley.

47.  Hafen and Hafen, 315–39. The articles appear in Bagley, 258–62.

48.  Ricketts, *Consumnes*, 13–17, 56.

49.  Walter Colton, *Three Years in California* (Stanford: Stanford University Press, 1949), 272–314; "Daniel Rhoads," *History of Tulare County, California* (San Francisco: Wallace W. Elliot & Co., 1883), 180. Mead's presence is inferred from Sutter's complaint that all his workmen left.

50.  Ricketts, *Battalion*, 338 n. 12. The author gives no source for the amount of $17,000, but probably used a speech by Brigham Young, quoted in Leonard J. Arrington, *Great Basin Kingdom* (Cambridge, Mass.: Harvard University Press, 1958; reprint, Lincoln: University of Nebraska Press, 1966), 65–66. However, see Bancroft, *California*, vol. 6, 42–49. California's military governor, Col. Richard B. Mason, visited Mormon Island on July 5. He found about 4,000 miners at work and estimated the daily take at $30,000 to $50,000 "if not more," all of it taken with ease. Quoted in J. S. Holliday, *The World Rushed In* (New York: Simon and Schuster, 1981), 40.

51.  Eugene Campbell, *Establishing Zion* (Salt Lake City: Signature Books, 1988), 48, claims that the LDS Church actually authorized a "gold mission."

52.  Ricketts, *Consumnes*, 56; J. Kenneth Davies, "Thomas Rhoads, Forgotten Mormon Pioneer of 1846," *Nebraska History* 64, no. 1 (Spring 1983): 83; Arrington, 65, 441 n. 7. An account of a meeting with the Rhoades Party en route to Salt Lake City claims that Thomas displayed a hundred pounds of gold, which at $16 an ounce, would equal a total of $25,600. See William Wellington White, "An Autobiography," *Quarterly of the Society of California Pioneers*, 4, no. 4 (December 31, 1927): 208.

53. Davies, 83.
54. Col. Joseph M. Locke, quoted in Kate B. Carter, ed., *Our Pioneer Heritage*, vol. 9 (Salt Lake City: Daughters of Utah Pioneers, 1966). A similar version is reported in Arrington, 441, n.7.
55. Quoted in Arrington, 65–66.
56. *Church Almanac*, 45; Harold Schlinder, *Orrin Porter Rockwell* (Salt Lake City: University of Utah Press, 1983), 184; Eugene Edward Campbell, "A History of the Church of Jesus Christ of Latter-day Saints in California, 1846–1946" (Ph.D. diss., University of Southern California, 1952), 142–44.
57. Belle Harris Wilson, "History of Justus Wellington Seeley," LDS History Dept., Salt Lake City, 1; John Henry Evans, *Charles Coulsen Rich* (New York: The Macmillan Company, 1936), 180–83; Leroy R. Hafen and Ann W. Hafen, eds., *Journals of the Forty-niners, Salt Lake City to Los Angeles* (Glendale, CA: Arthur H. Clark Co., 1954), 296; Seely Family History, LDS History Dept.; David Seely, "Autobiographical Sketch," c. 1885, MS C-D 779, H. H. Bancroft Collection, University of California, Berkeley, 7; Mildred E. Brown, "Justus Wellington Seeley II," 1970, typescript, copy in possession of the author.
58. According to historian Klaus Hansen, a third "shadow government" in the highly secretive LDS Council of Fifty operated, with one hiatus, from the 1840s into at least the 1890s as a precursor of a literal, political "Kingdom of God" (ruled by Mormons) on earth. Klaus Hansen, *Quest for Empire* (Lansing, Mich.: Michigan State University Press, 1967; reprint, Lincoln: University of Nebraska Press, 1974).
59. Dale L. Morgan, *The State of Deseret* (published as vol. 8 of *UHQ*, 1940; reprint; Logan: Utah State University Press, 1987), 30–31, 92–96.
60. Richard V. Francavigilia and Jimmy L. Bryan, Jr., "'Are We Chimerical in the Opinion?' Visions of a Pacific Railroad and Westward Expansion before 1845," *Pacific Historical Review* 17 (May 2002): 179–202.
61. William H. Goetzmann, *Army Exploration in the American West, 1803–1863* (New Haven: Yale University Press, 1959), 286.
62. Quoted in Goetzmann, 218–19.
63. Goetzmann, 274–284.
64. Hafen and Hafen, *Trail*, 307.
65. James Schiel, *Journey Through the Rocky Mountains and the Humboldt Mountains to the Pacific Ocean* (1859), in Nolie Mumey, trans., *John Williams Gunnison* (Denver: Artcraft Press, 1955), 85.
66. Hafen and Hafen, *Trail*, 306–7.
67. Quoted in Charles T. Lipton, "Geology and Coal Resources of Castle Valley in Carbon, Emery, and Sevier Counties, Utah," *USGS Bulletin* 628 (Washington, D.C.: Government Printing Office, 1916), 9.
68. Schiel, in Mumey, 86.
69. See Sondra Jones, *The Trial of Don Pedro Leon Lujan* (Salt Lake City: University of Utah Press, 2000), especially 61–106; and Sanchez, 126–27.
70. Duncan, 188.
71. Van Hoak, 327–28.
72. Robert S. McPherson, "Ute Indians—Southern," in Allan Kent Powell, ed., *Utah History Encyclopedia*, (Salt Lake City: University of Utah Press, 1994), 609–11.
73. Schiel, in Mumey, 86.
74. Albert C. T. Antrei and Allen D. Roberts, *A History of Sanpete County* (Salt Lake City: Utah State Historical Society, 1999), 71–72. In the winter of 1849–50, already noted for its severity, over 700 Utes camped at Manti

helped save the handful of newly-arrived Mormon settlers. Less than four years later, that ratio had been reversed. See 26–27 and 70–72.

75. Carvalho, 309.

76. Goetzmann, 285; Brigham D. Madsen, "John Williams Gunnison" in Allan Kent Powell, ed., *Utah History Encyclopedia* (Salt Lake City: University of Utah Press, 1994), 241. Madsen notes that the attack was believed to be in retaliation for earlier destruction wreaked by white emigrants, but the whole incident is still controversial.

77. Carvalho, 167, 186–91.

78. Goetzmann, 286.

79. Eugene Campbell, in "Brigham Young's Outer Cordon—A Reappraisal," *UHQ* 41, no. 3 (Summer 1973): 220–53, questions the concept of an "outer cordon" that would protect the trails into Utah, a then-standard view of the reasons for this and other colonizing measures. Campbell's work makes the more modest proposal of simply holding the land. See particularly 221–26 and 230–31. See also Morgan.

80. Orange Seely, "Told by himself, History of Orange Seely, Sr.," unpublished typescript, LDS Church Archives, LDS Historical Department, Salt Lake City, Utah, 1; David R. Seely, "Sketch," MS in Beattie Collection, #54, Folder 91, Huntington Library, San Marino, California, 13; Beattie and Beattie, 66–67.

81. Charles S. Peterson, *Utah* (New York: W. W. Norton & Company, Inc., 1977), 43; Jenson, 189–95, quote on 191–92.

82. Charles S. Peterson, *Look to the Mountains: Southeastern Utah and the LaSal National Forest* (Provo: Brigham Young University Press, 1975), 12–15, 62–64; McElprang, 200; Thomas M. Rees, "Mormon Missionary Work Among the Western Indians," (Master's thesis, University of Utah, 1922), 39–46; Jenson, 198–200.

83. See "Ordinances of the State of Deseret" in Morgan, especially 141–42,147–48,158–59, 162–70.

84. Howard R. Lamar, *The Far Southwest, 1846–1912* (New York: Yale University Press, 1966), 332–38; Gustive O. Larson, *The "Americanization" of Utah for Statehood* (San Marino: Huntington Library, 1971), 17–18.

85. Cross, 221–22; Allen and Leonard, 389–90; Will Bagley, *Blood of the Prophets: Brigham Young and the Massacre at Mountain Meadows* (Norman: University of Oklahoma Press, 2002), 6–9, 68–72, 80–81; Juanita Brooks, *The Mountain Meadows Massacre* (Palo Alto, CA: Stanford University Press, 1950; new edition, Norman: University of Oklahoma Press, 1970), 57–58.

86. Campbell, *Zion*, 234–237.

87. Bagley, *Blood*, 188–94; Beattie and Beattie, 181, 237–48; Edward Leo Lyman, *San Bernardino* (Salt Lake City: Signature Books, 1996), 175–76.

88. The most thorough study to date is Bagley, *Blood*; the seminal work is Juanita Brooks.

89. Bagley, *Blood*, 290–319; W. H. Lever, *A History of Sanpete and Emery Counties* (Salt Lake City: Tribune Job Printing Company, 1898), 681; Nels Anderson, *Desert Saints* (Chicago: University of Chicago Press, 1942), 188.

90. Seely, "Sketch."

91. James S. Brown, *Life of a Pioneer* (Salt Lake City: George Q. Cannon & Sons, Co., 1900), 1. Some evidence, including first-hand accounts and later archaeological investigation, indicates that the bodies went unburied. See Bagley, *Blood*, 157–58, 193–94.

92. James Brown, 1.

93. E. Carmon Hardy, *Solemn Covenant* (Urbana: University of Illinois Press, 1992), 39–126.

94.  Letter from David R. Seeley to George Beattie, 7 April 1937, Beattie Collection #54.

95.  Wilson lists three: the two sisters of his late wife and the daughter of one. Those who accepted polygamy became wedded not only to additional women but to life in the Mormon Zion. During the nineteenth century, when a man's reputation was everything, polygamists could only be "respectable" if they remained in Utah. Men who left faced two possible varieties of condemnation. If they took their plural families, they would be regarded as bigamists, harem-keepers, or worse in the outside world. Much uglier names dogged their plural wives. If men left plural families behind, they would be reprobates who abandoned dependent wives and children.

96.  Leonard J. Arrington, Feramorz Y. Fox, and Dean L. May, *Building the City of God*, 2nd ed. (Urbana: University of Illinois Press, 1992), 66–67.

97.  James Brown, 2.

98.  Edwin Brown Firmage and Richard Collin Mangrum, *Zion in the Courts* (Urbana: University of Illinois Press, 1988), 131.

99.  Alvin Josephy, *The Civil War in the American West* (New York: Random House, 1991); S. Lyman Tyler, "Ute Indians along Civil War Communication Lines," *UHQ* 46 (Summer 1978): 251–61; Brigham D. Madsen, *Glory-Hunter* (Salt Lake City: University of Utah Press, 1990), 60–90.

100.  John Alton Peterson, *Utah's Black Hawk War* (Salt Lake City: University of Utah Press, 1998), 320–71, quote on p. 370.

101.  Ibid., 16–18, 80–122; Lever, 594.

102.  O. Seeley, 7.

103.  Pearl Tidwell, "Local History of Pioneer Days," [Price] *Carbon County News*, 30 January 1913. As noted in Antrei and Roberts, 80, Black Hawk War veterans and their children gathered for encampments into the 1920s. This early story by a descendent of Jefferson Tidwell, a captain in Seely's cavalry, therefore has special value.

104.  John Alton Peterson, 320–71; Jones, 5.

105.  B. H. Roberts, *A Comprehensive History of the Church of Jesus Christ of Latter-day Saints, Century I*, vol. 5 (Salt Lake City: LDS Church, 1930), 198–206; Robert N. Baskin, *Reminiscences of Early Utah* (privately published, 1914), 5, 171–72.

106.  Roberts, V, 198–206; Baskin, 28. One of his assailants has been identified as Mormon "enforcer," Bill Hickman. See Baskin, 37 and D. Michael Quinn, *The Mormon Hierarchy: Extensions of Power* (Salt Lake City: Signature Books, 1997), 245.

107.  Roberts, V, 225–27.

108.  Roberts, V, 236–37, 315; Madsen, *Glory Hunter*, 188–89.

109.  Quoted in Quinn, *Extensions*, 263.

110.  Arrington, Fox, and May, 15–133.

111.  Arrington, 241–48, 303; Lamar, 372–73; David Haward Bain, *Empire Express* (New York: Viking, 1999), 659–60.

112.  Arrington, 241–42.

113.  Bain, 659–67.

114.  Arrington, 280.

115.  Robert A. Athearn, *Union Pacific Country* (Chicago: Rand McNally & Co., 1971), 98–100; Maury Klein, *Union Pacific* (New York: Doubleday & Company, 1987), 353–56.

116.  John Wesley Powell, *Report on the Lands of the Arid Region of the United States*, Wallace Stegner, ed., (Washington [D.C.], 1879; reprint, Cambridge, MA: Belknap Press of Harvard University Press, 1962), 60.

117.  Ibid., 171.

## Chapter Two

1.    Arthur Ridgway, "Denver and Rio Grande Development of Physical Property in Chronological Narrative," 1 January 1921, MS 513, Box 45, filed after "1921" divider, 3. Denver & Rio Grande Collection.

2.    Frederick Jackson Turner, "The Significance of the Frontier in American History," reprinted in *Major Problems in the History of the American West*, ed. Clyde Milner II (Lexington, MA: D. C. Heath and Company, 1989), 7.

3.    Dee Anne Finken, *A History of the San Rafael Swell* (Boulder, CO: Western Interstate Commission for Higher Education, 1977), 22–23.

4.    Ridgway, 3.

5.    For just two examples, see Andy Adams, *The Log of a Cowboy* (Boston: Houghton Mifflin and Company, 1903; reprint, Lincoln: University of Nebraska Press, 1964) and Robert Dykstra, *The Cattle Towns* (New York: Alfred A. Knopf, 1968).

6.    Terry G. Jordan, *North American Cattle-Ranching Frontiers* (Albuquerque: University of New Mexico Press, 1993), 159–64, 213, 242–69.

7.    Finken, 19–20; Eva Westover Conover, *The History of George Henry Westover and His Family* (Salt Lake City: Family Descendants, 1981), 89. Another good list of early stockmen can be found in Stella McElprang, comp., *Castle Valley: A History of Emery County* (Emery County Daughters of Utah Pioneers, 1949), 39. The debate over who was "first" into Castle Valley still rages warmly. Since the first Euro-American arrivals were herders, not settlers, they left very few records. Consequently, this list results from several reminiscences. According to Edward Geary, *A History of Emery County* (Salt Lake City: Utah State Historical Society, 1996), 57 n. 50, "An inscription in Coal Wash with Joe Swasey's name plus the date 7 February 1875, suggests that the Swaseys were in Castle Valley during the winter of 1874–75."

8.    John L. Jorgensen, "A History of Castle Valley to 1890," (Master's thesis, University of Utah, 1955), 53.

9.    James Liddell, "The Cattle and Sheep Industry of Carbon County," in *Centennial Echoes from Carbon County*, ed. Thursey Jesson Reynolds (Salt Lake City: Daughters of Utah Pioneers, 1948), 51.

10.   Robert V. Hine and John Mack Faragher, *The American West* (New Haven: Yale University Press, 2000), 304–10.

11.   Geary, 50.

12.   Owen McClenahan, *Utah's Scenic San Rafael* (Castle Dale, Utah: privately published, 1986), 61; McElprang, 293.

13.   McClenahan, 15, 36, 90.

14.   William H. Goetzmann, *New Lands, New Men* (New York: Viking Penguin, Inc., 1986), 407.

15.   G. M. Wheeler, *USGS Surveys West of the 100th Meridian Annual Report for 1874*, 5, and *Final Report*, vol. 3, 1875, 277, 279.

16.   Charles T. Lipton, "Geology and Coal Resources of Castle Valley in Carbon, Emery, and Sevier Counties, Utah," *USGS Bulletin 628* (Washington, D.C.: Government Printing Office, 1916), 11; W. H. Lever, *A History of Sanpete and Emery Counties* (Salt Lake City: Tribune Job Printing Company, 1898), 594.

17.   McElprang, 175.

18.   Lever, 635.

19.   Turner, in Milner, 14.

20.   Goetzmann, 408; David M. Wrobel, *The End of American Exceptionalism* (Lawrence: University Press of Kansas, 1993), 11.

21. Goetzmann, 413.
22. Albert C. T. Antrei and Allen D. Roberts, *A History of Sanpete County* (Salt Lake City: Utah State Historical Society, 1999), 111.
23. Leonard J. Arrington, *Great Basin Kingdom: An Economic History of the Latter-day Saints, 1830–1900* (Cambridge, Mass.: Harvard University Press, 1958; reprint, Lincoln: University of Nebraska Press, 1966), 323–24.
24. Antrei and Roberts, 111; Orange Seely, "Northern Sanpete Cooperative Institution Journal and Account Record" Mt. Pleasant, Utah, 1871–1881, n.p., Seely vault, Mount Pleasant, Utah, quoted in Edwin M. G. Seely, "A History of the Rambouillet Breed of Sheep in Utah" (Master's thesis, Utah State Agricultural College, 1956), 41.
25. McElprang, 70; Belle H. Wilson, "Mehitable (Bennett) Seeley," October 1985, unpublished typescript, Historical Department, Church of Jesus Christ of Latter-day Saints, Salt Lake City, Utah; Mildred E. Brown, "History: Justus Wellington Seeley II," 1970, typescript, copy in possession of the author, 3; Andrew Jenson, "History of Emery Stake," manuscript in the LDS Church Historian's Office, Salt Lake City. This work is written chronologically, with no page numbers. Orange Seely, "Autobiographical Sketch," typescript, LDS Church Archives, LDS Historical Department, Salt Lake City, 7. The family name is variously spelled "Seely" and "Seeley." The spelling chosen here is that used by Orange Seely in his biographical entry in Lever, 618–19.
26. McElprang, 70.
27. David Randolph Seeley, "Sketch of the Life of David Randolph Seeley," Beattie Collection, Box 7 (92), Huntington Library, San Marino, California, 11–13.
28. Leonard J. Arrington, Feramorz Y. Fox, and Dean L. May, *Building the City of God*, 2nd ed. (Urbana: University of Illinois Press, 1992), 7; Antrei and Roberts, 134.
29. D. Seely, 13.
30. F. S. Dellenbaugh, "Wellington," in Thursey Jesson Reynolds, ed., *Centennial Echoes from Carbon County* (Salt Lake City: Daughters of Utah Pioneers, 1948), 157. See also C. Gregory Crampton, ed., "F. S. Dellenbaugh of the Colorado: Some Letters Pertaining to the Powell Voyages and the History of the Colorado River," *Utah Historical Quarterly* [hereafter *UHQ*] 37, no. 2 (Spring 1969): 239.
31. Frances J. Blumberg, "History of Helper," [Price] *News-Advocate*, 24 February 1921. See also McElprang, 188.
32. William M. Phillipson, *The Life and Voyages of William M. Phillipson* (Sonora, CA: The Banner, 1924), 97.
33. "Interesting Career Is Drawn to a Close," n. d. [1913], Clip File, "Gilson, Sam," Utah State Historical Society, Salt Lake City, Utah. According to an article by Glynn Bennion, describing the experiences of his father, Israel, Gilson's move to Castle Valley came as a herder of Bennion stock. However, given Gilson's long experience as a stockman and his decision to set up his own ranch, the cattle were more likely his own. See Glynn Bennion, "Pioneer Cattle Venture, " quoted in Geary, 48.
34. McElprang, 39, 201.
35. Ibid., 200–201, 277–79.
36. Geary, 102.
37. Noble Warrum, ed., *Utah Since Statehood*, vol. 3 (Chicago-Salt Lake City: S. J. Clarke Publishing Company, 1919), 500; Nels Anderson, *Desert Saints* (Chicago: University of Chicago Press, 1942), 239.
38. Liddell, 51.

39. A. C. Watts, "Opening First Commercial Coal Mine Described," in Reynolds, 33.

40. George B. Matson, quoted in A. C. Watts, "Opening First Commercial Coal Mine Described," in Reynolds, 33–35; Hannah M. Mendenhall, "The Calico Road," in Reynolds, 150–51; Donald B. Robertson, *Encyclopedia of Western Railroad History* (Caldwell, ID: Caxton Printers, Ltd., 1986), 296.

41. Daniel Yergin, *The Prize* (New York: Simon & Schuster, 1991), 36–55.

42. Matthew Josephson, *The Politicos* (New York: Harcourt, Brace & World, Inc., 1938), 167–94.

43. B. H. Roberts, *A Comprehensive History of the Church of Jesus Christ of Latter-day Saints, Century I*, vol. 5 (Salt Lake City: LDS Church, 1930), 236–37, 315; Howard R. Lamar, *The Far Southwest, 1846–1912* (New York: Yale University Press, 1966), 380–84; Gustive O. Larson, *The "Americanization" of Utah for Statehood* (San Marino: Huntington Library, 1971), 34–35, 64–65; Anderson, 259–265; Poland Act, 18 Stat. 253 (1874).

44. "Pioneer Citizen Called by Death," [Price, Utah] *Carbon County News*, 27 November 1913; Jenson; Arrington, 354; Mildred Brown, "History: Justus Wellington Seely II," 1970, unpublished typescript, 2, copy in possession of the author.

45. Jenson.

46. Quoted in full in Geary, 58–59.

47. Lever, 594; Jorgensen, 49, 89. The portion of Orange Seely's autobiography that probably covers this period is missing. See Orange Seely, "Told by himself, History of Orange Seely, Sr.," unpublished typescript, LDS Church Archives, LDS Historical Department, Salt Lake City, Utah, 9.

48. McElprang, 70–71.

49. Ibid., 303, 71. Reportedly the last wolf in Castle Valley died in 1914, caught in some youngster's trap line. See Rolla West interview with author, Price, Utah, 29–30 March 1979, typescript 204–205.

50. James Albert Jones, "A Story of the Settling of Huntington, Utah," privately printed, 1975, 8–12.

51. Lowry Nelson, *The Mormon Village* (Salt Lake City: University of Utah Press, 1952).

52. McElprang, 73; Brown, 2; J. W. Seely, Jr., "Homestead Application, December 3, 1878," RG 49, Homestead Papers, File No. 4018, National Archives, Washington, D.C.

53. Belle Harris Wilson, "Orange Sr. and Hanna Olsson Seely, Both Utah Pioneers," unpublished typescript, LDS Church Historical Department, Salt Lake City, Utah, 3–5, 11–12; McElprang, 72.

54. Geary, 68–69.

55. McElprang, 92–93.

56. Jones, 12–14; McElprang, 271; Lever, 665.

57. McElprang, 151–53, 284; Lever, 595. The independence of plural wives, or lack of it, has been the subject of various studies. See overview and conclusions in Jessie L. Embry, *Mormon Polygamous Families* (Salt Lake City: University of Utah Press, 1987), 94–95.

58. McElprang, 154–56.

59. Ibid., 283–87.

60. "Wellington," Reynolds, 156–59.

61. McElprang, 101, 103, 105.

62. Lever, 596–97.

63. McElprang, 182.

64. Lever, 644; McElprang, 182–83.

65. Ernest S. Horsley, *Fifty Years Ago This Week At and Around Price*, [Price: privately published, 1929]. A word about sources. Latter-day Saints are generally avid journal-keepers and history-writers, particularly of revered ancestors. Usually several copies are made of these family histories and distributed to various family members. The account of the earliest settlement of Price, which follows, is therefore pieced together from several of these sources, including: "A Short Sketch of Dora Spencer's Father, John Amon Powell," unpublished typescript, in possession of the author. A similar account, "Life Sketch of John Ammon Powell [his middle name was spelled variously], written by Sara Jane Powell Snow as revealed to her during a conversation with her father on the front porch of the old family home at Salem, Utah, on May 31, 1928" is cited in Gale R. Rhoades and Kerry Ross Boren, *Footprints in the Wilderness: A History of the Lost Rhoades Mines* (Salt Lake City: Dream Garden Press, 1980), 145; see also 139–41. Other sources used here include "A History of Sarah Jane Shields Powell" by an unnamed granddaughter, and Mae Grames Brown, "Biography of Albert James Grames," both unpublished typescripts in possession of the author. Additional information comes from a personal interview with Caleb Rhoades's great-granddaughter, Marguerite Wilson, by author on 16 and 20 September 1980, in Carbonville, Utah, and from Frank Esshom, *Pioneers and Prominent Men of Utah*, (Salt Lake City: 1913; reprint, 1960), 126 and 127.

66. James Gay Homestead Papers, Record Group 49, File 2493, National Archives, Washington, D.C. Gay's role in Castle Valley settlement has historically been neglected in the aforementioned family histories, probably because he died a bachelor.

67. Ernest S. Horsley, "Caleb Baldwin Rhodes," attached to Horsley, "Sketch," no page. Horsley himself arrived in northern Castle Valley on April 5, 1884, and got to know the handful of people who preceded him. See Ernest S. Horsley, "Historical Sketch of Price," in MS 112, Jean M. Westwood Collection, Box 31, Fd. 1, Special Collections, Marriott Library, University of Utah, Salt Lake City, Utah, 7.

68. Horsley, "Sketch," 2. He also includes James Gay in the list for March 12, but the James Gay Homestead Papers, witnessed by Caleb Rhoades and Frederick Grames in 1883, are more likely to be accurate on this point.

69. "Frederick Empire Grames," attached to Horsley, "Sketch."

70. Mae Grames Brown, 3, claims Alfred came in 1879 with Rhoades. Horsley, "Sketch," says January 1880. In *Fifty Years Ago*, Horsley's dates for the Grames men also differ slightly from his "Sketch." However, the "Sketch" was completed in 1937, so I am assuming it has the more correct material—people surely read his published work and asked for corrections.

71. Horsley, "Sketch," 2.

72. Horsley, *Fifty Years Ago*, 1.

73. Horsley, "Sketch," 2.

74. Ibid.

75. McElprang, 154–56.

76. Lever, 597–98.

77. Ibid., 598.

78. Ibid., 598–99; McElprang, 92, 301–5.

79. McElprang, 155–56.

80. "Wellington," Reynolds, 156–59.

81. Clair C. Andersen, "History of Utah Grazing, Chapter IV," in B-100 WPA Grazing Notes, Box 1, Utah State Historical Society, Salt Lake City, Utah, 17.

82. Lever, 598.
83. McElprang, 271.
84. "Grazing, Chapter IV," 17.
85. Lever, 597, 593; Jorgensen, 92–94; Geary, 75; Charles S. Peterson, "Cowboys and Cattle Trails: A Centennial View of Emery County," in *Emery County*, ed. Allan Kent Powell (Salt Lake City: Utah State Historical Society, 1979), 81.
86. Edward Leo Lyman, *Political Deliverance* (Urbana: University of Illinois Press, 1986), 21.
87. The case was based on the Morrill Act, 12 Stat. 501 (1862), and influenced by the Poland Act, 18 Stat. 253. See Edwin Brown Firmage and Richard Collin Mangrum, *Zion in the Courts* (Urbana: University of Illinois Press, 1988), 131–59 and Gordon Morris Bakken, *"Reynolds v. United States,"* in Kermit Hall, ed., *The Oxford Guide to United States Supreme Court Decisions* (New York: Oxford University Press, 1999), 258.
88. Lyman, 21; Firmage and Mangrum, 227.
89. Kenneth E. Davison, *The Presidency of Rutherford B. Hayes* (Westport, CT: Greenwood Press, Inc., 1972), 210–17; Lyman, 20–22.
90. Geary, 76–79.
91. Quoted in ibid., 79–80.
92. Francis M. Lyman to Editor, *Deseret News*, 28 August 1880, quoted in Jenson, *Journal History*.
93. Robert Athearn, *The Denver and Rio Grande Western Railroad* (Lincoln: University of Nebraska Press, 1977), 8–15; Merle Armitage, *Operations Santa Fe* (Hawthorne, CA: Omni Publications, 1948), 10–15.
94. Athearn, 102.
95. George A. Storrs, "Reminiscences," 1–2, unpublished typescript, copy in possession of the author.
96. John S. H. Smith, "Census Perspectives: The Sanpete Origins of Emery County Settlement," in Powell, ed., 47.
97. M. T. Burgess, "Denver & Rio Grande Western Railway Company Annual Report of Chief Engineer for Year ending December 31st, 1881," MS 513, Denver & Rio Grande Western Collection, Box 42, Fd. "Annual Report of Chief Engineer, 1881," 1, Colorado Historical Society, Denver, Colorado.
98. Joseph Smith Black, journal excerpt, copy in possession of the author.
99. Athearn, 115–17.
100. Black journal.
101. Ibid.
102. Ibid.
103. Ibid.
104. Ibid.
105. Horsley, "Sketch," 3.
106. Black journal; Ellis Clark, Jr., to Gen. William Jackson Palmer, 11 October 1881, MS 513, Denver & Rio Grande Collection, Box 51, Fd. 865, 17–18, Colorado Historical Society, Denver, Colorado.
107. Clark to Palmer, 17–18.
108. "Samuel H. Gilson, Widely Known in West, is Dead," *Deseret Evening News*, 3 December 1913.
109. "State Land Board Minutes," 1 December 1896, Box 1: State Land Board Records, Administration Division; Series: Minutes, Utah State Archives, Salt Lake City, Utah.
110. John E. Pettit, *Tenth Biennial Report of the State Mine Inspector, 1913–1914* (Salt Lake City: The Arrow Press, 1915), 144.

111. Burgess, Chief Engineer's Report, 1881, 8–10.
112. "Denver & Rio Grande Western Railway Company Annual Report of Chief Engineer for Year ending December 31st, 1881," MS 513, Denver & Rio Grande Collection, Box 42, Fd. "Annual Report of Chief Engineer, 1881," 34, Colorado Historical Society, Denver, Colorado.
113. "A Little Mixed," *Salt Lake Daily Herald*, 14 May 1881.
114. For good, legal (or illegal) reasons, these transactions were not straightforward. A more complete description is found in Nancy J. Taniguchi, *Necessary Fraud* (Norman: University of Oklahoma Press, 1996), 10–16.
115. Ibid., 14.
116. M. T. Burgess to D.C. Dodge, 30 January 1882, MS 513, Denver & Rio Grande Collection, Box 41, Fd. 879, Colorado Historical Society, Denver, Colorado; "History of the Old Rio Grande Western Railroad," in McElprang, 22; National Register nomination, "Denver & Rio Grande Lime Kiln (Buckhorn Flat Lime Kiln)," Utah State Historical Society Records, Salt Lake City, Utah.
117. Lever, 601.
118. Teancum Pratt, "Diary," unpublished typescript by Frances B. Cunningham, copy in possession of the author, 11.
119. Ibid., 8–9.
120. Ibid., 18; Teancum Pratt Homestead Papers, RG 49, Homestead Papers, File 5387, National Archives, Washington, D. C.
121. Pratt typescript, 20–23.
122. Athearn, 117.
123. Carlos Schwantes, "The Concept of the Wageworkers' Frontier: A Framework for Future Research," *Western Historical Quarterly* 18, no. 1 (January 1987): 43, 49.
124. Lever, 599–600.
125. Robert G. Athearn, "Utah and the Coming of the Denver and Rio Grande Railroad," *UHQ* 27 (April 1959): 135–37.
126. Pratt typescript, 25.
127. J. Bracken Lee, "Price City, Its Organization and Presiding Officers," in Reynolds, 109.
128. Horsley, "Sketch," 5.
129. Ibid., 4.
130. Jenson on chart "Diagram of the Presidency of the Emery Stake"; Geary, 96–97, 118.
131. Horsley, "Sketch," 6; idem, "Statistics," attached to Horsley, "Sketch," MS 112, Jean M. Westwood Collection, Box 31, Fd. 1, Special Collections, Marriott Library, University of Utah, Salt Lake City, Utah; Jenson, chart "Emery Stake . . . Diagram of Wards," no page. It originally also included Moab, which went to Grand County in 1884.
132. McElprang, 173.
133. Ibid., 160.
134. Jones, 38–40.
135. Dora Seeley Otterstrom interview, with author, 23 April 1979, Castle Dale, Utah.
136. McElprang, 89.

## Chapter Three

1.   Teancum Pratt, "Diary," typescript by Frances B. Cunningham, copy in possession of the author, 55.

2. John A. Garraty, *The New Commonwealth, 1877–1890* (New York: Harper & Row, 1968), xiii.
3. Woodrow Wilson, *Congressional Government* (New York: Meredian Books, 1956), 171.
4. Matthew Josephson, *The Politicos* (New York: Harcourt, Brace & World, Inc., 1938), 287.
5. Howard R. Lamar, *The Far Southwest, 1846–1912* (New York: Yale University Press, 1966), 389–90.
6. Thomas V. Cooper and Hector T. Fenton, *American Politics (Non-Partisan) From the Beginning to Date* (Chicago: Charles R. Brodix, 1882), 268.
7. Edmunds Act, 22 Stat. 30 (1882).
8. Lamar, 391–92.
9. LDS Family Group Records, LDS Church Geneological Library, Salt Lake City, Utah, "John Ammon Powell;" Ernest Horsley, "Historical Sketch of Price," MS 112, Jean M. Westwood Collection, Box 31, Fd. 1, Special Collections, Marriott Library, University of Utah, Salt Lake City, Utah, 2 [hereafter "Sketch"]. The marriage date comes from the LDS Family Group Records. Slightly different dates are to be found in "A History of Sarah Jane Shields Powell" by an unnamed grandchild and "A Short Sketch of Dora Spencer's Father John Amon Powell" allegedly dictated a short time before his death, unpublished typescripts, copies of both in possession of the author.
10. Stella McElprang, comp., *Castle Valley: A History of Emery County* (Emery County Daughters of Utah Pioneers, 1949), 84, 303; Edward A. Geary, *Goodbye to Poplarhaven* (Salt Lake City: University of Utah Press, 1985), 17.
11. James Albert Jones, "A Story of the Settling of Huntington, Utah," privately printed, 1975, copy in possession of the author, A–E, 37, 39–41; quote on 41. (Beginning pages are lettered rather than numbered.) This list is not exhaustive, not even for Huntington.
12. Ibid., 33–34.
13. Pratt typescript, 27.
14. Samuel P. Hays, *Response to Industrialism, 1885–1914* (Chicago: University of Chicago Press, 1957), 6.
15. Robert H. Weibe, *The Search for Order, 1877–1920* (New York: Hill and Wang, 1967), 11.
16. McElprang, 185; "Wellington," in Thursey Jesson Reynolds, ed., *Centennial Echoes from Carbon County* (Salt Lake City: Daughters of Utah Pioneers, 1948), 159; Horsley, "Sketch," 6; W. H. Lever, *A History of Sanpete and Emery Counties* (Salt Lake City: Tribune Job Printing Company, 1898), 601.
17. Horsley, "Sketch," 6; John W. Van Cott, "Utah Place Names" in Wayne L. Wahlquist, ed., *Atlas of Utah* (Provo: Brigham Young University Press, 1981), 9.
18. McElprang, 186.
19. Ibid.
20. Ralph K. Andrist, *The Long Death* (New York: Collier Books, 1964), 178–79.
21. McElprang, 185.
22. Ibid., 186.
23. Ibid., 185.
24. Ibid., 186.
25. Alexander Saxton, *The Indispensable Enemy* (Berkeley: University of California Press, 1971); Chinese Exclusion Act, 22 Stat. 58 (1882); Roger Daniels, *Asian America* (Seattle: University of Washington Press, 1988), 55–57, 112.
26. A. C. Watts, "Opening First Commercial Coal Mine Described," in Reynolds, 37.

27.  Ibid.
28.  Eric Margolis, "Western Coal Mining as a Way of Life," *Journal of the West* 24, no. 3 (July 1985): 39; A. Dudley Gardner and Verla R. Flores, *Forgotten Frontier: A History of Wyoming Coal Mining* (Boulder: Westview Press, 1989), 46–50.
29.  Quoted in Gardner and Flores, 49.
30.  McElprang, 185–86.
31.  Teachers, Pupils, and Patrons of Carbon [School] District, "History of Carbon County," mimeographed, [c.1933], 12.
32.  Horsley, "Sketch," 6.
33.  Ernest Horsley, "Early History of Price," unpublished typescript, copy in possession of the author, 2.
34.  Ernest Horsley reported that Fred Grames "gave a piece of his ground [due west of Price, later known as the Whitmore farm] to the RR co to build a depot on for one dollar and built a small store next to it to sell merchandise." "Sketch," 6, 1. Since "from March 1881 to November 1882, Price was known as Castle Valley Junction," [Horsley, "Sketch," 1], this may have been the original depot, although most historians place it further south.
35.  Horsley, "Sketch," 1; idem, "Early History," 2.
36.  Horsley, "Sketch," 6.
37.  "Wellington," in Reynolds, 167.
38.  David Rich Lewis, *Neither Wolf Nor Dog* (Oxford: Oxford University Press, 1994), 34–53; Clifford Duncan, "The Northern Utes of Utah" in Forrest S. Cuch, ed., *A History of Utah's American Indians* (Salt Lake City: Utah Division of Indian Affairs and Division of State History, 2000), 196–201.
39.  "Wellington," in Reynolds, 163.
40.  Lewis, 53.
41.  "Wellington," in Reynolds, 163; Newell C. Remington, "A History of the Gilsonite Industry" (Master's thesis, University of Utah, 1959), 45–47.
42.  McElprang, 172.
43.  "Autobiography of Lydia Jane Metcalf Price," *Our Price Heritage* (privately published), no page, Emery County Archives.
44.  Ernest H. Stevenson, "E. H. Stevenson's History of Sunnyside, 1906–7 to 1923," *Carbon County Historical Society Journal* [hereafter *CCHSJ*] (October 2001): 34.
45.  Lucy Hansen Nielsen, "Recollections on the History of Molen, Emery County, Utah," April 13, 1976, unpublished typescript, copy in possession of the author, 7.
46.  Frederick E. Hoxie, "The Curious Story of Reformers and the American Indians," *Indians in American History*, Frederick E. Hoxie, ed., (Arlington Heights, IL: Harlan Davidson, Inc., 1988), 208.
47.  Eva W. Conover, "The History of George Henry Westover and His Family," (published by family descendants, Salt Lake City, 1981), 177, 255–56. This holiday commemorates the entry of the Saints into the Salt Lake Valley, and is still celebrated as festively as the Fourth of July throughout Utah.
48.  Bertrude Seely Mitchell, "Orange Sr. and Hanna Olsson Seely, Both Utah Pioneers," typescript, LDS Church Archives, LDS Historical Department, Salt Lake City, 24.
49.  Mildred Brown, "History of Justus Wellington Seely II," 1970, unpublished typescript, copy in possession of the author, 3.
50.  Ernest Horsley, "Sketch," 5, 7; idem, "Early History," 2. For wives, see International Society Daughters of Utah Pioneers, "Dorothy Chambers Birch; Mary Elizabeth Sylvester Birch," *Pioneer Women of Faith and Fortitude* (Salt Lake City: Publishers Press, 1998), 262–64. For Henry Bryner, see

Frank Esshom, *Pioneers and Prominent Men of Utah*, (Salt Lake City: Utah Pioneers Publishing Co., 1913; reprint, 1960), 777.

51.   Horsley, "Sketch," 7.
52.   Horsley, "Holidays, First May Day," attached to "Sketch," no page.
53.   Ibid.
54.   McElprang, 94.
55.   Nielsen, 6.
56.   McElprang, 96.
57.   Allan Kent Powell, "Castle Valley at the Beginning of the Twentieth Century," in *Emery County*, Allan Kent Powell, ed. (Salt Lake City: Utah State Historical Society, 1979), 30.
58.   Horsley, "First Public Show in Price," attached to "Sketch," no page.
59.   McElprang, 286–87.
60.   Horsley, *Fifty Years Ago This Week At and Around Price* (Price: privately published, 1929), 2–3; Mae Grames Brown, "Biography of James Albert Grames," unpublished typescript, 4, copy in possession of the author; Lever, 601; Horsley, "Sketch," 6.
61.   James Gardner, interview with author, Price, Utah, 25 April 1982.
62.   Lever, 601.
63.   Leonard J. Arrington, *Great Basin Kingdom* (Cambridge, Mass.: Harvard University Press, 1958; reprint, Lincoln: University of Nebraska Press, 1966), 312. Attracting a large number of "gentile" residents was a common nineteenth-century political solution to "the Mormon problem."
64.   Ovando James Hollister, *The Resources and Attractions of Utah* (Salt Lake City: Tribune Publishing and Printing Company, 1882), 93.
65.   Andrew Jenson, "A Visit To Emery Stake," *Deseret News*, 10 September 1884.
66.   Pratt typescript, 29. The Quorum of the Seventies, an organizational method, widely used by the Latter-day Saints, originated with the anti-abolition campaigns of Theodore Weld in 1836 and 1837 as he sent a group of seventy men around to northeastern churches preaching that slavery was a sin. The revival of the 1830s that launched the original Seventies also gave birth to the LDS Church. See Whitney R. Cross, *The Burned-Over District* (New York: Harper & Row, 1950), 218–20.
67.   Jenson.
68.   "First Annual Report of the Board of Directors of the Denver & Rio Grande Western Railway Company, Covering Operations to December 31st, 1883," MS 513, Denver & Rio Grande Collection, Box 42, Fd. 3927, Colorado Historical Society, Denver, Colorado, 10.
69.   Margolis, 11.
70.   Robert Athearn, *The Denver and Rio Grande Western Railroad* (Lincoln: University of Nebraska Press, 1977), 132–53.
71.   Arrington, 342.
72.   Quoted in Leonard J. Arrington, Feramorz Y. Fox, and Dean L. May, *Building the City of God*, 2nd ed. (Urbana: University of Illinois Press, 1992), 334.
73.   Horsley, "Sketch," 9; Mae Grames Brown, 4; McElprang, 253, 254.
74.   Gardner interview.
75.   Reynolds, 179.
76.   Ronald G. Coleman, "African-Americans in Utah," in Allen Kent Powell, ed., *Utah History Encyclopedia*, (Salt Lake City: University of Utah Press, 1994), 3; H. Bert Jenson, "Smith Wells, Stagecoach Inn on the Nine Mile Road," *Utah Historical Quarterly* [hereafter *UHQ*] 61, no. 2 (Spring 1993): 183–85; Michael J. Clark, "Improbable Ambassadors: Black Soldiers At Fort Douglas, 1896–99," *UHQ* 46, no. 3 (Summer 1978): 285.
77.   Horsley, "Sketch," 10–11.

78. H. Bert Jenson, 182–97; Arthur E. Gibson, "Industries, Other Than Coal, Which Were Important In The Development of Carbon County," in Reynolds, 44–45; Edward A. Geary, "Nine Mile: Eastern Utah's Forgotten Road," *UHQ,* Vol. 49 No. 1 (Winter 1981): 49.

79. Remington, 38–47.

80. Horsley, "Sketch," 10–11.

81. Athearn, 132–53; Arrington, 342–47.

82. Philip F. Notarianni, "Helper—the Making of a Gentile Town in Zion," in *Carbon County: Eastern Utah's Industrialized Island,* Philip F. Notarianni, ed., (Salt Lake City: Utah State Historical Society, 1981), 157.

83. *Second Annual Report of the Board of Directors of the Denver & Rio Grande Western Railway Co for year ending 31 July 1887* (New York: William H. Clark, 1887), MS 513, Denver & Rio Grande Collection, Box 42, Fd. 3931, Colorado State Historical Society, Denver, Colorado, 5.

84. Interstate Commerce Act, 24 Stat. 379 (1887); Edmunds-Tucker Act, 24 Stat. 635 (1887); Gustive O. Larson, *The "Americanization" of Utah for Statehood* (San Marino: Huntington Library, 1971), 208–10.

85. Edward Leo Lyman, *Political Deliverance* (Urbana: University of Illinois Press, 1986), 24.

86. *Clawson v. U.S.,* 114 U.S. 55 (1885); *Cannon v. U.S.,* 116 U.S. 55 (1885); *Snow v. U.S.,* 120 U.S. 274 (1886).

87. Larson, 110–14.

88. Margaret K. Brady, *Mormon Healer and Folk Poet* (Logan: Utah State University Press, 2000), 14–18, quote on 18.

89. Ibid., 18–19.

90. Pratt typescript, 30.

91. Orson Whitney, *History of Utah,* III, 332.

92. Charles S. Varian, quoted in R. N. Baskin, *Reply to Certain Statements by O. F. Whitney . . .* (Salt Lake City: Lakeside Printing Co., 1916?), 215–16.

93. Firmage and Mangrum, 167–75; Larson, 107–30.

94. Henry George Mathis, "Autobiography," typescript, 1957, LDS Church Historical Department, Salt Lake City, Utah, 27.

95. Ibid., 28–29.

96. Lyman, 110–19; Jean Bickmore White, "The Right to be Different: Ogden and Weber County Politics, 1850–1924," *UHQ* 47 (Summer 1979): 260–63; Thomas G. Alexander, "John Wesley Powell, the Irrigation Survey, and the Inauguration of the Second Phase of Irrigation Development in Utah," *UHQ* 37 (Spring 1969): 191–92.

97. "Memoirs of Rudger Clawson," typed summary, MS 143, Madeline R. McQuown Papers, Box 18, Fd. 25, Special Collections, Marriott Library, University of Utah, Salt Lake City, Utah, 7–10.

98. Mathis, 29.

99. Edward Geary, *A History of Emery County* (Salt Lake City: Utah State Historical Society, 1996), 104.

100. Pratt typescript, 32.

101. Ibid., 33.

102. Geary, 129.

103. Pratt typescript, 57.

104. Ibid., 55.

105. Ibid., 55–56.

106. Ibid., 56.

107. Ibid.

108. Ibid., 59.

109. Walter Nugent, *Into The West* (New York: Alfred A. Knopf, 1999), 120.
110. Sherman Anti-Trust Act, 26 Stat. 209; Garraty, 124.
111. *The Compiled Laws of Utah*, vol. 2 (Salt Lake City: Herbert Pembroke, 1888), quotes on 82, 98–99, 92–93. The statute regarding marriage was originally printed, "Marriages solemnized in any other county, State or Territory. . . ." The word "country" had to be laboriously pasted over "county," 93.
112. *The Late Corporation of the Church of Jesus Christ of Latter-day Saints v. U.S.*, 136 U.S. 1 (1890).
113. *Doctrine and Covenants* (Salt Lake City: Church of Jesus Christ of Latter-day Saints, 1968), 257.
114. For example, see Annie Clark Tanner, *A Mormon Mother* (Salt Lake City: University of Utah Library, 1976), 223–314.
115. For a full discussion, see B. Carmon Hardy, *Solemn Covenant: The Mormon Polygamous Passage* (Urbana: University of Illinois Press, 1992). Historians such as Leonard Arrington have characterized the so-called Woodruff Manifesto of 1890 as a reaction to the Supreme Court decision that had upheld the Edmunds-Tucker Law four months earlier. See Arrington, 377–78.
116. Stewart Lofgren Grow, "A Study of the Utah Commission, 1882–96" (Ph.D. diss., University of Utah, 1954), Table 22, 268.

## Chapter Four

1. Walter Nugent, *Into the West* (New York: Alfred A. Knopf, 1999), 129.
2. Teancum Pratt, "Diary," typescript by Frances B. Cunningham, copy in possession of the author, 58.
3. Book 6, 322–33 and Book 2, 26, Carbon County Recorder's Office, Carbon County Courthouse, Price, Utah.
4. *Eastern Utah Advocate*, [hereafter *EUA*] 7 August 1891, quoted in Pratt typescript, 73.
5. Henry George, *Progress and Poverty* (Garden City, NY: Doubleday, Page & Co., 1916); Laura Ann Ewell Dennis, "Biography of Francis Marion Ewell (Pioneer) Written by Laura Ann Ewell Dennis—His Daughter, of Camp Provo of Daughters of Utah Pioneers of Utah County, Provo, Utah," typescript, copy in possession of the author.
6. *Eastern Utah Telegraph*, 4 September 1891.
7. *Salt Lake Tribune*, 1 January 1892.
8. Philip F. Notarianni, ed., *Carbon County: Eastern Utah's Industrialized Island* (Salt Lake City: Utah State Historical Society, 1981), 157; Edward Geary, *A History of Emery County* (Salt Lake City: Utah State Historical Society, 1996), 191; Robert G. Athearn, *Union Pacific Country* (Chicago: Rand McNally & Company, 1971), 361–62.
9. Robert Forrester, "Annual Report of U.S. Mine Inspector, 1892," Secretary of Utah Territory, Territorial Executive Papers, Series 241, Box 5, Fd. 23, Utah State Archives, Salt Lake City, Utah, 13490.
10. Teachers, Pupils and Patrons of Carbon [School] District, "A Brief History of Carbon County," mimeographed, [c. 1933]; Forrester, 13491.
11. Paul Turner, *Sunnyside Memories* (Orem, UT: SunRise Publishing, 1997), 89–91.
12. A. Philip Cederlof, "Early History of Coal Mining in Utah," MS 277, Peerless Coal Company, Box 1 Fd. 1, Special Collections, Lee Library, Brigham Young University, Provo, Utah, 3–4.
13. James Gardner, interview with author, Price, Utah, 25 April 1982.

14. Cederlof, 3.
15. Ibid., 3–4.
16. Forrester, 13477.
17. Utah Department of Mines and Mining, *Report of the State Coal Mine Inspector* [hereafter *SCMIR*] 1896 (Salt Lake City: Deseret News Publishing Co., 1897), 18.
18. W. H. Lever, *A History of Sanpete and Emery Counties* (Salt Lake City: Tribune Job Printing Company, 1898), 602.
19. *Deseret News*, 25 November 1890.
20. "History of Peter Johnson," copy in possession of the author, 5.
21. Stella McElprang, comp., *Castle Valley: A History of Emery County* (Emery County Daughters of Utah Pioneers, 1949), 291.
22. Ibid., 223–224; "History of Peter Johnson," 5.
23. McElprang, 78–79; [no title], *Emery County Progress* [hereafter *ECP*],12 October 1901; "Dr. Kirkwood Coming," *ECP*, 29 February 1908.
24. McElprang, 75–77, 103–4, 178, 307–8, 310.
25. Samuella R. Hawkins, "Go Get Maggie," in Kate B. Carter, comp., *Our Pioneer Heritage*, vol. 6 (Salt Lake City: Daughters of Utah Pioneers, 1963), 540; "Margaret's Story," As Told to Samuella R. Hawkins, Winter 1952–Spring 1953, unpublished typescript, 12–14, and "The Obstetrics Course Finishing Its Studies," *ECP*, c. 20 April 1905, clippings file, both in Dottie Hawkins Grimes Collection, Emery County Archives, Castle Dale, Utah.
26. Bureau of the Census, *Historical Statistics of the United States, 1789–1945* (Washington, D.C.: Government Printing Office, 1949), 27, 32.
27. J. Bracken Lee, "Price City, Its Organization and Presiding Officers," in Reynolds, 109; Lever, 602.
28. Horsley, "Sketch," 13; Lever, 603.
29. Elizabeth J. Howard, "Eisteddfod: A Musical Festival and Contest," in McElprang, 29–31. Quote on p. 31.
30. Ibid., 31.
31. Peter N. Stearns, *The Industrial Revolution in World History* (Boulder, Co.: Westview Press, 1993), 51–52.
32. Robert G. Athearn, *Westward the Briton* (Lincoln: University of Nebraska Press, 1953), especially 102–15.
33. C. W. McCullough, "Briton Builds Rich Empire in Utah," in Reynolds, 64–65.
34. Coal Certificate 2972, Book 6, Carbon County Recorder's Office, Carbon County Courthouse, Price, Utah.
35. *United States v. Lewis A. Scott Elliott*, 7 Utah 39 (1891).
36. Ibid., 395.
37. James Liddell, "The Cattle and Sheep Industry of Carbon County," in Reynolds, 51–54; Civil Case 358, *Lewis A. Wallace v. Big Springs Ranch Co.* (1905), Seventh Judicial District Records, Carbon County Courthouse, Price, Utah; "Of A More Or Less Personal Nature," *EUA*, 15 February 1906.
38. "The McPhersons" in Reynolds, 53–54.
39. John H. Pace, "Recollections of a Carbon County Old-Timer," *New West Magazine* 11, no. 2 (February 1920): 23.
40. "The Whitmores of Carbon County," *New West Magazine* 11, no. 2, (February 1920): 17.
41. Rolla West, interview with author, Price, Utah, 29 March 1979, 214–16.
42. Liddell, 51.
43. "Whitmores of Carbon County," 17.
44. Reynolds, 189; Pearl Baker, *The Wild Bunch at Robbers Roost* (Lincoln: University of Nebraska Press, 1965; reprint, 1989), 67.

45. Baker, 67–69; Laura Evans and Buzz Belknap, *Green River Wilderness: Desolation River Guide* (Boulder City, NV: Westwater Books, 1974), 33, 43–45.
46. Lever, 681; Baker, 71–76.
47. Pace, 23; Horsley "Sketch," 16; "Old Files Reveal Story of the Killing and Capture of Notorious Bandits by Posse from Here in Book Cliff Region (Taken from the files of *The Eastern Advocate*, Thursday, May 19, 1898)," in Reynolds, 188–90; Baker, 76–81.
48. Leonard J. Arrington, *Great Basin Kingdom* (Cambridge, Mass.: Harvard University Press, 1958; reprint, Lincoln: University of Nebraska Press, 1966), 310.
49. Edwin M. G. Seely, "A History of the Rambouillet Breed of Sheep in Utah" (Master's thesis, Utah State Agricultural College [now Utah State University], 1956), 42–45.
50. "Many Herds of Sheep Now Changing Hands," *EUA*, 8 October 1903.
51. Edwin Seely, 79.
52. Mildred Brown, "History: Justus Wellington Seeley II," typescript, 1970, copy in possession of the author, 3.
53. Lucy Hansen Nielsen, "Recollections of the History of Molen, Emery County, Utah," typescript, copy in possession of the author, 13.
54. Walker Lowry, *Wallace Lowry* (privately printed, 1974), 167–69.
55. Lowry, 148–49; R. Hal Williams, *Years of Decision: American Politics in the 1890s* (Prospect Heights, IL: Waveland Press, Inc., 1978) 133–34.
56. Lowry, 69, 170.
57. Lee Anderson, "Stock Raisers," Price, Utah, 20 October 1940, in B-100, "WPA Grazing Notes," Box 4, Carbon County, Utah, Utah State Historical Society Library, Salt Lake City, Utah.
58. Lowry, 70.
59. Paul Young, *Back Trail of an Old Cowboy* (Lincoln: University of Nebraska Press, 1983), 126.
60. Edward Norris Wentworth, *America's Sheep Trails* (Ames, Iowa: The Iowa State College Press, 1948), 522–44.
61. Lowry, 166.
62. Ibid.
63. Athearn, *Rio Grande*, 180; Page Smith, *The Rise of Industrial America* (New York: McGraw-Hill Book Company, 1984), 464, 485; Williams, 75–77.
64. Horsley, "Sketch," 1; idem, "Caleb Baldwin Rhodes," attached to "Sketch," 2. The "Lost Rhoades Mine" has long been a Utah legend but has never been found.
65. Pratt typescript, 74.
66. Ibid., 80.
67. Ibid., 74.
68. Williams, 80–88; Smith, 508–16; Lever, 71–72.
69. Henry George Mathis, "Autobiography," typescript, 1957, LDS Church Historical Department, Salt Lake City, Utah, 30; speech quoted in Smith, 514.
70. Mathis, 29–31; Arva Smith, "Local history is memory for former Price Mayor Mathis," [Price] *Sun-Advocate*, 22 September 1987.
71. "Wellington," in Thursey Jesson Reynolds, *ed., Centennial Echoes from Carbon County* (Salt Lake City: Daughters of Utah Pioneers, 1948), 162–63.
72. McElprang, 247–48.
73. The documents connected with the mill show the activity for 1893 and 1895. See "Warranty Deed, George A. Humble and Olive M. Humble to Huntington Milling & Mfg. Co," 24 April 1893, Book B2 of Deeds, p. 5; and "Mortgage," Book D of Mortgages, p. 568, both in Emery County

Recorder's Records, Castle Dale, Utah. Luther M. Becker supposedly served as president, but Christopher Wilcox, supposedly his vice-president, signed as president on appropriate legal papers. See also McElprang, 241; Willard Sandberg, interviewed by Elizabeth Hanson, Huntington, Utah, typescript, May 1978; Lever, 645.

74.   Arrington, 227.
75.   Nielsen, 10.
76.   "History of Peter Johnson," 5; Mary Ann Cook, "The Silk Industry," McElprang, 235.
77.   McElprang, 236.
78.   *Minute Book of the Board of Education of Emery Stake, Castle Dale, Utah, 1890–1908*, 2–4; McElprang, 32–33; Geary, *History*, 118, 121–23.
79.   Joseph L. Rawlins, *The Unfavored Few: An Auto-Biography of Joseph L. Rawlins*, ed. Alta Rawlins Jensen (Salt Lake City: privately printed, 1954), 172–85, quotes on 179, 181, 185.
80.   Ibid., 185–86.
81.   "An Act to Enable the People of Utah to form a Constitution and State Government . . .," 28 Stat. 107 (1894).
82.   James S. Clarkson to Wilford Woodruff, 11 July 1894, copy, A. T. Volwiler Papers, Lilly Library, Indiana University, Bloomington, Indiana, 30–31. [Hereafter Clarkson letter.]
83.   "Memoranda made by Clio [Hiram B. Clawson] of the things he has learned . . . [over] the past four years," attached to Clarkson letter, 4.
84.   Jean Bickmore White, *Charter for Statehood* (Salt Lake City: University of Utah Press, 1996), 43–87.
85.   Alfred H. Kelly and Winfred A. Harbison, *The American Constitution*, 3rd ed. (New York: W. W. Norton and Co., Inc., 1963), 556–57.
86.   *Official Report of the Proceedings and Debates of the Convention . . . to Adopt a Constitution . . .*, vol. 2 (Salt Lake City: Star Printing Company, 1898), 1873–74.
87.   White, 43–87.
88.   Horsley, "Sketch," 14.
89.   Lever, 74. The tally gave Bryan 50,987 out of 77,877 votes cast.
90.   *SCMIR*, 1896, 9, 23, 33–35; *SCMIR* 1897, 5, 28–31; *SCMIR* 1898, 45.
91.   *SCMIR* 1896, 3; *SCMIR* 1898, 42, 45, 60.
92.   [Editorial], *EUA*, 15 January 1897.
93.   Williams, 136.
94.   Pratt typescript, 96, 101.
95.   Ibid., 101.
96.   Ibid., 109.
97.   Woodruff Journal, 30 December 1896, quoted in Edward Leo Lyman, *Political Deliverance* (Urbana: University of Illinois Press, 1986) 254 n. 73.
98.   Arrington, 386–95.
99.   "Happenings Ten Years Ago This Week," *EUA*, 4 July 1907.
100.  "Articles of Incorporation, Holladay Coal Co.," Special Collections, College of Eastern Utah, Price, Utah; *SCMIR*, 1897, 29; *Record: Mining Locations, Book 8*, Carbon County Recorder's Office, Price, Utah, especially 1–5, 100–101, 121. These holdings were expanded in 1899, as shown on 170–73. Part of the reason to use hard rock mining law (as recorded above) instead of coal land law was that the latter limited ownership to a maximum of 640 acres. See Coal Land Act of 1873, 17 Stat. 607.
101.  "Coal Lands Inquiry," *EUA*, 6 December 1906; W. P. Morrell, *The Gold Rushes* (London: Adam and Charles Black, 1940), 374–409.

102. "Coal Lands Inquiry."
103. "Articles of Incorporation, Holladay Coal Co.," especially 100–101, 121. The company's largest stockholder (at 47,437 shares) was Alvaretta C. Holladay, George's wife; her brother, James H. Jones, owned 19,437. George's father, Thomas, owned 10,437 shares. In addition to patriarch Jefferson Tidwell, stockholders included his wife, Sarah Seely Tidwell; her brother, Orange Seely; Tidwell's children William J., John F., Joseph Randolph, and Hyrum, and neighbor William S. Ronjue, each with 12,500 shares. The corporation's officers (in an unusual arrangement, not the major stockholders) included as president and treasurer Robert N. Baskin, who owned 9,125 shares of stock, as did the company secretary, Liberal supporter Judge Enos D. Hoge. George T. Holladay, the Vice President and company's namesake, personally owned a mere 439 shares. H. P. and E. L. Mason rounded out the participants. For Hoge, see Madsen, 270. Potential forces brokering the association of dedicated pioneers and a once-active enemy of the LDS Church deserve to be investigated. The company's mineral land holdings were expanded in 1899, as shown in *Mining Locations, Book 8,* 170–73.
104. *The Holladay Coal Company v. R. A. Kirker, et al.,* 20 Utah 192 (1899). This published opinion is all that remains of the case records, with the exception of one single page of the primary documents. The rest of the documents listed in *Register of Actions — Civil, 1896–1901,* Seventh Judicial District Court, Price, Utah, supposedly forwarded to the Utah Supreme Court, have disappeared.
105. "Peabody Tells His Story," *EUA,* 26 December 1907; "Happenings Ten Years Ago This Week," *EUA,* 24 October 1907; "Coal Lands Inquiry."
106. Rolla E. West, interview with author, Price, Utah, 29 March, 1979. See also Liddell, 51.
107. "Bold Outlaws Get $7000 In Gold," *EUA,* 22 April 1897.
108. "The Castlegate Hold Ups," *EUA* 29 April 1897; Horsley "Sketch," 16.
109. McElprang, 90–91.
110. "Castlegate Hold Ups."
111. "The County Commissioners," *EUA,* 8 July 1897.
112. Ronald G. Coleman, "The Buffalo Soldiers: Guardians of the Uintah Frontier, 1886–1901," *Utah Historical Quarterly* 47 (Fall 1979): 421–39.
113. Quoted in Williams, 140–41; Horsley, "Sketch," 16; "History of Peter Johnson," 7; Robert Athearn, *The Denver and Rio Grande Western Railroad* (Lincoln: University of Nebraska Press, 1962; reprint, 1977), 187.
114. "The Romance of Maxwell," *EUA,* 11 August 1898; "Happenings Ten Years Ago This Week," *EUA,* 15 August 1907; "Maxwell is Convicted," [Salt Lake City] *Daily Tribune,* 20 September 1898; "Gets Eighteen Years," *EUA,* 22 September 1898; [no title] *EUA,* 30 November 1899. "Maxwell Plans For Freedom," *Salt Lake Herald,* 14 July 1900; *Maxwell v. Dow* 176 U.S. 581 (1900).
115. "Maxwell Plans For Freedom."
116. Lever, 605.
117. [no title], *EUA,* 28 December 1899.

## Chapter Five

1. Mary Harris Jones, *The Autobiography of Mother Jones,* Mary Field Parton, ed., 3rd ed. rev. (Chicago: Charles H. Kerr Publishing Company, 1925; reprint, 1976), 105–106.
2. Samuel P. Hays, *The Response to Industrialism, 1885–1914* (Chicago: University of Chicago Press, 1957).

3.      "20 Years Ago," [Price] *Sun,* 1 August and 3 October 1919.
4.      Utah Department of Mines and Mining, *Report of the State Coal Mine Inspector* [hereafter *SCMIR*] 1899 (Salt Lake City: The Deseret News, 1901), 17.
5.      *SCMIR* 1899, 22–23.
6.      "The New Railroad," *Eastern Utah Advocate* [hereafter *EUA*], 15 June 1899; *SCMIR* 1899, 21–22; "Sunnyside Line Being Inspected," *Deseret Evening News,* 9 November 1899.
7.      "Coal Mines Go Out On A Strike," *Deseret Evening News,* 18 November 1899.
8.      "Italian Miners Arrive," *EUA,* 30 November 1899.
9.      Father Francis Pellegrino, "History of St. Anthony's Parish," *Carbon County Historical Society Journal* 2, no. 1 (Spring 1983): 22–23; Louis and Zelpha Vuksinick, interview with author, Spring Glen, Utah, 14 March 1979; Bureau of the Census, *Historical Statistics of the United States, 1789–1945* (Washington, D.C.: Government Printing Office, 1949), 32.
10.     Craig Fuller, "Finns and the Winter Quarters Mine Disaster," *Utah Historical Quarterly* [hereafter *UHQ*] 70 (Spring 2002): 125–28; Gary Ungrich, e-mail dated 19 October 1999, and Jussi Kemppainen, e-mail dated 22 October 1999, both in "Remembering Winter Quarters," published by the *Sun-Advocate* and *Emery County Progress,* 25 April 2000, 15, 18–19.
11.     "Corpses by the Hundred," *Los Angeles Times,* 2 May 1900; *SCMIR* 1899, 19; J. W. Dilley, *History of the Scofield Mine Disaster* (Provo, Utah: The Skelton Pub. Co., 1900; reprint: privately published by Paul and Linda Helsten, 2000), 46–49, 97, 102, 132. Coal gases include carbon monoxide, as a result of burning oxygen, plus "firedamp" (methane), "black damp" (carbonic acid) and "white damp" (carbonic oxide). See Thomas J. Schlereth, *Victorian America* (New York: HarperPerrenial, 1992), 50.
12.     Dilley, 49–52, 101–3, 113; "Death in Horrid Form," *Los Angeles Times,* 3 May 1900.
13.     Dilley, 101, 113.
14.     Ibid., 96–97.
15.     Ibid., 24–25, 27, 51, 101; *SCMIR* 1900, 62–63; "From the autobiography of Arni Julius Arnason, sent by Blanche Wilson," in "Remembering Winter Quarters," 10; Fuller, 136.
16.     Dilley, 53–62, 106, 212; "Upper Camps to Contribute to the Relief of Stricken People," *EUA,* 26 April 1906; "Message From President" and "Louret's Condolence," both in *Los Angeles Times* 4 May 1900; Allan Kent Powell, *The Next Time We Strike* (Logan: Utah State University Press, 1985), 32, 33; Fuller, 134–35; Noble Warrum, ed., *Utah Since Statehood,* vol. 3 (Chicago-Salt Lake City: S. J. Clarke Publishing Company, 1919), 267.
17.     Dilley, 56, 86, 99–100; Joseph J. Larsen "A Sketch of My Life," Harold B. Lee Library, Brigham Young University, Provo, Utah, quoted in Allan Kent Powell, "Castle Valley at the Beginning of the Twentieth Century," *Emery County,* ed. Allen Kent Powell (Salt Lake City: Utah State Historical Society, 1979), 13.
18.     *SCMIR* 1900, 42–95. See also Nancy J. Taniguchi, "An Explosive Lesson: Gomer Thomas, Safety, and the Winter Quarters Mine Disaster," *UHQ* 70 No. 2 (Spring 2000): 140–57.
19.     "Death in Horrid Form."
20.     Records for 1900–1901, Seventh District Court, Carbon County Recorders Office, Price, Utah; "The Upper Coal Camps Give To The Sufferers," *EUA* 3 May 1906; James Whiteside, *Regulating Danger* (Lincoln: University of Nebraska Press, 1990), 70–72. Montana had the other such law.
21.     Teancum Pratt, "Diary," typescript by Frances B. Cunningham, copy in

possession of the author, 102–7, quote on 112.

22. Ibid., 112. The *Eastern Utah Advocate* reported that Pratt fell down a shaft; the State Coal Mine Inspector said that he was killed by a fall of coal from the roof that struck him on the head. All agreed that he died instantly. See "Teancum Pratt Dead," *EUA*, 13 September 1900; *SCMIR* 1900, 112.

23. "Teancum Pratt Dead."

24. *SCMIR* 1900, 42, lists nine men killed and sixty-three injured beyond the Scofield total, but the usual details are not available on 111–15, where only seven deaths and forty-one injuries are described. Usually, all of them are. Therefore, it is impossible to tell the location of the remainder.

25. Robert Athearn, *The Denver and Rio Grande Western Railroad* (Lincoln: University of Nebraska Press, 1962; reprint, 1977), 194–96; Nancy J. Taniguchi, *Necessary Fraud* (Norman: University of Oklahoma Press, 1996), 42–46. Athearn, 195, correctly notes that formal consolidation took place in 1908.

26. Peter Collier and David Horowitz, *The Rockefellers* (New York: Holt, Rinehart and Winston, 1976), 29, 45; "Oil Notes," *Emery County Progress* [hereafter *ECP*], 25 May 1901; "Oil and Ores," *ECP*, 25 January 1902; *SCMIR* 1901, 42–45, 52–56; Letter from Royal Swasey to Miss Eva Larsen, 6 December 1913, Emery County Landscape Collection, Emery County Archives, Castle Dale, Utah.

27. Lee Anderson to C. C. Anderson, 27 November 1940, in B-100 "WPA Grazing Notes," Box 4 "Carbon County, Utah," Utah State Historical Society, Salt Lake City, Utah; "Big Springs Ranch," in Thursey Jesson Reynolds, ed., *Centennial Echoes from Carbon County* (Salt Lake City: Daughters of Utah Pioneers, 1948) 52; Pearl Baker, *The Wild Bunch at Robbers Roost* (revised, Lincoln: University of Nebraska Press, 1989), 90–93.

28. "Biography of William Henry Price," *Our Price Heritage* (privately published), 7.

29. Edward Geary, *A History of Emery County* (Salt Lake City: Utah State Historical Society, 1996), 177–78.

30. Murat Halsted, *The Illustrious Life of William McKinley* (no place: Murat Halsted, 1901), 35–52; R. Hal Williams, *Years of Decision: American Politics in the 1890s* (Prospect Heights, IL: Waveland Press, Inc., 1978), 155–58.

31. Theodore Roosevelt, *Ranch Life and the Hunting-Trail* (New York: Century, 1901; reprint, Lincoln: University of Nebraska Press, 1983), 1.

32. William D. Rowley, *Reclaiming the Arid West* (Bloomington: Indiana University Press, 1996), 71–103.

33. Donald Worster, *Rivers of Empire* (New York: Oxford University Press, 1985), 157; Thomas G. Alexander, "John Wesley Powell, the Irrigation Survey, and the Inauguration of the Second Phase of Irrigation Development in Utah," *UHQ* 37 (Spring 1969): 201.

34. Geary, 185; James R. Kluger, *Turning on Water with a Shovel* (Albuquerque: University of New Mexico Press, 1992), 22–27.

35. Geary, 174.

36. Udella Peterson Johansen, Owen McClenahan and Jane McClenahan, Castle Dale, Utah, interview with author, 20 March 1979.

37. Keith Wright, "Clawson," in Montell Seely, LaVora Kofford, Owen and Jane McClenahan, and Roma Powell, eds., *Emery County, 1880–1980* (Castle Dale: Emery County Historical Society, 1981), 92.

38. Stella McElprang, comp., *Castle Valley: A History of Emery County* (Emery County Daughters of Utah Pioneers, 1949), 130.

39. George A. Thompson, *Some Dreams Die* (Salt Lake City: Dream Garden Press, 1982), 112; McElprang, 127–31.

40.  McElprang, 132–34; Geary,179–80; Charles and Maude Jones, "Elmo," in
     Seely, et al., eds., 176.
41.  *ECP*, 10 August 1901, 4.
42.  Charles S. Peterson, *Look to the Mountains* (Provo: Brigham Young University
     Press, 1975), 122–23, quoting *ECP* of 9 and 16 March and 10 August 1901.
43.  Geary, 130, 176, 186–87; Montell Seely, "Irrigation on Cottonwood Creek,"
     in Seely, et al., eds., 79, 86.
44.  Geary, *History*, 188.
45.  Powell, "Castle Valley," 17.
46.  Rowley, 107–8.
47.  Geary, *History*, 174.
48.  Powell, "Castle Valley," 18–19.
49.  Samuel P. Hays, *Conservation and the Gospel of Efficiency* (Cambridge: Harvard
     University Press, 1959), 28–44.
50.  Lee Anderson, "Stock Raisers," B-100 WPA Grazing Notes, Box 4, Carbon
     County, Utah, Utah State Historical Society, Salt Lake City, Utah.
51.  Virginia N. Price and John T. Darby, "Preston Nutter: Utah Cattleman,
     1886–1936," *UHQ* 32 (1964), 245–46.
52.  Clair C. Andersen, "History of Grazing, Chapter IV," B-100 WPA Grazing
     Notes, Box 1, Carbon County, Utah, Utah State Historical Society, Salt Lake
     City, Utah.
53.  C. C. Andersen, interview with Lew Peterson, Emery, Utah, B-100 WPA
     Grazing Notes, Box 4, Carbon County Utah, Utah State Historical Society,
     Salt Lake City, Utah.
54.  Thomas E. Bryson, "Interview With A Large Cattleman" 5 March 1941, and
     "Interview With An Average Cattleman" 5 March 1941, both in B-100, WPA
     Grazing Notes, Box 4, Emery County, Utah, Utah State Historical Society,
     Salt Lake City, Utah.
55.  Ruben Brasher and Stella McElprang, "The Livestock Industry," in
     McElprang, 41–43; Peterson, 123–24; see especially 123 n. 50.
56.  "Diary of Albert F. Potter, Associate Chief of the Forest Service," May 1902–
     November 1902, Entry for 7 October 1902, Emery County Archives.
57.  John Peterson, "Beginnings of the Manti-LaSal National Forest: Draft #7,
     Timber in the Manti Division of the National Forest," 1991, Emery County
     Archives.
58.  Velma Peterson, "Ferron," in Seely, et al., eds., 112.
59.  Eva Westover Conover, *The History of George Henry Westover and His Family*
     (Salt Lake City: Family Descendants, 1981), 52–53, 56.
60.  Ibid., 56, 63–64.
61.  Roxie W. Nelson, personal history, prepared 28 February 1994, Emery
     County Archives.
62.  McElprang, 156–59.
63.  [no title], *EUA*, 20 March 1902.
64.  [no title], *EUA*, 3 and 17 July 1902.
65.  Frederick Lewis Allen, *The Big Change* (New York: Harper & Brothers, 1952),
     83.
66.  "Coal Mines Go Out On Strike," *Deseret Evening News*, 18 November 1899;
     Powell, *Next Time*, 37–54.
67.  Powell, *Next Time*, 69–70.
68.  Powell, "Castle Valley," 15.
69.  Powell, *Next Time*, 79–80.
70.  Jones, 104–7.
71.  Ibid., 107.

72.  Photograph in the Utah State Historical Society collections and Western
     Mining and Railroad Museum, published in *UHQ* 58, no 2 (Spring 1990): 149.
73.  Powell, *Next Time*, 75, 81; Melvyn Dubofsky, *Industrialism and the American
     Worker, 1865–1920* (Arlington Heights, Ill.: Harlan Davidson, Inc., 1985),
     63–64; idem, *We Shall Be All* (Chicago: Quadrangle Books, 1969), 71–75.
74.  "Good Wages," *EUA*, 17 March 1904; *SCMIR* 1904, 91; Helen Z.
     Papanikolas, "The Great Bingham Strike of 1912 and the Expulsion of the
     Padrone," *Toil and Rage in a New Land*, special edition of the *Utah Historical
     Quarterly*, 2nd issue, rev., reprinted from vol. 38, no. 2 (Spring 1970), 121–
     33; Tsurutani Hisashi, with Betsy Scheiner assisted by Yamamura Mariko,
     trans., *America-Bound* (Tokyo: The Japan Times, 1977), 148; [no title], *EUA*,
     25 April 1901; [no title], *EUA*, 10 May 1901; Powell, *Next Time*, 70.
75.  Powell, *Next Time*, 74–78.
76.  "Strikers Move On," *EUA*, 11 May 1905.
77.  Carbon County Tax Rolls, Spring Glen School District, 1901. For a complete
     study of the first ethnic farming village in Utah, see Nancy J. Taniguchi,
     "Common Ground: The Coalescence of Spring Glen, 1878–1920" (Master's
     thesis, University of Utah, 1981).
78.  J. B. Oberto, personal communication, 19 March 1980; quote from Peter
     Clerico and Margaret Clerico Paluso, interview with author, Spring Glen,
     Utah, 30 August 1978.
79.  Carbon County Tax Rolls, Spring Glen School District, 1905.
80.  *Utah State Gazetteer*, 1906; "News of Town and County in Brief," *EUA*, 14
     November 1907; Ernest and Gladys Saccomanno, interview with author,
     Spring Glen, Utah, 1 May 1979; Hugh and Charles Saccomanno, interview
     with author, Spring Glen, Utah, 5 May 1979.
81.  Taniguchi, "Common Ground."
82.  Dubofsky, *We Shall*, 76.
83.  Idem, *Industrialism and the American Worker, 1865–1920*, 2nd ed. (Arlington
     Heights, Ill.: Harlan Davidson, Inc., 1985), 106.
84.  This marriage of the WFM and IWW did not last long: in the 1906 convention,
     the IWW and the WFM had a major falling-out, although the WFM remained
     the formal mining department of the IWW until 1908. See Sally Zanjani and
     Guy Louis Rocha, *The Ignoble Conspiracy* (Reno: University of Nevada Press,
     1986), 13; Sally Zanjani, *Goldfield: The Last Gold Rush on the Western Frontier*
     (Athens, OH: Swallow Press of Ohio University Press, 1992), 48–58.
85.  Zanjani and Rocha, 8–18. Despite a temporary rift in 1906, the WFM and
     IWW continued this relationship until July 1908.
86.  "Is Free Man," *EUA*, 26 November 1903; "Town and County News," *EUA*, 9
     March 1905; *SCMIR* 1904, 126; *SCMIR* 1905, 38; "Town and Country News,"
     *EUA*, 9 March 1905; "Truth and Gossip," *EUA* 26 January 1905; "Petition
     Totally Ignored," *EUA*, 30 October 1907.
87.  Zanjani and Rocha, xi–xiii, 1–2, 14–16, 153–54; Zanjani, 48–58.
88.  "Big Increase in the Wealth of the World," *EUA*, 22 November 1906.
89.  "Utah Leads in the Production of Coal," *EUA*, 8 August 1907.
90.  Athearn, *Rio Grande*, 200–210.
91.  Fred Voll, interview with author, Helper, Utah, 13 April 1982.
92.  Ernest S. Horsley, "Caleb Baldwin Rhodes," attached to Horsley, "Historical
     Sketch of Price," in MS 112, Jean M. Westwood Collection, Box 31, Fd. 1,
     Special Collections, Marriott Library, University of Utah, Salt Lake City, Utah, 2.
93.  "Pioneer Rhoades Passes On," *EUA*, 8 June 1905; "It Looks Bad," *EUA*, 10
     March 1904; *SCMIR* 1905, 40–41.
94.  [Editorial], *EUA*, 10 March 1904.

## Chapter Six

1.  Anna Marolt Tolich, interview with author, Spring Glen, Utah, 13 May 1982.
2.  Bureau of the Census, _Historical Statistics of the United States, 1789–1945_ (Washington, D. C.: Government Printing Office, 1949), 33.
3.  Robert H. Wiebe, _The Search for Order, 1877–1920_ (New York: Hill and Wang, 1967), xii–xiv.
4.  Wink's first wife, Anna Eliza Reynolds, had been thrown from a buggy on 19 November 1895 and died from her injuries the same day. He married Mary J. Jorgenson on 16 September 1896. See "'Wink' Is Sixty," _Emery County Progress_ 25 June 1910; Obed C. Haycock, "Electric Power Comes to Utah," _Utah Historical Quarterly_ [hereafter _UHQ_] 45 (Spring 1977): 186.
5.  Belle Harris Wilson, "Orange, Sr. and Hanna Olsson Seely, Both Utah Pioneers," typescript, LDS Historical Department, Salt Lake City, Utah, 15; "'Wink' Is Sixty;" Mildred Brown, "History: Justus Wellington Seeley II," typescript, 1970, copy in possession of the author, 4; Stella McElprang, comp., _Castle Valley: A History of Emery County_ (Emery County Daughters of Utah Pioneers, 1949), 98; Dora Seeley Otterstrom, interview with author, Castle Dale, 23 April 1979.
6.  "History of Olof [sic: Olaf] William Sandberg," unpublished typescript, copy in possession of the author, 1–3, 6–18.
7.  Willard Sandberg, interview with Elizabeth Hanson, Huntington, Utah, May 1978, copy in possession of the author; Lynn Collard, interview with Elizabeth Hanson and author, Huntington, Utah, 9 November 1978.
8.  Thomas J. Schlereth, _Victorian America_ (New York: HarperPerennial, 1991), 115, 164–65; Haycock, 187; Keith Wright, "Clawson," in Montell Seely, LaVora Kofford, Owen and Jane McClenahan, and Roma Powell, eds., _Emery County, 1880–1980_ (Castle Dale: Emery County Historical Society, 1981), 98; Eva W. Conover, "A Time To Remember," (privately printed, 1977), 153–54; Cecelia Bryner, "Miller Creek," in Castle Country Chapter of the League of Utah Writers, _Legends of Carbon & Emery Counties_ (privately printed, 1996), 49.
9.  Schlereth, 188–90.
10. Lavora Kofford and Paulette Kelly, "Lawrence," in Seely, et al., eds., 233; Michael Dame, "Telephone 'old days' still exist in area," [Price] _Sun-Advocate_, 30 January 1985; quote from Tom McCourt, _The Split Sky_ (Springville, UT: Bonneville Books, 2002), 198–99.
11. Edward A. Geary, "Reuben G. Miller: Turn-of-the-Century Rancher, Entrepreneur, and Civic Leader," _UHQ_ 67 (Spring 1999): 123–39; J. Bracken Lee, "Price City, Its Organization and Presiding Officer," in Thursey Jesson Reynolds, ed., _Centennial Echoes from Carbon County_ (Salt Lake City: Daughters of Utah Pioneers, 1948), 110; "Eastern Utah Telephone Company," _New West Magazine_, 17.
12. Rolla West, interview with author, Price, Utah, 29 March 1979.
13. Edward A. Geary, "Reuben G. Miller," 139–45. Only after he and Emma agreed to discontinue marital relations in 1923 could he return to the LDS Church. He was rebaptized in 1925. Apostle Reed Smoot backed a circular sent to all stake presidents and their counselors in 1910 urging church trials for polygamists, and influenced President Smith's rebuke of polygamists at the fall, 1910 general conference. See B. Carmon Hardy, _Solemn Covenant_ (Urbana: University of Illinois Press, 1992), 292.
14. Edward Geary, _A History of Emery County_ (Salt Lake City: Utah State Historical Society, 1996), 223.

15. Milton R. Merrill, *Reed Smoot: Apostle in Politics* (Logan: Utah State University Press, 1990), 16–29; R. Davis Bitton, "The B. H. Roberts Case," *UHQ* 25 (January 1957): 27–46; "Personalities," *Eastern Utah Advocate* [hereafter *EUA*], 23 February 1899; "Owen Consults Streeper Today," *Deseret Evening News,* 14 October 1899; "C. Mostyn Owen After Roberts," *Deseret Evening News,* 16 October 1899; B. H. Roberts, *A Comprehensive History of the Church of Jesus Christ of Latter-day Saints, Century I,* vol. 6 (Salt Lake City: LDS Church, 1930), 362–64.

16. "Charles Mostyn Owen Makes Strong Charges," *EUA* 14 May 1903. In November, he made the same accusation against Smoot's fellow Apostle, Heber J. Grant. See "After Grant," *EUA,* 12 November 1903. *Times* quoted in Merrill, 51.

17. Hardy, 261, 268, 286; Thomas Alexander, "Political Patterns of Early Statehood, 1896–1916," in Richard D. Poll, ed. *Utah's History* (Provo: Brigham Young University Press, 1978), 416, 425; Merrill, 80, 231–32.

18. Sen. Boies Penrose of Pennsylvania, quoted in Francis T. Plimpton, "Reminiscences," *Reader's Digest* 72 (1 June 1958): 142.

19. Union Pacific Coal Company, *History of the Union Pacific Coal Mines, 1868 to 1940* (Omaha: Colonial Press, [1940]), 41, 43, 59, 165; M. C. Burch to solicitor general, 26 March 1909, RG 60, U. S. Department of Justice Straight Numerical Files, Box 654, Case 48590, National Archives, Washington, D.C.; "Wyoming Coal Lands Restored," *EUA* 29 July 1909; "David Graham Phillips Attacks A National Boss," in Richard Hofstadter, *The Progressive Movement, 1900 to 1915* (New York: Simon and Schuster, 1963), 108–12.

20. "President Sends Official Message," *EUA,* 10 December 1903; "Light Cast On Methods Used To Grab Coal Lands," *Salt Lake Herald,* 12 March 1905; see also Samuel P. Hays, *Conservation and the Gospel of Efficiency* (Cambridge: Harvard University Press, 1959), especially 70.

21. H. G. Williams to C. H. Schlacks, 22 May 1905. See also R. Forrester to H. G. Williams, 22 May 1905; R. Forrester to C. H. Schlacks, 8 March 1905, W. J. T[idwell] to R. Forrester, 17 July 1905, and W. J. Tidwell to H. G. Williams, 20 July 1905, all in MS 154, Utah Fuel Company Records, Lee Library, Brigham Young University, Provo, Utah, Box 8, Fd. 5; J. Harwood Graves to Attorney General, 30 August 1905, RG 60, U.S. Department of Justice Straight Numerical Files, Box 654, Case 48590.

22. "Talk of New Coal Camps," *EUA,* 8 June 1905.

23. "Democrats Get Majority," *EUA,* 8 November 1906; Robert Forrester to H. G. Williams, 5 July 1905, MS 154, Utah Fuel Company Records, Lee Library, Brigham Young University, Provo, Utah, Box 17, Fd. 2.

24. W. J. Tidwell to H. G. Williams, 20 July 1905, MS 154, Utah Fuel Collection, Box 17, Fd. 2, Lee Library, Brigham Young University, Provo, Utah. See also W. J. T[idwell] to Robert Forrester, 11 July 1905, MS 154, Box 17, Fd. 2.

25. Clark deposition, attached to Ernest Knaebel to Attorney General, 28 July 1911, RG 60, U. S. Department of Justice Straight Numerical Files, National Archives, Washington, D. C., Box 655, Case 48590.

26. Carl J. Mayer and George A. Riley, *Public Domain, Private Dominion* (San Francisco: Sierra Club Books, 1985), 122–27; "Land Board Will Make No Contest," *EUA,* 13 December 1906; "And Still More Coal Lands Are Withdrawn From Entry in Utah," *EUA,* 25 October 1906.

27. Arthur A. Sweet, Coal Certificate 172, GLO #1947, Book 6, Records of Carbon County, Recorder's Office, Carbon County Courthouse, Price, Utah; Noble Warrum, ed., *Utah Since Statehood,* vol. 3 (Chicago-Salt Lake City: S.

J. Clarke Publishing Company, 1919), 232; *Arthur A. Sweet v. Charles Mostyn Owen*, Civil 272, Utah 7th Judicial District, Carbon County Clerk's Records, Carbon County Courthouse; "Coal Lands Inquiry" *EUA*, 6 December 1906.

28.  "Earliest Mining Ventures," [Price] *Sun Advocate and Helper Journal*, 2 January 1975; "Wade Sues His Son-In-Law," *EUA*, 1 August 1907; "Curtis Tells What His Company Is Now Doing," *EUA*, 7 March 1907; "'Jack' Woodhead Tells of The Early Doings," [Price] *Sun*, 19 March 1926; *SCMIR* 1907, 24; "Independent Company to Condemn Spring Glen Realty," *EUA*, 17 January 1907; "Dr. Clark Offered Place At Independent Mines," *EUA*, 8 August 1907; "Of A More Or Less Personal Nature," *EUA*, 25 July 1907; "Big Strike Soon Settled," *EUA*, 31 October 1907; "Of A More Or Less Personal Nature," *EUA*, 12 December 1907; "Of A More Or Less Personal Nature," *EUA*, 3 October 1907.

29.  Bureau of the Census, *Historical Statistics*, 33, 35; Leonard J. Arrington, *Great Basin Kingdom* (Cambridge, Mass.: Harvard University Press, 1958; reprint, Lincoln: University of Nebraska Press, 1966), 382; "Truth and Gossip," *EUA*, 21 July 1904; "Truth and Gossip," *EUA*, 9 February 1905; "Of A More Or Less Personal Nature," *EUA*, 12 December 1907; Yamato Ichihashi, *Japanese in the United States* (New York: Arno Press, 1969).

30.  *SCMIR* 1905, 25.

31.  "Italian Population of Utah Grows Each Year," *EUA*, 25 June 1908. The statistics showed 606 from northern Italy plus 365 from the south.

32.  Helen B. Leavitt, "The Lives and Times of Joseph and Jennie Barboglio," typescript, copy in possession of the author.

33.  Philip F. Notarianni, "Italian Fraternal Organizations in Utah, 1897–1934," *UHQ* 43 (Spring 1975): 173–77.

34.  "Slovene National Benefit Society, Subordinate Lodge Charter," revised 1 July 1928; Joseph Stipanovich, "The Yugoslavs," in Helen Z. Papanikolas, ed., *The Peoples of Utah* (Salt Lake City: Utah State Historical Society, 1976) 370; Tolich interview.

35.  William, August, and Mary Krissman Topolovec, interview with author, Spring Glen, Utah, 17 January 1979; "The Christmans of Sunnyside: They've Mined for Four Generations," *The Ingot* [of Kaiser Steel Corp.], March 1975, 4 R.

36.  Rose Katalin Brajkovich, interview with author, Spring Glen, Utah, 1 March 1979.

37.  Frances Dupin Vouk, interview with author, Price, Utah, 10 October 1978.

38.  "Of A More Or Less Personal Nature," *EUA*, 14 November 1907; "News Of Town and County in Brief," *EUA*, 28 November 1907; "Map of County Is Bought," *EUA*, 2 April 1908.

39.  Dorothy Millarich Losik to Frances B. Cunningham, 2 April 1977, copy in possession of the author.

40.  Marie Auphand Fidell, interview with Frances B. Cunningham, 16 March 1976, Spring Glen, Utah.

41.  "Town and County," *EUA*, 7 October 1909; *John Diamenti* [sic] *v. Independent Coal and Coke Company*, Civil 537, 7th Judicial District, Price, Utah; quote from "Kenilworth Injunction," *Carbon County News* [hereafter *CCN*], 5 August 1910.

42.  Martin Marchello, Sr., interview with author, Spring Glen, Utah, 1 October 1978.

43.  U.S. Census 1900, Castle Gate Precinct, Carbon County, Utah; Pete Clerico and Margaret Clerico Paluso, interview with author, Helper, Utah, 30 August 1978; "Independent Coal People Lose Suit," *EUA*, 20 June 1912.

44.  Pearl Baker and Ruth Wilcox, "Greenriver," in McElprang, 191; Geary, *History*, 192.

45. Baker and Wilcox, 184, 191; Nelson Wadsworth, "Green River Is Still Town On Frontier," [Price] *Sun-Advocate*, 25 July 1979.

46. Baker and Wilcox, 188; Geary, *History*, 191; Barbara Ekker to Jim Ramsay, 23 February 1971, copy in possession of the author; Wadsworth, "Green River."

47. Roderick Nash, *Wilderness and the American Mind*, 3rd ed. (1967; reprint, New Haven: Yale University Press, 1982), 141–60; Hayes, 141–46; Geary, *History*, 247.

48. John B. Rae, *The Road and the Car in American Life* (Cambridge, MA: MIT Press, 1971), 35; Geary, *History*, 217; McElprang, 193; Charles S. Peterson, *Look to the Mountains* (Provo: Brigham Young University Press, 1975), 222.

49. Quoted in Nelson Wadsworth, "A Town Struggles For Survival," *Sun-Advocate*, 1 August 1979.

50. Geary, *History*, 193–94, 225–26; McElprang, 194.

51. Quoted in Geary, *History*, 224.

52. Brigham D. Madsen, *Corinne* (Salt Lake City: Utah State Historical Society, 1980), 208–11; Joseph A. Vinatieri, "The Growing Years: Westminster College from Birth to Adolescence," *UHQ* 43 (Fall 1975): 344–51, 356–57; Geary, *History*, 224–25, 246; Allan Kent Powell, "Castle Valley at the Beginning of the Twentieth Century" in *Emery County*, ed. Allan Kent Powell (Salt Lake City: Utah State Historical Society, 1979), 21–22; Velma Peterson, "Ferron," in Seely et al., eds., 114–15; McElprang, comp., 158–59, 164. Female moral authority and its beneficial effect on society through education can be traced back at least as far as the pre-Civil War efforts of female reformers such as Catharine Beecher. See Sarah M. Evans, *Born For Liberty* (New York: Free Press, 1989), 70–73.

53. *SCMIR* 1900, 104; *SCMIR* 1901, 26.

54. Civil 227, *George C. Whitmore v. Utah Fuel Company and Rio Grande Western Ry. Co.*, filed 21 January 1902; refiled 13 January 1906, 7th District Court, Carbon County, Utah; "Whitmore Wins Out in His Two Water Cases," *EUA*, 8 October 1903; Civil 504, *Joseph R. Sharp v. George C. Whitmore, et al.*, filed 15 September 1909, 7th District Court, Carbon County, Utah; Kay Preston and Emma Civish, "Early History & Lore of East Carbon Area of Carbon County, *Carbon County Historical Society Journal* (Spring 2002): 29.

55. "Everything is Going Sky High," *EUA*, 27 June 1907.

56. Quoted in Robert H. Wiebe, *Businessmen and Reform* (Chicago: Ivan R. Dee, Inc., 1962), 70.

57. "News of Town and County in Brief," *EUA*, 29 August 1907.

58. Wiebe, *Businessmen*, 70–75; Nell Irvin Painter, *Standing at Armageddon* (New York: W. W. Norton and Company, 1987), 212–15; "Salient Points of President's Message," *EUA*, 5 December 1907.

59. Theodore Roosevelt, *The Autobiography of Theodore Roosevelt*, Wayne Andrews, ed. (New York: Charles Scribner's Sons, 1958), 233.

60. *SCMIR* 1907, 5–6; "Of A More Or Less Personal Nature," *EUA*, 3 October, 21 November, and 28 November 1907.

61. "Price of Coal Is Reduced," and "Employees Are Discharged," *EUA*, both 9 January 1908 and "More Mines Are Closed Monday," *EUA*, 27 February 1908; "Utah Fuel Company Is Curtailing Its Output," *EUA*, 16 January 1908; Robert Athearn, *The Denver and Rio Grande Western Railroad* (Lincoln: University of Nebraska Press, 1962; reprint, 1977), 213–14.

62. "Of A More Or Less Personal Nature," *EUA*, 28 November 1907; Thomas E. Bryson, "Interview With A Large Sheepman," 7 March 1941, B-100, WPA Grazing Notes, Box 4, Emery County, Utah, and Lee Anderson, "Stock Raisers," B-100 WPA Grazing Notes, Box 4, Carbon County, Utah, Utah

State Historical Society, Salt Lake City, Utah; "Sheepherding family home is studied," *Sun-Advocate*, 19 September 1980; Mary Grace Paquette, *Basques to Bakersfield* (Bakersfield, CA: Kern County Historical Society, 1982), 57; "Bernard Iriart, Sr.," [Price] *Sun-Advocate*, 23 January 1980; "Kiz," in Teachers, Pupils and Patrons of Carbon [School] District, "A Brief History of Carbon County," mimeographed, [c. 1933], 25–26.

63.  Thomas E. Bryson, "Interview with a Large Sheepman [Karl Seely]," 7 March 1941, WPA Grazing Notes Collection, Box 4, Fd. Emery County, Utah, Utah State Historical Society, Salt Lake City, Utah.

64.  "Salt Lake Banks Issue Some Certificates," *EUA*, 14 November 1907; "Green River Bank Closed," *EUA*, 19 December 1907.

65.  [Editorial], *EUA*, 14 November 1907.

66.  West interview, 115–18.

67.  H. S. Alden to Gomer Thomas, 24 January 1908, Coal Mining Collection, Utah State Coal Mine Inspector's Correspondence, Special Collections, Marriott Library, University of Utah, Salt Lake City, Utah.

68.  "Big Strike Soon Settled," *EUA*, 31 October 1907.

69.  Eva W. Conover, "The History of George Henry Westover and His Family," (published by family descendants, Salt Lake City, 1981), 35–37; "Is Increasing Its Forces," *EUA*, 4 June 1908; "Independent People Behind on Big Orders," *EUA*, 24 September 1908; Ernest and Gladys Saccomanno, interview with author, 1 May 1979; "Fuel Famine Is Predicted," *EUA*, 13 August 1908.

70.  *Utah State Gazetteer and Business Directory* (Salt Lake City: R. L. Polk, 1900), 210 ; West interview, 235–36; "Second Only to Salt Lake City," *CCN*, 25 September 1913.

71.  H. Bert Jenson, "Smith Wells, Stagecoach Inn on the Nine Mile Road," *UHQ* 61, no. 2 (Spring 1993): 182–97; Arthur E. Gibson, "Industries, Other Than Coal, Which Were Important In The Development of Carbon County," in Reynolds, ed., 44–45; Edward A. Geary, "Nine Mile: Eastern Utah's Forgotten Road," *UHQ*, 49, no. 1 (Winter 1981): 49; "News of Town and County In Brief," *EUA*, 1 November 1906.

72.  W. J. Tidwell to H. G. Williams, 19 August 1905, MS 154, Box 17, Fd. 2, Utah Fuel Company Records, Lee Library, Brigham Young University, Provo, Utah; "John B. Millburn Shot Down," *EUA*, 12 October 1905.

73.  Quoted in Walker Lowry, *Wallace Lowry* (Stinehour Press: privately printed, 1974), 73. He has misidentified Millburn as Milner.

74.  West interview, 85.

75.  [Editorial], *EUA*, 5 April 1906.

76.  Madge Tomsic, "The Lowenstein Building," in *A Tour of Historic Helper Main Street* (pamphlet, 2002), 7–8; Jack Goodman, "Jews in Zion'" in Papanikolas, 201–10.

77.  Teachers, et al., 12; Francis J. Blumberg, "History of Helper," *News-Advocate*, 24 February 1921.

78.  Marion M. Robinson, no title [History of the Episcopal Church in Carbon County], 1967, copy in possession of the author.

79.  *SCMIR* 1907, 6–7.

80.  *SCMIR* 1909, 31; "Big Railroad and Coal Mining Deal Is Sure To Go," *EUA*, 22 July 1909; "Road Will Build To Cedar Creek," *EUA*, 9 September 1909; "Coal Road to End at Castle Gate," *CCN*, 6 November 1913; "Map Showing Location of the Coal Mines in Carbon & Emery Co.'s Utah," RG 134, Records of the Interstate Commerce Commission, Docket 7933, National Archives, Washington, D.C.

81. "Denver and Rio Grande Have Merged," *EUA*, 30 July 1908; "Harriman and Gould Have Buried Hatchet," *EUA*, 22 April 1908; "Great Things For Future," *EUA*, 28 May 1908; "Ogden Gateway Open To Carbon County Coal," *EUA*, 1 October 1908.
82. "Castle Valley Coal Property," *EUA*, 23 March 1911; "Eastern Men At Mohrland Mine," *EUA*, 6 July 1911; Will C. Higgins, "The Castle Valley Coal Company," *Salt Lake Mining Review* 13 No. 6 (30 June 1911): 15–17; Higgins, "Business Men Examine Hiawatha Mines," *Salt Lake Mining Review* 13 No. 4 (30 May 1911): 15–17.
83. "Coal Company Is Incorporated," *EUA*, 12 May 1911.
84. "Eastern Utah Road Assured," *EUA*, 6 April 1911.
85. "Independent Is Going to Front," *EUA*, 30 July 1908.
86. "Map of County Is Bought," *EUA*, 2 April 1908; "Of A More Or Less Personal Nature," *EUA*, 26 November 1908; *SCMIR* 1907, 24; *SCMIR* 1908, 70; "Truth and Gossip," *EUA*, 13 August 1908.
87. "C. L. Maxwell Discharged," *EUA*, 17 October 1907; "Both Men Improving Now," *EUA*, 3 October 1907; "Petition Totally Ignored," *EUA*, 3 October 1907; "Have Buried the Hatchet," *EUA*, 10 October 1907; "Reidel and Mack Marry at Ogden," *EUA*, 7 November 1907; Charles N. Strevell, *As I Recall Them* (Salt Lake City: Stevens & Wallis, [1944?]), 199–200; "C. L. Maxwell Is Killed By Deputy Sheriff Johnstone," *EUA*, 26 August 1909; "C. L. Maxwell Reported To have Married Rich California Widow," *EUA*, 20 February 1908; "Maxwell to Live at Zion," *EUA*, 27 February 1908; "Mrs. Maxwell Files Suit," *EUA*, 12 March 1908; "She Loses Money and Diamonds," *EUA*, 2 April 1908; "Maxwell Holds Up Wells-Fargo," *EUA*, 18 June 1908; "C. L. Maxwell Is Now Out On Bond," *EUA*, 31 December 1908; "C. L. Maxwell Is Again In Trouble," *EUA*, 25 March 1909; "Maxwell Goes To Castle Dale," *EUA*, 22 April 1909; "Lots of Powder, But Little Smoke," *EUA*, 3 June 1909; "News of Town and County," 17 June 1909.
88. "C. L. Maxwell Is Killed. . . ."
89. "Dead Man Found To Be Hop Fiend," *EUA*, 26 August 1909.
90. Interviews with Sam Taylor, Moab, Utah, 14 September 1979; Rolla West, Price, Utah, 29 March 1979; Lorenzo Dow Young, Price, Utah, 6 August 1979. See also "News of Town and County," *EUA*, 9 September 1909.
91. "Mark P. Braffet Talks About His Bodyguard," *EUA*, 26 August 1909.

## Chapter Seven

1. Rolla West, interview with author, Price, Utah, 29–30 March 1979, 33, 35–36.
2. Richard Hofstadter, "Introduction," *The Progressive Movement* (New York: Simon & Schuster, Inc., 1963), 4–5.
3. Edward Geary, *A History of Emery County* (Salt Lake City: Utah State Historical Society, 1996), 144; "Sarah Ann Stevenson Fullmer," "Mary Ann Price Fullmer," "Olive Amanda Smith Cook Fullmer," all in Daughters of Utah Pioneers, *Pioneer Women of Faith and Fortitude*, vol. 2 (U.S.A.: Publishers Press, 1998), 1033–36; Ina Poulsen, "Orangeville," in Stella McElprang, comp., *Castle Valley: A History of Emery County* (Emery County Daughters of Utah Pioneers, 1949), 304; Clara Fullmer Bullock, "Edwin Fullmer," typescript, copy in possession of the author.
4. "Instructions to Workers for the Woman Suffrage Petition to Congress," attached to Annie Maria Allen to Ada Ostberg, 18 January 1909, copy in possession of the author.

5.   Eleanor Flexner, *Century of Struggle* (New York: Athenaeum, 1974), 249.
6.   W. F. Olson, "Looking Backward," [Price] *Sun Advocate*, 29 May 1947.
7.   "Housefly Safeguards," *Emery County Progress* [hereafter *ECP*], 13 July 1910.
8.   "Swat the Flies and Swat the Garbage," *Eastern Utah Advocate* [hereafter *EUA*], 31 July 1913.
9.   Rolla West, interview with author, Price, Utah, 29 March 1979, 13.
10.  McElprang, 168–69.
11.  Ida M. Tarbell, *The History of the Standard Oil Company*, briefer version, ed. David M. Chalmers (New York: W. W. Norton & Co., 1904; reprint, 1966); David Graham Phillips, *The Treason of the Senate* (New York: Monthly Review Press, 1906; reprint, 1953); Lincoln Steffens, *The Shame of the Cities* (New York: Hill and Wang, 1904; reprint, 1960). All of these were originally serialized in magazines, in *McClure's*, 1902–1904; in *Cosmopolitan*, 1906, and in *McClure's* 1902–1903, respectively.
12.  Richard Hofstadter, *The Age of Reform* (New York: Vintage Books, 1955), 188; Hal G. McKnight, "History of Price's Newspapers," in Thursey Jesson Reynolds, ed., *Centennial Echoes from Carbon County* (Salt Lake City: Daughters of Utah Pioneers, 1948), 124–25; Geary, 204; Allan Kent Powell, "Castle Valley at the Beginning of the Twentieth Century," in *Emery County*, ed. Allan Kent Powell (Salt Lake City: Utah State Historical Society, 1979), 7–8.
13.  "The Editor's Column," [Price] *Carbon County News* [hereafter *CCN*], 19 September 1912.
14.  Nancy J. Taniguchi, *Necessary Fraud* (Norman: University of Oklahoma Press, 1996), 151–54.
15.  For details on the 1912 elections, see John Milton Cooper, Jr., *The Warrior and the Priest* (Cambridge: Belknap Press of Harvard University Press, 1983), 139–221.
16.  "Moroni Heiner, Coal Company President, Dies," [Salt Lake City] *Deseret News*, 26 January 1948.
17.  [Theodore Roosevelt] to Moroni Heiner, 12 June 1912, microfilmed Theodore Roosevelt papers, Series 3A, Reel 377, Library, College of Eastern Utah, Price, Utah.
18.  Olson.
19.  Scott Molloy, "Eugene V. Debs (1855–1926)" in Mari Jo Buhle, et al., eds., *Encyclopedia of the American Left* (Urbana: University of Illinois Press, 1992), 184–86.
20.  Paul Buhle, "Socialist Party," in Buhle et al., 716; John R. McCormick, "Hornets in the Hive: Socialists in Early Twentieth-Century Utah," *Utah Historical Quarterly* [hereafter *UHQ*] 50 (Summer 1982): 225–27; Geary, 216–17; "Socialists Name Ticket," *CCN*, 7 October 1910; "William A. Jameson," *CCN*, 24 October 1912.
21.  Quotes from "Socialist Column—Resolution of the Helper Federation," *CCN*, 19 September 1912. See also "Official List of Nominations for the General Election, November 5th, A.D. 1912," *CCN*, 24 October 1912.
22.  Hepburn Act, 34 Stat. 584 (1906); "Does the New Law Interfere," *EUA*, 23 August 1906.
23.  "Memorandum" accompanying M. C. Burch to attorney general, 26 March 1909, RG 60 Justice Department Straight Numerical Files, Box 654, Case 48590, National Archives, Washington, D.C.
24.  Bills in Equity 867, 868, 870, 27 July 1906, ibid.; Bill in Equity 282, 22 January 1907, in Transcript of Record, *U.S. v. Sweet*, RG 267, S. Ct. Appellate Cases, 25120, National Archives, Washington, D.C.

25. Nancy J. Taniguchi, "The Shifting Significance of *United States v. Sweet*," *Western Legal History* 9, No. 2 (Summer/Fall 1996): 131–46.
26. *Utah v. U. S.* 284 U.S. 534 (1932); Taniguchi, *Necessary Fraud*, 245–46.
27. "Utah Fuel Cases Are Now Settled," *EUA*, 1 April 1909; "Some Figures of Coal Case Fines," *EUA*, 22 April 1909; "Some Facts About Coal Lands Frauds," *Salt Lake Tribune*, 16 April 1909; "Were Not Confined To The One Company," *EUA*, 8 April 1909.
28. E. N. Clark to C. H. Schlacks, 10 April 1909, RG 513, Denver and Rio Grande Collection, Box 13, Fd. 4586, Colorado Historical Society, Denver, CO; "Carbon County Man Higher Up," *EUA*, 20 May 1909; Nancy J. Taniguchi, "No Proper Job for a Stranger: The Political Reign of Mark Braffet," *UHQ* 58 (Spring 1990): 145–64.
29. "Letter from Scofield," *CCN*, 7 October 1910.
30. "Wages Raised," *CCN*, 11 November 1910.
31. "Republicans Carry Carbon County," ibid.
32. "Woodrow Wilson on The Meaning of the New Freedom 1912," in Hofstadter, *The Progressive Movement*, 169–70.
33. J. F. Vaile to M. P. Braffet, 4 January 1912; 9 January 1912; 1 February 1912, all in MS 154, Box 9, Fd. 2, Utah Fuel Company Records, Lee Library, Brigham Young University, Provo, Utah; "Uncle Sam Recovers Valuable Coal Land," *CCN*, 26 April 1912.
34. F. A. Sweet to the Interstate Commerce Commission 3 January 1912; F. A. Sweet to James S. Harlan, 20 January 1912; E. N. Clark to James S. Harlan, 3 February 1912, "Stipulation: Consolidated Fuel Company and Castle Valley Coal Company v. Atchison, Topeka and Santa Fe Railway Company, et al.," 17 June 1913, all in RG 134, Records of the Interstate Commerce Commission, Docket #3811, National Archives, Washington, D.C.
35. "Sunnyside Closed to Progressives," *CCN*, 31 October 1912.
36. "Official Figures on the Late Unpleasantness," *CCN*, 14 November 1912.
37. "Presidential Elections in Utah, 1896–1976," Richard D. Poll, Thomas G. Alexander, Eugene E. Campbell, David E. Miller, eds., *Utah's History* (Provo: Brigham Young University Press, 1978), 700.
38. Olson.
39. Geary, 216; "Official Figures on the Late Unpleasantness," *CCN*, 14 November 1912; Ann B. O'Brien to Nancy Taniguchi, 28 June 1990, copy in possession of the author.
40. Olson.
41. Arthur S. Link, *Woodrow Wilson and the Progressive Era, 1910–1917* (New York: Harper & Brothers, 1954), 31–53, 68–74. Regarding Wilson's anti-Rio Grande litigation, see Taniguchi, *Necessary Fraud*, 177–217.
42. "County Commissioners Are On The Warpath," *CCN*, 16 January 1913; "Doings At The Courthouse," *CCN*, 30 January 1913; "Peace Now Prevails at the Courthouse," *CCN*, 6 February 1913; "District Judge Sustains County Commissioners," *CCN*, 6 February 1913; "War Declared At Sunnyside," *CCN*, 10 April 1913; *Leonard DeLue and Charles H. Vinton v. C. H. Stevenson*, Utah 7 Civil 836 (1914); "Republican Ticket Makes Clean Sweep," *CCN*, 6 November 1913; "County Commissioners Make Serious Charges," *CCN*, 1 January 1914; "So the People May Understand," *CCN*, 29 January 1914; "Impeachment Case Started," *CCN*, 19 February 1914; "Women Organize Betterment League," *CCN*, 26 February 1914.
43. "Hundreds of Women Petition the Council," *CCN*, 5 March 1914.
44. Alfred H. Kelly and Winfred A. Harbison, *The American Constitution*, 3rd ed. (New York: W. W. Norton & Co., Inc., 1963), 586–99; "White Slavery Has No

Place," *EUA*, 23 February 1911; "Women Made To Leave Forthwith," *EUA*, 7 December 1911; "City and County," *CCN*, 25 July 1912; "'Sassiety' News," *CCN*, 1 August 1912.

45. "Local News Briefs," *CCN*, 20 November 1912.
46. "A Spring Poem," *CCN*, 2 April 1914.
47. "Progressive Equalization Means Reduced Levy," *CCN*, 11 June 1914.
48. "Supt. Williams States Utah Fuel's Position," EUA, 10 September 1914.
49. "Bull Moose Party Dead" and "Progressive Party Sweeps the County," *EUA*, 5 November 1914.
50. "Republican Voteslide Hit Price Last Tuesday," *News-Advocate*, 5 November 1915; Braffet to McAllister, 18 April 1916, MS 513, Denver and Rio Grande Collection, Box 15, Fd. 3271, Colorado Historical Society, Denver, Colorado.
51. "Election of Smoot is Assured In Senate," *EUA*, 5 November 1914; Milton R. Merrill, *Reed Smoot: Apostle in Politics* (Logan: Utah State University Press, 1990), 178, 207–9; Larry E. Nelson, "Utah Goes Dry," *UHQ* 41 (Fall 1973): 342–56; Michael Katsanevas, Jr., "The Emerging Social Worker and the Distribution of the Castle Gate Relief Fund," *UHQ* 50 (Summer 1982): 242; "Republicans Get but Three Places on County Ticket," [Price] *News-Advocate* [hereafter *N-A*], 9 November 1916; McAllister to Braffet, 10 January 1917, MS 513, Box 29, Letterbook 12, Colorado Historical Society, Denver, Colorado. See also Taniguchi, "No Proper Job," 145–64.
52. Link, 56–75.
53. John Peterson, "Cattlemen, woolmen debate grazing on Manti mountains," *Sun Advocate*, 11 June 1991.
54. C. C. Anderson, "Interview with Harry Mahleres," July 1940, WPA Grazing Notes Collection, Box 4, Fd.: "Carbon County, Utah," Utah State Historical Society, Salt Lake City, Utah.
55. Elizabeth Hanson, "Cattle drive not what it was," *ECP*, 28 June 1979.
56. "Elk Are Take From Car Here For Emeryites," *N-A*, 21 January 1916; Jim Peacock, "Elk Transplant—(1915–1916)," in Montell Seely, LaVora Kofford, Owen and Jane McClenahan, and Roma Powell, eds., *Emery County, 1880–1980* (Castle Dale: Emery County Historical Society, 1981), 332–33.
57. "Arthur A. Sweet Dead," *Deseret Evening News*, 21 July 1910; "Coal Deal Consummated," *Salt Lake Mining Review* 14 (15 June 1912): 19; "Official Manual of Utah Railway Company . . . No. 2, January 1, 1937," 12.
58. "Denver and Rio Grande Takes Over Two Roads," *EUA*, 26 June 1913.
59. "'Uncle' Jesse Knight Makes Another Buy," *EUA*, 12 June 1913; Utah Department of Mines and Mining, *Report of the State Coal Mine Inspector* [hereafter *SCMIR*] 1913–1914 (Salt Lake City: The Arrow Press, 1915), 5–6.
60. George A. Storrs, "Reminiscences," typescript, n.d., copy in possession of the author, 21–22. Local tradition erroneously holds that the town of Storrs never had a saloon. See "Commissioners Cause Arrests," *CCN*, 11 September 1913.
61. Nedra Monroe Richardson and Kay Leavitt, "Memories of Standardville," in Castle Country Chapter of the League of Utah Writers, *Legends of Carbon & Emery Counties* (privately published, 1996), 161.
62. Arthur E. Gibson, "In the Coal Fields of Eastern Utah, Carbon and Emery Counties, Spring Canyon District, Carbon County," in Reynolds, ed., 228–29.
63. Peter Wiley and Robert Gottleib, *Empires in the Sun* (Tucson: University of Arizona Press, 1982), 142; SCMIR 1914, 133–39, 147–48; SCMIR 1915, 6; SCMIR, 1916, 281; Taniguchi, *Necessary Fraud*, 184–249; "Carbon Fuel Incorporates," *N-A*, 17 September 1915; *Carbon Fuel Company v. Standard Coal Company and C. W. Bemis*, Civil 941 (1915), Utah Seventh Judicial District;

"Moroni Heiner, Coal Company President, Dies," [Salt Lake City] *Deseret News*, 26 January 1948.

64. John B. Rae, *The Road and the Car in American Life* (Cambridge, MA: MIT Press, 1971), 36–37.

65. Geary, 216.

66. McElprang, 193.

67. Ronald G. Watt, *A History of Carbon County* (Salt Lake City: Utah State Historical Society, 1997), 82–83; quote from "Midland Trail Better Than Northern Roads," *EUA*, 31 July 1913.

68. Edward Leo Lyman, "The Arrowhead Trails Highway: The Beginnings of Utah's Other Route to the Pacific Coast," *UHQ* 67 (Summer 1999): 242–64.

69. McElprang, 177; Geary, 217.

70. West interview, 75–76.

71. Richard E. Behling, personal interview, Ferron, Utah, 26 April 1994, Emery County Archives.

72. "Local News Briefs," *CCN*, 27 November 1913.

73. McElprang, 173.

74. Watt, 83.

75. "Strikers Killed Thomas Jackson," *EUA*, 9 February 1911; "All Quiet Now at Kenilworth," *EUA*, 16 February 1911.

76. *SCMIR* 1909, 6.

77. Peter Aiello interview with author, Price, Utah, 23 November 1979.

78. "All Now Quiet . . .;" Aiello interview.

79. "Accused Passed Through Price" and "Men Taken Through Price Last Tuesday," *EUA*, 27 April 1910.

80. Melvyn Dubofsky, *We Shall Be All* (Chicago: Quadrangle Books, 1969), 96–105.

81. Philip Taft, *Labor Politics American Style* (Cambridge, MA: Harvard University Press, 1968), 48–51; Michael Kazin, *Barons of Labor* (Urbana: University of Illinois Press, 1987), 204–8.

82. Helen Zeese Papanikolas, "The Great Bingham Strike of 1912 And Expulsion of the Padrone," *Toil and Rage in a New Land*, 2nd ed. rev. (1974) of the *Utah Historical Quarterly* 38, no. 2 (Spring 1970), 121–33; Idem, "The Exiled Greeks," in *The Peoples of Utah*, Helen Zeese Papanikolas, ed., (Salt Lake City: Utah State Historical Society, 1976) 413; "Company After Grafters," *EUA*, 30 July 1908.

83. "Strike at Tucker," *CCN*, 12 June 1913; "Fear Trouble At Tucker," *CCN*, 12 June 1913; "Conflicting Reports," *CCN*, 19 June 1913; "Agitators Jailed; Strike Is Broken," *EUA*, 19 June 1913; "No Room Here For 'Never Workers,'" *EUA*, 26 June 1913. Quote from "No Room Here."

84. Gibbs M. Smith, *Joe Hill* (Salt Lake City: Peregrine Smith Books, 1984), 115–19.

85. Ibid., 67–177; "Deputy Ed Johnstone Bounces I.W.W. Sympathizer From Capitol," [Price] *Sun*, 28 January 1916.

86. Laurence LaFore, *The Long Fuse* (Philadelphia: J. B. Lippincott Company, 1965); "War Hits Coal Mines," *EUA*, 26 November 1914. See also Nancy J. Taniguchi, "World War I, the American Interior, and Pacific Markets: A Look at Distant Impacts," in Dennis O. Flynn, Arturo Giraldo, and James Sobredo, eds., *Studies in Pacific History: Economics, Politics and Migration* (England, U.K.: Ashgate Publishing, Ltd., 2002), 123–39; "Coal Operators Seek Contracts," *EUA*, 24 September 1914; David McCullough, *The Path Between the Seas, 1870–1914* (New York: Simon and Schuster, 1977), 608–9; Kevin Starr, *Americans and the California Dream, 1850–1915* (New York: Oxford University

Press, 1973), 296–306; Gertrude Atherton, *My San Francisco* (Indianapolis: Bobbs-Merrill Company, 1946), 78; Orson P. Madsen, "Potential Wealth of Carbon County, Utah," *New West Magazine*, 11, no. 2 (February, 1920): 12; "Coal Claims Attention," *EUA*, 19 March 1915; "Enthusiastic Letter From Senator Brinkerhoff," *ECP*, 15 May 1907; McElprang, 146.

87. Robert Knight, *Industrial Relations in the San Francisco Bay Area, 1900–1918* (Berkeley: University of California Press, 1960), 307–68.

88. Watt, 365; Geary, 244–45; Frances Vouk, interview with author, Price, Utah, 10 October 1978; "Supposed Alien Enemy," *Sun*, 22 February 1918; Frances Cunningham, "Utacarbon exemplified the loyalty of local citizens . . ." *Sun Advocate*, 25 June 1979.

89. Quoted in "Biography of William Henry Price, *Our Price Heritage* (privately published), 12–13.

90. Nick Salvatore, "Eugene V. Debs: From Trade Unionist to Socialist," in *Labor Leaders in America*, Melvyn Dubofsky and Warren Van Tine, eds., (Urbana: University of Illinois Press, 1987), 108.

91. Salvatore, 106–8; Preston William Slosson, *The Great Crusade and After, 1914–1928* (New York: Macmillan Company, 1930), 67.

92. Woodrow Wilson to Josephus Daniels, in Ray S. Baker, *Woodrow Wilson*, vol. 1 (New York: Greenwood, 1927), 506.

93. "Strevell Helping," *N-A*, 31 May 1917; Charles R. Van Hise, *Conservation and Regulation in the United States During the World War* (Washington, D.C.: Government Printing Office, 1917) in facsimile reprint as *The United States in World War I* (no place: Jerome S. Ozer, 1974), 139–41.

94. Slosson, 56; W. W. Armstrong to W. E. Hope, 19 March and 29 March, 1918, Record Group 67, Records of the Fuel Administration, "Bureau of State Organizations, Utah," Box 841, Folder 1, National Archives, Washington, D.C.

95. "Heiner Made The Distributor of Coal," *Sun*, 14 June 1918.

96. "Why The Greeks Don't Volunteer," *N-A*, 16 August 1917; Papanikolas, *Toil and Rage*, 146–47; "Gunderson Gets Contract," *CCN*, 27 November 1913.

97. "Carbon Hellenes Organize For Their Own Protection," [Price] *Sun*, 2 August 1918.

98. "Greeks Resent Uncalled For Slur," *Sun*, 12 April 1918. The Crocketts had sold their newspaper and then reclaimed it but neglected to include its name in the paperwork. The *Carbon County News* bought the name of the *Eastern Utah Advocate* and became the *News-Advocate*. Robert Crockett kept his paper, and opted to call it *The Sun*, publishing it continuously until his death in 1930. See Edith Allred, "The Pages Tell a Tale," *Carbon County Journal* vol. 1 (1982):9–13.

99. "John 'Johnny' Sampinos, 58, Rancher, Shepherd, Businessman," in Leslie G. Kelen and Eileen Hallet Stone, eds., *Missing Stories* (Salt Lake City: University of Utah Press, 1996), 427. The full family name is given in Helen Z. Papanikolas, *Emily-George* (Salt Lake City: University of Utah Press, 1987), 284.

100. Quoted in Papanikolas, "Toil and Rage," 156.

101. "Goodbyes Said To More Soldier Boys," *Sun*, 31 May 1918; Kay Preston and Emma Civish, "Early History of East Carbon Area of Carbon County," *Carbon County Historical Society Journal* (Spring 2002): 29.

102. West interview, 58–63.

103. Roger Rowley, "Life History of George Albert Rowley," in *Legends*, 37–38.

104. Richard Pipes, *The Russian Revolution* (New York: Alfred A. Knopf, 1990), 489–603; 624–62; Fred Voll, interview with author, Helper, Utah, 13 April 1982; Robert K. Murray, *Red Scare* (New York: McGraw-Hill, 1955), 40–45.

105. "Start New Coal Camp," *N-A*, 5 April 1917; "Wattis Begins To Ship Coming Week," *Sun*, 29 March 1918; "Lion Coal Company," *New West Magazine*, 11, no. 2 (February 1920): 30; Geary, 224.
106. "Dr. C. T. Rose," *N-A*, 27 December 1917; "Hospital Name Changed," *Sun*, 3 May 1918; "Hospital in New Hands," *Sun*, 16 August 1918; "Buys Local Hospital," *Sun*, 24 June 1921.
107. "Activities of Carbon County Women," *New West Magazine*, 11, no. 2 (February 1920):15.
108. "One Shovel of Coal Each Day Now Being Asked For," *Sun*, 11 January 1918.
109. Watt, 49–52; "1919 fire threatened town's very existence," Helper Centennial supplement to the *Sun Advocate*, September 1981, 13.
110. Slosson, 44; Vouk interview; Gina Kolata, *Flu* (New York: Farrar, Straus and Giroux, 1999), 4–8.
111. Margaret K. Brady, *Mormon Healer and Folk Poet* (Logan: Utah State University Press, 2000), 25, 84.
112. Wilhelmina Holdaway, interview with author, 20 July 1982, Price, Utah.
113. David M. Kennedy, *Over Here* (Oxford: Oxford University Press, 1980), 189.
114. Holdaway interview.
115. "Doughboy statue dedicated to veterans' memory," *Sun Advocate*, 13 November 1990.
116. "Government-Operated Star Route," *New West Magazine*, 11, no. 2 (February 1920): 24; Ravell Call, "Star Route drive recalls area's early mail service," *Sun Advocate*, 10 July 1979; John H. White, "Bank By Mail," *American Vignettes* (Covent Station, New Jersey: TravelVision, 1976), 172–74.
117. Don Carlos Grundvig, "Evolution of the Mind of Man," (privately published, 1965), copy in possession of the author, 217–19.
118. Andrew Hunt, "Beyond the Spotlight: The Red Scare in Utah," *UHQ* 61, no. 4 (Fall 1993): 357–80; Murray, 48–78, 153–55, 231–42; Allan Kent Powell, *The Next Time We Strike* (Logan: Utah State University Press, 1985), 112–20; Dubofsky, *We Shall*, 455–56.
119. Ellis W. Hawley, *The Great War and the Search for A Modern Order, 1917–1933*, 2nd ed. (New York: St. Martin's Press, 1992), 31–36.

## Chapter Eight

1. Eva W. Conover, *A Time To Remember* (privately published, 1977), 33.
2. Robert H. Wiebe, *The Search for Order, 1887–1920* (New York: Hill and Wang, 1967), 301–2.
3. Arthur E. Gibson, "Industries, Other Than Coal, Which Were Important In The Development of Carbon County," in Thursey Jesson Reynolds, ed., *Centennial Echoes from Carbon County* (Salt Lake City: Daughters of Utah Pioneers, 1948), 48–49; Jackie Thayne, "I Remember Wellington," in Castle Country Chapter of the League of Utah Writers, *Legends of Carbon & Emery Counties* (privately printed, 1996), 81.
4. Orson P. Madsen, "Potential Wealth of Carbon County, Utah," *New West Magazine* 11, no. 2 (February 1920): 11–12.
5. Fullmer Allred, "The History of Carbon County Agriculture," in Reynolds, 61.
6. Madsen, 11.
7. J. B. Forrester, "Carbon County Coal Properties," *New West Magazine*, 30, 33.
8. Arthur E. Gibson, "In The Coal Fields Of Eastern Utah, Carbon and Emery Counties, Spring Canyon District, Carbon County," in Reynolds, 228; Thomas Varley, C. C. Stevenson and W. Spencer Reid, *Utah's Mineral Wealth* (Salt Lake City: Commercial Club—Chamber of Commerce, 1921), 25.

9.  "History of Spring Canyon's Latuda Property," [Price] *Sun*, 19 March 1926; Irene O'Driscoll, "Columbia," in Reynolds, 236; "Permit for Railway Granted New Company," [Price] *News-Advocate*, 17 August 1922.

10. *Bulletin No. 4 of the Industrial Commission of Utah* (1 July 1926 to 30 June 1928) (Salt Lake City, Utah, 1929), 64; Helmut Hans Doelling, *Central Utah Coal Fields* (Salt Lake City: University of Utah, 1972), 546; M. Henry Robison, "A Brief Economic History of Utah's Coal Industry," *Utah Economic and Business Review* 37 (April 1977): 4.

11. Wayne K. Hinton, "The Economics of Ambivalence: Utah's Depression Experience," *Utah Historical Quarterly* [hereafter *UHQ*] 54 (Summer 1986), 270–71.

12. Allan Kent Powell, *The Next Time We Strike* (Logan: Utah State University Press, 1985), 201–2.

13. Owen McClenahan, "Days of Prohibition." quoted in Edward A. Geary, "History Written on the Land in Emery County," *UHQ* 66 (Summer 1998): 213.

14. Owen McClenahan, *Utah's San Rafael Swell* (Castle Dale: privately printed, 1986), 100.

15. Helen Zeese Papanikolas, "Bootlegging in Zion: Making the 'Good Stuff,'" in John S. McCormick and John R. Sillito, eds., *A World We Thought We Knew* (Salt Lake City: University of Utah Press, 1995), 286–303.

16. T. L. Burridge, "Diary," 1924–25, typescript, copy in possession of the author.

17. Conover, 33–34.

18. Alda Vee Lambson Alger and Edith Lambson, interview with author, Price, Utah, 4 May 1982.

19. Frederick Lewis Allen, *The Big Change* (New York: Harper and Brothers, Publishers, 1952), 134–35; Noel A. Carmack, "Before the Flapper: The Utah Beginnings of John Held, Jr.," *UHQ* 66 (Fall 1998): 299, 301.

20. Arthur Knight, *The Liveliest Art* (New York: New American Library, 1957), 14–30.

21. Ibid., 51.

22. "Moving Pictures at Price Town Hall," *Eastern Utah Advocate* [hereafter *EUA*,] 7 January 1908; Ernest H. Stevenson, "E. H. Stevenson's History of Sunnyside, 1906–7 to 1923," *Carbon County Historical Society Journal* [hereafter *CCHSJ*] (October 2001): 25; Elvie Marie Hurskainen Stevens, interview with author, Price, Utah, 26 July 1979.

23. Helen B. Leavitt, "The Lives and Times of Joseph and Jennie Barboglio," typescript, copy in possession of the author.

24. [Editorial], *EUA*, 27 April 1911; "Moving Pictures That Talk," *Carbon County News*, 23 January 1913

25. Stella McElprang, comp., *Castle Valley: A History of Emery County* (Emery County Daughters of Utah Pioneers, 1949), 170.

26. Ibid., 171, 178; Edward Geary, *A History of Emery County* (Salt Lake City: Utah State Historical Society, 1996), 273, 293–94; Madge Tomsic, "A Tour of Historic Helper Main Street," (pamphlet, 2002), 15, 19.

27. "Memories of Willie Plese," in *Memories of Kenilworth*, Frances Blackham Cunningham, comp. (privately printed, 1990), 26.

28. Joe Myers and Walt Borla, interview with author, Helper, Utah, 29 June 1982.

29. Nedra Monroe Richardson and Kay Leavitt, "Memories of Standardville," *CCHSJ* (Spring 2002): 6.

30. John Higham, *Strangers in the Land* (New York: Athenaeum, 1970), 167.

31.  Joseph Stipanovich, "South Slav Settlements in Utah, 1890–1935," *UHQ* 43 (Spring 1975): 170.

32.  Kosuye Tsugawa Okura, translator Ferry Okura Taniguchi, interview with author, Carbonville, Utah, 8 January 1989.

33.  Higham, 311.

34.  Nick Bikakis, interview with Jimmy Robertson, 15 February 1988; Jimmy Robertson, "My 'Rizzis'—(Roots): The Story of an Immigrant," copies in possession of the author.

35.  Higham, 323–24.

36.  Allan Kent Powell, "Utah and the Nationwide Coal Miners' Strike of 1922," *UHQ* 45 (Spring 1977): 137.

37.  Ibid., 136.

38.  Stanley Harvey interview with Mark Hutchings, 12 June 1976, Labor Oral History Project Collection, Charles Redd Center for Western Studies, Brigham Young University, Provo, Utah, 5.

39.  Powell, " Strike of 1922," 140–41; Hilda Kraync Yoklovich, "Kraync Family," *CCHSJ*, 2, no. 1 (Spring 1983):12.

40.  Powell, "Strike of 1922," 142; Harvey interview, 6.

41.  "Howard Browne, Sr., Coal Miner, Farmer, Redcap," in Leslie Kelen and Eileen Hallet Stone, eds. *Missing Stories* (Salt Lake City: University of Utah Press, 1996), 83–84.

42.  "Browne," Kelen and Stone, 84.

43.  Powell, *Next Time*, 123.

44.  Helen Z. Papanikolas, "Women in the Mining Communities of Carbon County," in *Carbon County: Eastern Utah's Industrialized Island*," Philip F. Notarianni, ed., (Salt Lake City: Utah State Historical Society, 1981), 95.

45.  Wilhelmina Steckleman Holdaway, interview with author, Price, Utah, 20 July 1982.

46.  Albert Vogrenic, interview with author, Price, Utah, 3 May 1982.

47.  Anna Marolt Tolich, interview with author, Spring Glen, Utah, 13 May 1982.

48.  Papanikolas, "Women," 94–95.

49.  "Filomena Fazzio Bonacci," in Kelen and Stone, 278.

50.  Annie Matekovich Kosec, John Kosec, John Skerl, Jr., and Rose Kosec Skerl, interview with author, Spring Glen, Utah, 25 April 1979.

51.  Martin Kromich, private interview with Allan Kent Powell, Spring Glen, Utah, 8 April 1976; Dorothy Millarich Losik to Frances B. Cunningham, 2 April 1977, copy in possession of the author; Frances Dupin Vouk, interview with the author, Price, Utah, 10 October 1978.

52.  Rochino (Keno) Ariotti, Margaret Marzo Ariotti, and Battista Jack Marzo, interview with author, Spring Glen, Utah, 21 March 1979.

53.  Helen Zeese Papanikolas, "Toil and Rage in A New Land," 2nd ed. rev., 1974, reprint, *UHQ* 38, no. 2 (Spring 1970): 167.

54.  Helen Zeese Papanikolas, "The Exiled Greeks," in *The Peoples of Utah*, Helen Zeese Papanikolas, ed., (Salt Lake City: Utah State Historical Society, 1976), 431.

55.  Powell, *Next Time*, 129; Papanikolas, "Toil and Rage," 169.

56.  Powell, "Strike of 1922," 146–47; Ariotti-Marzo interview; "Official Manual of Utah Railway Company," 17; Mike and Virginia Fugate Magliocco, interview with author, Price, Utah, 8 November 1978.

57.  Wilhelmina Steckleman Holdaway, interview with author, Price, Utah, 28 October 1982.

58.  Sam King, quoted in Papanikolas, *Toil and Rage*, 172.

59.  Papanikolas, "Toil and Rage," 171–75.

60. Vito and Filomena Bonacci, interview with author, Spring Glen, Utah, 15 November 1978.
61. Powell, *Next Time*, 133–34; Marzo-Ariotti interview.
62. "Remembrance of Elizabeth Jackson Ciochette," in Cunningham, 17.
63. Charlie Saccomanno, "Early Kenilworth Memories," in ibid., 7.
64. Powell, *Next Time*, 136; Charlie Saccomanno, "Early Kenilworth Memories," in Cunningham, comp., 7.
65. McElprang, comp., 161; Geary, 261, 274–75.
66. "Remembrances of Ronald Jewkes" and Mabel Jewkes Robertson, "Kenilworth, Utah—No Other Place Quite Like It," in Cunningham, 16, 39; Ronald G. Watt, *A History of Carbon County*, (Salt Lake City: Utah State Historical Society, 1997), 101; Emma Lou Stevenson, "Tribute to Cal Jewkes," in *Legends*, 28.
67. Margaret Burton Stephens, "Fond Memories of Kenilworth," in Cunningham, comp., 22.
68. John, Sr., and Annie Vuksinick Skerl, interview with author, Spring Glen, Utah, 5 July 1979; Joe Rolando, Jr., "Helper firm thriving after some 55 years," [Price] *Sun-Advocate* [hereafter *S-A*], 6 June 1979; "Mutual Furniture to close doors for last time," *S-A*, 8 July 1997.
69. Mineral Leasing Act, 41 Stat. 437 (1920).
70. Teachers, Pupils and Patrons of Carbon [School] District, "A Brief History of Carbon County," mimeographed [c. 1933], 15, 21, 28; Civil Case 2819, *Marrazani v. U. S. Fuel Company*, Exhibits and Attachments, Dept. of Finance, Utah State Archives, Salt Lake City, Utah; Arthur E. Gibson, "A Brief History of the Development of the Gordon Creek Coal District," in Reynolds, 241–42.
71. Robert F. Zeidner, "From Babylon to Babylon: Immigration from the Middle East," *The Peoples of Utah*, Helen Zeese Papanikolas, ed. (Salt Lake City: Utah State Historical Society, 1976), 392.
72. George A. Storrs, "Reminiscences," n. d., typescript, copy in possession of the author, 39.
73. Ibid., 35.
74. "Beulah Storrs Leaves," *Sun*, 10 March 1916.
75. Storrs, 37.
76. Knight, 44–55, 142–51; Bradford A. Jenson, "Castle Dale's Most Famous Cowboy, Artimus Ward Acord," in Montell Seely, LaVora Kofford, Owen and Jane McClenahan, and Roma Powell, eds., *Emery County, 1880–1980* (Castle Dale: Emery County Historical Society, 1981), 384.
77. Frederick Lewis Allen, *Only Yesterday* (1931; reprint, New York: Harper & Row, 1964), 155.
78. Storrs, 37–38.
79. Quoted in Ibid., 38–39; "Utah Mauler Making Ready To Put Money Into Gordon Creek Mines," [Price] *Sun*, 19 October 1923; Ronald C. Brown, *Hard Rock Miners* (College Station: Texas A & M University Press, 1979), 164; Chuck Zehnder, "Carbon Ghost Town Was Boxer's Home," *S-A*, 12 October 1984; Teachers, Pupils, and Patrons, "Coal City," 28; Emma Lou Stevenson, "Coal City," in *Legends*, 34.
80. "Official Manual of Utah Railway Company: Maps and Mileage Tables, Equipment Roster, Historical Data, and Other Information, No. 2, January 1, 1937," 24–25.
81. Allen, 174–75; Allan Kent Powell, "Population" in Allen Kent Powell, ed., *Utah History Encyclopedia*, (Salt Lake City: University of Utah Press, 1994), 432–33.

82. John B. Rae, *The Road and the Car in American Life* (Cambridge, MA: MIT Press, 1971), 50, 57.
83. Rolla West, interview with author, Price, Utah, 29 March 1979, 75.
84. Thomas J. Schlereth, *Victorian America* (New York: HarperPerrenial, 1992), 25–26; quotes from "The Autobiography of Clifford Smith," [1974], LDS Church Historical Department, Salt Lake City, Utah, 29.
85. J. Bracken Lee, "Price City, Its Organization and Presiding Officers," in Reynolds, 110; L. A. McGee, "Pure Water, Paving and Parks for Price," *New West Magazine* 11, no. 2 (February 1920): 10; Nevin Wetzel, "Mohrland-Revisited," [c. 1985], 6; Alger-Lambson interview; Geary, 265.
86. "Kiz," in Teachers, Pupils, and Patrons of Carbon [School] District, "A Brief History of Carbon County," mimeographed, 26.
87. Geary, 218; Watt, *Carbon County*, 84; William Grogan, "History of the Price, Utah Post Office," in Reynolds, 107; "Star Line is Barred," *Sun*, 14 June 1918.
88. "Of A More Or Less Personal Nature," *EUA*, 28 October 1908; Merril Bearnson, telephone interview with author, 18 September 1980.
89. Max Finley, "Mohrland," in *Legends*, 129.
90. Arva Smith, "Marsing is named as rancher of the year," *S-A*, 21 May 1986.
91. Luke Cormani, interview with author, Helper, Utah, 4 November 1978.
92. Preston William Slosson, *The Great Crusade and After, 1914–1928* (New York: Macmillan Company, 1930), 74–75.
93. Janet Prince Spark, "Childhood Remembrances of Francis Prince," *CCHSJ*, 3, no. 1 (1984): 49.
94. Lucy C. Nelson, "Molen," in McElprang, 294.
95. Irma Peterson Snow, personal interview, Ferron, Utah, 4 February 1993, Emery County Archives.
96. Jules Tygiel, *Past Time* (New York: Oxford University Press, 2000), 3–34.
97. Teancum Pratt, "Diary," typescript by Frances B. Cunningham, copy in possession of the author, 100.
98. Photograph, Montell Seely, LaVora Kofford, Owen and Jane McClenahan, and Roma Powell, eds., *Emery County, 1880–1980* (Castle Dale: Emery County Historical Society, 1981), 75.
99. Ernest S. Horsley, "Historical Sketch of Price," MS 112 Jean Westwood Collection, Box 31, Fd. 1, Special Collections, Marriott Library, University of Utah, Salt Lake City, Utah. 17.
100. Myers-Borla interview.
101. Al Latimer, "Documentary slated to premier at Helper," *S-A* 19 August 1997; Watt, *Carbon County*, 334–38.
102. Cormani interview.
103. Conover, 343.
104. Powell, "Population," 432; Mark H. and Terry Lyn Williams, "Mohrland," *ECP*, 17 October 2000.
105. Lee Allen, *The American League Story* (New York: Hill & Wang, 1962), 91–100; Joseph L. Reicher, "The Black Sox Scandal," in *The World Series,* Joseph L. Reicher, ed., (New York: Simon and Schuster, 1978), 142–47, 202; Robert M. Smith, *Baseball in America* (New York: Holt, Rinehart and Winston, 1961), 179–82.
106. Myers-Borla interview.
107. Remo Spigarelli, interview with author, Carbonville, Utah, 5 May 1982.
108. Myers-Borla interview.
109. James L. McClain, *Japan: A Modern History* (New York: W. W. Norton & Company, 2002), 389; "Concert and Dance Coming For Japanese Funds," *Sun*, 7 September 1923.

110. John and Ann Slavensky Spensko, interview with author, Helper, Utah, 7 May 1982.
111. "Anthony 'Tony' Kontgas, 81, Businessman," in Kelen and Stone, eds., 381.
112. Harvey interview, 1–3.
113. Ibid., 5.
114. Burridge diary; Geary, 265; Reynolds, 13, 78, 93; Michael Katsanevas, Jr., "The Emerging Social Worker and the Castle Gate Relief Fund," *UHQ* 50 (Summer 1982): 244.
115. Papanikolas, "Women," 96.
116. Burridge diary.
117. Spensko interview.
118. Burridge diary.
119. Harvey, 1–7.
120. Burridge diary.
121. Frances Dupin Vouk, interview with author, Price, Utah, 12 October 1978.
122. Tolich interview, 33.
123. "Kontgas," in Kelen and Stone, 381.
124. Burridge diary.
125. Tolich interview, 32–33.
126. Burridge diary.
127. Harvey, 8.
128. Katsanevas, 245–51.
129. Larry R. Gerlach, *Blazing Crosses in Zion* (Logan: Utah State University Press, 1982), 88.
130. Leavitt.
131. Ronald L. Lewis, *Black Coal Miners in America* (Lexington: University Press of Kentucky, 1987), 103–10; Gerlach, 2–28, 41–75.
132. Gerlach, "Crosses," 98–99.
133. "Stan John Diamanti, 72, Mining Engineer," in Kelen and Stone, eds., 398.
134. Gerlach, "Crosses," 110, 112, 215 n. 140; Papanikolas, "The Exiled Greeks," 430.
135. Stevens interview.
136. Allan Kent Powell, "A History of Labor Union Activity in the Eastern Utah Coal Fields: 1900–1934" (Ph.D. diss., University of Utah, 1976), 304 n. 10. Since his guilt was never proven in a court of law, his crime can only be alleged.
137. Powell, "Labor Union," 279–84; telegrams E[dward] E[ynon] J[ones] to C. B. H. [Claude P. Heiner?] and A. C. W[atts] 16 June 1925; J. P. to C. B. H. and A. C. W[atts], 16 June 1925; J. P. to C. B. H. and A. C. W[atts], 17 June 1925; E[dward] E[ynon] J[ones] to C. B. H., A. C. W[atts], and F[erdinand] Ericksen, 18 June 1925, all reprinted in J. Eldon Dorman, *Confessions of a Coal Camp Doctor* (Price: Peczuh Printing, 1995), 147–50.
138. Janet Prince Sparks, "Dad Was There—The Lynching of Robert Marshall," *Carbon County Journal* 2, no. 3 (Fall 1983), 26.
139. Larry R. Gerlach, "Justice Denied: The Lynching of Robert Marshall," *UHQ* 66 (Fall 1998): 358.
140. For example, at the grisly southern lynching of seventeen-year-old Jesse Washington in 1917, when a "professional photographer . . . documented the lynching for the inevitable souvenir postcards," Philip Dray, *At The Hands of Persons Unknown* (New York: Random House, 2002), 218.
141. "Lynched by a Mob!" *Sun*, 19 June 1925.
142. They named the company men who had accompanied Marshall from Castle Gate to Price: Henry East and John Daskalakis; Joseph Parmley, Utah Fuel chief clerk; Edward Eynon Jones, Castle Gate mine superintendent; Joseph

E. Caldwell, Utah Fuel employee; and Levi (or Lafe) Davis, manager of the Castle Gate company store. Five more of those arrested came from Price: Warren Peacock, the city marshal; Morgan King, city electrician; Joseph Richard Golding, of Golding Brothers Vulcanizing Works, and barbers George O'Neil and Charles Atwood. See Powell, "Labor Union," 286. See also copies of legal documents (warrants, information, and complaints) in Dorman, 147–50.

143. Gerlach, "Lynching," 358–59.
144. Sparks, 27.
145. "Event organized to reconcile '25 hanging incident," *S-A*, 31 March 1998; "Event focuses on eliminating racism," *S-A*, 7 April 1998; Kevin Ashby, "Reconciling or rewriting history?" [Editorial], *S-A*, 31 March 1998; Michael McAinsh, "Favors reconciling mob violation of lynching victim's constitutional rights," [Letter to the Editor], *S-A*, 9 April 1998.
146. Gerlach, Lynching," 362; "Day of reconciliation concentrates on abolishment of racism," *S-A*, 7 April 1998.
147. E. U. Essein-Udom, "Garvey and Garveyism," in Eric Foner, ed., *America's Black Past* (New York: Harper & Row, 1970), 357–65; Nathan Irvin Huggins, ed., *Voices From the Harlem Renaissance* (New York: Oxford University Press, 1995).
148. Robert L. Zangrando, *The NAACP Crusade Against Lynching, 1909–1950* (Philadelphia: Temple University Press, 1980), 6–7.
149. Utah Department of Mines and Mining, *Report of the State Coal Mine Inspector* 1905–1906 (Salt Lake City: The Deseret News, 1907), 21; idem., 1909–1910 (Salt Lake City: Tribune-Reporter Printing Company, 1911), 76; idem. 1915–1916 (Salt Lake City: Tribune-Reporter Printing Company, [1917]), 156.
150. Poll, 691.
151. Wetzel, 5; Okura interview.
152. Iris Mangum Potts, interview with author, Price, Utah, 6 March 1979.
153. "Largest Crowd Mining Town Has Ever Seen Attends Services," *Sun*, 12 March 1926.
154. "Clear Creek Team Wins Another Football Game," *EUA*, 31 July 1913.
155. Teachers, Pupils, and Patrons of Carbon [School] District, "A Brief History of Carbon County," mimeographed [c. 1933], copy in possession of the author, 33.
156. Charlotte Hamaker, "Balanced Rock and Victory Drum," *CCHSJ* (Spring 2003): 2–8.
157. David A. Shannon, ed. *The Great Depression* (Englewood Cliffs, N. J.: Prentice-Hall, Inc., 1960), 1–4.
158. Robert S. McElvaine, *The Great Depression: America, 1929–1941* (New York: Times Books, 1993), 72–90, 137; James B. Allen, "The Great Protectionist, Sen. Reed Smoot of Utah, *UHQ* 45 (Fall 1977): 338–45.

## Chapter Nine

1. Helen E. Bunnell, "Depression Memories," *Utah Historical Quarterly* [hereafter *UHQ*] 54 (Summer 1986), 266.
2. Caroline Bird, *The Invisible Scar* (New York: David McKay Co., 1965) cited in Studs Terkel, *Hard Times* (New York: Pantheon Book of Random House, 1970), 3–4.
3. Teachers, Pupils, and Patrons of Carbon [School] District, "A Brief History of Carbon County," mimeographed [c. 1933], 17.

4.  Edward Geary, *A History of Emery County* (Salt Lake City: Utah State Historical Society, 1996), 261, 274–75.

5.  Warranty Deed, recorded in Book 5M, 467; "Plat of Central Cemetery," Plat Book A, 14–a, both in Carbon County Recorder's Records, Price, Utah; Frances Dupin Vouk, interview with author, 10 October 1978, Price, Utah; John Skerl, Sr., interview with author, Spring Glen, Utah, 5 July 1979; Annie Matekovich Kosec, John Kosec, John Skerl, and Rose Kosec Skerl, interview with author, Spring Glen, Utah, 25 April 1979.

6.  Robert S. McElvaine, *The Great Depression* (New York: Times Books, 1993), 91–94, 134.

7.  John and Ann Slavensky Spensko interview with author, Helper, Utah, 7 May 1982.

8.  Bunnell, 267.

9.  Eva W. Conover, *A Time to Remember* (privately published, 1977), 40–42, 100.

10. Kosuye Tsugawa Okura and Ferry Okura Taniguchi, interview with author, Carbonville, Utah, 8 January 1989.

11. Stella McElprang, comp., *Castle Valley: A History of Emery County* (Emery County Daughters of Utah Pioneers, 1949), 37.

12. Ida Snow, "Banks," in Montell Seely, LaVora Kofford, Owen and Jane McClenahan, and Roma Powell, eds., *Emery County, 1880–1980* (Castle Dale: Emery County Historical Society, 1981), 50–51; Walker Lowry, *Wallace Lowry* (privately published, 1974), 142–44.

13. McElvaine, 140–56.

14. Melvyn Dubofsky and Foster Rhea Dulles, *Labor in American History*, 6th ed. (Wheeling, IL: Harlan Davidson, Inc., 1999), 251.

15. Isaac Marcosson, *Anaconda* (New York: Dodd, Mead & Company, 1957), 147.

16. *National Miners Union Membership Book* (Women's Auxiliary, Book No. 2724), South Slavic Archives, Special Collections, Marriott Library, University of Utah, Salt Lake City, Utah.

17. Francis Dupin Vouk, interview with author, Price, Utah, 12 October 1978.

18. Allan Kent Powell, *The Next Time We Strike* (Logan: Utah State University Press, 1985), 173–74.

19. Ronald G. Watt, "Price Band Days: The Intermountain Music Festival" *UHQ* 68 (Summer 2000): 244–57, *Sun Advocate* quote on 249; "Dorr Williams Hanson," in Seely et al., eds., 595; Arva M. Smith, "Joseph LaMar and Thelma Mathis Jewkes," in Castle Country Chapter of the League of Utah Writers, *Legends of Carbon & Emery Counties* (privately printed, 1996), 19; "Williams Named To Committee on Patriotic Music," *Sun Advocate* [hereafter *S-A*], 19 March 1942.

20. Spensko interview.

21. Remo Spigarelli, interview with author, Carbonville, Utah, 5 May 1982.

22. Allan Kent Powell, *The Next Time We Strike* (Logan: Utah State University Press, 1985), 165–70.

23. Ibid., 174–78.

24. Nicholas Fontecchio, *The New Deal For the Coal Mining Industry*, [1933], copy in possession of the author.

25. Powell, 178–79.

26. Joseph Myers and Walter Borla, interview with author, Helper, Utah, 29 June 1982.

27. Powell, 180–81.

28. Myers-Borla interview.

29. Myers-Borla interview; "Joseph Myers [obituary]" *S-A*, 12 February 1991, J. Eldon Dorman, "Death of Sheriff Marion Bliss," in *Confessions of a Coal Camp*

*Doctor* (Price, Utah: Peczuh Printing Company, 1995), 155–58.

30. Helen Z. Papanikolas, "Unionism, Communism, and the Great Depression: The Carbon County Coal Strike of 1933," *UHQ* 41 (Summer 1973):279–300. Quote on 294.
31. Ibid., 295.
32. Richard C. Cortner, "The Wagner Act and the Constitutional Crisis of 1937," in John W. Johnson, ed., *Historic U. S. Court Cases, 1690–1990* (New York: Garland Publishing, 1992), 684–91.
33. Wayne K. Hinton, "The Economics of Ambivalence: Utah's Depression Experience," *UHQ* 54 (Summer 1986): 284–85.
34. Myers-Borla interview.
35. Myers-Borla interview.
36. "Coal Bill Favorable to Carbon County Passed by Senate," *S-A*, 23 February 1933; "Royalty Money Apportioned; Some Warrants to Be Paid," *S-A*, 23 November 1933.
37. Committee to Study Operations of [Utah] State Government, Works Progress Administration, *An Economic Study of the Development of Utah's Coal Resources* (Salt Lake City, October 1936), 19, 28, 72–73, 88–89, 97, 120–24.
38. Hinton, 270–71.
39. Edward A. Geary, "History Written on the Land in Emery County," *UHQ* 66 No. 3 (Summer 1998): 213; Albert Vogrenic, interview with author, Price, Utah, 3 May 1982.
40. Geary, *History*, 276–84.
41. Remo Spigarelli, interview with author, Carbonville, Utah, 5 May 1982.
42. Geary, *History*, 275; Willard Sandberg, interview with Elizabeth Hanson, Huntington, Utah, May 1978; "Willard Sandberg" [obituary], *S-A*, 11 April 1996.
43. Keith Wright, "Clawson," in Seely, et al., 100; Geary, *History*, 285–87.
44. Bunnell, 266–67.
45. Arva Smith, "Half-Century New Century Club is gone," *S-A*, 19 June 1985.
46. Bunnell, 265. Italics in original.
47. Leonard J. Arrington, "Utah's Great Drought of 1934," *UHQ* 54 (Summer 1986): 249; McElprang, 48.
48. Hinton, 268–85.
49. Homer Edwards and Calvin L. Moore, "Moore," in McElprang, 298.
50. Thomas E. Bryson, "Interview with an average cattleman [James F. Allred]," WPA Grazing Notes Collection, Box 4, Fd.: "Emery County, Utah," Utah State Historical Society, Salt Lake City, Utah.
51. Tom McCourt, *The Split Sky* (Springville, UT: Bonneville Books, 2002), 34, 163; quote from Virginia N. Price and John T. Darby, "Preston Nutter: Utah Cattleman, 1886–1936," *UHQ* 32 (1964): 250.
52. Clair C. Anderson, "History of Grazing, Chapter V, Growing Crisis on the Range," B-100 WPA Grazing Notes Collection, Box 1, Fd.: "History of Grazing," Utah State Historical Society, Salt Lake City, Utah; Carl Abbott, "The Federal Presence," in *The Oxford History of the American West,* Clyde Milner II, Carol A. O'Conner, and Martha A. Sandweiss, eds., (New York: Oxford University Press, 1994), 478.
53. Stanford J. Layton, *To No Privileged Class* (Provo: Brigham Young University Press, 1988), 88.
54. C. C. Anderson, "Interview with Harry Mahleres," July 1940, WPA Grazing Notes Collection, Box 4, Utah State Historical Society, Salt Lake City, Utah; Warranty Deed, Book 195, page 127, Carbon County Recorder's Office, Carbon County Courthouse, Price, Utah.

55. Arrington, 248–259, 262; Geary, *History*, 277–79.

56. Hinton, 268–85.

57. Wright, 98; "Helper meeting describes Depression arts activity," *S-A*, 5 December 1984; "Special Delivery—Murals for the New Deal Era," *S-A*, 29 March 1989.

58. "Building projects lift town out of Depression," *Helper Centennial* supplement to the *Sun Advocate*, September 1981.

59. "Special Delivery"; "National museum displays photograph of post office in downtown Helper," *S-A*, 21 April 1998; Hinton, 281–82.

60. "The Price Mural by muralist Lynn Fausett," [pamphlet], n.p., n.d.

61. *History C.C.C. Company 959, 1933 to 1936* (privately published), no page. This spiral-bound volume was prepared for the CCC reunion in 1983. At Emery County Archives, Castle Dale, Utah.

62. "CCC built friendships, families and character," ibid.

63. Arva Smith, "After 75 years, business calls it quits," *S-A*, 31 March 1987.

64. Beth R. Olsen, "Utah's CCCs: The Conservators' Medium for Young Men, Nature, Economy, and Freedom," *UHQ* 62, no. 3 (Summer 1994): 261–74; McElprang, 172; Geary, "History Written," 215; Geary, *History*, 283–84; "C.C.C. to Observe 8th Birthday This Week At Main and Side Camps," *S-A*, 3 April 1941; "CCC Projects Completed On The Ferron Ranger District, Manti-LaSal National Forest," in *History C.C.C. Company 959*, no page.

65. Thursey Jesson Reynolds, ed., *Centennial Echoes from Carbon County* (Salt Lake City: Daughters of Utah Pioneers, 1948), 68–69; Ronald G. Watt, *History of Carbon County* (Salt Lake City: Utah State Historical Society, 1997), 52–53.

66. "Autobiography of Henry George Mathis, 1861–1959," MS 15457, LDS Church Historical Department, Salt Lake City, Utah, 38–39.

67. Roderick Nash, *Wilderness and the American Mind*, 3rd ed. (New Haven: Yale University Press, 1982), 161–81.

68. David M. Kennedy, *Freedom From Fear* (New York: Oxford University Press, 1999), 147–48; Joseph E. Stevens, *Hoover Dam* (Norman: University of Oklahoma Press, 1988), 19–46; Donald E. Wolf, *Big Dams and Other Dreams* (Norman: University of Oklahoma Press, 1996),13–29, 38.

69. Reed Thompson, 24 December 1931 at rear of Teancum Pratt, "Diary," typescript by Frances B. Cunningham, copy in possession of the author, 213. After Pratt's death, other family members made sporadic entries until 1963.

70. Stevens, 52–64, 243–44.

71. Rue L. Clegg to Fred A. Weller, 10 March 1936; Jonathan Fletcher to Edward J. Rowell, 5 February 1936; Paul S. Taylor to William Palmer, 20 March 1936, all in RG 96 Subgroup FSA, San Francisco, Series RR UT Correspondence, 1935–37, Box 2, Fd. RR UT 11 Price River 100–, Sierra Pacific Branch, National Archives, San Bruno, California; Peter S. Briggs, curator and Brian Q. Cannon, essay, *Life and Land* (Logan: Utah State University Press and Nora Eccles Harrison Museum of Art, 1988), 9–12. All the photographs bear the original caption, presumably provided by Garst, Taylor, and Lange.

72. Dorman, 67–68; "Many families hold memories of Consumers," *S-A*, 25 June 1980.

73. William I. Palmer to Omar Mills, 1 February 1936, RG 96 Subgroup FSA, San Francisco, Series RR UT Correspondence, 1935–37, Box 2, Fd. RR UT 11 Price River 100–, Sierra Pacific Branch, National Archives, San Bruno, California.

74. Jonathan Garst to Henry H. Blood, 7 May 1936, RG 96, Subgroup FSA San Francisco, Series RR UT Correspondence 1935–37, Box 2, Fd. RR UT 11 Price River 100–, Sierra Pacific Branch, National Archives, San Bruno,

California; Melvin W. Buster to C. O. Stott, 18 April 1936, RG 96, Subgroup FSA San Francisco, Series RR UT Correspondence 1935–37, Box 2, Fd. RR UT 11 Price River 400–, Sierra Pacific Branch, National Archives, San Bruno, California.

75. Val H. Cowles to Abe Murdock, 17 February 1937; Administrator to Abe Murdock, 5 March 1937, both in RG 96, Subgroup FSA San Francisco, Series RR UT Correspondence 1935–37, Box 1, Fd. SH-UT 6, Sierra Pacific Branch, National Archives, San Bruno, California.

76. Carbon College, "This Is Your College," in Reynolds, 132–37; Watt, *Carbon County*, 295.

77. Arva Smith, "By-gone days hold pleasant memories," *S-A* 12 June 1985; Leonard Shield, interview with author, Price, Utah, 14 July 1983; Lease record card SL–051279–063188, Bureau of Land Management Office, Price, Utah.

78. Clair C. Anderson, "History of Grazing," 31–32; Leonard J. Arrington and Thomas G. Alexander, "World's Largest Military Reserve: Wendover Air Force Base, 1941–1963" *UHQ* 31 (Fall 1963): 324–32.

79. Rochino (Keno) Ariotti, Margaret Marzo Ariotti, and Battista Jack Marzo, interview with author, Spring Glen, Utah, 21 March 1979.

80. Claire Anderson, 67.

81. Fred Wataru Taniguchi, interview with Robert I. Taniguchi, 31 July 2000, Ogden, Utah.

## Chapter Ten

1. Owen McClenahan, "Uranium Mining in the Colorado Plateau," typescript, Emery County Archives, Castle Dale, Utah, copy in possession of the author, 9.

2. Helmut Hans Doelling, *Central Utah Coal Fields* (Salt Lake City: University of Utah, 1972), 546; Max Finley, "Mohrland," in Castle Country Chapter of the League of Utah Writers, *Legends of Carbon & Emery Counties* (privately printed, 1996), 133; Edward Geary, *A History of Emery County* (Salt Lake City: Utah State Historical Society, 1996), 305; quote from Vernon Leamaster, "Leamaster Coal Company," 24 February 1994, Emery County Archives, Castle Dale, Utah; "Safety standard combats diesel dangers in underground mines," *Sun-Advocate* [hereafter *S-A*], 29 October 1996. Although wartime statistics show only total state production, Castle Valley had always supplied some ninety per cent of the total.

3. Hilda Kraync Yoklovich, "Kraync Family," *Carbon County Historical Society Journal* [hereafter *CCHSJ*], 2, no. 1 (Spring 1983): 15.

4. Clifford Smith, "The Autobiography of Clifford Smith," LDS Church Historical Department, Salt Lake City, Utah, 43.

5. J. Eldon Dorman, "How a 'Stay at Home' Doctor Fought World War II in Carbon County," unpublished typescript, copy in possession of the author, 14–15. [A part of this manuscript was published as "J. Eldon Dorman" in Allan Kent Powell, *Utah Remembers World War II* (Logan: Utah State University Press, 1991).]

6. Dorman, 1–7; Ronald G. Watt, *History of Carbon County*, (Salt Lake City: Utah State Historical Society, 1997), 88–89.

7. Arva Smith, "By-gone days hold pleasant memories," *S-A* 12 June 1985; Leonard Shield, interview with author, Price, Utah, 14 July 1983.

8. Shefton and Roxella Behunin Gordon, interview with author, East Carbon, Utah, 1 April 1982.

9. Nancy J. Taniguchi, "Stigmatizing Okies," in Gordon M. Bakken, ed., *California History: A Topical Approach* (Wheeling, IL: Harlan Davidson, Inc., 2003), 146–72.

10. James Noble Gregory, *American Exodus* (New York: Oxford University Press, 1989); Jeanette McAlpine, "Rains: A Memoir," *CCHSJ*, 2, no. 1 (Spring 1983):38–39; Nadine Marx, "Memories of a Small Mining Town," in *Legends*, 36.
11. Dorman, 14.
12. Ross and Fern Boyack, "Like Father, Like Son," *CCHSJ* (Spring 2003): 17.
13. "Victory Cooking School Is Planned for Price; Defense Council In Charge of Plan," *S-A*, 16 April 1942.
14. Katie Clark Blakesley, "'Save 'em, Wash 'em, Clean 'em, Squash 'em: The Story of the Salt Lake City Minute Women," *Utah Historical Quarterly* [hereafter *UHQ*] 71 (Winter 2003): 36–51; Eva Conover to Nancy Taniguchi, 15 September 2000; Lucy Hansen Nielsen, "Recollections on the History of Molen, Emery County, Utah," typescript, copy in possession of the author, 17–18.
15. Wilhelmina Steckleman Holdaway, interview with author, Price, Utah, 20 July 1982.
16. Finley, 133; C. A. Hamaker, "Helper's Boy Scout Troop #78," *CCHSJ* (April 2000): 60.
17. Karen Anderson, *Wartime Women* (Westport, CT: Greenwood Press, 1981), 4.
18. "Price Woman Paint Crew Restriping Canyon Road; Pictures On Cover Page," *S-A*, 14 October 1943.
19. "Twenty-Nine Women Working For Carbon Coal Companies; Hire 300 Men, More Needed," *S-A*, 25 November 1943.
20. Powell, xii. It is unclear if this total is also meant to include women.
21. "More Men [sic; and women] Listed Discharged from Military Service Units," *S-A*, 3 January 1946; Eva Trauntvein Dixon, "My Memories of Kenilworth," in *Memories of Kenilworth*, Frances Blackham Cunningham, comp. (privately printed, 1990), 45.
22. Arva Smith, "Ann Self's tireless efforts built school," *S-A*, 3 November 1987.
23. "Had Unusual Record," *S-A*, 20 January 1944.
24. Dorman, 13–14.
25. Watt, *Carbon County*, 381.
26. Jackie Thayne, "I Remember Wellington," in Castle Country Chapter of the League of Utah Writers, *Legends of Carbon & Emery Counties* (privately printed, 1996), 80; Meloney Rigby, "Hoffman radio graduate recalls troop train's stopover at Helper," *S-A*, 14 May 1996.
27. Eva Conover to Nancy Taniguchi, 15 September 2000.
28. Arva Smith, "After 75 years, business calls it quits," *S-A*, 31 March 1987.
29. J. Eldon Dorman, *Confessions of a Coal Camp Doctor* (Price, Utah: Peczuh Printing Company, 1995), 28–29; Nevin Wetzel, "Mohrland-Revisited," [c. 1985], typescript, copy in possession of the author, 6.
30. Powell, 193–96.
31. Dorman, "'Stay-At-Home' Doctor," 132–37.
32. Roger Daniels, *Asian America* (Seattle: University of Washington Press, 1988), 196.
33. Ibid., 198.
34. Paul Turner, *Sunnyside Memories* (Orem, UT: SunRise Publishing, 1997), 258.
35. Peter Irons, *A People's History of the Supreme Court* (New York: Penguin Books, 1999), 356–63. The literature on the internment is voluminous and growing. See, for example, National Park Service, *Confinement and Ethnicity* (Tucson: Western Archeological and Conservation Center, 1999); Louis Fiset, *Imprisoned Apart* (Seattle: University of Washington Press, 1997), and

on the United States imprisonment of Peruvian Japanese, Seiichi Higashide, *Adios to Tears* (Honolulu: E. & E. Kudo, 1993).

36.  Commission on Wartime Relocation and Internment of Civilians, *Personal Justice Denied*, foreword by Tetsuden Kashima, (Seattle: University of Washington Press, 1997), 459.

37.  Daniels, 246–57.

38.  Fred Wataru and Ferry Hiroko Okura Taniguchi, interview with author, Ogden, Utah, 17 February 2001.

39.  Ibid., "Japanese Couple From Sweet Mine Licensed To Wed," *S-A*, 16 December 1943; Dixon, 45.

40.  "Sego Takita Matsumiya," in Powell, 226.

41.  Gordon interview.

42.  "Japanese Move To Green River Area This Week" *S-A*, 2 April 1942; Herbert G. Folken to Rex Willard, 2 April 1942, RG 83, War Relocation Records, 1942, Relocation Camp Sites, Utah-Wyoming, Series 284, Box 36, Fd. Utah, National Archives Pacific Sierra Branch, San Bruno, CA; Edward A. Geary, "History Written on the Land in Emery County," *UHQ* 66 (Summer 1998): 215; Nancy J. Taniguchi, "Japanese Immigrants in Utah," in Allan Kent Powell, ed., *Utah History Encyclopedia*, (Salt Lake City: University of Utah Press, 1994), 281–83.

43.  "Hold Carbon Coal Land Most Safe Investment," *Eastern Utah Advocate* [hereafter *EUA*], 6 April 1911; "Sharp Interests Are Figuring On Horse Canyon Coking Coal," *EUA*, 4 April 1912.

44.  Leonard J. Arrington and Thomas Alexander, *A Dependent Commonwealth* (Provo: Brigham Young University Press, 1974), 73; Irene O'Driscoll, "Columbia," in Thursey Jesson Reynolds, ed., *Centennial Echoes from Carbon County* (Salt Lake City: Daughters of Utah Pioneers, 1948), 236, 258.

45.  Roger D. Launius and Jessie L. Embry, "A Transforming Force: Military Aviation and Utah in World War II," *UHQ* 63 (Summer 1995): 233.

46.  Arrington and Alexander, 73; O'Driscoll, 236, 258; Arthur E. Gibson, "The Kaiser Mine, Sunnyside," in Reynolds, 261.

47.  Thomas G. Alexander, "Utah War Industry during World War II: A Human Impact Analysis," *UHQ* 51 (Winter 1983): 79–85.

48.  Frank Peczuh, "Sunnyside," in *Legends*, 159.

49.  Gerald D. Nash, *The American West Transformed* (Lincoln: University of Nebraska Press, 1985), 26; "Lease," Book 3W, 222, Carbon County Recorder's Records, Carbon County Courthouse, Price, Utah.

50.  Gibson, 261–62; "Here High In Carbon County Mountains The War Built A Town In Six Weeks," Pennie Olsen scrapbook; Henry Malaby, "History of Carbon County Railway Company," in Reynolds; Turner, 224, 228; Rosann Fillmore, "'Still in it' after a century of sales," *S-A*, 13 November 1990.

51.  "Scofield Dam Case Decided Favorably," *S-A*, 27 January 1944; Cecelia Bryner, "Miller Creek," in *Legends*, 49.

52.  Allan Kent Powell, "Population," in Powell, *Utah Encyclopedia*, 432–33.

53.  Geary, *History*, 307–8; Roma N. Powell, "A History of Emery County Schools," in Montell Seely, LaVora Kofford, Owen and Jane McClenahan, and Roma Powell, eds., *Emery County, 1880–1980* (Castle Dale: Emery County Historical Society, 1981), 303.

54.  Eva Conover to Nancy Taniguchi.

55.  Dixon, 45; "Victory Ends World War," "Coal Production Is Curtailed By V-J Day In Carbon Area," "Ration Relaxed On Gas, Canned Goods," "Celebration Is Orderly, Says County Sheriff," *S-A*, 16 August 1945.

56. Joseph Arave, "The Forest Service Takes to the Slopes: The Birth of Utah's Ski Industry and the Role of the Forest Service," *UHQ* 70 (Fall 2002); 341–55; quote from Turner, 220–21.

57. Elvie Marie Herskainen Stevens, interview with author, Price, Utah, 26 July 1979.

58. C. H. Madsen, "Clear Creek," in Reynolds, 209.

59. Elliott Roosevelt, *As He Saw It* (New York: Duell, Sloan and Pearce, 1946), 233–46; Tom Balsley, interview with Bill Cook, Moab, Utah, 13 February 1988.

60. M. Henry Robison, "A Brief Economic History of Utah's Coal Industry," *Utah Economic and Business Review* 37, No. 4 (April 1977): 6.

61. Gerald J. Goodwin, Richard Current, and Walter Freidell, *A History of the United States*, 2nd ed. (New York: Alfred A. Knopf, 1985), 794–95; Edward A. Geary, *Goodbye to Poplarhaven* (Salt Lake City: University of Utah Press, 1985), 117–18.

62. William H. Chafe, *The American Woman* (New York: Oxford University Press, 1972); Reva Beck Bosone, "Biography" in Register 20 and "Autobiography," both MS 127, Box 1, Fd. 11, Special Collections Department, Marriott Library, University of Utah, Salt Lake City, Utah, 40–54; Stanford J. Layton, "Ivy Baker Priest," in Colleen Whitley, ed., *Worth Their Salt* (Logan: Utah State University Press, 1996), 223–27; John Heilprin, "Bosone Blazed Trail For Women in Utah," *Salt Lake Tribune*, 17 September 1999; Maureen Ursenbach Beecher and Kathryn L. MacKay, "Women in Twentieth-Century Utah" in Richard Poll, ed., *Utah's History* (Provo: Brigham Young University Press, 1978), 576–77; Albert Fried, ed., *McCarthyism* (New York: Oxford University Press, 1997).

63. Walter LaFeber, *America, Russia, and the Cold War, 1945–1967* (New York: Wiley, 1967), 56.

64. Howard Balsley, untitled paper prepared for the Southeastern Utah Chapter of the American Institute of Mining Engineers [hereafter Balsley Remarks], c. 1975, copy in possession of the author, 1.

65. Balsley Remarks, 5; Owen McClenahan, *Utah's Scenic San Rafael* (Castle Dale; privately printed, 1986), 105–6; Lucy C. Nielson, "Ferron," in Stella McElprang, comp., *Castle Valley: A History of Emery County* (Emery County Daughters of Utah Pioneers, 1949), 292.

66. "75 Years Ago: The Work Of An Emery County Man," *S-A*, 27 June 1979.

67. "Deposit of Uranium Discovered in Utah," *EUA*, 3 June 1909; "Utah Uranium Shipped to Eastern Markets," *EUA*, 5 January 1911; Dee Anne Finken, *A History of the San Rafael Swell* (Boulder, CO: Western Interstate Commission for Higher Education, 1977), 32–33; "Price and Vicinity," *EUA*, 13 August 1914; Balsley Remarks, 2–4.

68. Balsley Remarks, 5; J. Eldon Dorman, interview with author, Price, Utah, 24 July 1998; Raye Ringholtz, *Uranium Frenzy* (New York: W. W. Norton, 1989), 70, 100.

69. Ringholtz, 59–67.

70. Dorman interview.

71. McClenahan, "Uranium Mining," 12.

72. Geary, *History*, 330–31; McClenahan, *San Rafael*, 43, 107–15 and idem, "Uranium Mining," 1–8; Ringholtz, 72–76.

73. McClenahan, "Uranium Mining," 28.

74. Dorman interview.

75. Ibid., (reading from a newspaper clipping).

76. "Price native signs mine contract," *S-A*, 14 July 1982; "Kalatzes expands various gold mining operations," *S-A*, 13 November 1990.

77.    Ringholtz, 132–34; McClenahan, "Uranium Mining," 33.
78.    McClenahan, *San Rafael*, 107–9; Arminta Hewitt, "Temple Mountain," in
       Seely et al., eds., 335–36.
79.    Quoted in Finken, 33.
80.    Utah Mining Association, *Utah's Mining Industry* (Salt Lake City: Utah
       Mining Association, 1967), 39.
81.    Ringholtz, 116–22; McClenahan, *San Rafael*, 116.
82.    Dorman interview.
83.    Ringholtz, 179–93.
84.    Ibid., 108–10, 157–58; "Carter signs tailings bill," *Deseret News*, 10 November
       1978; Ernest H. Linford, "Let's All Hope Tailings Plans Will Get Needed
       Attention," *Salt Lake Tribune*, 29 May 1978.
85.    Amber Saupan, "Carbon County native meets with the 17 scholarship
       recipients he funded," [Price, College of Eastern Utah] *The Eagle*, 30
       October 1997; Ringholtz, 166–78, 194–206, 230–51; McClenahan, *San
       Rafael*, 81; Sara M. Evans, *Born for Liberty* (New York: Free Press, 1989), 274.
86.    Paul Foy, "Scam Artists Thrive on Easy Pickings in Utah," *San Francisco
       Chronicle*, 24 November 2000.
87.    A. E. Gibson, "Atomic Energy In Emery County," in Reynolds, 259.
88.    Layne Miller, "MK Tunnels are part of San Rafael Swell's dark past," *S-A*, 21
       May 1998.
89.    Arthur R. Gomez, *Quest for the Golden Circle* (Albuquerque: University of New
       Mexico Press, 1991), 187–91.
90.    McClenahan, *San Rafael*, 90, 115–16; idem, "Uranium Mining," 29.
91.    Saupan.
92.    Nash, vii.
93.    Ibid., 24.
94.    "1947 Production of Utah Coal Loading Truck Mines For 1947 By
       Counties," MS 277, Peerless Coal Company, Box 55, Fd. 9, Lee Library,
       Brigham Young University, Provo, Utah; "Production By Counties," *Report of
       the Industrial Commission*, 1 July 1950 to 30 June 1952, Utah State Archives,
       Salt Lake City, Utah, 31; "Southeastern Utah 1974 Coal Production By
       Mine," Southeastern Utah Association of Governments, *Economic Report*
       (privately published, 1976), 39.
95.    U.S. Bureau of Mines, *Mineral Yearbook*, applicable years.
96.    Robison, 6.
97.    Rochino Ariotti, Margaret Marzo, and Battista Jack Marzo, interview with
       author, Spring Glen, Utah, 21 March 1979.
98.    Powell, "Population," 433–38.
99.    Quoted in *CCHSJ* (April 2000): 44, and "Eastern Utah Broadcasting,"
       *CCHSJ*, (October 2001), 54.
100.   John Peterson, "Livestock Grazing on the Manti Division of the Manti-LaSal
       National Forest," 1991, Emery County Archives; "General Authorities: The
       First Presidency," *1991–1992 Church Almanac* (Salt Lake City: Deseret News,
       1990 [sic]), 12; Powell, "Population," 433–38.
101.   J. Bracken Lee, "Price City, Its Organization and Presiding Officers," in
       Reynolds, 112; Dennis R. Lythgoe, *Let 'Em Holler* (Salt Lake City: Utah State
       Historical Society, 1982), 26–39. Quote in Lythgoe, 39.
102.   Lythgoe, 58–64.
103.   Louis Galambos and Joseph Pratt, *The Rise of The Corporate Commonwealth*
       (New York: Basic Books, Inc., 1988), 128; Lythgoe, 127–43, 178–87.
104.   Lythgoe, 178–87, 207–8; Watt, *Carbon County*, 296–98; Powell, "Population,"
       432–33; Smith, "After 75 years"; quote from "Carbon College Wins Battle

For Survival," *S-A*, 4 November 1954.

105. Watt, *Carbon County*, 278; "Information on Dragerton Houses Given," *S-A*, 17 January 1946.

106. J. Eldon Dorman, "The Carbon College Prehistoric Museum," paper presented to the Utah Statewide Archeological Society, 26 May 1962, copy in possession of the author.

107. *Progress Report on the Status of Women*, First annual report, quoted in Margaret Mead and Frances Bagley, eds., *American Woman* (New York: Charles Scribner's Sons, 1965), 161.

108. Eva Conover, *A Time To Remember* (privately printed, 1977), 236–50, 270–94; quote from Eva Conover to Nancy Taniguchi, 21 January 2000.

109. Conover, *Time*, 294.

110. Gary R. Tomsic, "Emery County: The Second Hundred Years," in *Emery County*, Allan Kent Powell, ed., (Salt Lake City: Utah State Historical Society, 1979), 126–27.

111. Geary, *Poplarhaven*, 162.

## Chapter Eleven

1. Mrs. Roy W. Cook to Chuck Zehnder and J. Eldon Dorman [letter to the editor], *Sun-Advocate* [hereafter *S-A*], 18 August 1987.

2. Ibid.

3. Kirk Olsen, personal communication, Price, Utah, 27 May 2003.

4. Allan Kent Powell, personal communication, 14 March 2004.

5. Rodolfo Acuna, *Occupied America*, 4th ed. (New York: Longman, 2000), 279–80; Brown decision quoted in Robert P. Green, Jr., "Separate Education Is Not Equal Education," in John W. Johnson, ed., *Historical U. S. Court Cases, 1690–1990* (New York: Garland Publishing, 1992), 389.

6. Helen Z. Papanikolas, *Emily-George* (Salt Lake City: University of Utah, 1987), 271–72; quote from Paul Turner, *Sunnyside Memories* (Orem, UT: SunRise Publishing, 1997), 111.

7. Arminta Hewitt, "Temple Mountain," in Montell Seely, LaVora Kofford, Owen and Jane McClenahan, and Roma Powell, eds., *Emery County, 1880–1980* (Castle Dale: Emery County Historical Society, 1981), 336.

8. Acuna, 280–81, 348–49; Vincente V. Mayer, "After Escalante: The Spanish-speaking People of Utah," in Helen Z. Papanikolas, ed., *The Peoples of Utah* (Salt Lake City: Utah State Historical Society, 1976), 464–67; Jose Jesus Palacios, interview with Margie Archuleta and Vincent Mayer, Dragerton, Utah, 13 July 1972, Utah Minorities Number S–59, Special Collections, Marriott Library, University of Utah, Salt Lake City, Utah.

9. Frank Farlaino, comp., "The History of Good Shepherd Parish," *Carbon County Historical Society Journal* (Spring 2003): 47–62.

10. "Epilogue: Dahlia Cordova," in Leslie Kelen and Eileen Hallet Stone, *Missing Stories* (Salt Lake City: University of Utah Press, 1996), 501.

11. Rosa Sandoval, interview with Chuck Lobato, Katarina Trujillo, and Margie Archuleta, East Carbon, Dragerton, Utah, 13 June 1972, Utah Minorities Number S–46, Special Collections, Marriott Library, University of Utah, Salt Lake City, Utah.

12. Valentine Arambula, interview with Floyd O'Neil and Vincent Mayer, Sunnyside, Utah, 5 February 1972, Utah Minorities Number S–31, Special Collections, Marriott Library, University of Utah, Salt Lake City, Utah.

13. Mr. and Mrs. Richard Martinez, interview by Vincent Mayer and Bernice Martinez, Dragerton, Utah, [n.d., c. 1972], Utah Minorities Number S–22,

Special Collections, Marriott Library, University of Utah, Salt Lake City, Utah.

14.   Roger D. Hardaway, "A Case Of Black And White: Removing Restrictions Against Interracial Marriages," in Johnson, 636–38.

15.   Joanne Taniguchi Kanehara, personal e-mail, 10 June 2003; Jeanne Taniguchi Ogden, personal e-mail, 9 June 2003.

16.   Charles S. Peterson, *Utah: A History* (New York: W. W. Norton & Company, Inc., 1977), 202.

17.   Deseret News, *1991–1992 Church Almanac* (Salt Lake City: Deseret News, 1990 [sic]), 296–99; F. LaMond Tullis, "The Church Moves Outside the United States," in Thomas G. Alexander and Jessie L. Embry, eds., *After 150 Years: The Latter-day Saints in Sesquicentennial Perspective* (Provo: Charles Redd Center for Western Studies, 1983) 150; Dean L. May, "A Demographic Portrait of the Mormons, 1830–1980," in ibid., 57. For this insight, I am indebted to Todd Olsen, personal communication, 28 May 2003.

18.   Jan Shipps, "In the Presence of the Past: Continuity and Change in Twentieth-Century Mormonism," in Alexander and Embry, 27.

19.   *Church Almanac*, 297.

20.   Preston Huntington, "Translator System," in Seely et al., eds., 321.

21.   Tom McCourt, *The Split Sky* (Springville, UT: Bonneville Books, 2002), 242.

22.   Edward A. Geary, *Goodbye to Poplarhaven* (Salt Lake City: University of Utah Press, 1985), 67.

23.   Walt Borla, "Helper was once baseball center of southeastern Utah," *Helper Centennial* supplement to the *S-A*, September 1981, 23.

24.   Allan Kent Powell, personal communication, 14 March 2003; *The Spartan* [Emery High School Yearbook], various years.

25.   South Emery High School, *The Bark* [yearbook], 1954, 46; 1955, 53; Roma N. Powell, "A History of Emery County Schools," in Seely et al., 303; "Dinosaurs Win First Region Eight Championship," *S-A*, 25 February 1960; "Dinosaurs Capture Third in State Tournament," *S-A*, 17 March 1960; "Third In State," *ECP*, 24 March 1966.

26.   "Enter State Class B High School Tournament," *S-A*, 18 March 1965; "CEU Wins First ICAC Title; To Host Regional JC Tourney," *S-A*, 25 February 1965; "Cunningham, Watkins Rate on ICAC, All-Tournament Teams," *S-A*, 18 March 1965; "ICAC, NJCAA Region Champion Eagles Eye National Tournament," *S-A*, 11 March 1965; "Huge Crowd Greets National Third Place Eagles at Airport Sunday Eve," *S-A*, 25 March 1965.

27.   Borla, 22–23; Roma N. Powell, 309–10.

28.   Borla, 20–22; Ronald G. Watt, *A History of Carbon County*, (Salt Lake City: Utah State Historical Society, 1997), 336–37; "Price National Gang Nabs County Boys' League Title," *S-A*, 1 August 1957.

29.   Layne Miller, "Coal Town Turning to Dust," *Historic Preservation News* (December 1992): 10–12; Kristine Fredriksson, *American Rodeo* (College Station: Texas A&M University Press, 1985), 5, 65; Jean Christiansen and Arminta Hewitt, "Emery Town Including the Muddy and Quitchumpah," in Seely, et al., eds., 250–58; Irene Allred, "Cleveland, Utah," in ibid., 169; idem, "Veda Merlene Jones," in ibid., 641.

30.   McCourt, 187–90.

31.   Ibid., 158.

32.   "Local History of Pioneer Days," [parts one and two], *Carbon County News*, 23 January and 30 Jan, 1913; "History of Helper," *News-Advocate*, 24 February 1921; Teachers, Pupils, and Patrons of Carbon [School] District, "A Brief History of Carbon County, mimeographed [c. 1933].

33. Ernest S. Horsley, "Historical Sketch of Price," MS 112 Jean Westwood Collection, Box 31, Fd. 1, Special Collections, Marriott Library, University of Utah, Salt Lake City, Utah.

34. Papanikolas, "The Greeks of Carbon County," *Utah Historical Quarterly* 22 (1954); Miriam B. Murphy, "Helen Zeese Papanikolas," in Colleen Whitley, ed., *Worth Their Salt* (Logan: Utah State University Press, 1996), 253. Among those Murphy quite correctly lists are Philip F. Notarianni, Allan Kent Powell, Ronald G. Coleman, Joseph Stipanovich, Vincente V. Mayer, and me (f. 24, 296). Craig Fuller also belongs on this list.

35. John D. Fitzgerald, *Papa Married A Mormon* (New York: Prentice-Hall, 1955).

36. John D. Fitzgerald, *The Great Brain* (New York: Dial, 1967), lists additional works facing the title page: *More Adventures of the Great Brain, Me and My Little Brain, The Great Brain at the Academy, The Great Brain Reforms, The Return of the Great Brain,* and *The Great Brain Does It Again.*

37. Melvin T. Smith, "Report to the Board of State History," 24 January 1986, unpublished typescript, copy in possession of the author, 4; "Allan Kent Powell," in Seely, et al., eds., 727; Philip F. Notarianni, personal communication, Salt Lake City, Utah, 7 August 2002; Murphy, 253; Helen Z. Papanikolas, telephone interview by author, 25 May 2003.

38. Allan Kent Powell, personal communication, 20 May 2003; "Emery County Museum" in Seely, et al., eds., 322. A majority of the State Board of History had to vote to list a building on the State and National Registers of Historic Places.

39. Francis Dupin Vouk, interview with author, Price, Utah, 10 October 1978.

40. "National Register of Historic Places Inventory—Nomination Form" for Martin Millarich Hall/Slovenian National Home, copy in possession of the author; "Spring Glen hall named," *S-A,* 17 December 1980.

41. Nomination forms in possession of the author.

42. "Castle Valley Historical Society, Articles of Incorporation and Bylaws, July 1978," copy in possession of the author, 2–3.

43. "Ferron Woman to lead C. V. Historical Society," *S-A,* 29 July 1978; "Society disbanded but two are formed," *S-A,* 18 June 1980.

44. Montell Seely, "The Castle Valley Pageant," in Castle County Chapter of League of Utah Writers, *Legends of Carbon and Emery Counties* (privately published, 1996), 90–94.

45. Geary, *Poplarhaven.*

46. "Historical Society writing contest deadline near," *S-A,* 26 April 1980; Frances B. Cunningham, [Message from the editor], *Carbon County Journal* 1 (1982): preceding p. 1.

47. Kristin Diamanti Taylor, "The Patchwork Piece," *S-A,* 19 March 1980.

48. Allan Kent Powell, ed., *Emery County: Reflections on its Past and Future* (Salt Lake City: Utah State Historical Society, 1979); Philip F. Notarianni, ed., *Carbon County: Eastern Utah's Industrialized Island* (Salt Lake City: Utah State Historical Society, 1981); Seely et al., eds.

49. Edward Geary, *A History of Emery County* (Salt Lake City: Utah State Historical Society, 1996); Watt, *Carbon County;* Montell Seely and Kathryn Seely, *Castle Valley Pageant History* (privately published, 2003).

50. Pearl Baker and Ruth Wilcox, "Greenriver," in Stella McElprang, comp., *Castle Valley: A History of Emery County* (Emery County Daughters of Utah Pioneers, 1949), 191; Lucy C. Nielson, "Ferron," in McElprang, 294; "Hiawatha Native Wins BYU Award," *S-A,* 20 November 1985; "Life's Career Opens in Old Lard Bucket," *Utah Natural History* 3, no. 3, (1971): no page, clipping at Museum of the San Rafael; Owen McClenahan, *Utah's San Rafael Swell* (Castle

Dale: privately printed, 1986), 121; quotes from "Dinosaur Expert Preaches Devout Evolution," *Salt Lake Tribune*, 18 February 1990; BLM, "Meet 'Al,'" [pamphlet, n.p., n.d.]; Donald L. Burge, interview with author, 30 May 2003.

51. Don Burge, quoted in J. Eldon Dorman, "The Carbon College Prehistoric Museum," paper presented to the Utah Statewide Archeological Society, 26 May 1962, copy in possession of the author; Alice and Art Rasmussen, "The Founding Fathers of the Castle Valley Museum," in *Legends*, 82.

52. "Museum celebrates 30th birthday with grand opening," *S-A*, 28 May 1991; quote from Dorman, "Museum."

53. Dorman, "Museum."

54. Ibid.; Telephone interview with Dr. J. Eldon Dorman, 12 November 1999, notes in possession of the author.

55. "Museum celebrates."

56. Dorman, "Museum"; Burge interview; J. Eldon Dorman, *Confessions of a Coal Camp Doctor* (Price, Utah: Peczuh Printing Company, 1995), 145; "Local Physician chosen as 'quiet pioneer,'" *S-A*, 23 July 1991.

57. Dorman, "Museum."

58. Watt, *Carbon County*, 298; "Museum celebrates"; quote in "Dream comes true as new prehistoric museum is dedicated," *S-A*, 4 June 1991.

59. Dorman, "Museum"; "Museum celebrates."

60. "Burge signs dinosaur stamp; a historical day for CEU," *The Eagle* 21, no. 10, 8 May 1997; Burge interview.

61. "Prehistoric museum welcomes paleontologist to CEU," [CEU] *Alumni News* 40 (Fall/Winter 2003): 5.

62. Fred Voll, interview with author, Helper, Utah, 13 August 1982.

63. Jan Halladay, "Remembering railroads, art, museum," *S-A*, 9 October 1990; Watt, *Carbon County*, 92; "City gives its tribute to coal," *S-A*, 4 June 1980; Bill and Albert Fossatt, personal communication, 19 April 2004.

64. Arva Smith, "Women's history important, curator says," *S-A*, 20 June 1984.

65. "Mining museum curator, couple research Carbon County history," *S-A*, 16 May 1996; "Helper's historical preservation law implemented to protect, enhance commercial district," *S-A*, 28 April 1994.

66. "Recapping effort to obtain longwall for repository site," *S-A*, 4 February 1998.

67. Geary, *History*, 356–57; Michael Leschin, electronic communication to author, 13 August 2003.

68. Larry W. Davis, "Columbian Mammoth unveiled at U of U ceremony," *Emery County Progress* [hereafter *ECP*], 11 August 1992.

69. Tom Martin, "Museum becomes one of three [sic, four] to be accredited in Utah," [CEU] *Eagle*, 14 November 1991. The others are the Hansen Planetarium, the University of Utah Natural History Museum, and the University of Utah Museum of Fine Arts.

70. Larry W. Davis, "Museum opening includes county displays," *ECP*, 3 August 1993; "Dinosaur Diamond" [pamphlet, n.p., n.d.].

71. Christiansen and Hewitt, 255.

72. Geary, *History*, 352–55.

73. Peggy Foote and Genevieve Force, "The Catholic Church in Huntington," adapted by Roma N. Powell in "History of Churches of Huntington," in Seely, et al., eds., 198.

74. "The First Baptist Church of Emery County," in ibid., 475.

75. Rachel Carson, *Silent Spring* (Boston: Houghton Mifflin Company, 1962); David E. Nye, *Consuming Power* (Cambridge, MA: MIT Press, 1999), 225.

76. Sen. William Proxmire, quoted in Carl J. Mayer and George A. Riley, *Public Domain, Private Dominion* (San Francisco: Sierra Club Books, 1985), 224.

77. Mayer and Riley, 216–18; The President's Commission on Coal, *Coal Data Book* (Washington, D.C.: Government Printing Office, 1980), 8–9, 211–13; Peter Wiley and Robert Gottlieb, *Empires in the Sun* (Tucson: University of Arizona Press, 1982), 150–52; Utah Power and Light Company, "Hunter and Huntington Projects," (n.p., 1978), 2; Robert Taniguchi, "Castle Country Community Profile," Utah Department of Employment Security (July 1980), 4; "Projected Mines Carbon/Emery Counties," mimeographed (Price: Utah Job Service, 1980).

## Chapter Twelve

1. Kent R. Petersen, oral history interview, 22 April 1994, Emery County Archives, Castle Dale, Utah.
2. Ibid.
3. Louis Pestotnik, Jr., interview with author, Price, Utah, 5 May 1982.
4. Special Warranty Deed, Book 107, 506; Warranty Deed, 2 January 1968, Book 107, 424; Judgment of Disincorporation, 25 June 1974, Book 152, 680, all in Carbon County Recorder's Office; [no title], *News-Advocate*, 11 January 1917; "Ask Deed to Mining Land in Hard Scrabble Canyon," *Sun-Advocate* [hereafter *S-A*], 23 March 1939; MS 277, Peerless Coal Co. Records, especially Box 3, Fd. 14 and Box 15, Fd. 9, Lee Library, Brigham Young University, Provo, Utah; Ronald G. Watt, *A History of Carbon County*, (Salt Lake City: Utah State Historical Society, 1997), 122–23; Interviews with Walker J. Diamanti and Stan John Diamanti, in Leslie J. Kelen and Eileen Hallet Stone, eds., *Missing Stories* (Salt Lake City: University of Utah Press, 1996), 382, 398–401.
5. Thelma Mills, "Coal Industry," in Montell Seely, LaVora Kofford, Owen and Jane McClenahan, and Roma Powell, eds., *Emery County, 1880–1980* (Castle Dale: Emery County Historical Society, 1981), 290–93; idem, "A Brief History of Emery Mining Corporation, Yesterday and Today, Meeting the Energy Need of Utah," in ibid., 480.
6. Ibid.
7. Utah Power and Light Company, *How Electricity is Generated* (pamphlet: c. 1982).
8. Eva Conover to Nancy Taniguchi, 21 January 2000; Edward Geary, *A History of Emery County* (Salt Lake City: Utah State Historical Society, 1996), 348–52.
9. Geary, 348–52.
10. LaVora Kofford and Paulette Kelly, "Lawrence," in Seely, et al., eds., 233–34; Kent Powell, personal communication, 14 March 2004.
11. Elizabeth Hansen and Sylvia Nelson, "The Huntington Emery County Airport," in Seely et al., eds., 496–97.
12. Jean Christiansen and Arminta Hewitt, "Emery Town Including the Muddy and Quitchumpah," in Seely, et al., eds., 250–58, 257–60.
13. Montell Seely, "Irrigation on Cottonwood Creek," Seely et al., eds., 88–89; "1970 to be big year for UP&L," *S-A*, 1 January 1970.
14. LaVora H. Kofford, "Livestock," Seely et al., eds., 54.
15. Roger D. Curtis, "Comments," in *Emery County: Reflections on Its Past and Future*, Allan Kent Powell, ed., (Salt Lake City: Utah State Historical Society, 1979), 127.
16. William K. Wyant, *Westward in Eden* (Berkeley: University of California Press, 1982), 326–31.
17. Daniel Yergin, *The Prize* (New York: Simon & Schuster, 1991), 780.
18. "Independent mines are few, due to consolidation," *S-A*, 31 December 1980.
19. Angie Hyre, "Planner says Price has grip on energy boom," *S-A*, 5 August 1981.

20. Layne Miller, "More Layoffs For Utah Coal Mines," *Salt Lake Tribune*, 28 June 1982; Hal Edwards, "Coal Mine Idles 96 Workers," *Salt Lake Tribune*, 1 December 1982.

21. James A. Eaquinto, "Dragerton," in Castle Country Chapter of the League of Utah Writers, *Legends of Carbon & Emery Counties* (privately printed, 1996), 138.

22. "A conversation with Richard Walker," *S-A*, 22 October 1982.

23. Yergin, 717, 726.

24. "Jobless flee coal country," *S-A*, 6 July 1983; Layne Miller, "Officials monitor Thistle slide," *S-A*, 1 May 1997; quote from "Japanese, Energy Independence Caused Slump in Utah Coal Use," *Salt Lake Tribune*, 26 October 1983.

25. Yergin, 721–22.

26. Carl J. Mayer and George A. Riley, *Public Domain, Private Dominion* (San Francisco: Sierra Club Books, 1985), 209–10.

27. Yergin, 716; "Tar sand developers to receive DOE funding [sic: they were not funded]," *S-A*, 14 June 1980; "Texas firm to extract Sunnyside tar sands," *S-A*, 22 July 1981.

28. "Of a More Or Less Personal Nature," *Eastern Utah Advocate*, 15 August 1907; quote in "Promises Much For Carbon County," *Carbon County News* [hereafter *CCN*], 11 July 1912.

29. "A Boom for Carbon Asphalt," *CCN*, 11 December 1913.

30. Paul Turner, *Sunnyside Memories* (Orem, UT: Sunrise Publishing, 1997), 8, 19–24; James E. Taylor, "Rock Asphalt Quarry/Tramway Operations," *Carbon County Historical Society Journal* [hereafter *CCHSJ*] (October 2001): 37–41; Michael Dame, "Local tar sands project is on again," *S-A*, 28 November 1984; Michael Dame, "Optimistic tar sands reports released," *S-A*, 27 February 1985.

31. Thomas Michael Power, *Lost Landscapes and Failed Economies: The Search for a Value of Place* (Washington, D.C.: Island Press, 1996), 112.

32. Ibid., 106.

33. "Castle Gate to be leveled," *S-A*, 17 January 1974; Stanley C. Harvey, interview with Mark Hutchings, 12 June 1976, Charles Redd Center for Western Studies, Brigham Young University, Provo, Utah; "Commission holds key to building," *S-A*, 28 March 1974.

34. Eldon Miller, "The Standardville Bandstand Finds a Home at Long Last," *CCHSJ* (April 2000): 9–11.

35. "State winners for young woman of the year," *S-A*, 15 October 1970.

36. "Trumka applauds women," *S-A*, 6 July 1983.

37. "Women organize for mining work," *S-A*, 4 February 1981; quotes from Frances Farley, "A Meeting of the miners: The National Convention of Women Miners," *Network*, August 1985, 14–15.

38. "Women miners' workshops warn of sexual harassment," and "Women miners hold conference in Price," both *S-A*, 26 June 1985.

39. Mike Gorrell, "Wilberg Miner Survived The Fire, But Can't Escape the Memories," *Salt Lake Tribune*, 18 December 1994.

40. "Miners still trapped in Wilberg," *S-A*, 21 December 1984; "Final body recovery made at Wilberg," *S-A*, 18 December 1985; "Wilberg aftermath," *S-A*, 28 December 1984; "Memorial service honors lost miners," *S-A*, 28 December 1984; "Community Faces Economic Impact of Mine Disaster," *Washington Post*, 27 December 1984; "Wilberg mine near being sealed today," *S-A*, 28 December 1984; "Testimony pinpoints fire location," *S-A*, 5 April 1985; "Blake Testimony released by MSHA after hearings," and "Emery Sheriff looks at Wilberg mine fire," *S-A*, both 10 April 1985; "FBI Investigating Disaster At Wilberg Mine," *Salt Lake Tribune*, 21 September 1985; "MSHA blames compressor for fatal Wilberg fire," *S-A*, 18 August

1987; "Mine Official Tells Investigators of Out-of-Date Safety Plan," *Salt Lake Tribune*, 16 April 1985; "Jury places blame for fire on UP&L, Emery Mining," *S-A*, 28 June 1990.

41.  "Counselors help families after tragedy," *S-A*, 2 January 1985.
42.  Chuck Zehnder, "Objections to mine request stop Kaiser," *S-A*, 31 March 1987; Joe Rolando, "Geneva Reluctantly Agrees to Buy Kaiser Coal's Sunnyside Mines," *Salt Lake Tribune*, 28 January 1988; Joe Rolando, "Kaiser Coal Seeks Court Approval To Sell Mines to Power Agency," *Salt Lake Tribune*, 15 August 1988; Joe Rolando, "Sale of Kaiser Mines To Colorado Firm Awaits Court Ruling," *Salt Lake Tribune*, 20 February 1989; quote in Steve Christensen, "First train leaves Sunnyside mine," *S-A*, 30 March 1989.
43.  Emmet Pierce, "The Town That Loves Trash"; Pierce, "Mayor's aim: Dig out revival"; Pierce, "Town was shafted, she claims," all *San Diego Union-Tribune*, 6 June 1993; Lynnda Johnson, "Court denies injunction motion, dismisses CAN lawsuit," *S-A*, 23 June 1994; "ECDC Environmental landfill reaches milestone," *S-A*, 5 September 1995.
44.  Yergin, 778–79.
45.  "UMWA reiterates union's opposition to U. N. Treaty," *S-A*, 30 December 1997.
46.  "Mining project approved," *S-A*, 25 June 1980; Joe Rolando, "Mine Development Plans 'on Hold,'" *Salt Lake Tribune*, 6 July 1982; Joe Rolando, "Coastal Moves Western Coal Operations to S. L.," *Salt Lake Tribune*, 27 April 1996; Layne Miller, "Limited deposits threaten successful mining history," *S-A*, 10 December 1996; Nancy J. Taniguchi, "Perceptions and Realities: Progressive Reform and Utah Coal" (Ph.D. diss., University of Utah, 1985), 193–94; "Carbon County experiencing climbing joblessness in 1998," *S-A*, 7 July 1998.
47.  Southeastern Utah Association of Governments, "Table X: Southeastern Utah Coal Production," *Castle Valley* (privately printed, 1976), 36; "Utah coal production registers all-time high," *S-A*, 5 February 1998.
48.  Layne Miller, "Experts predict bleak future for Utah's coal," *S-A*, 10 December 1996.
49.  Layne Miller, "PacifiCorp details power plant issue," *S-A*, 10 December 1996.
50.  "Geophysical crew and machines look for oil, gas," *S-A*, 19 November 1980; Overthrust Industrial Association, "The Overthrust Belt," *Overthrust News*, 1, no. 1 (n.d.; c.1980): 2. As this book goes to press, the fate of the Escalante-Grand Staircase National Monument is once again a political football.
51.  Mayer and Riley, 296–97.
52.  Kevin Ashby, "Future gas development hot issue in Carbon, Emery area," *S-A*, 7 September 1995; "Officials exploring options in gas drilling water issue," *S-A*, 18 July 1996.
53.  Layne Miller, "Texaco exploratory natural gas well flares at Emery drilling site," *S-A*, 28 September 1995.
54.  Layne Miller, "Defending Carbon area's lifestyle," *S-A*, 12 October 1995.
55.  Layne Miller, "U. S. Forest Service considering applications on drilling projects," *S-A*, 21 December 1995; Layne Miller, "Field dubbed Utah's 'single largest' drilling project," *S-A*, 24 September 1996; Layne Miller, "Anadarko details drilling objectives," *S-A*, 17 December 1996; "Anadarko presents introduction to local residents," *S-A*, 28 May 1998; Miller, "Officials exploring."
56.  Brent Israelsen, "Energy firms seek Book Cliffs wells," *Salt Lake Tribune*, 10 August 2003.
57.  Layne Miller, "Tourism rapidly becoming key driving economic force," *S-A*, 6 February 1997.

58.   Raymond Wheeler, "Southern Utah: The Trauma of Shifting Economies and Ideologies," in Ed Marston, ed., *Reopening the Western Frontier* (Washington, D.C.: Island Press, 1989), 165–66.

59.   *Utah's Castle Country*, pamphlet, n.p., n.d., no page; "Christmastown, Utah is already in the holiday spirit," CEU *Eagle*, 31 October 1996.

60.   "County preserves open spaces"; Michael Dame, "Community Wants Ghost Towns Saved," *Salt Lake Tribune*, 7 February 1985; "Tour guide directs visitors to abandoned coal camps," *S-A*, 9 May 1991; "County takes possession of Ledges," *S-A*, 12 November 1996; "The Castle Valley Ridge Trail System," *S-A*, 10 July 1997; "Manti Forest is favorite playground for local residents," *S-A*, 25 June 1991; "Golfing abounds in area" and "Carbon Country Club expands to 18 holes," *See & Do in Castle Country*, May 1996, 7; "Sheep herd takes over Carbon's golf course," *S-A*, 23 April 1996; Layne Miller, "Officials strive to resolve quarry security issue," *S-A*, 24 October 1996; "Grant focuses on quarry, Nine Mile improvements," *S-A*, 28 August 1997; Steve Christensen, "Recreation facility becomes reality for Nine Mile Canyon," *S-A*, 8 July 1997; "Goblin Valley is a great place," *See & Do Castle Country*, May 1996, 10; Layne Miller, "Emery County preparing for Utah's first 'televillage,'" *S-A*, 7 December 1996; "Emery residents at meeting endorse San Rafael proposal," *S-A*, 14 October 1997; "Trail group, SUWA debate BLM's plan for San Rafael," *S-A*, 18 December 1997; Emery County, Utah website, http://www.emerycounty.com, accessed 3 May 2003.

61.   Michael Dame, "Two Utah Craftsmen Still Fashion Stone Following Old World Ways," *Salt Lake Tribune*, 30 March 1985; Original Creations [Gary Prazen], "A Statement in Bronze," Helper, 1992; Layne Miller, "Italian stonemasons left an impression in Carbon County," *S-A*, 2 January 1997; George A. Thompson, "Martin," *Some Dreams Die* (Salt Lake City: Dream Garden Press, 1982), 98–99; Ross Gigliotti, personal communication, Price, Utah, 9 August 2003; Arva Smith, "Miners killed in disaster remembered," *S-A*, 6 October 1987; "The Scofield Disaster," *S-A*, 3 November 1987; Chuck Zehnder, "He has passed the torch," *S-A*, 19 January 1988; "Carbon County immigrants are remembered by monument," *S-A*, 28 September 1989.

62.   "Remembering Winter Quarters," and Mike Gorrell, "Descendants, Town Mark 100th Anniversary of Deaths," *Salt Lake Tribune*, 2 May 2000; "Program, Winter Quarters, Utah 100 Year Commemoration, The Scofield Mine Disaster," pamphlet, copy in possession of the author.

63.   Mike Gorrell and Rhina Guidos, "Immigrant miners take on Kingstons," *Salt Lake Tribune*, 12 October 2003; Elaine Jarvik, "Kingstons exploitative, protesters say," *Deseret News*, 18 January 2004; Stephen Hunt, "Polygamist heads to jail for incest," *Salt Lake Tribune*, 27 January 2004; Utah Jobs With Justice web site, http://www.utahjwj.org, accessed 9 March 2004.

64.   Wyant, 280–84.

65.   Lee Johnson, telephone interview with author, 19 May 2003.

66.   David Diamond, "What's best for the West," *USA Weekend*, 3–5 November 1995, 4–6; Michael McCabe, "Utah Battle Over What Constitutes Wilderness," *San Francisco Chronicle*, 1 April 1996; Layne Miller, "Emery committee devises San Rafael protection plan," *S-A*, 2 October 1997; Layne Miller, "Plan includes potential to unite counties," *S-A*, 2 October 1997; quote from "Local officials discuss plan to create national heritage area," *S-A*, 14 July 1998.

67.   David Darlington, "Untracked Utah," *Sierra* 88, no. 1 (January/February 2003): 24–31.

68.   Dennis R. Worwood to Interested Party, 14 February 2003, on Emery County website, http://www.emerycounty.com, accessed 24 July 2003.

69. "Local officials discuss plan;" John A. Jakle, *The Tourist* (Lincoln: University of Nebraska Press, 1985), 288–99.

70. Hal K. Rothman, *Devil's Bargains* (Lawrence: University Press of Kansas), 370.

71. Patrick T. Long, "For Residents and Visitors Alike: Seeking Tourism's Benefits, Minimizing Tourism's Costs," in David M. Wrobel and Patrick T. Long, eds., *Seeing and Being Seen* (Lawrence: University Press of Kansas, 2001), 87.

72. Bryce Petersen, Jr., "It's Swell," [Ogden] *Standard-Examiner Explore Outdoors* [supplement], 6 August 2003.

73. National Trust for Historic Preservation, "Press Release: National Trust Names Utah's Nine Mile Canyon One of America's 11 Most Endangered Historic Places," 24 May 2004, http://www.nationaltrust.org/news/docs/20040524_11most_ninemilehtml.htm, accessed 25 May 2004.

74. Sharon Peacock McCully, "Women and the Law," speech delivered at College of Eastern Utah, 10 October 1986, copy in possession of the author.

75. Edward A. Geary, "Castle Valley: The World We Have Lost," in Powell, ed., 99.

76. Turner, 268.

77. Steven D. Bunnell, "The Birth of My Values" and "My One Real Adventure," in *Guess Who Got The Last Hotdog? & Other Stories*, Books In Motion #438 (1992), dramatic readings by Jack Sondericker.

78. Mary Rynio, "Former teacher, principal at Latuda shares coal canyon memories," *S-A*, 19 July 1998.

# Index